T0375489

Who I Am in Christ

Maegen Neely

Copyright © 2019 Maegen Neely.

All rights reserved. No part of this book may be used or reproduced by any means, graphic, electronic, or mechanical, including photocopying, recording, taping or by any information storage retrieval system without the written permission of the author except in the case of brief quotations embodied in critical articles and reviews.

WestBow Press books may be ordered through booksellers or by contacting:

WestBow Press
A Division of Thomas Nelson & Zondervan
1663 Liberty Drive
Bloomington, IN 47403
www.westbowpress.com
1 (866) 928-1240

Because of the dynamic nature of the Internet, any web addresses or links contained in this book may have changed since publication and may no longer be valid. The views expressed in this work are solely those of the author and do not necessarily reflect the views of the publisher, and the publisher hereby disclaims any responsibility for them.

Any people depicted in stock imagery provided by Getty Images are models, and such images are being used for illustrative purposes only.
Certain stock imagery © Getty Images.

ISBN: 978-1-9736-7818-2 (sc)
ISBN: 978-1-9736-7820-5 (hc)
ISBN: 978-1-9736-7819-9 (e)

Library of Congress Control Number: 2019916969

Print information available on the last page.

WestBow Press rev. date: 10/29/2019

Scripture quotations taken from The Holy Bible, New International Version® NIV® Copyright © 1973 1978 1984 2011 by Biblica, Inc. TM. Used by permission. All rights reserved worldwide.

"Scripture taken from the NEW AMERICAN STANDARD BIBLE®, Copyright © 1960,1962,1963,1968,1971,1972,1973,1975,1977,1995 by The Lockman Foundation. Used by permission. www.Lockman.org"

Scripture quotations marked (NLT) are taken from the Holy Bible, New Living Translation, copyright © 1996, 2004, 2007 by Tyndale House Foundation. Used by permission of Tyndale House Publishers, Inc., Carol Stream, Illinois 60188. All rights reserved.

Scripture taken from the New King James Version®. Copyright © 1982 by Thomas Nelson. Used by permission. All rights reserved.

Scripture taken from the Amplified Bible, Copyright © 1954, 1958, 1962, 1964, 1965, 1987 by The Lockman Foundation. Used with permission.

"Scripture quotations are from the ESV® Bible (The Holy Bible, English Standard Version®), copyright © 2001 by Crossway, a publishing ministry of Good News Publishers. Used by permission. All rights reserved."

Introduction

Dear reader,

I am so excited that you have decided to embark on this journey with me in discovering more fully what the Bible says concerning your identity in Christ. This devotion is intended to be a tool in your arsenal. Each day begins with Scriptures related to that day's truth of who we are in Him, followed by an explanation of this truth, and ending with a portion of prayer. Please don't let any of these be an exhaustive list of study or time of prayer or reading of Scripture. Delve as deep into these truths, into God's Word, and into prayer as you want to go. There are 130 days in this devotion. It is set up for you to read one devotion a day, Monday-Friday, for six months. That way if you ever fall behind, there is built-in time to catch up.

This topic is incredibly personal to me. I've been following Jesus for a long time but have wrestled with my identity in Christ. After several conversations with other fellow-believers, I've realized that others wrestle with who they are in Him too. For me, I need to remind myself daily, be grounded daily, so this devotion was written largely from that place. I pray it helps and encourages you as much as the process of writing it has helped and encouraged me. Be blessed in the LORD.

In Christ,
Maegen Neely

⇜⇝

Day 1: I Am More Than a Conqueror!

> *"Who will bring any charge against those whom God has chosen? It is God who justifies. Who then is the one who condemns? No one. Christ Jesus who died—more than that, who was raised to life—is at the right hand of God and is also interceding for us. Who shall separate us from the love of Christ? Shall trouble or hardship or persecution or famine or nakedness or danger or sword? No, in all these things we are more than conquerors through him who loved us."* (Romans 8:33-35, 37 NIV)

You are more than a conqueror through Christ who loves you! I believe there is significance in how the Scriptures word this phrase. You are not just a victor, an overcomer, a winner; you are more than that. Your capacity as a conqueror in Christ is greater than the parameters that word could possibly contain; thus, Paul uses the phrasing "more than" to describe your stance of victory. Oh friend, that is truly awesome! You see, you and I are not fighting for victory. The enemy of your soul and you are not on equal playing fields despite his tactics of intimidation. You already have the victory; you are already an overcomer in Christ. You are fighting from a stance of victory. It is part of your identity in Him. Look at the scripture above. It asks who could possibly bring any charge against those whom God has chosen because it is God who justifies. Who brings charges against you? Satan does! Yet even in this Satan is fighting a losing battle for it is God who has justified you. The Scriptures then ask who then could condemn someone whom God has justified? No one! Not even Satan! Christ died for you, rose to life for you, and is at the right hand of God right now interceding for you! So who could separate you from the love of Christ? Could hardship or trouble or persecution or danger ever hinder Christ's love for you? No! Even in all these things you are still more than a conqueror!

When David was king of Israel he surrounded himself with some pretty amazing warriors. These men were fearless in battle, they had a reputation for victory, and the Word of God says that just one of these men could take on insurmountable odds-such as Abishai who slaughtered three hundred enemies at one time. That's incredible! Second Samuel 23 lists these men and some of their feats of victory, calling them David's mighty men. These men had such a reputation of victory for David that the armies of Israel exacted fear throughout enemy nations. The Philistines, the Ammonites, the Moabites, and the Amalekites were all squelched by David and his men. The King didn't just know who they were, they weren't just known around the Israelite camp, but the enemy also knew who they were. Can I tell you, child of God, that your enemy knows who you are? Satan is fully aware that you are more than a conqueror through Christ. You have a reputation of valor and victory because of Jesus. Even if your life is currently filled with hardship, trouble, persecution, or danger, Satan's lies cannot prevail over the truth of who you are in Christ, and according to the irrefutable Word of God, you are not just a conqueror, you are more than a conqueror! Jesus has made you so victorious that human vocabulary can't even express how victorious you are. It's time to rise up out of a stance of fear, of shame, of complacency into a stance of victory. It is who you are!

Father,

> Thank You for Jesus. Thank You that He died for me, that He rose for me, and that He is seated at Your right-hand interceding for me. The odds are in my favor because Jesus has already made me victorious. Would You help me to remember who I am in Christ and to approach my day, my schedule, my life, and even my setbacks from the stance of being more than a conqueror in Christ. You are an awesome God and today I choose to praise You. Let it be so in Jesus's name, amen!

Day 2: I Am Highly Esteemed

> *"He said, 'Daniel, you who are highly esteemed, consider carefully the words I am about to speak to you, and stand up, for I have now been sent to you.' And when he said this to me,*

> *I stood up trembling. Then he continued, 'Do not be afraid, Daniel. Since the first day that you set your mind to gain understanding and to humble yourself before God, your words were heard, and I have come in response to them."* (Daniel 10:11-12 NIV)

In the third year of Cyrus the king of Persia, on the twenty-fourth day of the first month, Daniel is standing on the Tigris River. He looks up and sees a vision of a magnificent angel who speaks to him these incredible words. The angel addresses Daniel as being one who is highly esteemed, highly respected, valued, regarded, and admired. What an honor to be spoken to in such a manner by a heavenly messenger from God. This angel instructs Daniel not to be afraid and then tells him that his words, his prayers were heard from the very first day that Daniel humbled himself before God.

If you read the book of Daniel and study his life, you'll realize that Daniel experienced some incredible favor from God. But before we discredit ourselves from such favor because we are not Daniel, can I submit to you that Daniel was so highly regarded by the LORD because he chose to humble himself before God. Reread the angel's words above if you need to. Being so exalted by God is not just something that was available to Daniel but is promised to us as well. First Peter 5:6 admonishes us to humble ourselves under the mighty hand of God so that He will lift us up in honor. According to the Bible, humility brings honor in God's eyes. If you want God to favor you, if you want Him to exalt you, to esteem you, I challenge you to keep your heart in a position of humility before the LORD. And if you are already a child of God, then you are already highly esteemed because it requires humility to repent before the LORD and it requires humility to continuously submit to the Lordship of Jesus Christ in your life. How cool would it be to actually speak with an angel of God, but because of Jesus, we have access to communicate with Someone much greater than an angel, the Holy Spirit of the Living God! The humility it takes to call upon the name of Jesus and continuously live under His Lordship, qualifies you as being highly esteemed with God. He hears you when you pray and more than that, He responds! As a child of God, His Spirit is always with you; speaking to you. May you have ears to hear what the Spirit is saying. And just as the angel addressed Daniel, the Spirit of God through His Word also calls you highly esteemed!

Father,

I readily admit that You are God and I am not. You are greater, wiser, and higher than I could ever imagine or possibly attain to. Therefore, I choose to humble myself before You. Holy Spirit help me to continuously choose a position of humility before God. May my heart remain humble in Your eyes LORD because being esteemed by You is of far greater importance than being esteemed by man. I thank You for favoring me, for hearing me when I pray, and for responding to my prayers. I want to commune with You so I invite You to speak to me through Your Word and to give me ears to hear what Your Spirit is saying today in Jesus's name, amen!

Day 3: I Am No Longer a Slave to Sin

"For we know that our old self was crucified with him so that the body ruled by sin might be done away with, that we should no longer be slaves to sin—because anyone who has died has been set free from sin. In the same way, count yourselves dead to sin but alive to God in Christ Jesus. Therefore, do not let sin reign in your mortal body so that you obey its evil desires. Do not offer any part of yourself to sin as an instrument of wickedness, but rather offer yourselves to God as those who have been brought from death to life; and offer every part of yourself to him as an instrument of righteousness. For sin shall no longer be your master, because you are not under the law, but under grace." (Romans 6:6-7,11-14 NIV)

Sin can initially be very appealing and often justified at the expense of having fun and doing what one wants to do. From this perspective, God and the Bible seem very rigid and stoic. However, the goal of sin is always mastery. You may start out thinking that you are just doing what you desire to do, but eventually you realize that your desires are dictating what you do. Paul describes it this way in his letter to the church in Rome, "I do not understand what I do. For what I want to do I do not do, but what I hate I do." (Romans 7:15 NIV). Paul goes on to say that he had the desire to do what was good, but he couldn't carry it out. This sounds like someone who is fighting a losing battle with their own willpower. Willpower is never enough to conquer sin. If it were, there would have been no need for Jesus, but the Bible says that our old self was crucified with Him so that the body ruled by sin might be done away with. As such, we should no longer be slaves to sin.

Can I tell you that if you have made Jesus your LORD and Savior then you are no longer a slave to sin! Sin is no longer your master; Jesus is! That means whenever Satan tempts you with lust, with fear, with guilt, with shame, with anger, or with any of the old vices that used to rule over you, you do not have to give into those temptations. Why? Because lust is no longer your master, fear is no longer your master, shame is no longer your master, anger is no longer your master. Sin is no longer your master! Slaves do not have the authority to say no to their masters, but Jesus has broken sin's authority over you. In Christ, you now have the authority to say no to sin! That old self that used to be ruled by all these things, according to the Word of God, was hung on the cross with Jesus. They are dead and gone, and anyone who is dead has been set free from sin. That is the power of grace! The grace of Jesus Christ is not a ticket to do whatever you want to do and still be forgiven. No! It is freedom from the mastery of sin.

Paul says, "We were therefore buried with him (Jesus) through baptism into death in order that, just as Christ was raised from the dead through the glory of the Father, we too may live a new life." (Romans 6:4 NIV). This is a truth Satan very much does not want you to understand. If you have surrendered to Christ and His Lordship in your life, then spiritually, your old self died with Christ. Can a dead person sin? Why would Satan waste his time tempting a dead person? That would be completely ridiculous! As the Bible admonishes, consider yourself and make the enemy consider you dead to sin because in Christ, you absolutely are! And just as the glory of the Father rose Jesus from the grave, so too His glory raises you to live a new life in Him. That is powerful! Can I challenge you that whenever you feel tempted, remind yourself and remind the enemy that you are no longer a slave to sin! You are dead to sin! Yes, God can and will forgive you if you fall and then confess your sin to Him, but as a child of God, you do not have to continue to live under the mastery of the enemy when Christ has identified you as no longer being a slave to sin. A child of God who continuously lives under the bondage of sin is absolutely experiencing a crisis of their identity. It's imperative that you know who you are and, according to the Bible, you are no longer a slave to sin!

Father,

> I thank You for Jesus and all that His death and resurrection accomplish for me. I thank You that because of Jesus I am no longer a slave to sin. I thank You that sin no longer has any mastery in my life because I have chosen Jesus as my LORD and Master instead. Holy Spirit, would You help me to continue to choose Jesus, to continue to submit to His Lordship in my life, and to be an instrument of righteousness rather than one of wickedness. Give me discernment; give me courage and boldness today. May I be fully dead to sin, but fully alive to Christ. And I praise You and thank You that the power of grace is always greater than the power of sin in Jesus's name, amen.

Day 4: I Am a Child of God

> *"For those who are led by the Spirit of God are the children of God. The Spirit you received does not make you slaves, so that you live in fear again; rather, the Spirit you received brought about your adoption to sonship. And by him we cry, 'Abba, Father.' The Spirit himself testifies with our spirit that we are God's children. Now if we are children, then we are heirs—heirs of God and co-heirs with Christ, if indeed we share in his sufferings in order that we may also share in his glory."* (Romans 8:14-17 NIV)

A few verses prior to these that are written up above explain how those who belong to Christ have the Spirit of God living in them. When you make Jesus your LORD and Savior, the Spirit of God comes to live in you. God sets His seal of ownership upon you, which is His Spirit, as a deposit guaranteeing your inheritance as a son/daughter. His Spirit declares you as belonging to God. You no longer belong to darkness; you no longer belong to sin; you no longer belong to even yourself. You belong to the LORD, your God! However, the Spirit you received does not make you a slave again so that you must fear. Sin enslaves, darkness enslaves; even our own fleshly desires often enslave us and, in the end, bring death. But the Spirit of God you have received makes you a child of God, freeing you forever from the enslavement of sin, which brings death, and making you instead God's child, which gives you eternal life. The Spirit of God living in you legally brings about your adoption into God's family. The infinite, incomprehensible God is now your Father and as a sign that you truly do belong to Him, He gives you His precious Spirit to bear witness with your own spirit that you are a child of God.

In Matthew 3 we read the account of Jesus' baptism in the Jordan River. As soon as Jesus was baptized, John the Baptist saw heaven open and the Spirit of God descended like a dove upon Jesus. Then John hears a voice from heaven declare, "This is my Son, whom I love; with him I am well pleased." (Matthew 3:17 NIV). God set His seal of ownership upon Jesus and declared Him to be His Son. In similar fashion, when you surrender to Jesus and His Lordship in your life, God gives you His Spirit, His seal of ownership upon you. By His Spirit, He declares you to be His son/daughter whom He loves and with whom He is well pleased. Oh friend, let that sink in for a minute. You are God's child. He loves you and is well pleased that you are His son/daughter. Don't let the enemy distort your view of God's heart towards you. You are a son; a daughter of God.

Now as a child of God you have become an heir of God and a co-heir with Christ. Satan hates this! Your being God's child ultimately displays the enemy's defeat. Satan would rather label you or have you label yourself almost anything other than a child of God. But as God's child, you share in the glory of Jesus! By God's Spirit, His magnificence, His brilliance, His splendor resides in you. That is incredible! Just as Paul says to the Corinthian church, "But we have this treasure in jars of clay to show that this all-surpassing power is from God and not from us." (2 Cor. 4:7 NIV). Your identity as a child of God testifies to the whole world the power of God. Only God could make a slave a son. Only God could make the old new and the dead live. Only God's power could accomplish such a radical spiritual transformation. May the Spirit that has made you a son/daughter of God cause you to cry out to Him,

"Abba, Father." You are not a slave. You are a son! May you truly know Him intimately as your Father.

Father,

> I thank You for Your Spirit that has made me a child of God. Thank You for declaring me as belonging to You and for adopting me into Your family. Thank You for translating me from a slave to a son. Help me Holy Spirit to remember my identity as a child of God. As Your child, may I be led by the Spirit rather than the flesh. May the glory of Jesus shine bright in my life and may I know You intimately and personally as my Father in Jesus's name, amen.

Day 5: I am Born of the Imperishable Seed

> *"For you have been born again, not of perishable seed, but of imperishable, through the living and enduring word of God. For, 'All men are like grass, and all their glory is like the flowers of the field; the grass withers and the flowers fall, but the word of the LORD stands forever.'"* (1Peter 1:23-25 NIV)

You are a part of God's lineage since the Word He has planted in you has saved you. Who has saved you? Jesus! The Bible says, "The Word (Jesus) became flesh and made his dwelling among us… "(John 1:14a NIV). You have been redeemed by the precious blood of Christ and now His blood identifies you as God's child, His offspring, or His seed. Therefore, you are not just born of the perishable seed of your earthly father Adam; you have been reborn by the imperishable seed of Jesus. Consider this for a moment. The seed of man is subject to death. Romans 5 explains how sin entered the world through one man, Adam, and how death was passed upon all men through his seed. In our flesh, we are also born of this perishable seed, "for we have all sinned and fall short of the glory of God," (Romans 3:23 NIV). According to the aforementioned Scripture, all men are like grass, and their glory is like the flowers. Grass withers and flowers fall. So, man's life withers and all of his glory eventually falls as a result of sin since the penalty of sin is death (Romans 6:23 NIV). But Jesus, the Word made flesh, changes everything!

Paul says, "Concerning his Son Jesus Christ our LORD, which was made of the seed of David according to the flesh; and declared to be the Son of God with power, according to the spirit of holiness, by the resurrection from the dead." (Romans 1:3-4). Jesus is the greatest miracle of all time because, like us, He was born of the perishable seed of David (you can find the genealogy of Jesus in Matthew 1), but, unlike us, the spirit of holiness declares Him as the Son of God. By His resurrection from the dead, He is now the Imperishable Seed, the Word made flesh that will endure forever. Satan may discredit you because of your earthly lineage, he may taunt you because of your pedigree and your background; but he absolutely cannot tarnish, dishonor, or destroy the imperishable seed you have been born of in Jesus. "For since death came through a man (Adam), the resurrection of the dead comes also through a man (Jesus). For as in Adam all die, so in Christ all will be made alive." (1 Corinthians 15:21-22 NIV). Jesus being born of the seed of Adam and being born as the Son of God by the spirit of holiness qualifies Him to exact the penalty for sin which is death. Yet His resurrection from the dead displays His power over sin and death, making Him absolutely imperishable; the Word made flesh, the seed that will never die. Jesus is everlasting; He is immortal and eternal and those who are born again in Him will also live forever. Satan cannot annihilate the seed that Jesus has made imperishable!

Father,

> I thank You again for Jesus. I thank You that because of Him, I am born again of an imperishable seed, a beginning that will last forever. Holy Spirit, would You help me to remember that regardless to what the circumstances of my life might currently look like, I will always have a future and a hope because of Jesus. May the knowledge of living eternally with You give me proper perspective for this day. I thank You that the troubles I have faced in life will one day seem light and momentary in comparison to the glory that outweighs them all and will last for all eternity. Overwhelm my heart with hope this day in Jesus's name, amen.

Day 6: I am Loved by God

> *"For one will scarcely die for a righteous person—though perhaps for a good person one would dare even to die--But God shows his love for us in that while we were still sinners, Christ died for us."* Romans 5:7-8 ESV

> *"For I am sure that neither death nor life, nor angels nor rulers, nor things present nor things to come, nor powers, nor height nor depth, nor anything else in all creation, will be able to separate us from the love of God in Christ Jesus our Lord."* Romans 8:38-39 NIV

God's love is woven throughout the entire fabric of the Bible. From the initial fall of man in the Garden of Eden, we see God's plan to reconcile all of humanity unto Himself through Jesus. "For God so loved the world that he gave his only begotten Son, that whosoever believes in him should not perish, but have eternal life." (John 3:16 NIV). Jesus obliterates all questions, all doubt, all skepticism about God's love. Does God love you? Absolutely, yes! How can you know? He gave you Jesus!

It is rare to find someone willing to die for a righteous person, to step in and suffer in the place of one who is unjustly suffering at no fault of their own. Perhaps someone might possibly dare to die for the sake of a good person, but God shows His love for us in that while we were still sinners; while we were still selfish, still reliant upon ourselves, still very much a willing friend of the world and an enemy of God, Christ died for us. "… don't you know that friendship with the world means enmity against God? Therefore, anyone who chooses to be a friend of the world becomes an enemy of God." (James 4:4 NIV). There is no greater love than the love of Christ simply because He chose to lay down His life for the sake of God's enemies in order to make them friends. In Christ, you are no longer an enemy of God. God's anger is no longer upon you. Jesus has made you a friend of God and nothing can now separate you from God's love!

The sin that used to separate you from God was done away with through Jesus (Romans 5:9)! No power, no height, no depth, no ruler, nothing that could happen today, nothing that could happen in the future, not even death itself; absolutely nothing in all of creation can separate you from God's love in Christ! That is awesome! You are not just a recipient of the love of God; in Christ, being the object of God's love is now part of your identity. Everyone is considered loved by God since He gave Jesus in response to His love for the whole world; His love for everybody, but those who are in Christ are now identified by that love. Look how Paul addresses the Christians living in Rome, "To all those loved by God ..." (Romans 1:7 NIV). Being loved by God is now who you are! The enemy of your soul has always tried to thwart God's plan of salvation through Jesus because Jesus is the ultimate proof of God's love for you. Why does Satan tempt you, why does he constantly remind you of your faults, your failures; why does he continuously look for accusations to bring against you? Because he wants you to die for your sins. He wants you to bear the wrath of God yourself. He wants you to be God's enemy just like he is. He wants you to forget Jesus. But He couldn't stop Jesus from living. He couldn't stop Jesus from dying and he couldn't stop Jesus from being resurrected from the dead though he certainly tried to. He couldn't stop God's love for you because he couldn't stop Jesus. So, if you feel unloved, remember Jesus. If the enemy tries to convince you that you are unwanted, that God couldn't possibly love you, remind him of Jesus. If you are living in sin and are currently considered an enemy of God, run to Jesus! Jesus is the way, the truth, the life. In Christ, you are no longer separated from God's love. The LORD is not slow to love and abounding in anger. On the contrary, Psalm 103:8 describes God as being "compassionate and gracious, slow to anger and abounding in love." Your need to be loved by God will never exceed the supply of love that He has for you. You are not just loved; you are loved extravagantly, exceedingly. In Christ, there is no limit to God's love for you. That is worth celebrating!

Father,

> I thank You for loving me enough to give me Jesus. I thank You that Your wrath against me has been fully met in Jesus so that I am no longer separated from You. Holy Spirit, would You help me to grasp how deep and wide and high is Christ's love for me and to know this love that

surpasses all understanding? I want to approach this day, my challenges, and my life from the vantage of knowing fully how abundantly I am loved by You. Open my eyes to Jesus Who is and will always be the proof of Your love. May I never forget, and may I never let the enemy forget Jesus! It's in His name, Jesus, that I pray, amen.

Day 7: I Am Forgiven

"In him (Christ) we have the redemption through his blood, the forgiveness of sins, in accordance with the riches of God's grace" Ephesians 1:7 NIV

"In the case of a will, it is necessary to prove the death of the one who made it, because a will is in force only when somebody has died; it never takes effect while the one who made it is living. This is why even the first covenant was not put into effect without blood. When Moses had proclaimed every command of the law to all the people, he took the blood of calves, together with water, scarlet wool and branches of hyssop, and sprinkled the scroll and all the people. He said, 'This is the blood of the covenant, which God has commanded you to keep.' In the same way, he sprinkled with the blood both the tabernacle and everything used in its ceremonies. In fact, the law requires that nearly everything be cleansed with blood, and without the shedding of blood there is no forgiveness....The blood of goats and bulls and the ashes of a heifer sprinkled on those who are ceremonially unclean sanctify them so that they are outwardly clean. How much more, then, will the blood of Christ, who through the eternal Spirit offered himself unblemished to God, cleanse our consciences from acts that lead to death, so that we may serve the living God! For this reason, Christ is the mediator of a new covenant, that those who are called may receive the promised eternal inheritance—now that he has died

> *as a ransom to set them free from the sins committed under the first covenant."* Hebrews 9:16-22, 13-15 NIV

In reading the Old Testament practices of purification for sin under the Law with all the shedding of blood, we are sometimes tempted to think that this whole thing seems a little barbaric. But there is incredible significance in the blood. God in His righteousness, in His holiness, in His grace gave the Law, the Ten Commandments, to Moses and the people. Sin already being present in the world was absolutely complicating life and creating a great chasm between God and His people. Because of sin, people were justifying their lying, stealing, their killing of each other, their adultery, their sin and separating themselves from a Holy God in the process. Paul explains to the Galatian church, "Why, then, was the law given at all? It was added because of transgressions (sin) until the Seed (Jesus) to whom the promise referred had come." (Galatians 3:19 NIV). Though we tend to view the Law and the Commandments as rigid and harsh, God in His grace and love gave His standard of living to the people to keep them in right relationship with Him until Jesus. And He gives them a process of purification for sin that required the shedding of blood.

We have already established that the wages of sin, the penalty of sin is death. Despite our underestimation of the severity of sin, the God of the Bible, a truly Holy God, cannot tolerate it. Why? Because He is life and sin's goal is death. Don't miss this friend. It is not God's desire to kill people in their sin. "As surely as I live, declares the Sovereign LORD, I take no pleasure in the death of the wicked, but rather that they turn from their ways and live." (Ezekiel 33:11 NIV). "The LORD is not slow in keeping his promise, as some understand slowness. Instead he is patient with you, not wanting anyone to perish, but everyone to come to repentance." (2 Peter 3:9 NIV). Satan wants you to think that God hates you, that God is too stern and uncompromising to follow. However, God did not bring sin into the world; Satan did! The goal of the enemy, the goal of sin is death, your death; but God's goal for you is life!

Hebrews 9 explains in detail the process of purification through the shedding of blood. When the people failed to keep the Law given to them, the price, the sentence was death. Yet so that they wouldn't die for their sin, God required them to shed the blood of bulls and goats and lambs annually on the Day of Atonement as a sacrifice for their sin so that sin could be atoned for (Leviticus 16 NIV). Why the blood? Because as according to the Law, "the life of every creature is in its blood." (Leviticus 17:14 NIV). Sin demands your life;

it requires blood and without this shedding of blood there was no forgiveness. Yet once a year this blood of goats and bulls and lambs was shed so the people could be cleansed and purified. The Day of Atonement was a yearly reminder of sin that was a copy and shadow of what was to come through Jesus.

Why was Jesus's blood shed on the cross? Because without the shedding of blood there is no forgiveness! His blood has redeemed you. His blood has cleansed you. His blood has purified you. His blood has brought about the forgiveness of all your sins! There is power in the blood! In the Old Testament God required goats and bulls and lambs that were without defect, without any fault; only their blood was acceptable. And Jesus being without any sin became the perfect Lamb of God, an acceptable sacrifice for sin whose blood, being more potent than any blood offered previously, provided once for all the cleansing for sin. Jesus died so that you could live! There remains no more sacrifice for sins because the blood of Jesus was enough! His blood is enough to cleanse you! It is enough to save you, enough to redeem you and to forgive you of all your sins! In Christ, you are forgiven! You are pardoned, excused, absolved forever of all your guilt, of all your shame, of all your sin because of the precious blood of Jesus! There truly is wonder-working power, redeeming power in the blood of the Lamb!

Father,

> You are so holy, so pure, so righteous and good. How could I ever get close to such brilliance, to such holiness?! It seems unfathomable! Yet in Your grace and love, You've made a way through Jesus. So, I thank You today for Jesus. Thank You for His blood that has pardoned me, that has cleansed me, that has forgiven me. Even if I feel like I have nothing else to thank You for today, I will thank You for the redeeming power of Christ's blood. Holy Spirit help me to live a life worthy of such a sacrifice. I praise You for the blood, I am so grateful for the blood, I plead the blood over me and my house today in Jesus's name, amen.

Day 8: I Am Justified Before God!

> *"Therefore, since we have been justified through faith, we have peace with God through our LORD Jesus Christ."* Romans 5:1 NIV

> *"He (Jesus) was delivered over to death for our sins and was raised to life for our justification."* Romans 4:25 NIV

Have you ever sinned? Have you ever broken any of God's Laws? The Word of God clearly tells us in Romans that all have sinned and fallen short of God's glory; everyone has sinned, including me, and including you. However, many of us consider ourselves good in comparison to others. We aren't perfect by any means, but we aren't exactly criminals deserving of condemnation. Yet Jesus says in the Bible, "No one is good—except God alone." (Mark 10:18 NIV). Our definition of good is usually relative to other people who we consider not as good as ourselves. Yet God's definition and standard of good is relative to Himself and there is no living soul who meets those criteria. According to the Bible, if you have not accepted Jesus as your LORD and Savior then you do not have peace with God. There is uproar, upheaval, and a severing of relationship between you and the One who made you. But in Jesus, that separation, that disunity is completely absolved, and you are brought close to God. "But now in Christ Jesus you who were once far away have been brought near by the blood of Christ." (Ephesians 2:13 NIV). Don't let Satan convince you that you can't talk to God. That God has no business listening to you. You are not far off anymore! The blood of Christ has brought you near. You have peace with God and now you can approach His throne of grace with confidence. In Christ, you and God have unity! You agree with God and He is in agreement with you; that is perfect peace! What a shame it would be to live your life at a distance from God when He has done everything possible to bring you near to Him!

How are you justified? How are you absolved of your guilt before God so that you can get close to Him? How are you cleared of the sin that separates? How are you released from the charges that stand against you? According to the Scripture above, you have been justified through faith in Jesus Christ! Your works can't justify you. Your good deeds aren't enough to justify you. Even all of your good intentions can't bring you justification before a Holy God. Faith alone in Jesus Christ completely vindicates you. You are exonerated in Christ! Satan may remind you of who you used to be, of all that you used to do. He may try to charge you again with those things that used to stand against you before God. But those accusations are completely empty; they carry no weight because Jesus has justified you! If Satan reminds you of your past sin, you remind him of Jesus!

Romans says that Jesus died for our sins, but it also tells us that He was raised to life for our justification. Don't miss this, friend. Yes, Jesus died for you, for your sins. But He rose to life for your vindication, so that you might be justified before God. "For Christ did not enter a sanctuary made with human hands that was only a copy of the true one; he entered heaven itself, now to appear for us in God's presence." (Hebrews 9:24 NIV). A few verses later in Hebrews Paul says that people are destined to die once and after that to face judgment. So, Christ was sacrificed once to take away the sins of many people. Jesus died once, appeared before God on your behalf, and rose to life for your justification. His resurrection is your vindication! It is the evidence that, in Him, you are cleared before God! Don't let Satan forget about the resurrection of Jesus Christ! Christ's resurrection is the enemy's defeat! His resurrection is the proof that the love of God, the grace of God is greater than the power of sin! That is truly awesome!

Father,

> I thank You for Jesus. I thank You that in Him, I have peace with You, that I am not distanced from you any longer because of my sin, but that I have been brought near to You by Christ's blood, that I am justified through faith. Holy Spirit help me not to be apathetic and lazy and uncaring about how close I draw to the LORD since because of Jesus I can now draw as close to God as I am willing to. So today I choose to draw near to You, Father. I want to hear Your voice. I want to feel Your heartbeat. I want to know You intimately because Jesus has made a way for me to know You. I am excited because Your Word says that if I draw

near to You, You will draw near to me. Let it be so in Jesus's name, amen.

Day 9: I Am Chosen!

"Before I formed you in the womb, I knew you, before you were born, I set you apart..." Jeremiah 1:5 NIV

"But you are a chosen people, a royal priesthood, a holy nation, God's special possession, that you may declare the praises of him who called you out of darkness into his wonderful light." 1 Peter 2:9 NIV

God chose you! I know it seems a novel idea, but we seldom stop to consider the power of this simple truth. The LORD chose to make you! Psalm 139 says how He created your inmost being, and how He knit you together inside your mother's womb. It describes how your frame was not hidden from Him while you were being made inside that secret place in the womb, but that He saw your unformed body and all the days made for you were written in His book before a single one of them came to existence. You are not a mistake despite the circumstances that may have surrounded your conception and birth. You are not just the byproduct of genetics nor are you some evolutionary happenstance. You are much more valuable than that to the heart of your Father. Every detail of your being was designed fearfully and wonderfully by God. And guess what the Bible also says in Psalm 139? His works, God's creations, what His hands have made are wonderful! You are one of His works; therefore, you are wonderful (you're welcome☺)!!

Those in your life may or may not have wanted you, but one thing is for sure: God has always wanted you! How do I know? Because He chose to make you! Look at the Scripture mentioned above in Jeremiah. The LORD tells Jeremiah that even before He formed Jeremiah in the womb, God knew him, before he was ever born, God set him apart. Wow! If you read the book of Jeremiah, you'll quickly discover that Jeremiah wasn't very well liked. The messages he gave to the people were not very popular or well received. He was known as the "weeping prophet", mostly delivering words of warning to the Israelites during the reigns of five different kings of Judah; words that were seldom heeded; words that often landed him in jail. He was persecuted, ridiculed, and made fun of; yet God chose him to be His prophet. The LORD set him apart from before he was ever born. Can I tell you something? People may or may not like you. People may or may not receive you. Man often decides your value based on your usefulness or the things about you that are outward and visible; your works, your appearance, your charm (just read 1 Samuel 16:7 NIV). But God chose you before you ever did anything. He chose you before anyone made any sort of judgments about your looks or your personality. He doesn't need the persuasion of popular opinion; even your opinion. He settled it from before your very beginning: you are chosen!

Satan is a liar, my friend! If he's told you that you're a nobody, that no one wants you, that no one likes you. If he's used the conditions of your arrival into this world against you or made you feel like you are somehow nothing more than a combination of chromosomes, then he is absolutely downplaying your significance. The Word of God declares that you are wanted; you are chosen! "Can a mother forget the baby at her breast and have no compassion on the child she has borne? Though she may forget, I (God) will not forget you!" (Isaiah 49:15 NIV). Oh friend, that is powerful! Even if those who were supposed to love you, supposed to care for you, supposed to want you somehow forgot to do these things, the LORD declares that He will not forget you!

God not only chose to create you; He chose to love you! "But God demonstrates his own love for us in this: while we were still sinners, Christ died for us." (Romans 5:8 NIV). Before you knew Him, He chose to know you! Before you ever loved Him, He chose to love you! He chose to make a way for you to know Him through Jesus. He chose to lay down His life for you. He chose to forgive you. He chose to set you apart. He chose to set His seal of ownership upon you, the Holy Spirit of the Living God. There is nothing accidental about it; God chose you so that you might declare the praises of Him who has brought you out of darkness into His marvelous light! You are not in darkness anymore! Why? Because the LORD, your God, chose to bring you out! Praise God, He chose you!

Father,

> I thank You that I am chosen. I am not an accident, a mistake, I am not forgotten. You saw me, You knew me, You chose me before I was ever born. Thank You for valuing me that much. Thank You for securing my significance from the very beginning. Holy Spirit, would You help to remember that I am chosen by God? Even when others don't choose me or it seems like I'm not anyone's first choice for anything, still I will praise You because I am Your choice. You will never forget me and for that I am so thankful. May Your Word prevail in my life in Jesus's name, amen.

Day 10: I Am Free!

> *"Therefore, there is now no condemnation for those who are in Christ Jesus, because through Christ Jesus the law of the Spirit who gives life has set you free from the law of sin and death."* Romans 8:1-2 NIV
>
> *"You; my brothers and sisters, were called to be free. But do not use your freedom to indulge the flesh; rather, serve one another humbly in love."* Galatians 5:13 NIV
>
> *"So, if the Son sets you free, you will be free indeed."* John 8:36 NIV

Did you know that apart from Christ you are a slave to sin? Most people don't want to classify it in those terms, but Jesus says, ".... everyone who commits sin is the slave of sin." (John 8:34 NIV). Paul also says, "When you were slaves to sin, you were free from the control of righteousness." (Romans 6:20 NIV). Sin is binding. It entraps, it enslaves, it seeks to rule over us, to master us. According to the Scripture in Romans 8, there is a law of the Spirit which gives life, but there is also a law of sin and death. Yet through Christ you have been set free from the law of sin and death! You are no longer bound to lust! You are no longer bound to fear! You are no longer bound to deception! You are no longer bound to sin in any way, shape, or form! Christ has set you free! Satan may entice you with those things that used to hold sway over you. He may set traps for you, he may tempt you, but the Word of God says that with every temptation God has provided a way of escape for you (1 Corinthians 10:13 NIV). Take the way of escape! Flee temptation! Run away, my friend! Running away doesn't make you a coward or somehow weak; rather, it implies that you are very much strong in the LORD. Those who are free will run away from any and all prospects of being enslaved again. Those who truly know that they were slaves and have now been completely liberated would seem foolish to willfully choose to return to that yoke of slavery. Don't let the enemy trick you; if the Son has set you free, then you are free indeed!

In Christ, what have you been freed of? You have been freed from guilt; freed from shame! There is now no condemnation for you because you are in Christ Jesus. "He (Jesus) canceled the record of the charges against us and took it away by nailing it to the cross." (Colossians 2:14 NIV). You are free from the record of charges that stood against you! That record has been cancelled in Christ. In fact, the Bible says that Jesus literally took it away and nailed it to the cross! So, if Satan ever has the audacity to bring up that record to you, remind him that Jesus nailed it to the cross. Please friend, leave it there!

Mark 2 records the account of Jesus healing a paralyzed man that was brought to him by four friends. These men couldn't get their friend to Jesus because of the crowd that had gathered to hear Jesus teach so they made a hole in the roof and lowered their friend down. In verse 8, the Bible says that when Jesus saw these men's' faith, He said to the paralyzed man, "Son, your sins are forgiven." (Mark 2:8 NIV). Jesus has the power to forgive sins! Some teachers of the law were there who began to question in their minds how Jesus could forgive anyone of their sins and immediately Jesus knew in His Spirit that this is what they were thinking and He responds by saying, "Which is easier to say to this paralyzed man, 'your sins are forgiven,' or to say, 'get up, take up your mat and walk?" (Mark 2:9 NIV). Wanting them to know that the Son of God had authority on earth to forgive sins, He goes on to heal the paralyzed man. Jesus has the power to heal! He has the power to set you free from your past! Jesus has the power to forgive you of all your sins! Jesus has broken the chains of imprisonment for you! "It is for freedom that Christ has set you free! Stand firm, then, and do not let yourself be burdened again by a yoke of slavery." (Galatians 5:1 NIV). Don't let the enemy oppress you again with those things that Christ has freed you from! Don't willingly pick up the chains that Jesus has broken off of you. You have been freed, my friend. Satan wants you to continue to consider yourself a slave to sin even though Christ has set you free. He wants you to think that you're too weak not to give into a certain sin. He wants you to think that you'll always struggle with that one area that you've seemed to always struggle with. No! That is a lie! God's strength is made perfect in weakness according to the Bible (2 Corinthians 12:9 NIV). In Christ, you can do all things (Philippians 4:13 NIV). Jesus has set you free from the tyranny of sin! Praise His name forever, you are free!

Father,

> I thank You that I am no longer condemned in Christ. Thank You that the written record of charges against me has been completely taken away by Christ and nailed to the cross. Thank You, Jesus, for setting me free from the power of sin, from the confinement of sin, from the enslavement of sin. Holy Spirit, would you help me to live free in Christ? Help me not to return to a yoke of slavery after already being set free. Give me wisdom and discernment to see the traps of the enemy for what they are and to flee from temptation. You always provide a way of escape. Help me to see that way and to have the courage to take it. I praise You and thank You LORD for setting me free. Let it be so in Jesus's name, amen.

Day 11: I Am Corrected

> *"...my son do not regard lightly the discipline of the LORD, nor be weary when reproved by him. For the LORD disciplines the one he loves and chastises every son whom he receives."* Hebrews 12:5-6 ESV

> *"It is for discipline that you have to endure. God is treating you as sons. For what son is there whom his father does not*

> *discipline? If you are left without discipline, in which all have participated, then you are illegitimate children and not sons. Besides this, we have had earthly fathers who disciplined us and we respected them. Shall we not much more be subject to the Father of spirits and live? For they disciplined us for a short time as it seemed best to them, but he disciplines us for our good, that we may share his holiness. For the moment all discipline seems painful rather than pleasant, but later it yields the peaceful fruit of righteousness to those who have been trained by it."* Hebrews 12:7-11 ESV

Most of us balk at the idea of a loving God punishing people for their wrongs. From that perspective, it seems so harsh. Disobey and He's going to squish you like a bug. Most of us are aware of how people or our parents respond to our faults and failures and outright sins and disobedience. They get mad. There's punishment and consequences to our choices and oftentimes there's rejection. Part of growing up is realizing this. Some of us, because of our experiences especially at an early age, associate confession with rejection. So, we don't want to confess our sins to anyone let alone God. We think to do so will bring His wrath, His punishment; we think it will bring rejection from Him and those closest to us who we confess to. And we're sort of caught in this catch 22. We refuse to confess because we're afraid of rejection, then we hide and cover things up, but your sin always finds you out. So, eventually what needed to be confessed is brought into the light and the results are typically not very pretty at all. But the Bible gives us a different perspective that isn't cruel or unkind; still painful and unpleasant yes, but Hebrews tells us not to regard lightly the LORD's discipline or to become weary in the midst of it, for the LORD disciplines the ones He loves and has received. Wait, what? God's disciplining me because He loves me. Yes! The writer of Hebrews goes on in expounding to us this comparison of earthly fathers who discipline their children as they see best, and God disciplining us for our good that we may share in His holiness. What is God's motivation for correcting you, for training you to obey Him, for chastising you for your disobedience? He does it for your good so that you can share in His holiness. Why should you resist that?

We see this displayed all throughout the Bible. Think of the children of Israel who God often referred to as being stiff-necked or the equivalent to a stubborn child. If you're a parent of a stubborn child, you probably understand the LORD's frustration. The children of Israel often wouldn't receive God's warnings, His verbal correction coming through the prophets and leaders of Israel. They often said one thing and did another. There were many times they failed to learn what God was trying to teach them the easy way. Instead they would resist, they would stubbornly refuse and balk at God's correction and would be forced to learn things the hard way. There have been times I have been that stubborn child. God has tried to show me things about my heart that were wrong, sinful. He has tried to bring them to my attention so that I could repent and deal with them, but I resisted. I wouldn't willingly go through the painful, unpleasant process of Him disciplining me, and would thus have to learn things the hard way. Yuck! Learning things the hard way is no fun and, well, just unnecessary. And I think that is the most frustrating part of learning things the hard, stubborn way. You know that it really didn't have to be this way. My advice to any child of God being disciplined by God: He loves you! He's not correcting you or punishing you because He hates you or is against you or He enjoys taking things out of your life. What parent enjoys taking things away from their kids right? But we'll do it to teach them responsibility in those areas and to teach them to grow-up and God will do the same with us. Settle it in your heart from the beginning. No discipline is pleasant and it's still going to be painful, but He's correcting you because He loves you. It's not a matter of Him rejecting you as His child. He loves you! The very fact that He's correcting you is proof that you are His son/daughter. It's proof of His love for you. So, just don't even go there in your mind. You may have angered Him, but His anger only lasts for a moment, His favor lasts a lifetime. You may have disappointed Him, but He's never disappointed that you're His son/daughter so just refuse to go there. Furthermore, I'd advise any child of God undergoing God's discipline to be humble and cooperate with what He's trying to teach you. The Bible tells us that God opposes the proud but gives grace to the humble. The more we resist and disagree and are too proud to admit our sin, the more God is opposing us. And if it's God vs. you, who do you think is going to win that match right? So, it's always best to agree with Him and cooperate with Him, not to resist or be stubborn because then you'll just have to learn the lesson the hard way. We need grace. I need God's grace and the Word of God tells us that He gives grace to the humble. Let's be humble and let Him correct us graciously.

Father,

Forgive me for my wrong perspectives and attitude about Your discipline of me. Help me Holy Spirit to get this truth way down in my heart today. I am corrected by God because He loves me, because I am His son/daughter. He's correcting me for my good so that I might share in His holiness. Yes, it's still painful and unpleasant, but knowing this makes it much easier to humbly cooperate. Thank You for loving me through discipline. Thank You for never leaving me or forsaking me. I thank You that I don't have to resist Your correction. I know I've messed this up in the past and I've been that stubborn child who's had to learn things the hard way. Forgive me. Help me, Holy Spirit, to cooperate with my Father and to learn quickly and easily the things He's trying to grow me into. Let it be LORD in Jesus's name, amen.

Day 12: I Am Strong in God's Standard

"He (God) will be a spirit of justice to the one who sits in judgment, a source of strength to those who turn back the battle at the gate." Isaiah 28:6 NIV

"I can do ALL things through Him who gives me strength." Philippians 4:13 NIV

"He gives strength to the weary and increases the power of the weak." Isaiah 40:29 NIV

"Therefore, I am well content with weaknesses, with insults, with distresses, with persecutions, with difficulties, for Christ's sake; for when I am weak, then I am strong." 2 Corinthians 12:10 NASB

I love the truth that God is the source of my strength. I love to remind myself that I can do all things through Christ who strengthens me. I love that even when I am weak, God is not intimidated by my weaknesses, rather His grace is sufficient for me and He makes me strong in the midst of those weaknesses. Those weaknesses are opportunities for His strength to be perfected in me. How cool is that? I love that He gives strength to the weary and increases the power of the weak. I love that He is my source of strength in the battle even the battle that goes on between my ears. Sometimes renewing our minds is exhausting, but He is the source of strength to do it and not just know that we should do it. I love that. Yet Isaiah 28:6 makes an interesting connection between His strength and His justice. I believe there's a correlation here between His justice, His judgments, His standards and His strength. He is the source of strength to the one who has embraced His justice; His standards.

Let me explain further. When you become a follower of Jesus the Bible has a lot to say about who you are now: you are a new creation, you are a son and no longer a slave, you are adopted into God's family, etc. These were things that were not true of who you were before Jesus but are absolutely true of you now that you have accepted Jesus as your LORD and Savior. Your identity, who you are, has completely changed. Now the source of your identity is no longer rooted in yourself or in what you do for a living or in your family name or social status or any of those outward things. Those things may still powerfully influence you and your life, but the real source of who you are is now the standards God has established for who you are as a new creation in Him and those standards are found in His Word. He is the strength of your identity. No one or nothing can destroy that identity, but in order for this to truly hold up in your life, you have to know and make what He says about you the standard of your identity. Does that make sense? How can I expect to be strong in who I am in Him if I don't know and embrace His standards of who I am?

The first example I can think of to illustrate this in Scripture is the story of Gideon. In Judges 6 an angel comes down from heaven to speak with Gideon who was threshing wheat in a winepress and who, along with all of Israel, was hiding out from the enemy, the Midianites. The angel appears to Gideon and says, "The LORD is with you, mighty warrior." (Judges 6:12 NIV). He calls Gideon a mighty warrior which is interesting because Gideon had never even fought in any battles and was currently behaving rather cowardly in that he and his whole family was hiding out from the enemy. Not exactly a great candidate to be labeled as a mighty warrior by the Great I AM. Gideon responds to this angel by saying, "Pardon me, my lord." (Judges 6:13 NIV). I love that! He's like, "excuse me; are you talking to me?" Then Gideon proceeds to question how God could be with him when all these horrible things have been happening at the hand of the Midianites. And then the angel of the LORD turned to him and said, "Go in the strength you have and save Israel out of Midian's hand..." (Judges 6:14 NIV). The LORD told Gideon to go in the strength he had; not in the strength he didn't have. You see, Gideon was stronger than he realized. God would be the source of Gideon's strength if Gideon would embrace the standards God would give to him on how to defeat this enemy. And it all started with Gideon first embracing that he was who God said he was a mighty warrior. This wasn't easy for Gideon. He responds, "Pardon me, my lord, but how can I save Israel? My clan is the weakest in Manasseh, and I am the least in my family." (Judges 6:15 NIV). Gideon knew who he was outwardly. His family was the weakest in his whole tribe and he, himself, was the least in his entire family. But he doesn't refuse or dismiss God outright. He doesn't say I can't save Israel because I'm the weakest and the least. No, Gideon instead asks God how he can save Israel. Friend don't dismiss God's plans for your life because you don't think you can do them, or you aren't worthy of them. There's a difference between asking God how and telling God, "I can't." It's ok to ask how, but it's time you eliminate the "I can't" from your vocabulary. You can do all things through Christ who strengthens you remember? He'll be the source of your strength for whatever He has for you if you'll embrace His standards for what He has for you.

The LORD answers Gideon's inquiry by informing him or perhaps reminding him, that He will be with Gideon. How will Gideon save Israel from the Midianites? God would be with him! How can this man who was one of the weakest in Israel and the least of his family defeat an enemy that had everyone in hiding? God would be with him! How could this outwardly unlikeliest of candidates, this man who was acting a bit cowardly be a mighty warrior as the LORD had said? God would be with him! God was not intimidated by Gideon's apparent weaknesses. Rather; the LORD saw them as an opportunity to show forth His strength. Gideon asks God for a sign and has this incredible encounter with God then the LORD tells him to go that night and tear down his father's altar to Baal and to build a proper altar to the LORD in its place. Gideon did what God had told him to, but he was afraid of his family and the townspeople so he did it at night instead of during the day and when everyone woke up in the morning to see what had been done, they were enraged. They wanted to kill Gideon, but Gideon's father replies that if Baal is really a god, he can defend himself so the people waited to see if Gideon would be struck down by Baal. And when nothing happened to Gideon, the people decided that Gideon had indeed defeated Baal and they no longer called Gideon by his original name, but they gave him the name Jerub-Baal and from that day forward he became known as the one who contended with Baal and won. Sounds a lot like a mighty warrior. Friend, God will be the strength of your identity, of who you are but you must embrace His standards of who you are. Gideon went out to do what God had told him during the night with just ten men and he was shaking in his boots the whole time. He was terrified. And it seems his feelings were validated when everyone woke up mad and ready to kill him. But even though his feelings didn't match what God said and his circumstances didn't immediately match either, still Gideon embraced the standard God gave to him. You have to embrace those standards enough to live by them, to obey God even when you're scared. There was a reason he believed that he was the least in his whole family, but still he followed the standard God gave to him and the LORD became the strength of who he was. Are you getting this? Gideon was a mighty warrior in God's eyes before he ever became a mighty warrior in anyone else's eyes. No matter how crazy it sounds or how much your feelings don't line up with what God says right now or even how much your circumstances may currently protest God's truth, make God's Word of who you are your standard and He'll be the source of the strength of who you are. It's time to stop saying, "I can't," and start responding with, "LORD, show me how." It's time all the cowards became mighty warriors for Jesus. Let it be God in Jesus's name.

Father,

> I thank You for being my source of strength and my standard. Forgive me for desiring Your strength but forfeiting Your standards. It simply doesn't work that way. Help me, Holy Spirit, to embrace the standards God has outlined in His Word of who I am. Help me to know these standards, to believe them, and live by them so that God would be the strength of who I am. I don't want to be a coward. I want to be a mighty warrior. Help my unbelief LORD in Jesus's name, amen.

Day 13: I Am Personally Restored

"Peter said to him, 'LORD, why can't I follow you now? I will lay down my life for your sake.' Jesus answered him, 'Will you lay down your life for my sake? Most assuredly, I say to you, the rooster shall not crow till you have denied me three times." John 13:37-38 NIV

"Jesus said to them, 'Come and have breakfast.' None of the disciples dared asked him, 'Who are you?' They knew it was the LORD. Jesus came, took the bread and gave it to them, and did the same with the fish...When they had finished eating, Jesus said to Simon Peter, 'Simon, son of John, do you love me more than these?" John 21:12-13, 15 NIV

Before Jesus's crucifixion, in John 13, Jesus predicts to Simon Peter his personal denial of Jesus and that this denial will take place three times before the rooster crows. Simon Peter had told Jesus that he was willing to lay down his life for His sake, but he really wasn't even willing to be identified with Jesus when the pressure was on. Why would he tell Jesus that he was willing to lay down his life for Him when he really wasn't? Did Simon know what was in his own heart or was he trying to make himself look good in front of the other disciples? Regardless, Jesus obviously knew what was in Simon's heart and brought it to his attention. Yet still Simon failed. The events that Jesus predicted unfold in John chapter 18 and we see Simon Peter questioned three times if he knew Jesus or was associated with Him as one of His disciples and each time Simon denies it. He even becomes very agitated and upset about the questioning of his association with Jesus. He knew this was going to happen right? Jesus told him it was going to happen! He had the advantage of foreknowledge that could have helped him prepare better for the moment or be more on guard against it or to search his own heart beforehand to make sure his heart was as with Jesus as his mouth said it was. But Peter didn't do that or if he did it wasn't a very deep, fruitful search. He thought he was right, he was okay. He thought he knew who he was to the point that it doesn't seem that he believed Jesus about this denial prediction until after that rooster had crowed and he had realized what he had done. Jesus had given Peter a prophetic word. Jesus had exposed Simon Peter's own heart to him, and it must have gotten to him a little because Luke 22 records that after being told by Jesus that he would deny the LORD three times, he goes out and weeps bitterly. This was a man in conflict; a man who loved Jesus, who wanted to serve Jesus, but who was afraid of what people thought about him and when Jesus tried to bring that to Simon's attention, it was certainly a sore spot. Ever been there?

Can you imagine the pain of denying your friend, your master, your LORD three times? Can you imagine the pain of failing quite miserably in a public way? He had been Jesus's disciple, he had boasted that he was willing to lay down his life for Jesus; he had the opportunity to repent beforehand, to have gone to Jesus with his broken heart before that rooster ever crowed, to have handled the whole thing differently, but he didn't. He denies Jesus then must witness the very One He loves, but had denied even knowing, be killed. I'm sure the finality of the whole thing was crushing to Peter. I'm sure he felt horrible, but what could he do now? He had failed and now the One he had failed was dead. He had cared more about what people thought of him than of being who Jesus had made him, a disciple. Was Simon a fake, a farce? He was one of the disciples, but he obviously didn't have it all together. He had tried to make himself look better than the other disciples, tried to prove himself, but now he had failed in a very big way. Was he doomed to forever be known as the disciple who denied Jesus? What a horrible reputation to live with. What would validate his credibility now? Every time he or someone else identified him as a disciple of Jesus, now there would be this sting associated with it because he would have to recall these moments, these denials, and how he had been asked that question before but failed to answer correctly because he was more afraid of man's response. Ouch! What a tough reality for Simon to live with for the rest of his life. Ever been in a similar reality?

After the resurrection, as news began to spread among the disciples of Jesus being alive, we see this desperation in Simon as he is one of the ones who runs to the empty tomb after Mary Magdalene's report about Christ. He runs and runs probably hoping to be restored to the One he denied only to find Jesus isn't there. Jesus appears to all the disciples and I'm sure Simon is trying to grapple with the whole reality just like the rest of them, but still we see no personal restoration between Jesus and Simon. Yet in John chapter 21 Jesus, the One who had been denied, who had been lied to and deceived about, the One who had been hurt by one of His followers, His friends, goes to Simon and some of the other disciples who were out fishing. He has breakfast with these disciples and three times personally asks Simon if he loves Him. What in the world is going on here? Jesus was restoring Simon to Himself, redeeming the whole failure. Of course, Simon had been forgiven by Jesus a long time ago, but still Jesus personally restores Simon. Jesus didn't say, "See, I told you so. I tried to tell you and show you what was in your heart Simon, but you didn't listen. I warned you. This could have been avoided, this could have gone differently, but you chose this. You care more about what people think about you than you do about really following Me. You need to grow up Simon. You've said that you're not my disciple, so I guess you're not My disciple anymore. I had such big plans for you too. I equated you to a rock that I was going to build My church upon. I guess all of that is null and void now because of what you've done, because of the choices you've made, because of the way you've handled all of this. I love you Simon, but I don't want anything to do with you anymore. You're a fake. You were just pretending to be My disciple. I forgive you, but you're on your own now. Good luck."

Jesus's response to all of this is amazing and so unlike most people's response to sins done against them. He goes to Simon Peter. He didn't wait for Simon to come to Him. Wow! He acts amicably toward Simon and doesn't give Him a piece of His mind, though He very well could have. Nor does Jesus beat him up for his actions or humiliate him in front of the other disciples there. Instead, He welcomes Simon, includes Simon as if nothing had happened, as if Jesus hadn't been hurt by Simon's actions; although I'm sure He was hurt by them. And not only that, Jesus redeems those three denials for Simon Peter. Now Simon doesn't have to live with those denials haunting him for the rest of his life. Jesus redeemed them personally. This is beautiful. This is powerful. This is grace! Now, the last encounter Simon has with Jesus isn't his biggest failure, it isn't how he denied Him and disappointed Him. No. Now, the last earthly encounter he shares with Jesus is this meal between friends; this personal restoration where Jesus validates Simon's love for Him. Wow! He did it for Simon Peter. He'll do it for you as well. Friend, you can search the Bible inside and out, but you'll never find a single person in the whole history of those who God used, other than Jesus Himself, who was perfect, who didn't mess up in some pretty big ways, who didn't have dysfunction and brokenness as a part of their story somehow. Jesus doesn't write these people off. He doesn't look for the most pristine track records or walk away from those who failed when they failed even when those failures were professing believers. No. Jesus exposes their hearts, heals their hearts, and restores their hearts to Him. Jesus goes to the ones who've failed Him and hurt Him not to lecture them or beat them up or punish them somehow, but to rather restore them with His love. Who in the world is like You, Jesus? No one!

Father,

> Thank You for loving me and for forgiving me when I've failed You. Thank You for coming to those broken places and restoring them. I don't deserve You being so good to me. Thank You, LORD. Help me to forgive and love like You in Jesus's name, amen.

Day 14: Abounding in Grace

> *"Moreover, the law entered that the offense might abound. But where sin abounded, grace abounded much more, so that as sin reigned in death, even so grace might reign through righteousness to eternal life through Jesus Christ our LORD."*
> Romans 5:20-21 KJV

> *"So, he got up and went to his Father. But while he was still a long way off, his Father saw him and had compassion for him; he ran to his son, threw his arms around him and kissed him."*
> Luke 15:20 NIV

Jesus tells three parables in Luke 15, two of which are about lost things being found. And in these parables, we see the heart of God for those who don't know Him, who aren't serving Him. But the last parable, famously known as the parable of the prodigal son, though also illustrating God's heart for the lost, is slightly different than the other two. In this illustration we see God as a Father who has a son who took his share of his Father's estate, left his Father's house, and went to spend his wealth on wild living. This wasn't a servant or a stranger, but a son. He already had a deeply personal relationship with the Father. If anyone should know the heart of the Father, it would surely be one of His sons, right? Yet even so, this son, for whatever reasons, left his Father's house completely and squandered his rightful inheritance on things unworthy of that inheritance. He overstepped a boundary, broke a trust when he asked for that which belonged to him only after His Father's passing, then he leaves without looking back. And we see the Father, though I'm sure deeply hurt by His son's actions and still absolutely loving His son, the Father does an amazing thing. He lets His son go. I'm sure He wanted to run after His son, to go rescue him from himself, to chase him down and drag him back home, but that would very much violate the son's free will and God honors our ability to choose. So, the Father stays, letting His son go, but His heart doesn't become hard and angry towards His son. Everyone would probably understand if this Father chose to cut all ties with this disgraceful son, to be so hurt and dishonored that He chose never to have anything to do with that son again. Legally the son already had his inheritance, so the Father had no legal ties to His son anymore, but still His heart loved and longed for that son. How do I know? The Father saw the son while he was still a long way off and has compassion for him. The Father runs to His son, throws His arms around him and kisses him. Those are the actions of someone who loves you, who forgives you, whose heart is still towards you and has always been for you. Those actions convey a love that was never lost and a longing that has finally come to fruition. But the fact that the Father saw His son while he was still a long way off suggests that the Father was already looking and waiting for His son. He was already expectant of that son's return. Oh, He would honor that son's free will to choose, but if that son ever decided to come home, that Father would be ready, waiting, and willing to run to His precious son, love him, and restore him. It truly is an incredible story.

I'm sure the son was pleasantly surprised. He had only hoped to return as a servant. He was ready to beg and crawl and plead his case. He probably thought his Father was still angry, disappointed, and upset with him. But the Father blows all of that away by reacting to His returned son the way that Jesus described. The Father never even gave the son a chance to beg and plead and grovel. The son might have been dirty and smelly and very unkempt. He had been working in the pig slops remember. Yet still the Father runs to him, throws His arms around him, and kisses him. All that garbage and dirtiness did not detract from the fact that this was His son, a son He loved; a son who had come home. That's amazing! The son made one decision; a decision of humility. He was willing to humble himself enough to go back home and receive whatever he deserved. He thought that he had lost his position as son forever but was willing to just be a servant. Yet the Father showed abounding grace in response to that one act of humility. Wow! Paul says in Romans "... that where sin increases, grace increases all the more." (Romans 5:20 NIV). Friend, the Father has enough grace for you. His grace is more, abounds more than any sin you may be guilty of. Your Father is thriving with plentiful grace to accommodate your sin. You may still be dirty and smelly from the bad choices you have made, but when you humble yourself enough to come home to the Father, you won't find an angry, disappointed Dad who doesn't want to see you or talk to you anymore. No, you'll find a Father who abounds in grace towards you, One who sees you coming from afar and takes off running towards you just to welcome you home. You'll find a Father who will embrace you even in the aftermath and filth of your sin and kiss you because you are His son; you've always been His son. Legally you may have severed all ties with Him, but His love towards you never wavered. You'll find a Father more than willing to restore you to your rightful position; a position of dignity and honor and love. That is the heart of the Father towards all those sons or daughters who have royally messed up. It's time to come to our senses. It's time to humble ourselves. It's time to receive abounding grace. It's time to be restored and know that we have an outstanding Father whose love respects our ability to choose, but whose love looks for us and waits for us and runs to us when we come to Him. Wow, thank You Jesus!

Father,

> Oh, I'm sorry today. For turning from You, for leaving You, for choosing something else besides You; forgive me for doubting You. I'm coming home today. I don't deserve anything; I just want to come back to You today. Please forgive me. Please receive me and restore me in Jesus's name, amen.

Day 15: I Am Never Forsaken

> *"For you formed my inward parts; you knitted me together in my mother's womb. I praise you, for I am fearfully and wonderfully made. Wonderful are your works; my soul knows it very well. My frame was not hidden from you, when I was being made in secret, intricately woven in the depths of the earth. Your eyes saw my unformed substance; in your book were written, every one of them, the days that were formed for me, when as yet there was none of them."* Psalm 139:13-16 ESV

> *"Where shall I go from your Spirit? Or where shall I flee from your presence? If I ascend to heaven, you are there! If I make my bed in Sheol (hell), you are there!"* Psalm 139:7-8 NIV

Psalm 139 is one of my favorite Scriptures. It speaks of a God who isn't far off or aloof to you, but One who is very near, who is with you when you are living on the proverbial cloud 9, but also One who is with you as you wake up and lay down in utter misery; even misery that you have made your own bed in. I don't mean that to be offensive but read the Scripture. "Sheol" in the Bible often refers to the grave, death, and hell. Sometimes we find ourselves in crummy circumstances that are largely a result of what's going on around us, our environment, and the poor decisions others have made that have affected us. But sometimes we find ourselves in a crummy place mostly by our own doing, the results of our own poor decisions. No one has made this bed for us; we've made it ourselves, but even then, God is with us. Wow! Let that bless you for a second.

The LORD hasn't forsaken you! Even if you've made your bed in the depths of the earth, still He's there! I doubt He's there to tuck you in that bed of misery every night, to make sure you're comfortable where you are. He overcame that place through Jesus. Why in the world would He want you to stay there? And I believe His Spirit is continually beckoning to yours, echoing the words Jesus spoke to another invalid paralyzed for a long time, who had been laying on his own bed of misery (mat) for 38 years, "Get up! Pick up your mat and walk." (John 5:8 NIV). He's already conquered that place, took ownership of it for you, opened the doors and took the keys away from Satan so that you don't have to make your bed there. What a good Father; what an awesome God! Friend, even if you've been laying on that bed for a long time, all of your life maybe, waking up and going to bed in absolute misery, a misery you've pretty much made your own bed in; still the Living God is with you calling to you over and over and over again, "GET UP! Don't get comfortable there. GET UP!" I don't care what kind of darkness you may be in or have been in, even the darkness is as light to Him. He is not intimidated, scared off, or disgusted away by that grave because He's already overcome it in Christ.

It's time to get up, friend. It's time to get out of that bed, to take up your mat and walk. You aren't forsaken or forgotten; not by the One who made you! He isn't intimidated by what you don't have, who you aren't, or how dark of a place you've made your own bed in. He is the Light. He is the Creator. He is your Father; a very good One! He didn't just form your body, your inward parts in that secret place. He formed your days, every single one of them; believed in them and in Him in you enough to write them in His book before even one of them came to be. He dreamed for you, believed for you long before you could ever dream or believe for yourself. And these days of making your bed in the grave, He saw them too. He saw them and didn't want them for you so bad that He went there first, overcame them first for you so that He could call you out of them. Oh friend, I don't care how much you think your potential has been wasted, how miserable your circumstances are, how forsaken you believe your own bed of misery is. God hasn't forsaken you; He hasn't forgotten you. Yes, you have the free will to make your own bed wherever you so please whether that be on the clouds of heaven or in the depths of the earth, and by all means you can choose to stay there for the rest of your life if you want to. He won't drag you out, force you to get up, but as a good Father, He never stops calling you out of that place. He's very accustomed to working and creating and forming wonderful things from nothing, from things that absolutely have no substance, no potential whatsoever. He can work with your lack of substance. He can work even in the darkness. He can knit together something wonderful out of the brokenness of your own life. It's what He does. It's who He is, the Creator, the Conqueror; your Father!

Oh God, I've got nothing to bring to You, nothing to offer you but these shattered fragments of my life, my heart. I'm a mess and my life is a mess. What good could possibly be salvageable for me? But I know that even as I've made my own bed of misery that I've been living in, still You are here. So, I choose to get up out of this bed. I choose to bring to You my own lack of substance in this dark place. I surrender all that I am and all that I'm not to You, the Creator, my Father. You made me something of purpose and value and wonder before, would You do it again? I invite You to form and intricately weave together this brokenness, to make me whole again. I invite You to breathe potential and purpose back into me again. I invite You to dream for me and call those things that are not as though they are. Let my dreams match Yours, God. Let who I am match who You call me to be. I've been here a long time, but You've been here long before I ever got here. You came here and conquered it for me, took the keys of the devil himself and unlocked the door, swung it wide open so that all I must do is get up and get out. So, I choose to get up today by Your grace, to take up my mat and walk out of this place. Those days You've written for me in Your book, those are the days that I want as my reality. O God let them be in my life as they are in Your book. If I'm anything of wonder, anything of substance, anything of value, let it all reflect Your craftsmanship. I take up this bed of misery, this bed I've largely made for myself or at least stayed in on my own doing and I lift it up to You. It won't any more be the thing that keeps me from walking with You. You have never forsaken me not even while I was laying on this bed of misery. O God keep me from ever making my bed on this mat, in this place again! It's only by Your strength, Your healing, Your craftsmanship that I can even carry this mat out of here. What was impossible for me, You make possible. Thank You Jesus! Let the only one who experiences any shame in this be the devil himself who has no right, no authority, no keys to keep me here another day. You are my Conqueror, my Creator, my Father, my LORD. I'm getting up, I'm walking out in Jesus's name. Praise Your name forever!

Day 16: I Am Purged with Hyssop

"Purge me with hyssop, and I shall be clean; wash me, and I shall be whiter than snow." Psalm 51:7 ESV

> *"Later, knowing that everything had now been finished, and so that Scripture would be fulfilled, Jesus said, 'I am thirsty.' A jar of wine vinegar was there, so they soaked a sponge in it, put the sponge on a stalk of the hyssop plant, and lifted it to Jesus' lips. When he had received the drink, Jesus said, 'It is finished." With that, he bowed his head and gave up his spirit."* John 19:28-30 NIV

In Leviticus 14 the Law denotes the requirements in order to declare a person with leprosy clean. The priest would take a live bird and dip it along with some cedar wood, scarlet yarn, and hyssop into the blood of another bird that was killed over fresh water. The priest would then sprinkle this blood on the one to be cleansed seven times in order to pronounce them officially "clean" of their defiling skin disease. Afterwards, the priest would release the live bird in the open field. This was an interesting and precise requirement for cleansing that God orchestrated and gave to His people. Leprosy was a very destructive, degenerative skin disease of which there was no medical cure for during Biblical times. It was a terrible, horrendous disease that eventually could not be concealed by those who were infected; a disease that isolated individuals and caused people to be ostracized by communities and families as a result, left to die a very lonely death. David makes a parallel between the physical disease of leprosy and his own sinful condition in a prayer he recorded in Psalm 51. He pleads with God to "purge me with hyssop, and I shall be clean." (Psalm 51:7 NIV). Here is that same reference to hyssop, an herbal, medicinal plant used in the sprinkling of the unclean by the priests as God designed in order to declare them clean. Yet David doesn't ask to be sprinkled seven times but purged with hyssop signifying that the condition of his soul was much worse than the degenerative disease of leprosy. You can sense his desperation. Oh God, I don't want to be ostracized because of my sin; left to die a lonely, isolated death. I need to be purged!

The word "purge" is an abrupt or violent removal of something; an eradication of sorts in this case referring to the violent eradication of sin and its effects on the soul. It's widely accepted that Psalm 51 was a prayer David penned after he committed adultery with Bathsheba then schemed to have her husband, Uriah killed in battle when he failed to cooperate with the King's manipulative plan to avoid responsibility for the corresponding child that was conceived by Bathsheba; a child that David was the father of. David says that he knows his sin, that it is ever before him and he asks God to have mercy on him according to God's steadfast love and abundant mercy. David felt that he didn't just need a sprinkling with hyssop as was customary for someone with physical leprosy. His soul was so degenerated from sin that he needed a purging, a violent removal and eradication of his sin in order to be clean in God's eyes. Sigh, I can totally relate to this; can't you?

This guy who had committed a grievous sin that he needed God to purge him of later prophesies about Jesus in Psalm 69:21 that they will give Jesus vinegar for his thirst on the cross. This King who had broken several of the commandments including committing adultery, lying, and murder was the very one God chose to prophesy an important detail about Jesus's' death. And I don't think it was a coincidence that the detail David prophesied about Jesus's death was His taking a drink of wine vinegar on a sponge at the edge of a stalk of hyssop. Of course, this is exactly what transpired in John 19 when Jesus's last act on the cross is described before He declares, "It is finished," and gives up His spirit; an act that declared a cleansing with hyssop and a much more powerful blood of any bird, the precious blood of the Lamb. But who would have chosen David to make this messianic prophesy in light that he is the one who prayed for God to purge him with hyssop so he could be clean? Yet David didn't just pray a beautiful prayer that would resonate with a lot of people. He previously committed a grievous, horrendous sin that necessitated such a prayer and such a purging/cleansing. But this sin amazingly did not disqualify him from giving us this prophesy about Jesus. That's grace; that's awesome and I believe David, more than a lot of other people was the best candidate to make this prophesy because of what he learned about God after he sinned so badly. I don't think it's just coincidence or irony, but totally a divinely inspired factor. Sometimes it's easy to gloss over these details.

Friend, what I'm trying to say is that what you may think is your biggest failure, your biggest set-back in life, your biggest blemish against you is still redeemable according to God's abundant mercy and steadfast love for you. Jesus is still able to purge you, to make you clean by His precious blood.

LORD, I don't just need a sprinkling, I need a purging; a violent eradication of this sin from my life. Remove it LORD. Make me clean. I know violently eradicating things denotes a certain amount of pain and discomfort, but the results of being clean now are what I desire. So, do it LORD. Purge me. Wash me in Your blood and I will be clean in Jesus's name, amen!

Day 17: I Believe You!

"Now the serpent was more crafty than any other beast of the field that the LORD God had made. He said to the woman, 'Did God actually say, 'You shall not eat of any tree in the garden?" Genesis 3:1 NIV

"And the woman said to the serpent, 'We may eat of the fruit of the trees in the garden, but God said, 'You shall not eat of the fruit of the tree that is in the midst of the garden, neither shall you touch it, lest you die.' But the serpent said to the woman, 'You will not surely die. For God knows that when you eat of it your eyes will be opened, and you will be like God, knowing good and evil." Genesis 3:2-5 NIV

"And the LORD God commanded the man, saying, 'You may surely eat of every tree of the garden, but of the tree of the knowledge of good and evil you shall not eat, for in the day that you eat of it you shall surely die." Genesis 2:15 NIV

If you know something you are aware of it, you have developed a relationship with that information through spending time with that information; you are familiar with it. It's awareness, familiarity, regard, and an ability to distinguish. Most of us understand this with no problems. Yet if you believe something, you aren't just aware of it, but you also have accepted it as truth, you are sure of it; you have faith in it. There is a big difference between knowing and believing and with these working definitions in place it's easy to see that it is quite possible to know something but not believe it as true or at least not always believe it's true. Maybe this seems elementary but consider the account of the fall of man in Genesis 3.

Chapter 3 opens by telling us that the serpent, the devil, was more crafty than any of the other beasts that God had made, and the serpent says to the woman, "Did God really say..." (Genesis 3:1 NIV). The command to eat of any tree in the garden except for the tree of the knowledge of good and evil is recorded earlier in Genesis 2:15. God spoke this command directly to Adam, but it's interesting to note that this command came before Eve was even created so more than likely Adam was the one who relayed the command to Eve after she was fashioned by God in her Creator's image. The crafty serpent plays on this subtlety and goes to Eve with this ageless question of what God really said. Have you noticed that every temptation patterns a questioning of what God really says? Even when Jesus was tempted in the wilderness by the devil much later in Matthew 4, the enemy calls into question what God had just declared over Jesus at His baptism when the Father affirms, "This is My Son whom I love, with Him I am well pleased." (Matthew 3:17 NIV). Every one of the three temptations Satan crafts against Jesus in the wilderness right after this begin with him questioning, "If You are the Son of God..." Did you catch that? Satan calls into question what God had recently said about Jesus. Sounds a little familiar to that question in the Garden of Eden, "Did God actually say," doesn't it? I don't think that is an accident or coincidence, but a clear indication that the enemy constantly calls into question what God says and that his tactics haven't really changed. Satan knows what God says and he doesn't seem intimidated by our knowledge of what the LORD says, but whether we actually believe it or not.

Look at Eve's response in Genesis 3. The serpent asks her if God really said not to eat of the tree of the knowledge of good and evil and she quotes back to the enemy what God had said and she was accurate in her response. She knew what the LORD had said! So why did she fall for the temptation then. Doesn't seem to make much sense if she knew what God had said enough to quote it back to the enemy's face! The problem wasn't that she didn't know it, but that she didn't believe it! Did she doubt the message, the messenger, the source, or a little bit of all three? It doesn't really matter in the end because Satan knows that if he can play on any one of those doubts in your life, he can ultimately get you to doubt and disbelieve them all. If you don't believe the message, you won't trust the source of that message. If you doubt the trustworthiness of the messenger, you will more than likely question the message. They all play on one another, right?

Oh friend, I have spent a great portion of my life knowing what God says about me, my identity in Him. I can quote it to you. I can quote it to the enemy with chapter and verse, but this doesn't impress Satan much because he knows what God says about me too. Like Eve, I have known, but I haven't believed, and Satan will pounce on that lack of belief every single time. "Did God really say that you're His child? Did God really say that you're forgiven?

Did God really say that you are fearfully and wonderfully made? Did God really say?" It's a constant rhetoric, right? Satan is a relentless accuser and he realizes that it's possible for us to know what God has said, but to not always believe what God has said. That is the foothold that he's looking for, to cause us to question and doubt the message or the messenger, and ultimately the source of the message, God Himself and the validity of His Word. Personally, the issue for me hasn't been what God has said, but my belief in it and if I don't always believe, Satan knows that eventually I'll crumble. It's the same tactic over and over and over again. He even tried it with Jesus. It's time we wake up and become aware of his schemes so that he might not outwit us! If we disbelieve what God says, we'll be tempted to find what God offers us and has already given us through some other way apart from Him right?

It's time to not just know what God says, but believe what God says. It's more than time for me to accept as truth what God says about me, to have an unshakable faith in what God says about me so the enemy would be a fool to even go there with me anymore. It's time for us to believe what God really says! To believe all day, every day, no matter what, to establish our belief in the message and the source of that message! Satan persuaded Eve with the notion of being more like God which seems ridiculous because she was already like God, made in His image, His likeness. He tempted her with something that she already was but that she didn't believe that she was! Oh friend, it's high time that we wake up! You are a child of the living God. I am a daughter of the King of all kings. It's one thing for me to know this, to say this, express this, but it's another thing all together for you and me to emphatically believe it with everything that we have. Because if we believed it, truly believed it with everything that was in us; if it was settled as truth and etched as such on the very tablets of our hearts, it would deeply and dramatically affect how we live, how we talk, and even how we respond to our accuser. The redeemed Adam and Eve, those of us who have been restored to God through Jesus Christ would take hold of that crafty serpent by the neck and crush him under our feet where he belongs! I know we all have weak moments, weak days, times and areas of vulnerability in our lives, but we must settle in our hearts that we believe and will always believe what God has said even when it's hard, even when it doesn't feel true, even when others disbelieve it for us. Never stop believing! God doesn't speak to be heard; He speaks to be obeyed. My response is, "Yes Sir, You are right. I believe You." Let it be God in Jesus's name!

God,

> Help me to believe You today. Help me to choose to believe Your Word whether I feel like it or not, whether it feels true or not. Your Word is true no matter what. Today I choose to agree. Forgive me for my unbelief, my foolishness, my sin. Change me, Father in Jesus's name, amen.

Day 18: I Am Satisfied

> *"Jesus said to her, 'Everyone who drinks of this water will be thirsty again, but whoever drinks of the water that I will give him will never be thirsty again. The water that I will give him will become in him a spring of water welling up to eternal life.' The woman said to him, 'Sir, give me this water, so that I will not be thirsty or have to come here to draw water."* John 4:13-15 NIV

> *"So the woman left her water jar and went away into town and said to the people, 'Come, see a man who told me all that I ever did. Can this be the Christ?' They went out of the town and were coming to him."* John 4:28-30 NIV

Have you ever tried to get your needs met in an illegitimate way? I'm not talking about physical needs, but something much deeper; your need to be loved. We've all got that built-in need to be loved, a need intended to point us to the ultimate source of love, God. Yet most of us equate this need for other things and look to other means and sources to find nourishment and the love we so desperately long for. The story of the Samaritan woman at the well illustrates this whole process very well. In John chapter 4, Jesus, weary from His journey from Galilee, travels to Sychar and goes to Jacob's well to sit there and rest. Here he meets a Samaritan woman who comes to the well daily in order to draw the water she so desperately needs. I know this woman is desperate because she knowingly endures the shame associated with coming to this well every single day. Perhaps there isn't another well for her to go to or maybe this is the closest and most convenient spot in proximity to where she lives. Regardless, she is a Samaritan woman, looked down upon by the Jews, the lowest of the low culturally and socially and she treks to a well she isn't welcomed at to receive something she desperately needs until the day she meets a Jewish man there, Jesus, who tells her everything she ever did.

Jesus defies the cultural norm of His day by not only choosing to talk with a Samaritan who had a very clear and well-known enmity and division between the Samaritans and the Jews, but also by choosing to speak to a woman. He purposefully encounters this Samaritan woman, offering her living waters and completely changing her life by giving her a legitimate source for what she desperately needed.

This appeals greatly to the woman who comes to Jacob's well every day with her water jar to draw water out and have her thirst quenched and her need for water met. But there are a couple issues here. For one, the water she draws, though good and nourishing and needed, doesn't satisfy for long. The water serves its purpose then inevitably runs out, leaving this woman to travel back to the well every day in order to refill her water jar. In addition to that, Jacob's well was notoriously known as a Jewish watering spot. Being a Samaritan put her in a vulnerable position as she would more than likely wait until all the Jews had left before she could go fill her water jar. The very nature of going to this well for water brought with it shame and humiliation for the Samaritan woman. So when Jesus offers her a water source that will truly satisfy because one drink from it will produce a spring of living water to well up on the inside of the one who drinks it, she asks Jesus to give her this water so that she won't thirst again and so that she won't have to come to this well anymore.

Friend, just like the human body has a built-in need for water, emotionally at your core, you have a need for love, for acceptance, for approval. God fashioned you with such a need. So, you carry your water jar around emotionally until you find a well, a source of water that might supply what you need. The love, the acceptance, the approval is good; it's nourishing and needed, but most of us find wells with waters that don't truly satisfy. We go to the well of success or accomplishment thinking that the more we do, the more outstanding our achievements, the more impressive our resume, the more we will be loved and accepted and approved of not only by others, but also by ourselves. Sometimes, we even think God will like us better too. Yet those waters just don't satisfy for long. Or we go to the well of relationship thinking and hoping that if we could just get people to love us and accept us and approve of us then we'll be satisfied and all will be well, but instead we find ourselves coming back every day to draw water. We try repeatedly to quench a thirst that we just can't seem to quench. And like the Samaritan woman, there's a certain level of shame involved in this whole process. We need our water jars to be full, we crave so deeply the water (the love) that's inside, but those waters repeatedly run out, leaving us to trek back to an insufficient source, to draw water from a well we really aren't welcome at because most people are ok with giving you some water (some love), but no one is equipped to be your solitary source.

Oh friend, but Jesus has living waters. He offers living waters to you just like He did to this Samaritan woman. Waters that truly satisfy. One drink is enough. You don't have to keep trying, to keep working to get to these waters; you don't even have to bring your water jar to draw anything out of this well. One simple drink produces a spring of living waters to well up inside of you so that all you need and will ever need is already sourced inside of you. The source is Him, His Spirit now in you! There's no effort, no shame involved because Jesus satisfies that thirst and takes away the shame of drawing your own water from an illegitimate source with the Holy Spirit now housed in you. Do you need love; love Himself is in you. Drink up as much as you want; as much as you need. Do you need to feel accepted; the Spirit that brought about your adoption into sonship with God the Father is inside you. Get another drink of that acceptance if you want to. Do you need to feel approved of; that same Spirit that descended upon Jesus in the form of a dove where God declared Jesus to be His Son whom He loves and with whom He is well pleased is inside you. Drink again and know that your Father says that same thing over you; you are His son/His daughter whom He loves and with whom He is well pleased. The Samaritan woman had this encounter with Jesus, she drank from these living waters and afterwards verse 28 tells us that she went away and left her water jar. She left it! She didn't need it anymore, so she left that stupid thing behind! This tells me that she was coming to that well for more than just water! Her relationships were a mess. She had tried and failed to find love from the various people in her life. She was empty and needy, but now she had met Jesus! How absurd to keep carrying a water jar around, to keep drawing water from illegitimate sources when you already have a spring of living water inside of you. Oh friend, it's time to leave our water jars behind. Those water jars indicate an insatiable need that we continuously have, but if we've drank from the living water that Jesus offers, that need is now fully met in Him. So, we can cast off that thing that indicates our need. We don't need it anymore! She didn't need to come back to this well ever again. She didn't need to feel shamed and unsatisfied. She didn't need to carry around that water jar indicating that she needed water ever again. She wasn't in need any longer. Her need had been fully met with a source that was living, that would never run dry and one that brought no shame, no condemnation with it. Oh friend, it's time to take a drink of those waters. It's time to leave our water jars behind for good in Jesus's name!

LORD,

> I've been looking for love, for acceptance, for approval in all the wrong places. I've been carrying my water jug around begging people for water. I've been so desperate, so needy. Forgive me, God, for operating out of a love system that is contrary to Your system of love. I need You. You are my source. I recognize that You are the One with Living Waters. So, I come to You today. I want to drink deep of You, LORD. Change my appetite. Change my thirst. My I crave You, desire You, long for You in a dry and thirsty land where there is no water. I run to You today in Jesus's name, amen.

Day 19: I Am Rebuilt as I was at First

> *"Behold, I will bring to it health and healing, and I will heal them and reveal to them abundance of prosperity and security. I will restore the fortunes of Judah and the fortunes of Israel and rebuild them as they were at first. I will cleanse them from all the guilt of their sin against me, and I will forgive all the guilt of their sin and rebellion against me. And this city shall be to me a name of joy, a praise and a glory before all the nations of the earth who shall hear of all the good that I do for them. They shall fear and tremble because of all the good and all the prosperity I provide for it. Thus says the LORD: in this place of*

> *which you say, 'it is a waste without man or beast, in the cities of Judah and the streets of Jerusalem that are desolate, without man or inhabitant or beast, there shall be heard again the voice of mirth and the voice of gladness, the voice of the bridegroom and the voice of the bride, the voices of those who sing, as they bring thank offerings to the house of the LORD: 'Give thanks to the LORD of hosts, for the LORD is good, for his steadfast love endures forever!' For I will restore the fortunes of the land as at first, says the LORD."* Jeremiah 33:6-11 NIV

Do you have an area of your life that is just a mess? Maybe multiple areas? Places that have caused you issues most if not all your life. A place or places that you or others consider a waste, a desolate place no one wants to venture to, a broken area you're tempted to give up on? Hear the word of the LORD to you today, "I will bring to it health and healing, and I will heal them and reveal to them abundance of prosperity and security." (Jeremiah 33:6 NIV). This promise was declared over the nation of Israel after the Babylonians had come in to destroy the city of Jerusalem and take captive the people. This was something God warned Israel would happen many times, something He orchestrated to judge Israel of their sin because they refused to humble themselves and repent. The land was now desolate, in ruins, a wasteland. Maybe Israel doubted God's warnings before, but now they were a daily reality for them. I'm sure the whole thing seemed so final. They had blown it, big time. They had failed to listen to God, to obey, to repent before and although they were repentant now, I'm sure it felt like it was too late for them. Their land was already destroyed, desolate, in ruins; broken. Even if they set out to rebuild their home, things were such a mess, where should they begin? And to do so would require the favor and cooperation of their captors, a people that had executed this brutal devastation to begin with. I'm sure the whole thing seemed so overwhelming, defeating, a bit hopeless for Israel. Ever been there? But during all this, God promises to heal them, a revelation of abundance of prosperity and security.

Friend, God wants to reveal to you an abundance of prosperity and security. He wants to heal those desolate places of your heart, your life. Prosperity isn't just a reference to wealth or success, but also to well-being. The LORD is whole; there is no brokenness, no desolation about Him or His nature, and in Christ; He brings you to fullness, to wholeness. Sin brings brokenness, but Christ brings wholeness and a revelation of the profusion, the loads and loads of well-being that is God's and that you have access to through Christ. He wants to reveal to you an abundance of security, feeling safe and stable, free from danger and anxiety. He is here to restore your fortunes, not just a monetary thing, but a restoration of those things, people, and qualities that are useful and valuable to you, that are an asset to you, to rebuild them as they were at first, as they originally were supposed to be. Wow!

Jeremiah 33 speaks of a cleansing of all the guilt of Israel's sin and rebellion against God and that the city of Jerusalem will instead be a name of joy to the LORD, a praise and a glory to Him before all the nations of the earth who shall hear of God's goodness and His prosperity (well-being) to His people. This city and these people that had sinned and rebelled, who were ruined and destroyed and desolate would be healed by the LORD, their guilt removed, and instead of being known as a people who had sinned and rebelled and were thus desolate; they would be a name of joy to God; a praise and a glory to Him before all the people of the earth. Oh friend, when God heals you there is a cleansing of all the guilt associated with your sin and rebellion. He heals you to such a degree that where before people talked about your brokenness, shook their heads in shame, in disappointment at the mention of your name. God wants to heal you in such a way, bring you to so much well-being and wholeness that your name becomes His joy, a praise and glory to Him before everyone who witnesses the ruins being rebuilt in your life. Rebuilding is often a process. It takes time, hard work. Rarely is it an overnight job. God is God. He could have very well instantaneously rebuilt Israel's ruins, but He didn't. It was a long process that took time, lots of work; a process that illustrates God's patience, His endurance, His goodness and faithfulness; how His steadfast love bears with you forever! This word of promise came to Jeremiah while he was yet shut up in the court of the guard; a captive, a prisoner, the city he loved so much currently laying in ruins. God's promise, His healing, His wholeness did not at all line up with Jeremiah's reality, but, friend, God is not intimidated by your chains or your ruins nor is He limited by them. His love rebuilds!

Oh friend, I don't know what kind of ruins you have in your life, what brokenness, what areas of your heart remain desolate. I don't know what place of your life is like a no-man's land, a place without inhabitant, a place people are appalled at when they see it, so you do your best to keep them from seeing it right? Even a child will choose a whole cookie over a broken one if given the choice, so sometimes we personify a wholeness especially in the church that isn't authentic just because we want to be chosen or continue to be chosen and we're all too aware of people's propensity to abandon broken, desolate places. But God doesn't offer you a pretense of wholeness. He tends to expose pretenses because He wants the real thing for you. Rather He says to those desolate places, "I will bring to it health and healing." (Jeremiah 33:6a NIV). He wants to reveal to you an abundance of prosperity and security; an abundance of well-being and safety/stability. He desires to rebuild you as you were at first, as He originally designed you to be. Rebuilding takes time, it takes work, but go ahead and give thanks to Him for He is good, and His steadfast love will endure; it will bear with you forever. He's in it for the long haul. He won't give up on you. He won't walk away, get tired of the process, lose His patience with you and eventually decide that your ruins are too much, you're too broken; He can't bear with you for another day. His steadfast love bears all things with you. He is more patient with you than you could even imagine so that in those desolate places without inhabitant there will again be heard the voice of joy and gladness. I pray it is so in your life in Jesus's name.

Oh, God,

> I'm a mess. My life feels like a mess right now. Everything feels like it's in ruins and it's not that some horrible, unjust thing has happened to me. I know these ruins are a result of my sin, my choices. Oh God, I'm sorry. I wish I could go back and listen to You. I wish I could go back and choose differently. But I can't. Please help me to know where to go from here. Please help me to surrender to You in this rebuilding process. I thank You for hope. I thank You for healing. I thank You that You rebuild the broken down, devastated places of my heart and life. May those places bring You glory and praise in Jesus's name, amen.

Day 20: I Am Precious in God's Eyes, Honored, and Loved!

"But now thus says the LORD, he who created you, O Jacob, he who formed you, O Israel; 'Fear not, for I have redeemed you; I have called you by name, you are mine.…For I am the LORD your God, the Holy One of Israel, your Savior. I give Egypt as your ransom, Cush and Seba in exchange for you. Because you are precious in my eyes, and honored, and I love you, I give men in return for you, peoples in exchange for your life." Isaiah 43:1, 3-4 NIV

The LORD created you; He formed you. It is He who has redeemed you through Christ, called you by name. You are His! That's what this Scripture says in Isaiah 43. It says that the LORD gave Egypt as your ransom, Cush and Seba in exchange for you. Egypt was Israel's captors; their slave-drivers. Egypt was the nation that represented Israel's enslavement and, in many ways, represents our enslavement to sin. Romans 6:20 makes this comparison, likening us to slaves to sin, bound to that which displeases God, totally unable to free ourselves. Yet just like God brought deliverance to the nation of Israel through Moses and all the mighty acts of God in leading Israel out of Egypt and destroying Israel's captors, God in Christ has done the same thing for us with our enslavement to sin. He has set us free! The nations of Cush and Seba were also nations primarily known for their production of slaves and I believe these references to these nations represent what Christ did for us on the cross. He freed us from our enslavement, exchanged that enslavement for freedom. Hallelujah!

Because you are precious in His eyes, honored, and because He loves you, He has given the man, Jesus Christ, in exchange for your life. Isn't that the good news of the Bible, of the Gospel! For God so loved the world; God so loved you that He gave Jesus. Don't let that ageless truth lose its ability to move you. May it never get old to you! "The friendship of the LORD is for those who fear him, and he makes known to them his covenant." (Psalm 25:14 NIV). Why would friendship be the result of fearing God? Friendship, intimacy, closeness, forgiveness does not seem fitting with fear. Shouldn't the fear of the LORD produce punishment and friendship produce love? That would seem more logical, but Scripture equates closeness and friendship with God to fearing Him. Truly, no man more fully loves God than he who is most fearful to offend Him. Wow! That's what brings you close to God. Hating evil enough to not want anything to do with it just because you desire to please Him so much, you don't want to offend Him to that degree. Psalm 25 says that it's to those who fear Him that He makes known His covenant. He makes known His coming together, like a marriage, a life-long friendship commitment. Those who fear Him have access to a deeper level of relationship with the Almighty God. That's what I take away from this Scripture. Wow!

> Holy Spirit help me to truly fear God, to want to please Him above all else, to love God so much that I would be fearful of offending Him. Bring me to that place of intimacy with God. Let my heart be that caught up and connected to the Living God. I renounce all others because You have called me by name, and I am Yours. Let it be LORD in Jesus's name, amen!

Day 21: I Am Humbly Surrendered

> *"When the rule of Rehoboam was established and he was strong, he abandoned the law of the LORD, and all Israel with him."* 2 Chronicles 12:1 NIV

> *"Then Shemiah the prophet came to Rehoboam and to the princes of Judah, who had gathered at Jerusalem because of Shishak, and said to them, 'Thus says the LORD, you abandoned me, so I have abandoned you to the hand of Shishak.' Then the princes of Israel and the king humbled themselves and said, 'The LORD is righteous.'* 2 Chronicles 12:5-6 NIV

In 2 Chronicles 12 we learn of Solomon's son, Rehoboam, who became the king of Israel after his father's death. A few chapters earlier in 2 Chronicles 10 we see how foolishly Rehoboam acts in dealing with the people of Israel. Instead of listening to those who advised his father, he listens to his peers and answers the people harshly. The people were exhausted from their labor in building the Temple and the kingdom under Solomon's rule and were requesting a lighter load under Rehoboam's rule. He refuses them. Jeroboam was there trying to rally the unhappy people together against the king so that Rehoboam might be overthrown, and Jeroboam might reign instead. In response, Rehoboam assembles his troops to fight against Jeroboam and technically his own people, but the word of the LORD comes to him through the prophet Shemiah, instructing him not to go up to fight against his relatives. Rehoboam listened to the LORD. So, Rehoboam lived in Jerusalem and built cities for defense in Judah against Jeroboam, but they never actually went out to fight their relatives according to what God had said. So, God strengthened Rehoboam and his kingdom especially as they walked in the ways of David and Solomon, following the law of God.

Yet chapter 12 of 2 Chronicles opens by saying that when the rule of Rehoboam was established and he was strong, he abandoned the law of the LORD and all Israel with him. And because of this unfaithfulness, God sends Shishak the king of Egypt against Jerusalem. What does this tell me? There are consequences to sin! Then the LORD sends the prophet Shemiah to the King and to his princes saying, "You abandoned me, so I have abandoned you to the hand of Shishak." (2 Chronicles 12:5 NIV). Wow! Not exactly an encouraging message from the LORD. God equated an abandonment of His law, His word, His ways with an abandonment of Him personally. And so, He abandons the King and his people to the hand of the king of Egypt. Yet Rehoboam and the princes of Israel don't hide what they have done, they don't justify it or ignore it or excuse it. The Bible says that they humble themselves in response to this word from the LORD and all they say in response is, "The LORD is righteous." (2 Chronicles 12:6 NIV). The LORD pointed out their grievous sin to them and although this may seem unkind or unloving, God does so in order to give Rehoboam and his people opportunity to come back to Him. Thus, is the difference between condemnation and conviction. Condemnation points out your sin then convinces you that you must be punished for it. It is final. It pushes you away from God. It totally negates the work of Jesus on the cross. Conviction points out your sin by also providing the means to restoration. It invites you in to confess, to repent and to ultimately realign your heart with God's. It pulls you into God by realizing your own inadequacy to make things right but trusts in Jesus as your Advocate with the Father. It's important to detect the different spirits at work here.

Rehoboam and the princes of Israel respond to God's word to them with humility and all they declare is that God is righteous, thus implying that even in this personal word to them and this bringing of the king of Egypt against them, God is demonstrating His righteousness. They admit their sin, their guilt, they agree with God in humility and that's huge. In the next verse, when God sees that they have humbled themselves, He gives another word to Shemiah the prophet declaring that He will not destroy them but will grant them some deliverance. He declares that His wrath won't be poured out on Israel by the hand of Shishak the king of Egypt, but Israel will be servants to Shishak so that they may know God's service and the service of the kingdoms of the countries.

God responds to their humility. The LORD always responds to humility. He opposes the proud but gives grace to the humble. If you humble yourself before Him, He will exalt you, lift you up in due time. That's how God responds to humility. Wow! The LORD relents of this destruction that had been decreed against Rehoboam and Israel. He declares that they won't be destroyed, but He says that they will be servants to the king of Shishak so that they might learn the difference between the LORD's service and the service of the kingdoms of this world. God still in love chooses to discipline Israel that they may know God's service and the service of the kingdoms of the countries. He decides to do this in order to teach Rehoboam and all of Israel an important lesson; they needed to learn the difference between serving God and serving the kingdoms of the world. They seemed to have believed that serving God was burdensome and harsh, thus their choice to abandon God and His law. Maybe they thought serving other kingdoms would be "fairer" or "better." Yet God was about to show them otherwise, to teach them an invaluable lesson; His laws, His ways, who He is isn't burdensome or enslaving or imprisoning, they are quite freeing. They are protecting and providential in nature and this is not the case in man-made systems of enslavement. Apparently, Israel needed to learn this lesson first-hand and God knew this, so the LORD delivers them but not entirely this time. Out of love for His people, He permits this service not to punish them primarily, but to teach them. And verse 13 tells us that King Rehoboam grew strong in Jerusalem and reigned, so this act orchestrated by God truly served to help strengthen the king, not diminish him in any way.

Friend, the point is that we must trust God and His heart towards us and His nature in general. We must trust that He knows us better than we even know ourselves and anything that He has placed in our lives or not placed in our lives is done so for a reason even if it is to teach us something about Him. We must always approach Him with humility, in humility because He is God and we are not, and Scripture is replete with evidence that God responds favorably to humility. His heart towards us is good. His motives are pure and righteous and full of love. Even in His discipline He is good and righteous and loving. He's not out to crush you or destroy you. Sin is bent on doing that in your life. Rather He is out to restore and rebuild you but the only way He can do that is through your humble agreement with whatever is a problem in your life, in your heart, in your relationships. He will always honor your free will because He's the one who gave it to you, that's why humility is such a powerful thing. Humility reveals a heart that is surrendered to Him by choice not by force or coercion. And grace is a direct result of humility, something God gives to those who make the choice to repeatedly surrender to Him. Wow! It's time to surrender, to be a people truly humble before Almighty God. It's time to listen and obey and let Him lead us and teach us so that we don't have to experience things or learn lessons the hard way. It's time to grow up but remain humbly surrendered to Him. Let it be God in Jesus's name!

God,

> I've made some big mess-ups. I haven't just stumbled into wrong; I've gone looking for it, I've ignored Your warnings and what I know to be true and trusted in myself rather than You. Oh LORD, forgive me. I humble myself before You today. I repent today. I turn back to You today. I surrender in Jesus's name, amen.

Day 22: I Am Treasured

> *"You (God) keep track of ALL my sorrows. You have collected all my tears in your bottle. You have recorded each one in your book."* Psalm 56:8 NLT

> *"…It (love) keeps no record of wrongdoing but rejoices with the truth."* 1 Corinthians 13:6 NIV

Imagine being in a relationship with someone, with a Father, who absolutely keeps no record of your wrongs, nada, none whatsoever; zilch. Who does that? It's not that He doesn't know them or has forgotten them. He's God, He's all-knowing, to just magically forget your wrongdoings would seem impossibly ridiculous; counter intuitive considering who He is. Yet He does choose not to record them, not to hold them against you or chronicle them to your disadvantage in Christ. Why? Because He loves you. He loved you so much that He gave Jesus so that this could be a reality in your life and in your relationship with Him. That's amazing, but it gets better. This Father of yours not only chooses not to record your wrongdoings, but the Bible says that He does keep track of all your sorrows. So instead of recording your wrongs, your sins, He records your hurts; there's not a tear you've shed that He does not notice and keep track of. Wow! He collects each one of your tears in His bottle and records every single one of them in His book. So, instead of recording your wrongs, He records your tears! Are you getting this?

Your Father loves you enough not to record your wrongs, but to remove them in Christ. And He loves you enough to keep track of your sorrows, of what makes you cry. There's a book that He has with each one of your tears recorded in it. There's a personal bottle that He has that contains every single one of your tears. He doesn't scold you for crying, reprimand you for not being stronger in the face of sorrow, He doesn't ignore it or look away. Revelation 21:4 assures us that there is coming a day when He will wipe every tear from our eyes, but until then He collects them in His bottle almost as if He's keeping them safe in His care until that day when He can personally wipe them from your eye. Wow! This is the heart of your Father, a good,

good Father unlike any earthly father could ever live up to who has such a personalized knowledge and care of each of your individualized hurts. This is what He carries around with Him, what He notices, what He pays attention to, what moves Him, what He does for you because He treasures you that much. It's almost too much to wrap our minds around! Can you imagine what it will be like when you finally get to heaven and you get to see these things first-hand? I can hear Him saying, "Here, let me show you how much I love you. Here's your tear bottle that holds every tear you've ever cried. There's not a tear you shed in your lifetime that I did not notice. Here's the proof, this bottle, your bottle, your tears. Look, here's your book that contains the personalized details of every single sorrow you ever encountered, you have ever felt. I saw it all. I noticed it all. It all mattered to me. I have no record of your wrongs, that record ended up going through the paper shredder in Christ; it's hanging on the cross. But I do have these records about you because that is and has always been My heart towards you. Oh, how I love you!"

Maybe this seems silly, a little far-fetched, but I find it precious to know that I have a Father like this. Can you imagine how this truth if you really "got" it could absolutely transform your relationship with God; change how you view your Father forever? Today friend, if you feel broken, hurt, you've cried so many tears; tears you thought no one even saw. Today if you're hurting and you feel like no one sees, no one cares, no one even understands what you're going through. I'm here to tell you today that don't you dare believe that your Father doesn't care, that He doesn't notice. He's keeping a record of your tears; He's collecting them in His bottle. He's keeping track of all your sorrows. He cares, He cares, He cares! His love for you goes beyond just not recording your wrongs; His love also encompasses something as personal and precious as collecting and recording your tears. It's time to trade in the record you're keeping of your own wrongs for the record He is keeping of your hurts, your grief, your pain, and your tears. If for nothing else I pray that this truth from God's Word would overwhelm your heart today with the deep revelation of how high and wide and deep God's love for YOU is! Let it be LORD in Jesus's name!

God,

> Oh, how my heart is hurting today. I don't even know what to say. I just want to thank You for seeing my tears, for caring about my sorrows. Would You please be near me today? I ask

You to heal my heart, that this truth from Your Word would be a healing salve on my broken heart in Jesus's name, amen.

Day 23: I Am Compensated in Christ

"In Him (Christ) we have redemption (compensation) through His blood, the forgiveness of our trespasses, according to the riches of His grace." Ephesians 1:7 ESV

"But by His (God's) doing you are in Christ Jesus, who became to us wisdom from God, and righteousness and sanctification, and redemption (compensation)." 1 Corinthians 1:30 NASB

"Who gave Himself (Jesus) for us to redeem us (compensate, make up for) from every lawless deed, and to purify for Himself a people for His own possession, zealous for good deeds." Titus 2:14 NASB

Hear the Word of the LORD to you today from Isaiah. "Fear not, for you will not be ashamed (you won't be ashamed of your sin, of your past, of your failures); be not confounded (don't be surprised or confused), for you will not be disgraced (you won't be shamed, discredited; you won't lose reputation or respect as a result of a dishonorable action); for you will forget the shame of your youth (that shameful thing from your past, that faulty love system you learned as a child that has influenced your life and your relationships thus far), and the reproach (the disapproval and disappointment) of your widowhood (your isolation and loneliness) you will remember no more. For your Maker (God Himself) is your husband, the LORD of hosts...(Jehovah-Saboath, the God of an innumerable array of warring angels) is His name, and the Holy One of Israel is your Redeemer (He is the One who compensates for your faults and all of your bad aspects, your sin; the One who has regained possession of you in Christ), the God of the whole earth He is called. For the LORD has called you like a wife deserted (like a wife abandoned, left empty; a wife failed at a crucial moment when she needed someone the most), and grieved in spirit (one who is in sorrow, in great distress, pain, hurt, wounded inside); like a wife in youth when she is cast off (thrown away and discarded) says your God. For a moment I deserted you, but with great compassion I will gather you (assemble you, bring you together again, take you in from scattered places). In overwhelming anger for a moment I hid my face from you, but in everlasting love I will have compassion (sympathy, tenderness, mercy) on you says the LORD your Redeemer (the One who has compensated or made up for all of your faults and bad aspects)." (Isaiah 54:4-8 NIV-emphasis added)

Whew! Isn't that awesome? Friend, in Christ you are redeemed. He is your Redeemer. Most of us may be familiar with that terminology and we've heard it used before, but consider the truth that He, Jesus, is the One who has compensated or made up for all your faults, your sins; your bad aspects. This means that thing about you that seems too bad, too shameful, too much of a set-back or failure, that thing or maybe it's a whole slew of things that have disgraced you, that has caused you shame, has caused you to be discredited and to lose respect and reputation. God has made up for that in Christ. Wow! Let that sink in for a second. We often go through life discrediting ourselves and each other. We have logical reasons and explanations and limitations and excuses we readily place on our own lives as well as on one another's. It's easy for us to lose hope, to get jaded, to be confounded because most of us know our own faults and even each other's faults and bad aspects well. Those things are easy for us to notice and call out. But in God's everlasting love, He has compassion on you. He is tender and merciful even though He has reasons not to be; there is an overwhelming reason why He is tender towards you: His everlasting love! We would do well to be compassionate, to show tenderness and mercy to ourselves and to each other simply because of God's everlasting love for us. Imagine that kind of family, there truly would be no fear within that dynamic. There is another side to His character that makes His love complete and that is His justice, His holiness. There is order with Him. He is not a God of disorder but of peace. Still, His love for you is greater than your faults, your bad characteristics; your sin. This is the very reason Jesus came, to redeem you; to take all of that garbage away, to cancel it out, eradicate it from ever being an excuse in your life; to make up for what you think you don't have so that you can receive perfect relationship with God, your Maker.

It's time to forget the shame of your youth. It's time to remember no more the grief and pain of your isolation and loneliness. It's time to be assembled again, to have the LORD your God gather you together again including all those pieces of your heart that have been scattered to foreign places. He is in the business of wholeness, of healing; of restoration. He is an incredible God and the greatest Father. I pray you hear and feel His heart for you today.

God,

I need You. I need to be redeemed. I need to have all the sin and bad aspects of my life and heart and character eradicated, compensated for. I need a Savior! I admit it today. I can't save myself. No one else can do it for me either. I need You. I run to You today. Jesus, wash over me again. Cleanse my hands. Purify my heart. Do what only You can do in me. I praise You and bless You today in Jesus's name, amen.

Day 24: I Am Turning Around

"For 'who has known the mind of the LORD so as to instruct him?' But we have the mind of Christ." 1 Corinthians 2:16 NIV

"Have this mind among yourselves, which is yours in Christ Jesus, who, though he was in the form of God, did not count equality with God a thing to be grasped, but emptied himself, by taking the form of servant, being born in the likeness of men." Philippians 2:5-7 ESV

"From that time on Jesus began to preach, 'Repent, for the kingdom of heaven has come near." Matthew 4:17 NIV

The Word of God is replete with admonishments, commandments, and opportunities to repent; to not just be sorry for sins, transgressions, wrongdoing and asking for forgiveness, but to change one's heart, one's mind, and one's life. Full repentance happens when your heart, mind, and life have changed. It's much more than being remorseful about wrong behaviors and confessing those things to the LORD. We confess, we agree with Him on what we have done, who we have become as an act of humility and surrender so that He can change our hearts. That's the portion of repentance we are unable to accomplish. We cannot make our hearts right, our hearts pure; we are unable to change our own hearts, but God is well acquainted with our hearts and is able to change them. "I (God) will give you a new heart and put a new spirit within you; I will remove from you your heart of stone and give you a heart of flesh." (Ezekiel 36:26 NIV). He changes your heart, gives you a new heart. This is not something you can accomplish on your own. Only He can change your heart and repentance includes this confession and surrendering of your heart to Him so that He can change it; literally exchange the hard, stone-like, stubborn one prone to sin and lean on its own understanding for one that is soft and tender; a heart of flesh. Wow, thank You Jesus!

Yet there is a part that we play in repentance that goes beyond our confession and admission, our rendering our hearts before God so that He can change them. Repentance also includes a complete change of mind and this is something God has given us the responsibility for. It's up to you to change your own mind, to transform your mind by renewing it with God's Word, His truth. This alignment of your thoughts with truth, with God's Word does not happen automatically and it isn't something that He does for us supernaturally. It is a process that we engage in deliberately, every day over the course of our lives. Paul describes this as a battle in our minds and instructs us in 2 Corinthians 10:5 to take every thought captive and make them obedient to Christ. That is tedious, hard, but necessary work in the life of every believer. But 1 Corinthians 2:16 tells us that we have the mind of Christ. It's yours, friend, already given to you in Christ Jesus. If it's already yours then it is possible to have the mind of Christ in your life. This means you can think about yourself the way that Jesus thinks about you. You can think about others the way that Jesus thinks about them. You can think about sin the way Jesus thinks about sin. You can have the mind of Jesus about your life, your family, about eternity, about heaven; about everything. How is that even possible? Because you have the Word of God, which is a revelation of the Word made Flesh, Jesus!

Friend, it's time to repent, to rend your heart before the LORD and allow Him to change your heart. Only He can do that for you, so repentance is a necessary part of a changed life. But it's also time for you to change your mind, to change the way you think about yourself, about others, about your enemies, about the church, about sin, about eternity; about everything! It's time to change your mind with the truth of God's Word, to read His Word, to know His Word, to think about His Word; to align how you think about a certain topic to what the Bible says about that topic because what the Bible says is Christ's mind on the matter. And you have the mind of Christ! It's a battle, it's a process, it's something you must do over and over and over again day in and day out. It's something no one else can do for you and no one else can even see that you are doing generally, but it is necessary to having a changed life. If you'll change your thoughts, change your mind to think how Jesus thinks; you'll change your life. It's time to repent, completely; a changed heart, a changed mind, and a changed life. Let it be LORD in Jesus's name!

Father,

> I come before You today rending my heart in Your presence. I know that You see and know my heart much better than even I know it. You created it and You are familiar with all my ways. So, I ask You to search me, to search my heart, to know my thoughts, to see if there be any wicked way in me. Bring anything about me that is wicked or sinful or displeasing to You to my attention so that I can confess it, agree with You about it and allow You to change this heart of mine as I forsake it in pursuit of greater intimacy with You. That's what I want! And I thank You that I have the mind of Christ. Would You help me to think about things the way that Jesus does, especially when it comes to the way I think about myself. I know I must do the diligent, tedious, difficult task of taking every thought captive and making it obedient to what Your Word says. Please help me with this Holy Spirit. I am weak, but You are strong, and I know that I can do all things through Christ who strengthens. I take responsibility for my thought life and where it has brought me to thus far. Forgive me for not being a better steward of my thoughts. Forgive me for thinking about myself or any area of my life that is contrary to Your Word. I have the mind of Christ and for me to think in opposition to what the Bible says is contrary to this gift that You have given me. I repent. I plead Christ's blood over my life, my sin, even over my mind and thoughts. I don't want to have a mind that is hostile to You, but one that promotes the greatest level of intimacy with You. I realize that the way I have allowed

myself to think about myself is in opposition to Your Word and how Jesus thinks about me, this way of thinking has brought separation between You and I; a separation that I am responsible for since I am in control of what I think about. Forgive me LORD. Oh, how I need You, God! Bring revival to my life as a result of being closer to You. Change my life and draw nearer to me as I truly repent and change the way I think in Jesus's name, amen.

Day 25: I Am Christ's Joy...His Prize

"Look to Jesus, the founder and perfecter of faith, who for the joy set before Him (the prize set before Him) endured the cross, despising the shame, and is seated at the right hand of the throne of God." Hebrews 12:2 ESV

"In bringing many sons and daughters to glory, it was fitting that God, for whom and through whom everything exists, should make the pioneer of their salvation (Jesus) perfect through what He suffered." Hebrews 2:10 NIV

"And God raised us up with Christ and seated us with Him in the heavenly realms in Christ Jesus." Ephesians 2:6 NIV

"I press on toward the goal to win the prize for which God has called me heavenward in Christ Jesus." Philippians 3:14 NIV

As a believer, a follower, a disciple of Jesus, what is your goal? What are you pressing on towards? What is your prize, that one thing that keeps you going even when life is hard, and things are difficult? Paul says in Philippians that he is "pressing on toward the goal to win the prize that God has called him heavenward in Christ Jesus". (Philippians 3:14 NIV) What is Paul's prize? Jesus; unbroken and eternal connection with the LORD his God both now and forevermore. What a prize! Isn't that the prize for all of us or at least shouldn't that be the prize for all of us? He is our goal, our prize; what we are striving for. It's not the success, the glory, the recognition; the stuff He has done or will do for us. It's not even just escaping hell; it's Him. Relationship with Him is our aim, the absolute prize or at least that is intended to be what Christ purchased on our behalf; the possibility of Him being our prize becoming a reality in our lives both now and for all eternity. That's truly amazing if you stop and think about it. But did you know that you are His prize too?

Look at Hebrews 12. It says that Jesus endured the cross and all the shame associated with it for the joy that was set before Him. What was that joy? The Greek word for joy in this Scripture is *charas* which means "joy/ delight." It was Christ's delight, His joy to obey the Father. It wasn't His duty or obligation, but His joy; sheds a whole new light on what Jesus said, "If you love me, keep my commandments." (John 14:15 NIV). It's not a directive of having to keep His commandments in order to prove your love for Him. It's the other way around. Love Him, and keeping His commandments is born out of that love. Psalm 149:4 says that the LORD takes delight in His people and Zephaniah 3:17 tells us that God takes great delight in you, that He is rejoicing over you with singing. In addition to this, Hebrews 2:10 informs us that Jesus was made perfect through what He suffered in order to bring many sons and daughters to glory. Jesus is exalted and is seated at the right hand of the throne of God. He has perfect, unbroken fellowship with God the Father, but He had that before He came to this world. So why would He come; why go through the cross in the first place? "For God so loved the world that He gave His only begotten Son that whosoever believes in Him should not perish but have everlasting LIFE." (John 3:16 NIV). God so loved the world; He so loved you that He gave the world, He gave you Jesus in order that if you believe in Him you shouldn't perish, but instead have everlasting life with Him! That's it; hat's the prize, you!

Oh friend, you are precious in God's eyes, honored, and greatly loved. Yes, God hates sin. Yes, He convicts people of their sin, but He does it with the intent and purpose of wanting restored relationship with you because you are and have always been His prize! He doesn't need you; He wants you! Even the messiest, most sinful parts of you because Romans 5:8 makes it clear that while you were yet a sinner, Christ died for you. You were His prize before you cleaned up your act, before you ever loved Him in return, even while you were outright breaking His commandments and showing Him complete disregard; you were still His prize! Sometimes we think we must be so pristine and holy for God to love us, for Him to want us, but the whole Gospel tells quite the opposite story. Jesus proves that the nastiest, most revile, sinful parts of you are worth redeeming; hallelujah! Of course, He doesn't leave you in your sin, tolerate it, accept it. He hates what is evil. He does not tolerate sin. He is indeed holy. Yet He loved you enough, valued you enough to send Jesus to compensate for all your faults so that you could be with Him. Ephesians 2:16 says that God has raised you up with Christ and seated you with Him in the heavenly realms in Christ Jesus. Jesus endured the cross for you. He's seated at the right hand of God's throne making intercession for you and not only that, God has raised you up to sit with Christ in the heavenly realm. You couldn't sit there apart from the cross! Oh, He wants to be your prize, but it's foundational and truly remarkable to grasp that you already are His. Doesn't that revelation make you love Him more, make you want to be closer to Him? You aren't junk, you're not a fraud or some discarded, lowly thing, not in Christ Jesus! You're His joy, His delight, His prize, the very reason Jesus went to the cross to begin with! May this truly cause you to press on toward the goal to win the prize of eternal unbroken relationship with your Maker, your Creator, your Father through Christ Jesus both now and forever.

God,

> I thank You for redeeming me in Christ, for considering me a joy and delight to You. You are so good. Change my heart. Forgive my misgivings and hard-heartedness. You are my joy, my prize. You are worthy of it all. Thank You for who You are. In Jesus's name, amen.

Day 26: I Have No Lack

"And my God will meet all your needs according to the riches of his glory in Christ Jesus." Philippians 4:19 NIV

"For the LORD your God has blessed you in all that you have done; He has known your wanderings through this great

> *wilderness. These forty years the LORD your God has been with you; you have not lacked a thing."* Deuteronomy 2:7 NASB

You have no lack, no deficiency, no shortage in Jesus. Why? Because "my God will meet all of your needs according to the riches of His glory in Christ Jesus!" (Philippians 4:19 NIV). This Scripture pertains to finances and material needs at least in the context of what Paul was talking about in his closing statements to the church in Philippi. Here he thanks them for sharing in his troubles and for sharing with him in the matter of giving and receiving. Their financial aid and gifts helped Paul when he was in need specifically in Thessalonica, so Paul expresses his gratitude and assures the church of Philippi that God will also meet all their needs. Yet this supplying of needs is in accordance to the riches, the resources, the treasures of God's glory in Christ Jesus. How would you describe God's glory? Well, God's Word describes the glory of the LORD as very great, magnificent; awe-inspiring. In 1 Kings 8 the glory of the LORD filled the house of God and this glory was so great that the priests couldn't even stand on their feet to minister. God's glory is radiant, powerful, and incredibly great. Revelation 21:23 informs us that the new Jerusalem described in Scripture will not need the sun or the moon to give it light as we have needed here on earth, for the glory of God will give it light and the Lamb, Jesus, will be its lamp. And Hebrews 1:3 tells us that Jesus is the radiance of God's glory. That is some powerful glory, limitless glory; glory that has no equal, no comparison, no counterpart; glory that brings kings and priests and peasants all to the same position: on their faces. God's glory isn't discriminatory, it isn't influenced by socioeconomic status, popularity, prestige, accomplishments, or any man-made thing. His glory fills the expanse of the heavens and the earth and all your needs are supplied in accordance with the plentiful, powerful, radiant, rich glory of God; all of your needs are met in Jesus, the radiance of God's glory. Wow!

Oh friend, let this encourage you today. It's time to talk like you have no lack. It's time to live like you have no lack, to think like you have no lack, to pray and believe like you have no lack because according to God's Word, you have no lack! In Deuteronomy 2, the children of Israel had come out of Egypt, their land of slavery, of captivity, of bondage. And after coming to their land of promise from God and choosing to believe instead the negative report about the land, to be afraid of all the problems and technicalities of taking possession of the land. After allowing man's word to trump God's word, to believe that they were but grasshoppers in comparison to the giants already living in the land, Israel endures the consequence of not believing God, a delay in the fulfillment of the promise: to wander in the wilderness for forty years. Forty whole years! That's a long time, enough time for a whole generation of people to pass away. That's a long time to wake up and go to bed every day and be reminded that you aren't where you're supposed to be, where you're intended to be, where you've been promised to be because of your lack of belief, because of your disobedience, because of your failure to take God at His Word. How does one endure such regret? And to be sure that choice, their unbelief, that sin brought death to Israel, a whole generation dies; all the people who came out of Egypt die before they ever enter the land God promised them except Caleb and Joshua. Don't be fooled. Sin always brings death. It will always cost you something. No one wants to talk about the cost of sin, the penalty of sin, but God's Word says that the penalty of sin is death. Jesus paid that penalty for sure, but don't believe the lie that it's no big deal, that it doesn't matter; that it doesn't hurt anyone. If for nothing else, that sin hurt Jesus, brought death to Jesus and that is a big deal to God. Yet God's Word declares in Deuteronomy 2:7 that even during these forty years of wandering in the wilderness, still Israel has been blessed, still the LORD has been with Israel and they have not lacked a thing. Oh friend, the LORD your God isn't just with you in the Promised Land; He's with you as you wander in the wilderness! Not too many people may wander with you through the wilderness or at least wait on you to get done wandering there yourself, but God does. He is incredibly patient with you! And why did Israel fail to enter their promised land sooner? Because they chose to only see themselves as mere grasshoppers, incapable of conquering giants. They only saw themselves and all that they lacked instead of realizing that God's glory would supply and make up for all that they had a shortage of so that they would more than not lack anything! They failed to believe that because God was with them, they could truly be grasshoppers who destroyed giants!

Friend, can I tell you that God knows your wanderings, this long period of time where you have suffered delay to your promise because of your lack of belief in who He is and who you are as a result? He knows how you have lived on the outside of all that He has for you, how you have been given something greater and better. It's yours, but you've stumbled in the actuality of taking ownership of it. He knows how the enemies, the giants, the opposition has intimidated you and left you feeling like a grasshopper in comparison. He knows how your belief about yourself that you are just a grasshopper, something small and insignificant and easily squashed by the enemy; how this view of yourself and your own inabilities has trumped who God is and His word to you in your mind and this alone has prevented you from entering in. Oh friend, can I just tell you that He knows, your Father, your God knows! And even during this time, aimlessly wandering through this great wilderness still God has been with you. He hasn't left you! He provides for you even in the wilderness.

And can I also tell you that because He is with you, you lack nothing! Because He is with you, you can conquer giants, you will possess the promise if only you choose to believe! Yes, you very well may be a grasshopper, but the emphasis here is not on what you are or what you are not in and of yourself, but more on who you are in Him, because He is with you! Him being with you changes everything, it is the single most definitive truth that your victory hinges upon. The devil would like you to think that it hinges on you, that it's about you, your abilities, your power, your skill or lack thereof, because if you believe that it's about you then it all hinges upon your performance. Can I just take the pressure off you today by telling you that it's not about you? It's about Him. It all hinges upon who God is and only who you are as a result. Maybe today Satan is telling you that you're just a grasshopper, that you'll never amount to anything; accomplish anything because you're too weak, too unassuming, too small; that your voice is too quiet, and uninfluential to ever be heard by anyone. Maybe all you see when you look at yourself in the mirror is a grasshopper; this small, puny, insignificant thing that couldn't possibly take on the giants in its life. But I'm here to tell you today that you can! If God is with you, you can and will. He alone transforms grasshoppers into grasshoppers that kill giants. Satan very much doesn't want you to get a revelation of the greatness of God's glory largely because he knows that all of your needs, your deficiencies, and your lack is supplied in accordance to the riches of the limitless, plentiful glory of God, Jesus. He knows that whatever you are not God makes up for in who He is and in who you are in Christ. Do you know this? How embarrassing and shameful and laughable and humiliating for a giant to be annihilated by a grasshopper! But this is exactly the promise to you today! I don't know what kind of giants you are facing in your life right now. I don't know how weak you feel or how small you might feel in comparison, but I want to encourage you today to take heart because God is with you. And Him being with you gives you the victory over every giant. Him being with you makes you a grasshopper who slays giants. No one may notice when a giant steps on a grasshopper, but you better believe everyone takes notice when a grasshopper completely wipes out a giant. It's time to take down that giant today in Jesus's name!

Father,

I thank You for the greatness of Your glory and that You supply all my needs in accordance to Your glory. This is awesome. This is powerful. This is truly life-changing for me and I confess that I haven't really believed it. I haven't lived like this is true. I've been living my life like a grasshopper terrified of all the giants in my life, afraid of the enemy and just automatically assuming I can't really conquer anything as a result. Father forgive me. I choose today to lift my head up to You for You are with me. Thank You for being with me even in the wilderness. The enemy may not be intimidated by me, but I know he is already defeated by You and he should be scared out of his ever-loving mind by the truth that You are with me. Because You are with me, I have the victory. Because You are with me, I can do all things. Because You are with me, I possess the promise. Because You are with me, I defeat every giant in Jesus's name. I declare today that the LORD my God is with me. Oh, Holy Spirit, let this truth reach deep down into my heart and my spirit today and truly transform me. Let it wash over me and renew my mind. I declare victory over every giant, every enemy, every opposition in my life in the glorious name of Jesus. All of hell is trembling not at the force and might and grandeur of this grasshopper, but I know that I know that I know they are trembling because the LORD of all glory is with me. Jesus the very radiance of God's glory, the very One who has already conquered hell and took ownership of its keys is living in me and that changes everything. Thank You Jesus! Let it be in my life LORD. Help me to live, to think, to believe, to speak from that truth today in Jesus's name, amen.

Day 27: I Am Celebrated as a Son When I Return to the Father

"For you are all sons of God through faith in Christ Jesus." Galatians 3:26 NASB

"For all who are being led by the Spirit of God, these are the sons of God." Romans 8:14 NASB

"So he (the prodigal son) got up and went to his father. But while he was still a long way off, his father saw him and was filled with compassion for him; he ran to his son, threw his arms around him and kissed him. The son said to him, 'Father, I have sinned against heaven and against you. I am no longer worthy to be called your son.' But the Father said to his servants, 'Quick! Bring the best robe and put it on him. Put a ring on his finger and sandals on his feet. Bring the fattened calf and kill it. Let's have a feast and celebrate. For this son of mine was dead and is alive again; he was lost and is found,' so they began to celebrate." Luke 15:20-24

Your behavior is not indicative of your identity. Let me say that again; your behavior, good or bad, is not indicative of your identity. To be sure behavior may indicate a person's character or what is truly in a person's heart and behavior is certainly influenced by who someone is, but behavior alone is not the defining aspect of a person's identity. Most parents get this right? We love our children, are proud of our children just because they are our children. We certainly celebrate their successes and accomplishments and praise their good behavior, but just because they do or say something bad, even if it is a reoccurring behavior that isn't good at all, they do not somehow cease to be our child. Most parents never reach that end where they cut a child out of their life and declare them no longer to be their son/daughter because of poor behavior. And even if they verbally made this decision and declaration, that child would not and could not physically stop being that parent's child.

Words are powerful, names could be changed, and identities could be altered legally, but by blood that child cannot cease to be that parent's son/daughter. Oh friend, blood is always more powerful!

Someone needs to hear this today. God does not write you off because of your bad behavior just like a parent doesn't write their children off for negative behavior either. To be sure, He is holy and does not condone or approve of or tolerate sin. He does not turn a blind eye to bad behavior and use grace as an excuse for you to do whatever you want, not at all. Paul asks in Romans 6 how those who have died to sin can live in it any longer. He explains how that old sinful self has been crucified with Jesus on the cross, how it is dead and gone so that sin might be done away with in the life of a believer. And Hebrews 10 informs us that "if we deliberately keep on sinning after we have received the knowledge of the truth, there remains no more sacrifice for sins, but only a fearful expectation of judgment and of raging fire that will consume the enemies of God." (Hebrews 10:26 NIV). Jesus's sacrifice on the cross was a sufficient sacrifice for the sins of the whole world. There is no need for another sacrifice. To refuse Jesus and deliberately keep on sinning after you know the truth brings only a fearful expectation of judgment. His blood atones for your sins and makes it possible for you to receive His Spirit, the same Spirit that brought about your adoption into sonship. As the verse says above in Galatians, you are a son of God by Faith in Jesus Christ. You are not a son by good behavior or merit or anything else, but a son by Faith in Jesus.

I know we've already talked about it, but the story of the prodigal son that Jesus told in Luke 15 illustrates this truth so beautifully. Here a son, not a sinner, but one who was already considered a son in all legality and by blood, sins against his father in a very shameful and disgraceful and disappointing manner. That son chose not to be identified by his father anymore and we can make that choice too. But after that son comes to his senses and goes back to his father, thinking only that he might be permitted to be a servant, that son is welcomed personally by his father and treated like a son, restored like a son, loved like a son. The father's actions, illustrating God the Father's heart in this story, shows us how we, as sons and daughters who have sinned and are filthy with sin, when we come back to our Father and confess, we are not shamed or told how disappointing we are, we are not consigned to grovel and beg to just be servants, nor are we given what our poor behavior deserves. No, our Father runs and embraces us in the filthiness of our sin. We are kissed and showered with love. He puts the best robe on us, restores us back to honor and dignity and celebrates our return. Our bad behavior was bad for sure, sinful, and if we should choose to deliberately continue in it, there remains nothing else to be done for us. We may have been a son/daughter, but we've chosen to not be identified by our Father anymore. By our free will, we walked away from the Father. He did not cut us off even if He respects the free will that He gave us. But when we come to our senses and go back to the Father, that bad behavior doesn't trump His reception of us as sons/daughters.

I think it's telling how the prodigal son in this account expects and hopes just to be a servant. It's like he expects that his father could not receive him and accept him as a son anymore, that his behavior warrants this response. And don't we do the same thing, think the same thing; expect the same response from God. Sometimes we consign ourselves to servant hood and this lowly state with God after we've repented because we think that's what we deserve, that our rights as sons and daughters have been completely lost and it was our choice and we can't ever get that back. But the father from this parable of Jesus proves something else entirely. That prodigal, wasteful, reckless son never ceased to be that father's son. He's called the prodigal son, not the prodigal sinner or even servant. The father respected that son's free will to choose a different identity and live outside of his father's covering. The father didn't chase him down and force him to remain his son and legally that father had every right to cut that son out and off because of the son's disregard and disrespect towards the father. But in this parable, we don't see an angry, disappointed father, but one who has been waiting for his son's return, one who runs and welcomes that son, one who never stopped loving that son regardless to that son's poor behavior. Oh friend, when you confess and repent and come back to the Father, God, you are absolutely restored as His son/daughter. You haven't lost your sonship or your identity, nor are you written off or talked about in your Father's house as "that" son. You aren't shamed or dishonored or made to feel like or even told that you are a disappointment to your Father. Rather, your Father restores your honor and your dignity, and He commands those in His house to do likewise, to celebrate your return, to treat you like a son of His.

Oh friend, if you're in the pigpen today in your life because of your bad behavior, your sin, your wrong choices, your free will; know that God isn't punishing you. He respects your free will even if His heart yearns to bring you home, He won't make you come home, so He waits and looks for you. But that same free will you exercised to walk away can also be exercised to bring you back. You aren't too far gone; you can always change your choices. Regardless to all of the bad decisions, you can still come to your senses and make the decision to leave the pigpen and when you do come home, when you do humble yourself and repent though you may have expected to be shamed, demoted, or even to have lost what you had with the Father before; you'll find instead a Father who runs to you, embraces you, kisses you, honors you, and celebrates you. Oh, He is a good, good Father!

Father,

I thank You for being my Father, such a good, good Father. I know my poor behavior and my sin has been so foolish. I recognize that I'm in this pigpen not because You've abandoned me or You don't love me anymore, but I'm here because of my own free will and You respect the very free will that You gave to me when You made me. Today, I come to my senses and I come back to You. I confess that I have sinned against heaven and against You. I'm not worthy to be Your child anymore; I don't deserve it for sure, but Your Word tells me that because I've come back to You, I can expect to be embraced, to be honored, to be restored as Your child. Oh God, thank You. Thank You for loving me. Thank You for receiving me. Thank You for forgiving me and covering me with the best of Your robes, a robe of righteousness that covers the filth of my sin and where I've been. I know I still smell like I've been living in the pigpen, but that doesn't stop You from running to me, pulling me close, and kissing me. You are so good, so amazing, so incredible. I don't know how to even absorb how good You are. Pull me close today. Let me feel celebrated and honored and loved, for I was dead, I chose death even after knowing life, but now I'm alive again. I was lost because I chose to leave You and follow my own understanding, but now I'm found. Thank You LORD for the parable of the prodigal son. In Jesus's name, amen.

⥢⥤

Day 28: I Am Shielded

"In addition to all this, take up the shield of faith, with which you can extinguish all the flaming arrows of the evil one." Ephesians 6:16 NIV

"Surely, LORD, you bless the righteous, you surround them with your favor as with a shield." Psalm 5:12 NIV

"Now faith is confidence in what we hope for and assurance about what we do not see." Hebrews 11:1 NIV

"And I heard a loud voice saying in heaven, now is come salvation, and strength, and the kingdom of our God, and the power of His Christ: for the accuser of the brethren is cast down, which accused them before our God day and night. And they overcame him by the blood of the Lamb and the word of their testimony; and they loved not their lives unto the death." Revelation 12:10-11 NIV

The evil one, Satan, is your enemy. Revelation 12 refers to him as the "accuser of the brethren" who accuses you before our God both day and night. That's some relentless accusation, some continual tongue-waging. Your adversary is constantly bringing accusations, charges, allegations against you even when you're sleeping. Don't panic, 2 Kings 19 illustrates to us how God sent one of His angels for Israel in the night while the whole camp was sleeping to put to death 185,000 of their enemy so that when Israel woke up the next day, there were all the dead bodies. Satan may be accusing you throughout the night, but God is also fighting for you while you're asleep so that when you wake up the next morning, you've already got the victory. Wow!

Ephesians 6 tells us that Satan has flaming arrows that he is targeting you with. In Ephesians 6, Paul describes to us the armor of God by correlating it to the armor used by Roman soldiers in his day. He references a shield of faith that we are to take up in order to extinguish the flaming arrows of the evil one. Shields were commonly used by Roman soldiers as a defense mechanism against the enemy, yet most shields were made from wood, so a flaming arrow was intended to set an opponent's shield on fire and thus render it useless. If this was accomplished, that opponent would be entirely defenseless against the enemy. To combat this, Roman soldiers would cover their wooden shields with animal hide and douse this hide with water. They would also get close together with other Roman soldiers and combine their shields in order to create a much more substantial barrier to the enemy like an enclosure called a testudo or tortoise such as the protective shell of a tortoise. Here we see the significance of each other as fellow soldiers not just in Christian community, but also in spiritual warfare.

Yet the Greek word used for arrow in this Scripture is *bele* which can also mean "missile". An arrow, especially a flaming one, can certainly cause damage. It can wound, injure an opponent, and if positioned correctly, it could very well be considered lethal. But a missile is much more destructive by far. Friend, the Bible cautions us in 1 Peter 5:8 to be alert and vigilant because our adversary roams around like a roaring lion just looking for someone to devour. It's important for us to realize that Satan's goal is not just to hurt us, to trip us up, or even to cause us pain. His goal is to devour us. His flaming arrows are like missiles intended to completely obliterate us, to carry that level of destruction with them. His accusations, his temptations, his schemes are calculated to kill us, steal from us, and destroy our lives. But according to the Bible you have been given a shield of faith and we know from Hebrews 11 that faith is confidence in what we hope for and assurance about what we do not see. Faith is like the water Roman soldiers doused their shields in to extinguish those flaming arrows. Arguably, faith is choosing to believe God and His Word, to overcome by aligning the word of our testimonies to the Word of the Living God. The reality is that Satan's accusations cannot penetrate or override the truth of God's Word!

Oh friend, that flaming arrow, that missile sent by Satan, that accusation can be refuted by you when you align what you say about yourself with what God says about you in His Word; this is your inheritance from the LORD. No weapon formed against you, no flaming arrow, no missile of the enemy shall prosper in your life when you do this. That's what God's Word says! You overcome the accuser of the brethren by the blood of the Lamb and the word of your testimony. So, open your mouth, friend, and start overcoming! Psalm 5 says that surely the LORD will surround the righteous with His favor as with a shield. You not only take up the shield of faith every day to extinguish the flaming arrows of the enemy. You not only are in an army of fellow soldiers who have the opportunity to align their shields in order to build a more fortified enclosure and defense against the enemy's arrows, but you also are surrounded by the favor of the LORD Almighty whose support of you, whose kindness towards you, whose approval of you and esteem towards you completely enfolds you as a shield. God's favor acts as a shield to guard and protect and shelter and defend you against the enemy.

Oh friend, God has your back! So, take up your shield of faith. It's something you must choose to carry, to use, to take up as a defense against the enemy. And know that the favor of the Great I AM is also covering you and protecting you like a shield. You are not defenseless or powerless. In fact, you have been amply supplied with victory already. The real question isn't a matter of how you can defeat the enemy in your life, but how in the world could he possibly defeat you! Satan may roam around like a roaring lion but make no mistake he is no lion. It's time to shut him up today, to put him in his place, to extinguish all his flaming arrows and accusations by choosing to put your confidence in what God says over what the accuser says. Just a whisper of the name of Jesus, even the Word of the living God softly spoken out of your mouth will absolutely silence that roar of the enemy. You're in a fight, a war so, wake up! But know that this fight, this war has already been credited to your victory. You just have to believe it and keep on believing it until that day when the accuser of the brethren will finally be cast down forever. He's already been assigned to be cast down. Let's go ahead and get him used to the idea because we've cast him down every day of our lives already. Rise up, friend, take up your shield and stand in the victory that is yours in Jesus's name!

Father,

> I thank You for having my back, for surrounding me with Your favor, Your support, Your approval of me as a shield. How could the enemy's accusations destroy me when I am absolutely enclosed by Your esteem of me? That's where I choose to be today; in the middle of Your favor, Your approval, Your regard and good opinion of me. I don't need anyone else to approve of me and to have a good opinion of me. Those things are nice for sure and I appreciate being regarded by others. But I am not surrounded by the favor of man as a shield for the help of man is useless according

to Your Word. So, I choose today to rest in the enclosure, the protection of Your favor. I choose to believe and declare and trust in Your approval and good opinion of me outlined in the Scriptures. I declare that You, God, are who You say that You are, and I am who You have said that I am. I am Your child. I have been brought to fullness, to wholeness in Christ, I am alive, I have a future and a hope. I can do all things through Jesus living in me who gives me strength. I choose today to take up the shield of faith, to overcome and silence and cast down my accuser by the blood of the Lamb and the word of my testimony. I choose today to put my confidence, my assurance in You God and in Your Word. May every flaming arrow of the enemy in my life be extinguished today in Jesus's name. Let every weapon formed against me fail miserably and never prevail in my life or in my family's lives in Jesus's' name. I refute and silence the roaring lion in my life today. I cast him down and his accusations down in preparation for him being eternally cast down by You, God. He is defeated and I am victorious. I am covered, protected, shielded by Your favor and good opinion of me. Let it be in my life LORD in Jesus's name, amen.

Day 29: I Hate Evil

"To fear the LORD is to hate evil; I hate pride and arrogance, evil behavior and perverse speech." Proverbs 8:13 NIV

"The fear of the LORD is the beginning of wisdom, and knowledge of the Holy One is understanding." Proverbs 9:10 NIV

"When the angel of the LORD appeared to Gideon, he said, 'the LORD is with you, mighty warrior.'" Judges 6:12 NIV

There are truths that are absolute, they remain true regardless to your adherence to them or your agreement with them. For example, the truth that God is God. This truth is true no matter if you choose to believe that He is God or not. You could very well spend your whole life disbelieving the existence of God and His credibility as an ultimate deity or you could spend your life choosing to believe. Maybe you're unsure or indifferent, but everyone tends to sway one way or the other; everyone chooses to believe something. The hard reality is that the truth of His deity is not contingent upon your belief or lack thereof. He doesn't cease to be God simply because you choose not to believe that He's God. The same is true of gravity. You don't have to believe in gravity, but gravity's presence and laws influence your life whether you choose to mentally adhere to them or not. In fact, they have such a prominent effect on your life that to be a human who lives on planet earth and choose not to believe in gravity seems incredibly bizarre. My point is that belief is a choice. It's something you internally hold as true and that belief plays out in how you think, what you feel, and how you behave. If you don't believe in gravity despite all the evidence supporting its existence, you very well might jump off a cliff one day without considering the ramifications of gravity or of that decision. Seems absurd, but our beliefs affect how we think and how we live.

What the Bible says about your identity in Christ is true. How do I know? Because it's what the Bible says, and I trust the validity of the Word of God. Heaven and earth may pass away, but what God says, His Word, will never pass away. Think about that for a second. This means that I can choose to believe that what He says about me is true or I can choose not to believe it. My choice in this matter will affect how I think about myself and how I live my life. God is not a man that He should lie so the question isn't in what He has said about me, but in my choice to believe it or not. Can I just tell you from firsthand experience that to not believe what God says about who you are is detrimental? To not believe what God has said shows a lack of the fear of the LORD in one's heart. This is clear considering the Bible tells us that the fear of the LORD is the beginning of wisdom so to not fear God would be the epitome of stupidity. Not only so, the Bible also says that to fear the LORD is to hate evil. Most of us don't hate evil. We might hate the ramifications of evil, but we're otherwise tolerant of evil maybe especially in our own hearts. But a proper understanding of who God is produces a healthy fear of His deity; an understanding that He is God and you are not and because He is God, what He says is truth. To disbelieve, to choose not to believe shows a lack of fear of the LORD, it shows an improper understanding of who God is. Oh Jesus, forgive us; help us.

Friend, today you have a choice. Every day you get to choose, you can choose life, or you can choose death. You can choose to believe God or not to believe Him. You can choose to believe what He says about you in His Word or not to believe it. There will always be arguments and reasons and circumstances to persuade you not to believe, but there is one reason that will always prove credible in choosing to believe. Choose to believe because God said it! Your choice reflects your heart. It reflects your view of God. It reflects wisdom or it reflects foolishness. It reflects a fear of God or a lack thereof. I've chosen death, I've chosen not to believe, I've chosen foolishness so many times and I can't take back the regret or the pain of those choices. I can only tell you and warn you not to disbelieve God. But the incredible thing about truths that are absolute is that you can choose to believe them at any time! They've always been true, they'll always be true, so at any time you can choose to believe that they are absolutely truth. Make that choice today friend and choose to believe God every single day for the rest of your life. Believe because He is God and He does not lie. Choose life, choose blessing, and choose to believe in God and His Word. Choose that you are who He says you are because He is with you!

Father,

> You are absolutely God and I am not. You are high and exalted and holy and pure. You are so great, so vast, so awesome. I humble myself before You today and acknowledge that You are who you say You are, and I am who You say that I am. I confess my lack of belief, my lack of fear of You, my lack of wisdom. I have foolishly questioned who Your Word says that I am. I have relied on other things and other people and other words to affirm and validate my identity. Forgive me for not fearing You like I should. I acknowledge how detrimental this has been in my life, how my disbelief in what You say about who I am has impacted the way I think about myself and how I have lived my life and how my life is a summation of this stupid choice not to believe You or to waiver in this belief or to rely on other things and other people and other words to validate what You have already

established as truth in Your Word. Oh God, have mercy on me! I can't change those poor choices, but today I choose to believe that I am who You say that I am. I choose to accept it as truth simply because You said it and You are not a man that You should lie. Holy Spirit help me to make this choice every day and please let this choice to believe what Your Word says about me change the way I think about myself and the way I behave. I want to fear You God because You are God and that is undeniable to me. I want to hate evil, to despise it in my life, and to always turn from it. I want to think about myself the way that I ought to. I want to live in a way that pleases You. Let it radically change my life in Jesus's name, amen.

Day 30: I Have God's Attention

"How precious to me are your thoughts, God! How vast is the sum of them! Were I to count them, they would outnumber the grains of sand—when I awake, I am still with you." Psalm 139:17-18 NIV

"And my God will meet all your needs according to the riches of his glory in Christ Jesus." Philippians 4:19 NIV

Can I just tell you today that you have God's attention? He sees you; He knows you; He's paying attention to you. Let that sink in for a second. The thought should fill you with awe and trembling right? There should be this amazement that the God of the universe is thinking of you right now. He's so big, so vast, so sufficient in and of Himself, but He's absolutely thinking of you. It's amazing! And this truth should also deeply humble us to know that nothing about us escapes God's knowledge. He sees and knows our hearts. He sees and knows our motives. He sees and knows the very things we try to hide and this should cause us to fear Him, to be mindful that He is God and we are not.

We all want to be seen and heard and paid attention to. In fact, if we feel like we aren't receiving the attention that we think we need, we'll often act out in ways to receive it. This is evidenced in various behaviors even amongst children. Sometimes bad behavior is directly connected to wanting/needing attention so badly one will resolve that even negative attention is better than no attention at all. Some people lie and manipulate and scheme for attention. They dress a certain way, act a certain way for the attention they receive. They're desperate for someone to see them, to notice them. Some people believe they don't have personalities that attract a lot, if any, attention so they try to earn attention in other ways and these things can be attained in a healthy manner, but they can also be or become unhealthy. It seems a very shallow thing to admit our motives are perhaps too tied up with wanting attention, yet there's certainly a freedom in baring our hearts before a God who knows them anyway. But for those who feel they aren't seen, that people don't typically pay attention to them. To those who feel invisible or forgotten, to those who are or have been so desperate for attention often equating it with love that they've done unhealthy things and chosen unhealthy outlets to receive that attention they crave. Can I just tell you today that you don't need people's attention? I understand, we're all human and as such we all need a certain level of attention, but it's not something you have to be desperate for because God is already paying attention to you!

The Bible says that His thoughts about you are so vast that if you were to count them, they would outnumber all the grains of sand on the planet. Imagine that scenario! He's thinking about you constantly! You don't need anyone else to think about you all the time; God is! You already have His attention. It's not something you have to earn or work for or try and receive. It just is. Let His thoughts be precious to you. Your needs, even your need for attention, to be seen and heard and paid attention to, are fully met in God according to His riches in glory. Praise God! Not only so, Jesus has called you the light of the world. Lights by very nature and definition are visible; they are seen. Someone needs to grasp the implications of this today. You aren't invisible. You shine, you are seen; you are a light! Some of us need to stop trying to get other people's attention so much, to stop trying to be seen and noticed. Some of us need to lay down that need, to take even that to the feet of Jesus and realize that people's attention is futile. We don't need another person to constantly think about us. We don't need to fear being forgotten, that if we're somehow out of sight, we'll also be out of mind. That isn't true of God. You couldn't escape His sight even if you wanted to. He won't forget you or stop thinking about you. It's time to surrender that desire to Him, to realize that your need for attention may be out of balance, that it's become unhealthy and possibly destructive. It's time to relinquish that attention to Him and know that He's thinking about you. The God of the entire universe, your Father, your LORD is absolutely paying attention to you today. Oh, I pray this truth sets someone free, that it humbles someone, that it rekindles the fear of the LORD in our hearts and brings us to our knees in repentance. That it changes and heals someone's perspective even if it's just my own. Let it be LORD in Jesus's name!

Father,

> I thank You for thinking about me and for not just thinking about me from time to time, but for constantly thinking about me. Your thoughts are precious to me, they are so vast that I can't even possibly number them. So today I repent for all the unhealthy ways I've tried to get attention from others or even from You. I ask You to forgive me for being so desperate to be paid attention to when Your Word already settles the matter for me. Today I rest in this knowledge and in this truth that the God of the universe is thinking of me, paying attention to me. I'm not forgotten, and I am so grateful. I cast down the lie that I am invisible because Jesus has called me a light and lights ore visible. Holy Spirit help me to also maintain a position of humility as a result of this truth. I thank You for thinking of me so much, for considering me worth that much amount of thought. Thank You that all of my needs are truly met in You, so I lay down the right to meet my needs any other way. I surrender and release that need for attention today and leave it here at Your feet. Turn Your face towards me LORD and be gracious to me in Jesus's name, amen.

Day 31: I Am Taking heart

> *"...Paul advised them saying, 'Sirs, I perceive that the voyage will be with injury and much loss, not only of cargo and the ship, but also of our lives.'* Acts 27:9b-10 NIV
>
> *"Now when the south wind blew gently, supposing that they had obtained their purpose, they weighed anchor and sailed along Crete, close to the shore. But soon a tempestuous wind, called the northeaster, struck down from the land. And when the ship was caught and could not face the wind, we gave way to it and were driven along."* Acts 27:13-15 NIV
>
> *"...Paul stood up among them and said, 'Men, you should have listened to me and not have set sail from Crete and incurred this injury and loss. Yet now I urge you to take heart, for there will be no loss of life among you, but only of the ship."* Acts 27:21b-22 NIV

What do you do when regret threatens to suffocate you, when you feel like you are drowning in your own regrets? You're in a mess, a mess of your own making, a mess you may not have chosen, but one you feel responsible for. You heard God, but you disobeyed, and now you'd give anything to go back, but it seems like it's way too late for that. What are you supposed to do? How do you keep yourself from drowning in those waters?

In Acts 27, Paul finds himself on a boat to Rome, a prisoner for preaching the Gospel, along with some other men. After much time had passed and the voyage had become dangerous because of low food supplies, in verse 10 Paul advises the men to harbor their boat for the winter because he perceives the voyage onward will be with much injury and loss, not only of cargo but of their very lives. The centurion in charge; however, doesn't listen, but chooses to press on to find a more suitable spot to winter in.

So, they set out and at first the south wind blows gently behind them and they feel as though for a moment they have obtained their purpose, and all will go well with their voyage. But soon a tempestuous wind called the northeaster strikes down on them and their ship is caught, stuck, unable to face the wind, the ship gives way to the strong opposing wind and is driven along by it, forced backwards on the route by which they had already come. Isn't that just like sin? It's not just a mistake, a mess up. We all make mistakes and mess up from time to time, but there's this choice or series of choices to not listen and obey God's voice. And for a time, things appear to still go well with you, but there's a reason God warned you, because He saw and knew there was a tempestuous wind coming and He didn't want it to destroy you. Oh friend, listen to Him! This storm, this wind could have been avoided! God warned them through Paul, but they didn't listen, and they found themselves in a mess as a result, a mess that looked to be the very end of them. Now their boat was driven backwards, caught by this wind, and they were unable to face it, to overcome it.

Oh friend, have you ever been there, been caught in a storm, with the wind of regret pushing you back the way you came, waves of shame just beating down on you, nearly drowning you in the process? You feel you can't face it; can't overcome it because you feel it's your own fault, you're up against it. You wake up and go to bed day after day, night after night nearly drowning in your own regrets. The sun doesn't shine, the stars don't appear in your life. Things are so dark, so gloomy. What are you supposed to do then? Verse 20 says that neither the sun nor the stars appeared for many days and afterwards all hope of ever being saved for these guys, of getting out of this mess that they had gotten their own selves into was at last abandoned.

But the Bible says in verse 21 that Paul stood up in the middle of that mess and addressed those hopeless prisoners anyway by saying, "Men, you should have listened to me and not incurred this injury and loss. Yet now I urge you to take heart for there will be no loss of life among you." (Acts 27:21 NIV). Oh friend, I say this to myself as much as I say it to you. Yes, you should have listened! Yes, you should have chosen differently and perhaps avoided this mess altogether, but regardless to how badly you'd like to go back and do things another way, those decisions have been made and can't be unmade. You may not be able to go back, but you can move forward! However, Paul didn't just tell these guys what they should have done or could have done. He didn't read them their destiny's eulogy or replay the reel of disappointment for them, nor did he just sit there and let things unfold accordingly; he instead stands up in the storm, in the middle of those waves and that wind, in the midst of all that regret and says YET NOW it's time to take heart for this thing doesn't have to be the end of you! Oh, I hope someone today hears this. This isn't the end for you! His mercies are new every single morning. So, you have a choice to make this morning. You can choose to receive His mercy and move forward or you can choose to look back and let these waters of regret sweep over you. I know you don't deserve it. He knows you don't deserve it. It's not a matter of your worthiness, but a matter of His nature. He is merciful and gracious, slow to anger and abounding in love and faithfulness. He loves to show you mercy. Wow!

Paul was largely a victim of everyone else's poor choices on this one. He did everything right, tried to help these guys avoid this mess altogether, and still he finds himself in the middle of the outcome of their pride, their sin. But still he chooses not to be a victim of the storm, he chooses to not abandon the ship, or to just sit down and take it or even to stand up and let these guys have it; rather he stands up in the midst of it all, and gives hope to the very ones whose disobedience brought him to this mess. I imagine Paul had to scream to be heard above the sound of the storm. I imagine he was soaking wet from the waves and the rain. I imagine the sheer grit it took for him to stand up in that storm when everyone else had accepted their outcome and sat down to endure it, but still he does. Why? Because God had sent a message of hope in the middle of that mess: take heart! Oh friend, I don't know what you've done, I don't know what you regret or what you've lost, I don't know the details of why you are where you are today, I don't know all the things you wish you could go back and undo or at least do differently. Yet now God's Word urges you to take heart. It's not over; take heart! God doesn't want you to lose your life in this mess, take heart. He hasn't discarded you to your own regrets, take heart. He's got an island for you to run aground on. He's still got a place for you, a plan for you so take heart. Don't abandon the ship; don't you dare sit down and give up. You still have a future; you still have a hope. Hear the word of the LORD to you today and choose to take heart!

Father,

> Today I realize that I am where I am largely of my own doing, my own poor choices. I'm here because I didn't listen to You. Oh God, it's so destructive, so foolish not to listen to You! Forgive me for not paying attention to the warnings You gave me to avoid being where I've ended up. I confess that I should have listened, and I wish I could go back and

choose differently, but I can't. Father forgive me! God, I feel like I'm drowning in my own regrets. I'm so sorry. I don't know how to get back where I was or if it's even possible to do so. But today I find hope in Your Word that even though this is my situation, I can still take heart. So today I choose to stand up amid my regrets and declare a future and a hope for myself, today I choose to take heart. Oh, Holy Spirit, help me to take heart today. Please don't let this be the end of me in Jesus's name, amen.

Day 32: I Hate My Own Sin

"Have mercy on me, O God, according to your steadfast love, according to your abundant mercy blot out my transgressions. Wash me thoroughly from my iniquity and cleanse me from my sin! For I know my transgressions, and my sin is ever before me. Against you, you only, have I sinned and done what is evil in your sight, so that you may be justified in your words and blameless in your judgment....Purge me with hyssop, and I shall be clean; wash me, and I shall be wither than snow. Let me hear joy and gladness, let the bones that you have broken rejoice. Hide your face from my sins and blot out all my iniquities. Create in me a clean heart, O God, and renew a right spirit within me. Cast me not away from your presence and take not your Holy Spirit from me. Restore to me the joy of your salvation and uphold me with a willing spirit." Psalm 51:1-4, 7-12 NIV

Have you ever come to a place where your sin, not everyone else's, but your very own sin is ever before you? It's like you can't escape it, can't stop thinking about it, can't outrun it, or shrug it off as just a mistake or set-back? When your sin is ever, always before you, you quickly realize that you are utterly desperate for mercy. You realize that if God doesn't have mercy on you, you cannot and will not survive this. You realize that you have done what is evil in God's eyes and that He is completely justified in His words and blameless in His judgment towards you. What can you do in that situation but appeal to God's abundant mercy and steadfast love? O God have mercy on me not according to what I deserve, but in accordance to Your unwavering love for me and Your plentiful mercy! Wash me from my iniquity; cleanse me from my sin! Hide Your face from my sins and blot out all my iniquities. God, I'm asking You to hide Your face from my sin, to not look upon it, but to turn Your face away from it so that it isn't ever before You, so that my sin isn't what is magnified in Your eyes, so that You can look upon me with mercy and love.

Imagine someone knowing the evil thing you had done and still they choose to hide their face from it, they choose not to think about it, not to talk about it, not to highlight it, not to hold it against you, not to treat you accordingly or to influence others to treat you in accordance to that evil thing you had done. Sounds too good to be true. Sounds unfathomable, sounds too wonderful to even comprehend! Oh friend, but God's abundant, rich mercy is an act of Him hiding His face from your sin, of Him choosing not to look at and magnify that crime you committed. Wow! I committed the crime, Jesus didn't. This isn't about how good or bad I am in relation to other people. This is about how sinful I am and how sinless Jesus is, yet He went to trial for my sins. He was abandoned and mocked and ridiculed and humiliated for sins that He did not commit and did not deserve, but that I absolutely did commit and do deserve. Jesus was treated like a criminal so that I don't have to be. He was convicted a criminal and died a criminal's death even though He was completely innocent just because I am guilty. Wow. Oh friend, the Gospel is that personal!

I've come to a place recently where I hate my sin. I mean absolutely hate it. I'm disgusted by it, so grieved by my choices, by the condition of my heart, so broken over the depravity I have chosen. God, I don't need to be reformed, I need to be made completely new. I don't just need to be forgiven; I need to die 100% to self and be 100% reborn to You. I don't just rend my heart before You LORD, I'm asking You to give me a totally new one, a pure one. I see clearly the destruction of my sin, the outcome of it. It is always before me and I agree that it is nothing good. I despise it. I don't want anything to do with it anymore. I absolutely hate it. In the Psalm above David pleads with God to hide his face from David's sin; a picture of mercy. If God has hidden His face from your sin, why is it still ever before you? Nothing gets past God. He sees all and knows all, yet when you repent, He chooses to hide His face from your sins. He chooses to be merciful towards you. Considering His mercy, shouldn't you be merciful as well, not only towards others, but also towards yourself? If He's chosen to hide His face from your sins, shouldn't you hide your face from them too?!?

The Bible says that to fear the LORD, to reverence Him, to honor the position that He has as a just and holy God who absolutely has the authority to cast you, body and soul, into utter, eternal darkness. To fear Him is to hate evil. Not just to frown upon evil, but to absolutely despise it in yourself. All sin is a result of a lack of the fear of the LORD because if you really feared Him, you'd hate evil and if you really hated evil, you wouldn't participate in it.

> Oh God, forgive me for my lack of fear towards You. Forgive me for not hating evil enough to not partake in it. Forgive me for tolerating sin in my own heart, my own life; for fearing anything or anyone else more than I fear You and the position You hold as the ultimate authority, able to cast me into darkness for all eternity. You are God and I am not so I'm asking You to forgive me, to hide Your face from my sin. O God have mercy on me! Don't cast me from Your presence LORD. I know that's what I deserve, but Jesus has taken away my identity as a criminal and lawbreaker. He has brought me near to You again. So, I'm asking You to restore to me the joy of Your salvation in Jesus's name, amen.

Day 33: God is For Me

> *"What, then, shall we say in response to these things? If God is for us, who can be against us? He who did not spare his own Son, but gave him up for us all—how will he not also, along with him, graciously give us all things? Who then will bring any charge against those whom God has chosen? It is God who justifies. Who then is the one who condemns? No one. Christ Jesus who died—more than that, who was raised to life—is at the right hand of God and is also interceding for us."* Romans 8:31-35 NIV

If there's ever been a poster child for someone who has struggled to believe her identity in Christ, I have been that child. And it's not as if I've struggled because I don't know or haven't known what my identity in Christ is. I absolutely do know; I just haven't consistently believed it as truth for myself. I've been double-minded and according to the Bible, a double-minded person is unstable in all their ways. Explains a lot ha. After crying out to God and asking Him what was wrong with me, why I keep getting stuck in this same pattern, this same rut, I immediately felt the Holy Spirit gently whisper those two words to me: double-minded. I knew it wasn't my own thought because I don't typically talk to myself that gently and I knew it wasn't Satan because there was nothing accusatory about this revelation. It was truth and I knew it. The Holy Spirit was confronting me, and I had been running from this confrontation for a while, but I felt invited in at the same time. I quickly looked up the definition for "double-minded" so I knew precisely what to repent for and the definition hit me like a ton of bricks square in the gut. Someone who is double-minded is wavering in mind, insincere, and marked by hypocrisy, gulp. Oh God, is this who I've become? I'm so sorry. I'm so sorry for not consistently believing what You've already said about me in Your Word, for not considering the Living Word of God enough to settle this battle in my mind and my life once and for all. Oh God, I've said I believed it, acted like I believed it, thought I believed it, but I've also not believed it. I'm insincere, something about me isn't honest, isn't real, isn't genuine because I've known the truth, had countless opportunities to believe it, to transform my mind and life accordingly, yet I haven't consistently done the hard work of renewal. I've relied on other things to affirm my identity. I've often continued to believe the negative things about myself while proclaiming another, that's hypocritical. I have no excuse, no good explanation as for why; it's just the ugly truth. I agreed with God about everything, confessed my sin and made up my mind to finally make up my mind in this matter. I AM WHO GOD SAYS THAT I AM!

It's not as complex as we sometimes make it to be. Belief is a choice. You choose what you believe in and I can attest to the destructive nature of continually choosing not to believe what God says or being so wishy-washy in the matter. Yet the amazing thing about belief being a choice is that at any point you can start choosing differently. If you're breathing, there's still opportunity to align what you believe with what God's Word says. It's time to make that choice today, to choose and keep on choosing to believe what He says. It's time to make the devil very sorry for ever pushing you to this point of determination to become single-minded in your identity in Christ. We can't go back, but by His mercy we are moving forward!

Friend, God is for you, the King of the heavens and the earth is for you. He's for your life, for your salvation, for your freedom, for your hope, for your deliverance, for your victory, for your breakthrough; He's for you. Paul asks the believers in Rome, "If God is for us, who can be against us?" (Romans 8:31 NIV). The resounding conclusion is that no one, absolutely nothing, no power whatsoever could possibly stand against those whom God is for. Shame is not for you, fear is not for you, regret is not for you, sin is not for you, slander, accusation is not for you. The Word of God says that His favor surrounds you like a shield. His kindness and goodness and help and support fully encloses you, protecting you from outward accusation and slander. But friend, can I let you in on a little secret? You are on the inside of that shield; therefore, you are most vulnerable to your own words of accusation and slander. Some of us need to realize the amount of damage and destruction we have encountered isn't as much an outside job as it is an inside one, that we've nearly destroyed ourselves with our own negative thoughts and words. I know this has been my story. Oh God, forgive me! It's time to speak the truth. It's time to align what you say with what God says about you. It's time to make up our minds to be single-minded in how we think about ourselves as it relates to the Word of God. It's time to stop working against yourself when the all-powerful God is for you.

Father,

> Today I confess to You my insincerity, my hypocrisy; how double-minded I have been and how unstable as a result. My heart breaks for not believing what You say about me. You are God and I am not. I say that You are my LORD and yet I've been so wishy-washy in accepting what Your Word says about who I am? I can't imagine how this has grieved Your heart. You are my Father and I've foolishly leaned on other things for my identity instead of on You. God, forgive me! So today I come before You as Your child. You are so powerful, so big, so strong and yet Your heart is so tender towards me. I'm amazed. I feel so crushed, so broken, so ashamed. I need Your love to wash over me again. I can't take back the doublemindedness that has marked my relationship

with You thus far, but I am deciding that if I do nothing else from here on out, I will work to become single-minded in my identity in Christ. Help me, Holy Spirit. Let who I am match who You say that I am in Jesus's name, amen.

Day 34: I Am Walking on Water

In Matthew 14 we read the account of Jesus feeding a massive crowd of people with five loaves of bread and two fish. It's an incredible story of miraculous provision. Afterwards Jesus sends the disciples off in a boat to cross over to the other side of the waters while He dismisses the crowd and gets alone to pray. When evening came, the boat was a long way from land and was being beaten by the waves and the wind against them. Jesus doesn't go to them immediately, but in the fourth watch of the night the Bible says Jesus came to them walking on the sea. In fact, the account of this event in Mark says that Jesus intended to pass by them altogether. Yet when the disciples saw Him, they were terrified and cried out in fear, thinking He was a ghost. Jesus immediately spoke to them and said, "Take heart; it is I. Do not be afraid." (Matthew 14:27 NIV). Peter answered by requesting that Jesus command him to come to Jesus walking on the water. And Jesus says, "come." I think it's interesting that this whole thing was Peter's idea. Jesus wasn't asking Peter to do the impossible; Peter requested it. Wow give me that kind of faith, LORD!

So, Peter got out of the boat and started walking to Jesus on the water and we all know the story, right? When Peter saw the waves and the wind, he got scared and began to sink. So, he cries out, "LORD, save me," and Jesus immediately rescues him, asking Peter why he ever doubted and implying that the only reason he sank at all was his own fear. There are a lot of lessons that we can learn from this whole account, one being the truth that when we get our eyes off of Jesus and begin to focus on the wind and the waves in our life, when we start to be intimidated by fear we will generally sink as a result. Peter sank. He thought he was going to die and cries out to Jesus to save him and Jesus does which is remarkable. But sometimes I think we get a little too fixated on the fact that Peter sank; he was almost conquered by the wind and the waves. But isn't the more remarkable thing here that Peter walked on water! I don't know how long Peter he was up there or how far walked on water, but even if it was just a few steps still that's more than anyone else has ever done, still that's remarkable.

Peter did something that no one else had ever done before to my knowledge, he walked on water as if it were solid ground. That doesn't seem to coincide with the laws of physics. And it wasn't like this was a calm day at the lake with still, peaceful water to walk on. No, the Bible says that the wind and the waves were beating against the disciples' boat. These waters were rough, unpredictable, and dangerous but still Peter walked on those waters! Oh friend, most of us tend to focus on the fact that Peter sank. When we think of him walking on water, we immediately think of him sinking and crying out to Jesus for help. Even this incredible feat is framed a failure in our minds somehow. It seems people have a tendency to only notice your failures, all the times you've sank in life, all the times you've been desperate and cried out for help, all the times fear got the best of you; doubt threatened to drown you. Even the amazing things you've done are looked at through the lens of skepticism if you've ever gotten your eyes off Jesus and started sinking as a result. Oh, to God, if we would start noticing the good in each other; calling the good things out; highlighting each other's successes. I wonder what would happen if we started encouraging each other onward to higher things, greater things; even impossible things, but things that can be done through Christ. After Peter had been rescued by Jesus, Jesus asks him why he ever doubted, encouraging Peter to believe Jesus for greater things than even the impossible thing he had just done in walking on water. Peter's idea wasn't struck down by Jesus; Jesus said, "come." Peter wasn't scolded or humiliated or made to feel like a failure for being afraid, for doubting; for sinking. No, Peter was rescued and shown the truth by Jesus; encouraged to higher things. I don't think heaven frames Peter as the guy who sank, but the guy who walked on the water to Jesus. The fact that Jesus was on that water changed everything, made this impossible thing possible for Peter and Peter had the audacity to believe it even if he does lose his way in doubt and fear afterwards.

Oh friend, if you are going through the waters, if the wind and the waves are beating against you, the Word of God says that Jesus is with you and if He is with you, you can walk on the waters. You don't have to be swept away by the water, you don't have to be beaten to a pulp, you don't have to suffer loss, or even be afraid. Maybe you can rise above this impossible thing and walk all over it in Christ. And even if you've tried to do that and still started to waiver, to doubt, and to sink as a result, if you cry out to Jesus, He'll rescue you. He won't condemn you for sinking, but He will correct your doubt and fear so that the next time those waters rage, you'll know that He's with you and because He's with you, you'll walk on those waters too. I don't care how many times you've sank, I don't care how many times fear has kept you down, doubt has knocked you off course; today is the day to ask Jesus if you can come to Him even in these treacherous waters and I have a feeling He'll say, "come." Let it be LORD in Jesus's name!

Father,

> I thank You for being with me as I go through the rough waters of life. And I thank You that if You are with me, I can do all things even impossible things like walking on these waters. Holy Spirit, would You help me not to doubt, help me not to waiver in fear, help me not to sink? I need You and I am so thankful that You are here. Forgive me for all the times I've allowed fear to conquer me, for all the times doubt has caused me to sink. But even if I'm sinking today, I choose to cry out to You Jesus. Would You rescue me, would You teach me, would You give me the faith to walk on water to You in Jesus's name, amen.

Day 35: I Am Serving the LORD

> *"You shall have no other gods before Me."* Exodus 20:3 NIV

> *"But if serving the LORD seems undesirable to you, then choose for yourselves this day whom you will serve, whether the gods your ancestors served beyond the Euphrates, or the gods of the Amorites, in whose land you are living. But as for me and my household, we will serve the LORD."* Joshua 24:15 NIV (emphasis added)

For a moment, think about what it will be like to stand before Almighty God, the Maker of the heavens and all the earth, the One who sets up kingdoms and tears them down, your Creator, and hopefully your LORD. Isaiah 6 says that the glory of God fills the whole earth. The total surface area of the earth is roughly 197 million square miles just to put that in perspective a little bit. I'm not a numbers person, but I know that's a lot! Have you ever had a moment where the fear of Almighty God struck you with such ferocity that you end up on your knees? For sure this day is coming for everyone for the Bible says that every single knee in heaven, on the earth, and even in hell itself that has ever existed will bow before the King and confess His name, Jesus (Philippians 2:10). The fear of Him in His holy presence will bring this reaction out of you regardless to who you are. He's still God, you're still not, and you will face Him in all His glory one day. The thought is overwhelming and incredibly humbling.

Considering His holiness, our own unholiness is often brought to the surface so that we can confess it, turn from it, and be cleansed from all our unrighteousness. So, I'm ashamed to confess that other things and people have often crept up into positions and places they should never be in my own heart and life. Generally, at times people have been more lord of my life personally than Jesus has been. I know that's a strong statement to make, but I feel it's accurate. I know we all want to be liked; to be accepted, to please those around us to a certain degree, but my heart has overemphasized this throughout most of my life and my walk with God and it hasn't been pretty. A lot of my actions, thoughts, and feelings have correlated to people, have been wrapped up in people more than God; sometimes at the expense of God. We all might be able to relate to the experience of feeling like the Holy Spirit was telling us to do one thing and we chose not to for fear of someone's reaction and in that moment fear of man trumped the fear of God in our hearts. But what if the flow of your life, the decisions you make, and the stance of your heart tends to sway more towards fear of man than fear of God? What does this say, but that perhaps "man" is more the lord of your life than Jesus is! Oh God, have mercy on me!

The children of Israel would often abandon God to serve other idols, mostly the gods of the people around them or they would try to serve both God and these foreign deities that were really no deities at all. They did this over and over and over again and the prophets of their day would often equate them to a spiritual prostitute who had left their real Love to find pleasure with other lovers. I know that is a very intense picture to create but read the Bible and you'll find this comparison made several times. Friend, it's impossible to serve both God and other things. Jesus is either the LORD of your life or

He isn't. If you've made Him the LORD of your life, then you are His bride and He is your Bridegroom. To abandon Him to pursue other loves, other pleasures, to submit to any other lordship but His; to love anything else to the same degree as Him is the equivalent to spiritual adultery. Read the book of Hosea and you'll see God's heart to take back His people who have repeatedly prostituted themselves even after He's shown His love to them and taken them in to be His very own. Still He pursues them, still He loves them, but He does call them out in their sin. Still His heart breaks and is hurt by their continual choice to neglect His love and choose other gods, other lords, other loves. Oh friend, could it be that we have done the same thing in His eyes?

Joshua tells the children of Israel in Joshua 24 that if serving the LORD seems undesirable to them, that they should choose THIS DAY whom they will serve. You can serve yourself or someone else or anything other than God. You can fear man who can destroy your physical body, or you can fear the One who can cast you, body and soul, into utter darkness forever. It's time to choose THIS DAY whom you will serve, whom you will fear. Joshua declares that regardless to what all of Israel may decide on this, as for him and his house, they will serve the LORD. Oh friend, maybe you haven't made this choice yet, maybe you've made it, but you've also chosen other things too. Maybe you realize that you've loved other things to the same degree if not more than you've loved God and you need to choose THIS DAY to serve only the LORD. Oh, I pray you make this same decision and declaration today. I pray you choose this day to serve the LORD. Let it be God in Jesus's name!

Father,

> Today I rend my heart in Your holy presence completely aware that You are the Sovereign God and I am not. I acknowledge that there is no one comparable to You. You are holy, You are glorious, You are my Maker, You hold my life, my very breath in Your hands. I confess that I have feared man when I should have feared You. I confess that "people" have held an exalted position in my heart that they shouldn't hold. Your Word says that You are a jealous God and I repent today. I repent of having anyone or anything else in the position of lord in my heart and life. Forgive me, cleanse me. I renounce the lordship of man in my life and

say, THIS DAY, that as for me and my house, we WILL serve the LORD in Jesus's name, amen.

Day 36: I Am Being Brought to Completion

"being confident of this, that he who began a good work in you will carry it on to completion until the day of Christ JESUS." Philippians 1:6 NIV

It's not over, friend. Maybe you feel like too much has happened. You've been this way for far too long. You don't know if you'll ever successfully change or even if it's possible for you to do so. You want to do the right thing; you want to serve God and fulfill the plan that He has for your life. You desire what He has for you, but you fear it's just too late. It would literally take an act of God to turn things around at this point. Can I just say that you can be confident that it's not over because He who began a good work in you will carry it on to completion? And what's the time frame of this good work? Until the day of Jesus Christ! Friend, if you are breathing and Jesus hasn't come back yet, then it's not over for you. .He's still carrying on to completion the good work He first started in you. You can be confident of this. Oh, I pray we'll become confident of this.

Consider the long-suffering, the patience of the LORD your God. Unlike us, patience, suffering long with someone or something is not a quality He has to work on. It is part of His character; who He is. He took six days to create the heavens and the earth when He could have formed it all in an instant. There's approximately a 4,000-year period between the fall of man in Genesis and the birth of God's redemptive plan for man when He technically could have sent Jesus right away. There are 25 years between when the promise was given to Abraham by God and when Isaac, the birth of the promise, was born. Not only so, after coming out of Egypt and reacting to the Promised Land the way that they did, the children of Israel are consigned to wander through the desert for 40 years, long enough for a whole generation of people to pass away, yet God still brings them into their Promised Land even if they physically inherited it bit by bit. Israel also ends up in captivity in Babylon for 70 years because of their continual sin against God after numerous warnings and calls to repent, yet God doesn't give up on them, at the fullness of time He restores them. Yet even then it took four years for Nehemiah to lead the people to rebuild the walls around Jerusalem and it took just as long if not longer for the temple in Jerusalem to be rebuilt. Not only so, Jesus is alive for 30 years before He begins His earthly ministry at all then He fulfils everything in just 3 short years. Consider even the whole process of conception and birth. A human life, a baby isn't born instantaneously, but grows and develops inside its mother's womb for nine months per God's design before it is born into this world in a few short hours. Oh friend, the Bible is full of evidence to show how patient and long suffering the LORD God is. He does everything in the fullness of time, even the completion of the good work He's already started in you!

So, I don't know how off course you may feel today. I don't know if you've encountered yet another bump on the road, a delay, or a complete derailment. I don't know if you've taken things too far this time and you've got this sinking feeling that somehow things are over for you now, you've messed up too badly, you've messed up one too many times, this is finally the straw that sends the whole thing crumbling down; that somehow God has run out of patience with you. Oh friend, if you're still alive and if Jesus hasn't come back yet, then it's not over for you. He hasn't given up on you. He's still bringing to completion the good work He first started in you. He hasn't abandoned that work. Oh, don't you go and abandon it! Maybe it has taken longer than you expected, maybe things haven't gone perfectly and there are more twists and setbacks in your story than you'd care to admit, but it's not over, friend. I don't care how many people have walked away, how many times you've been labeled a certain way and deemed not worth the time or the effort or the energy. I don't care how often others have chosen to give up on you; the LORD your God hasn't.

In the Bible there are 430 years between the last book of the Old Testament, the last written words from a prophet of God to when Jesus is born into this world. And what are those last written words, but a promise that God is about to send an Elijah to the earth to prepare the way before the great an awesome day of the LORD; a promise that is fulfilled in John the Baptist 430 years later. I'm sure those 430 years seemed dark beyond compare. I'm sure it was horrendous to go 430 years without hearing a single recorded word from God. I'm sure many people thought that it was over, that God had given up on them, that there was no hope whatsoever for the future of mankind. I'm sure it seemed that darkness had finally won, that man was doomed to destruction, that sin had prevailed upon the world to such a point that there was nothing more that could be done. I'm sure those 430 years felt like an eternity, but when the fullness of time had come, Jesus, the hope for the entire world was born! There is no other sacrifice for sins. The next time Jesus comes to this world it won't be to serve and save it, but to judge and destroy it so that a new heaven and a new earth will be established in its place completely rid of the influence of sin and the devil. There's urgency because the timeline of events that are to occur before this day comes have already transpired and most scholars believe that the next major event to happen on the Biblical timeline is the rapture of the church of Jesus Christ. So, to be sure, the day of Christ is certainly coming, but until that day, God is still bringing to completion the good work He's already started in you. Don't you give up. Don't you listen to the enemy. It's not over for you, friend. Each breath you breathe is evidence of the mercy of God, of His patience. He isn't slow to fulfill His promise; rather, He is patient with man, not wanting anyone to perish, but ALL to come to repentance. It's time to repent. It's time to return to Him in Jesus's name!

Oh God,

> I thank You for Your patience and long suffering that I see evidenced in the Bible, that I see evidenced even in Your creation, and that I see evidenced in my own life. Thank You for being patient with me. Thank You for not giving up on me, but for carrying to completion the good work You started in me. I don't want to work against that work. I want to surrender fully to it, to be confident that You're the One who's bringing it to completion, not me. God, forgive me. I'm not a self-made man or woman. This work doesn't belong to me, but to You. Would You hasten this work in me? Help me, Holy Spirit, to cooperate with the work God has already started in me. I'm sorry for the failures. I'm sorry for the setbacks. I'm sorry for all the times I've gotten off course and have abandoned this work. But today I'm choosing to repent. Today I'm choosing to return to You with all that I have, all that I am. What I have, who I am may does not seem like much to me, but I give it to You anyways, I give it to You fully, knowing that You are what makes this work

good. Considering the coming day of Christ, would You hasten this work in me in Jesus's name, amen.

Day 37: I Am the Righteousness of God

> *"God made him (Jesus) who had no sin to be sin for us, so that in him we might become the righteousness of God* (2 Corinthians 5:21)." NIV

> *"Therefore no one will be declared righteous in God's sight by the works of the law; rather, through the law we become conscious of our sin. But now apart from the law the righteousness of God has been made known, to which the Law and the Prophets testify. This righteousness is given through faith in Jesus Christ to all who believe* (Romans 3:20-22)" NIV

The verse above in Romans tells us that no one is declared righteous in God's sight by the works of the Law, the Ten Commandments; rather, it's through the Law that we become aware of our own sin. Paul explains further in Romans 7 that he would not have known what sin was had it not been for the law. Therefore, the purpose of the Law is to make us conscious of our own sinfulness. Have you ever stolen? Have you ever lied? Even in a very small way? "For whoever keeps the whole law and yet stumbles at just one point is guilty of breaking all of it." (James 2:10 NIV). Seems a little harsh, but the God of the Bible is a righteous God. He is blameless, upright, honorable, and good. Considering how virtuous, how pure He is, all our righteous acts are like filthy rags. Therefore, no one is declared righteous in His sight by the works of the law since we have all sinned and fallen short of God's glory.

However, don't let Satan convince you that you've been set up for failure in this whole thing, because God made Jesus who had no sin to be sin for you so that in Christ you might become the righteousness of God. What does that mean? In Christ, you are blameless. In Him, you are upright, you are pure, you are clean! This righteousness has nothing to do with your works or your ability to keep the law. It has everything to do with faith in Jesus Christ.

In the Old Testament, God gave special instructions and special clothing the priests were to wear in order to come into His presence. Exodus 28 describes these various garments in detail. One piece of these priestly garments was something called the robe of the ephod, a seamless blue garment worn solely by the high priest. It was a sleeveless robe that went down to the ankles with an opening for the head in its center. Around this opening was a woven edge like a collar so that it wouldn't tear and around the hem imitation pomegranates were made of blue, purple, and scarlet yarn with finely twisted linen as well as gold bells. The gold bells and pomegranates were to alternate all the way around the hem of the robe. Many scholars believe this robe wore solely by the high priest was symbolic of Jesus's position and authority as the perfect High Priest. Yet they also believe this robe speaks of the robe of righteousness that is given to all who accept Christ's gift of righteousness by faith in His shed blood. "I delight greatly in the LORD; my soul rejoices in my God. For he has clothed me with garments of salvation and arrayed me in a robe of his righteousness, as a bridegroom adorns his head like a priest, and as a bride adorns herself with her jewels." (Isaiah 61:10 NIV).

Christ is your great High Priest! He is not unable to empathize with your weaknesses since He was tempted in every way just as you are yet was without sin (Hebrews 4:14-16 NIV). He has ascended into Heaven, is at the right hand of God, and because of Him you can now approach God's throne of grace with confidence! Because of Jesus you can now receive mercy and find grace to help you in your time of need! You have been arrayed in Christ's righteousness! You are clothed; you are covered in Christ and declared to be the righteousness of God! How awesome! Don't let the enemy alter your perspective. You are not trash, you are not a failure, you are not junk who can't seem to get anything right. In Christ, you are clean! In Christ, you are pure! In Christ, you are the righteousness of God! Your life, your testimony, how Christ has saved you and transformed you is an open declaration to the world, an open declaration to the enemy, and an open declaration to the heavens of God's righteousness! Knowing who you truly are in Christ should influence your outlook on the enemy, your outlook on sin, and on life. It's all because of Jesus!

Father,

I thank You for the power of Christ's blood to make me clean, to make me pure and righteous. I readily admit that all my righteous works are as filthy rags in comparison to how holy, how good, how upright You are. I could never earn or deserve to be in Your presence, but Jesus has made a way for me that has nothing to do with my works and has everything to do with faith in Him. Thank You, Jesus! So, I thank You that He is my great High Priest. I thank You that because of Jesus I can approach You with confidence, that I can receive mercy and find grace to help me whenever I'm in need. I thank You that I can now enjoy the splendor of Your presence because Jesus has made me Your righteousness. Holy Spirit help me to hold onto this truth and to live it out daily in Jesus's name, amen.

Day 38: I Am a New Creation!

"Therefore, if anyone is in Christ, he is a new creation. The old has passed away; behold, the new has come." 2 Corinthians 5:17 ESV

"Remember not the former things, nor consider the things of old. Behold, I am doing a new thing; now it springs forth, do you not perceive it? I will make a way in the wilderness and rivers in the desert." Isaiah 43:18-19 NIV

"To put off your old self, which belongs to your former manner of life and is corrupt through deceitful desires, and to be renewed in the spirit of your minds, and to put on the new self, created after the likeness of God in true righteousness and holiness." Ephesians 4:22-24 NIV

If Jesus is your LORD and Savior, then you are a completely new creation! The old you passed away! Paul declares, "I have been crucified with Christ and I no longer live, but Christ lives in me. The life I now live in the body, I live by faith in the Son of God, who loved me and gave himself for me." (Galatians 2:20 NIV). You are not the same, my friend. In fact, the Bible teaches that it's no longer you living, but its Christ living in you. Satan loves to try and disqualify you for the future because of your past. He'll remind you of all that you used to be, of all that you used to do and how God couldn't possibly use someone with your kind of track record. Even well-meaning people in your life may sometimes have a hard time letting go of the old you. Perhaps you, yourself, struggle to realize that the old you passed away, that they were crucified with Christ and are no more. The Scripture above in Isaiah encourages you to forget the former things! Stop considering the things of old for God is doing a new thing. Perceive it, my friend. Let it enter your mind and be firmly rooted within your heart. With God, all things are possible! If Satan brings up something from your past as a tool to exclude you from living for God or doing the very thing you feel like God is asking you to do, you tell Satan that it is no longer you who lives anyway. It's Christ who lives in you! Maybe with you, it IS impossible. Maybe on your own, you can't serve Jesus, you can't accomplish the will that God has for your life. But it's not on you anymore! Christ now lives in you and in His strength, you can do all things! If God can make a way in the wilderness and cause rivers to spring forth in the desert, He can certainly make you a new creation in Christ.

In Ephesians 4, Paul gives some instructions to the Christians living in Ephesus on how to live for Christ. Ancient Ephesus had both Greek and Roman customs one of which was the worship of different gods and goddesses. The goddess Artemis' temple was located in Ephesus and ancients believed the temple to be one of the Seven Wonders of the World until it was destroyed by a flood, was rebuilt in the 2nd century atop the previous location and was destroyed by a fire, was reconstructed again and was demolished by earthquakes, and was finally rebuilt again to be looted by the Goths one year later (I doubt that was a coincidence). Yet life in Ephesus revolved around the worship of Artemis in many ways. The Ephesians believed their relationship with Artemis was governed by a covenant between the city and the goddess; so much of society and culture was influenced by the worship of this goddess. If you grew up in Ephesus or lived there for any length of time, worshiping Artemis was sort of ingrained in you. It was your way of life. It was all you knew. Sin wasn't just something they chose to do occasionally; it was who they were. Sin permeated their entire culture. It was taught to them at a very early age. Sin was engrained in their brains and had deep, deep roots in their hearts. Yet Paul encourages those who had made Jesus their LORD and Savior living in Ephesus to put off their old self, to renew their minds, and to put on their new self, created after the likeness of God. Those Christians had to put off their old ways of doing things, those old practices and beliefs and ways of living since most of those ways were wrapped around idolatry and sin. And they had to put on their new self, created in the likeness of God in true holiness and righteousness. The same is true for you, my friend.

I don't care how wrapped up in sin you used to be. I don't care the degree it used to permeate your entire life. Perhaps like the Ephesians sin wasn't just something that you used to do occasionally; it was who you were. Other people identified you by your sin. Perhaps you identified yourself that way. It doesn't matter anymore because you are a new creation in Christ. So, put off that old self! They are dead, they are gone. They have been crucified with Christ and no longer exist. You are no longer identified by sin. You are identified by Christ! So, renew your mind with God's Word, with His truth and put on your new self, my friend. And don't ever let the enemy tell you that you can't live for Jesus, that you were too far gone into sin to faithfully serve the LORD because it's not just you living anymore; it is Christ living in you. Maybe it is too hard for you, but it isn't too hard for Christ! In His strength you can do all things!

Father,

> I thank You for making me a new creation in Christ. I thank You that the old me, my old ways, who I used to be is gone and the new has come. I thank You that you have given me a new heart and a new spirit. That You have taken out my heart of stone and given me a heart of flesh. Holy Spirit, would You help me to continuously put on my new self, created in the likeness of God? Would You help me to remember that Christ is now living in me and I can do all things through His strength? I can't do this on my own. I desperately need You, so I invite You today to make Your strength perfect amid my weakness. May I be strong in Christ in Jesus's name, amen.

Day 39: I Am Strong in the LORD!

> *"But he said to me, 'My grace is sufficient for you, for my power is made perfect in weakness.' Therefore, I will boast all the more gladly about my weaknesses, so that Christ's power may rest on me."* 2 Corinthians 12:9 NIV
>
> *"Finally, be strong in the LORD and in his mighty power."* Ephesians 6:10
>
> *"Through the praise of children and infants you have established a stronghold against your enemies, to silence the foe and the avenger."* Psalm 8:2 NIV

You are strong! You might not think of yourself that way and you might not feel very strong sometimes, but it's not about you anyways. It's about Christ in you! His grace is enough for you and His power is made perfect, complete, and absolute in weakness. Friend, this is excellent news! 1 Samuel 16:7 tells us that God doesn't look at the things people look at for people look at the outward appearance, but God looks at the heart. People make judgments about your strength based on your size, your skill, your charm, your stature, your track record. Yet God doesn't consider any of these things in gifting you His strength, He looks at your heart and how humble you are before Him, how reliant you are upon Him. This means that even the weakest person physically could be the mightiest in the LORD. God is not afraid of your weaknesses. In fact, He knows them well. It's okay to desperately need His help, His strength. So, if Satan brings up your weaknesses as a tactic to discourage you or somehow disqualify you from doing what God has asked you to do, go ahead and agree with your adversary. Yes, Satan, I am weak in this area and perhaps I've fallen many times as a result, BUT if I'll let it, the power of Christ is made perfect, whole, faultless in my weaknesses. The mighty power of Christ is resting on me and I am STRONG in the LORD! It's not on you, my friend. It's on Christ! And His power is greater than any weakness you have. His power is greater than that of the enemy!

According to the above Scripture in Psalm 8, even children and infants can silence the foe and the avenger and can establish a stronghold against the enemy through their praise. Even these ones who aren't physically strong yet by any means, these ones who are still very much dependent upon others for help and support and care can be mighty in the LORD. How is that possible? Because it's not about the stature of the person. it's all about Christ in the person and He alone makes you strong, makes you victorious, makes you mighty. It's all about Him!

1 Samuel 17 is the account of David versus Golaith, a very familiar and well-known Biblical story. A Philistine giant, a champion named Goliath defies the armies of Israel by asking for a man to come down and fight against him. If Goliath wins, the Israelites will become subject to the Philistines and if the Israelite man wins, the Philistines will become subject to Israel. The stakes are straightforward. The Bible says that when King Saul and all the Israelites heard these words, they were dismayed and terrified. Here are the enemy taunting God's people, boasting of his size, reminding everyone of his feats of victory. He is not just big and strong; he is a champion. He has been trained for battle and has seen victory many times. The people aren't just troubled and distressed about their current situation, they are terrified, absolutely paralyzed with fear because of their enemy. Can I tell you that is exactly Satan's goal for you? He wants to intimidate you, to mock you, to completely paralyze you with fear so that you won't even attempt to fight against him because he knows that when you do, you'll be victorious. Yet David, an unassuming shepherd boy, is sent to the line of battle by his father in order to take food to his brothers. And when he sees and hears what the enemy is saying, David asks, "Who is this uncircumcised Philistine that he should defy the armies of the living God?" (1 Samuel 17:26 NIV). He sees right through the stature, the intimidation of the enemy and volunteers himself to fight against Goliath. David isn't as strong, as big, as "buff", as "ripped" as his brothers. In fact, the king's armor nearly swallowed him whole. That's how little he was physically. He was just a boy at this point. But he goes against the enemy in the name of the LORD Almighty! David prophesies to Goliath, "This day the LORD will deliver you into my hands, and I'll strike you down and cut off your head. This very day I will give the carcasses of the Philistine army to the birds and the wild animals, and the whole world will know that there is a God in Israel. All those gathered here will know that it is not by sword or spear that the LORD saves; for the battle is the LORD'S!" (1 Samuel 17:46 NIV). And that's exactly what happened!

Don't be paralyzed with fear of your enemy. Don't let his mockery, his stature intimidate you. It doesn't matter how strong, how mighty, how big the enemy may appear to be in your life. It doesn't matter how he comes against you with sword or spear. It doesn't matter how weak you are or how unassuming you may be. You come against him in the name of the LORD Almighty! Prophesy to the enemy his own defeat for the battle is the LORD'S, my friend! Even an infant could triumph over the enemy because your victory isn't dependent upon how mighty you may or may not be, it is entirely dependent upon how mighty your God is and He is the LORD Almighty! If God is for you, who in their right mind could be against you!? No weapon the enemy could form against you will prevail! He can't stop you because he can't stop Jesus! The only way you lose is if you don't fight, my friend! Jesus will always be greater than the enemy! May you have the audacity to refute, to disprove, to counter every tongue that rises to accuse you even that of your Accuser. You are mighty in the LORD, my friend, so, be mighty in Him!

Father,

> I thank You for the power of Christ. I thank You that I don't have to be the best, the strongest, or even the most successful in order to overcome the enemy, I just must rely on Jesus. He is my strength. He is my victory. Holy Spirit, would you help me to be strong in the LORD? Help me to approach my day, my battles, my enemy in the name of the LORD Almighty. In my weaknesses, I run to You Jesus and ask You to make me strong. Let it be so in Jesus's name, amen.

Day 40: I Am the Temple of the Holy Spirit

> *"Do you not know that your bodies are temples of the Holy Spirit, who is in you, whom you have received from God? You are not your own; you were bought at a price. Therefore, honor God with your bodies."* 1 Corinthians 6:19-20 NIV

> *"Don't you know that you yourselves are God's temple and that God's Spirit dwells in your midst?"* 1 Corinthians 3:16 NIV

> *"And the priests could not perform their service because of the cloud, for the glory of the LORD filled his temple."* 1 Kings 8:11 NIV

In the Old Testament, God gave instructions to Moses on how to build the Tabernacle, a portable tent where God's presence would be housed as the Israelites traveled from their exodus of Egypt into the conquering of the land of Canaan. This was a place where man could meet with God, talk with God, and have God talk with them. Prior to this, Moses had met with the LORD atop Mount Sinai. This is where he went to receive from the LORD the Ten Commandments and this is where he also went to receive from God the instructions for the construction of the Tabernacle. It was upon this mountain that God revealed His glory to all the Israelites so that they might come close to Him in reverence, yet they chose to remain at a distance. "When the people saw the thunder and lightning and heard the trumpet and saw the mountain in smoke, they trembled with fear. They stayed at a distance and said to Moses, 'Speak to us yourself and we will listen. But do not have God speak to us or we will die." (Exodus 20:18-19 NIV). So, Moses became the mediator between God and His people. Later Moses appoints Aaron and his sons as priests to go into the holy of holies and carry out these instructions prescribed by God. The construction and the practices of the Tabernacle were very precise and were given by God so that if carried out completely, God's glory could come down and be with man.

The same was also true for the Temple that Solomon built later in Jerusalem. This Temple was a more permanent structure also having precise instructions and practices given in order to house God's presence. God's presence was always intended to be in these locations, yet at some instances, the cloud of God's presence would cover the Temple, or the Tabernacle and the glory of the LORD would fill these places until the priests couldn't even perform their service. Yet according to these instructions, only the priests could enter the presence of the LORD, the rest of the people remained at a distance from God's glory, from His presence, from speaking with Him. However, Jesus changed all of that for you! According to Hebrews 4, Jesus is your great High Priest. He went into God's presence for you as the perfect Lamb of God, an acceptable sacrifice for your sins, and tore the veil of separation that restricted you from entering the presence of the LORD. He brought you near to God through His shed blood on the cross. You don't have to stay at a distance anymore. Thank you, Jesus!

According to the Scriptures, you are now the temple of the Holy Spirit. You are the temple, the place where God's presence dwells. You are that sacred place where the glory of God resides. How awesome! My friend, Satan is a liar! You are not garbage. You are not the junk he tries to convince you of. Can I tell you; Satan doesn't want you to house God's presence, God's Spirit? He doesn't want you to carry God's glory with you wherever you go because that would drastically impact the world. He doesn't want you to know and understand that you are the temple of the Holy Spirit. So, he downplays the consequences of sin in your life so that you'll hopefully continue to permit it in your temple so the presence of God, the Holy Spirit would be hindered. However, you are not your own anymore! You were bought at a price; therefore, honor God with your body! Be the temple of the Holy Spirit! Let God's glory, God's presence fills you! When God's glory would fill the Temple and the Tabernacle in the Old Testament, it was obvious. The priests had to stop doing what they did every day. The people would see the cloud of God's glory and knew that God was there. Even Pharaoh saw the pillar of cloud, a sign of God's presence, with Israel as he perused them in the desert. It was evident even to the enemy that God was with His people! Let it be so with you, my friend. May it be apparent to all, even to your enemy that the LORD is with you for you are the Temple of the Holy Spirit of the Living God! Carry His glory!

Father,

> I thank You for Jesus, that because He tore the veil of separation, I can now get close to You and Your presence. I thank You for Your glory, for the holiness, the power, the brilliance of Your presence. Your presence changes everything and it is my desire to dwell in Your presence. And I thank You that I can now do that very thing because You have made me the temple of the Holy Spirit. Your Spirit is always with me, always talking to me, and I have every opportunity to commune with You without ceasing. Let it be so LORD. Help me to grasp this, to live this out every day. Holy Spirit help me to honor God with my body and to

be a carrier of Your glory. I invite You to come and fill this temple in Jesus's name, amen.

Day 41: I Am Redeemed!

> *"In him (Jesus) we have redemption through his blood, the forgiveness of sins, in accordance with the riches of God's grace."* Ephesians 1:7 NIV
>
> *"For all who rely on the works of the law are under a curse, as it is written: 'cursed is everyone who does not continue to do everything written in the Book of the Law.' Clearly no one who relies on the law is justified before God, because 'the righteous will live by faith.' The law is not based on faith; on the contrary, is says, 'The person who does these things will live by them.' Christ redeemed us from the curse of the law by becoming a curse for us, for it is written: 'Cursed is everyone who is hung on a tree."* Galatians 3:10-13 NIV

Jesus paid the necessary debt to clear you before God. The blood of Jesus has redeemed you! What was the necessary debt? Death. I know that seems harsh, but as we have already stated, Romans 6:23 says that the wages of sin, the penalty of sin is death. And according to Romans 3:23, we all have sinned and fallen short of God's glory. Sin was costing you your life, my friend, but Jesus has cleared your record before God. He took it away and nailed it to the cross. Now you are redeemed!

Look at the Scripture above in Galatians. It says that all those who rely on the works of the law are under a curse because the Bible says that everyone who doesn't continue to do everything written in the Book of the Law is cursed. What is the curse? Being separated from God, being spiritually dead. No one has kept the whole Law. "For whoever keeps the whole law and yet stumbles at just one point is guilty of breaking all of it." (James 2:10 NIV). We're all guilty. We've all stumbled. We were all under the curse of the Law. The above Scripture goes on to say that no one who relies on the Law is justified before God because the Bible says that the righteous will live by faith. The Law isn't based on faith; rather, it is entirely based on works. "...the person who does these things will live by them." (Galatians 3:12 NIV). The only way to be justified by the Law is to keep the Law and a person will live if they do everything that is written in the Law. Yet no one has done everything written in the Law; therefore, we are all under the curse of the Law. But Jesus redeemed you from the curse of the Law! He redeemed you from the inability to keep the Laws of God. He became a curse for you by being hung on the cross. He paid the necessary debt in order to redeem you. Thank You, Jesus!

You are not cursed! You are not a failure! You have been redeemed! The debt you owed has been paid in full. Now you have no outstanding debt with God. You have been cleared, justified! You don't have to rely on the works of the Law anymore to be declared righteous. You can rely on faith alone in Jesus Christ who has made you the righteousness of God! Jesus tells a parable in Matthew 18 about a man who owed a large debt to his master, ten thousand bags of gold. This man was brought before the master and the payment of his debt was demanded of him and since he couldn't pay the debt, the master ordered his entire family to be sold for repayment. But the servant falls on his knees and begs for mercy and the master takes pity on him, cancels his debt completely, and lets the servant go. Can you imagine being forgiven such a large sum of money? Yet somehow this servant seems to forget how mercifully he has been treated because he goes out and finds someone indebted to him, who owed him one hundred silver coins. He chokes this individual and demands payment, but when the servant begs for mercy, this guy refuses to be merciful and has the servant thrown into jail until the debt can be paid. When the master learns of this, he berates him for being so unmerciful especially when he has been shown such great mercy and has the man thrown into prison to be tortured as a result. Your debt has been canceled! You have been shown mercy because of Jesus, so don't continue to be unmerciful and unforgiving. Considering the great debt that you have been cleared of, celebrate, rejoice, share such mercy, such grace, such love with everyone! Do a black flip if you can; you have been redeemed!

Father,

> I thank You for the blood of Jesus that has redeemed me. I thank You that I am cleared before you in Christ, that I have been released from the debt that I owed. I thank You that I

am not under the curse of the Law anymore, but that I have been redeemed by faith in Jesus. Holy Spirit, would You help me to be merciful, to be thankful, to love and forgive freely. Considering how greatly I have been shown mercy, help me to be merciful. May I never forget what Christ has done for me in Jesus's name, amen.

Day 42: I Am Reconciled to God

"Therefore, if anyone is in Christ, the new creation has come: the old has gone, the new is here! All this is from God, who reconciled us to himself through Christ and gave us the ministry of reconciliation: that God was reconciling the world to himself in Christ, not counting people's sins against them. And he has committed to us the message of reconciliation. We are therefore Christ's ambassadors, as though God were making his appeal through us. We implore you on Christ's behalf be reconciled to God." 2 Corinthians 5: 17-20 NIV

"For God was pleased to have all his fullness dwell in him (Jesus), and through him to reconcile to himself all things, whether things on earth or things in heaven, by making peace through his blood, shed on the cross. Once you were alienated from God and were enemies in your minds because of your evil behavior. But now he has reconciled you by Christ's physical body through death to present you holy in his sight, without blemish and free from accusation— "Colossians 1:19-22 NIV

Through Christ, you have been reconciled to God, things have been put right in your relationship. You have been reunited with Him through Christ and the conflict between you and God because of your sin has been settled, resolved. "Come now, let us settle the matter,' says the LORD. 'Though your sins are like scarlet, they shall be as white as snow; though they are red as crimson, they shall be like wool." (Isaiah 1:18 NIV). Because of the blood of

Jesus, there is now peace between you and God, there is union. The conflict of sin has been done away with in Christ! Sin brings conflict. It causes trouble in your life and especially in your relationship with God. It causes separation and pain and brings enmity between you and the One who made you. Satan knows this full well, my friend. He always downplays the severity of sin. He'll try to convince you that one little mess up, one little time isn't that big of a deal. And perhaps it's not, but his goal for you is not the occasional slip-up. One compromise leads to another and another and still another until slowly you fade into something you never thought you'd be or do. Don't be deceived, the enemy's goal for you is always mastery. According to John 10:10 the enemy has come to kill you, to steal from you, and to destroy you; not to offer you occasional fun. So, don't be unaware of his schemes, his tricks, his lies. Flee temptation, run from sin because in Christ, you have been reconciled to God!

According to the above Scripture in Colossians, at one time you were alienated from God, but He has now reconciled you to Himself through Christ. Where He once saw you as an enemy because of sin, where He once saw the trouble, the conflict, the pain; in Christ you are now holy in His sight, without blemish and free from accusation! How awesome is that! Can I tell you that you didn't reconcile yourself to God because there's nothing you or I could accomplish to do away with sin? However, God reconciled you to Himself through Christ. He wanted things to be right between you both so much that He provided Jesus to reunite you with Him. That is amazing grace! That is real, authentic, transforming love!

Now you have been given the ministry and message of reconciliation. You are Christ's ambassador as if He were making His appeal through you, begging people, imploring the whole world, pleading with everyone to be reconciled to God. Please be reunited with God! Please let the conflict of sin in your life be settled through Jesus! Please come back to the One who formed you and fashioned you, Who knew you before you were ever born. I beg you to be reconciled to Him!

Father,

> I thank You for making a way for me to be reunited with You through Jesus. I thank You for the power of His blood to reconcile me to You. I am so thankful that my sins aren't counted against me, but that the conflict between me and You has been settled in Jesus. Holy Spirit, would You give

me eyes to see sin for what it really is? Would You give me discernment and wisdom to recognize the schemes of the enemy in my life for what they are? May every strategy of the enemy in my life be foiled in the name of Jesus. And may I carry this message of reconciliation with me wherever I go today. Help me, Holy Spirit, in Jesus's name, amen.

⇜⇝

Day 43: I Am Complete!

"For in Christ all the fullness of the Deity lives in bodily form, and in Christ you have been brought to fullness. He is the head over every power and authority." Colossians 2:9-10 NIV

"The LORD is my shepherd, I lack nothing! He makes me lie down in green pastures, he leads me beside quiet waters, he refreshes my soul. He guides me along the right paths for his name's sake. Even though I walk through the darkest valley, I will fear no evil, for you are with me; your rod and your staff they comfort me. You prepare a table before me in the presence of my enemies. You anoint my head with oil; my cup overflows. Surely goodness and love will follow me all the days of my life, and I will dwell in the house of the LORD forever." Psalm 23 NIV

"Therefore you do not lack any spiritual gift as you eagerly wait for our LORD Jesus Christ to be revealed. He will also keep you firm to the end, so that you will be blameless on the day of our LORD Jesus Christ. God is faithful, who has called you into fellowship with his Son, Jesus Christ our LORD." 1 Corinthians 1:7-9 NIV

In Christ, you are complete, you lack nothing! Christ has brought you to fullness, to richness! I'm not talking about how much money you have in your bank account. I'm talking about the fact that you have been brought near to, in union with the One who owns the cattle on a thousand hilltops. The Maker of the Heavens and the Earth, the unexplainable, uncontainable God of the cosmos Who has always been and will always be, the One with unlimited resources Whose very words call things that are not as though they are, and they are. You are now close to Him. In fact, the Word of God says that you are now His child. That is fullness! That is incredible!

Satan in his craftiness tries to make everything about you. Everything hinges on you. If a trial or problem arises in your life it rests on you and your ability to handle it, your resources, your intelligence, your endurance, your strength. If things in your life seem to be falling apart Satan twists, it into not just stuff that is falling apart but you are falling apart. If you don't seem to have the resources to meet a certain situation then you are lacking. You're poor, you're cursed, you're a failure, you're falling to pieces. It's all about you. No, no, no! Lift your eyes to the hills, my friend. Where does your help come from? Hopefully not just from yourself or even from your friends and family. Your help comes from the LORD, Maker of the Heavens and the Earth! You do not lack any spiritual gift according to the Bible (listed in 1 Corinthians 12:7-11)! In Christ, they are all yours! God is not holding out on you. He has given you everything! In Christ, you are kept firm to the end. You aren't barely making it, eeking by, just trying to hang on till Jesus comes. You are being kept firm, solid, completely unyielding to the enemy. God is faithful and He has called you into fellowship, companionship, friendship with Jesus! Shut up Satan, I am not falling apart! Things may be falling apart in my life, but I am not falling apart because in Christ I am being kept firm to the very end. In Christ, I have fullness!

Psalm 23 is a very well-known Scripture. Its words have been inscribed on thousands and thousands of cards, letters, and keepsakes throughout the years. Yet I pray these words and their truth would be inscribed on your heart forever. If the LORD is your Shepherd then regardless to what Satan says or what your circumstances may look like, you lack nothing! He is a good Shepherd, my friend! He will make you lie down in green pastures; He will lead you beside quiet waters, He will refresh your soul. He will guide you along the right paths for His name's sake. And even if you travel through the darkest valley you don't have to fear any evil for your Shepherd is with you. His rod and staff, His Word and His correction will comfort you. You don't even have to run from your enemies or hide from your enemies for He prepares a table for you in the presence of your enemies. He anoints your head with oil and causes your cup to overflow. If none of that sounds faintly familiar, then can I suggest to you that maybe the LORD isn't your Shepherd? Maybe something else or someone else or even you hold the position of shepherd in your life. Satan would rather you follow anything other than Jesus, so he magnifies the voices of lesser shepherds. I don't mean to be harsh but a shepherd leads, guides, and cares for his sheep and no one, not even you are as good a shepherd as God is. Listen to the LORD, your Shepherd, trust His goodness towards you. With God as your Shepherd, you lack nothing! On the contrary, goodness and mercy shall follow you all the days of your life and you will dwell in the house of the LORD forever!

Father,

> I thank You for bringing me to fullness in Christ. I thank You that I am complete, I lack nothing because You are my Shepherd. Would You forgive my heart for following the leading of other lesser shepherds when You alone are the Good Shepherd? Holy Spirit, I want to know Your voice, listen to Your voice, follow Your voice, trust Your leading. I forfeit the role of shepherd of my life to You LORD. Would You guide me today, would You speak to me today, would You be with me today? I desperately need You and wholeheartedly trust You. Based on Your Word, I boldly declare today that I am full, I am complete, I lack nothing in Jesus's name, amen!

Day 44: I Am a Saint!

> *"To the church of God, which is at Corinth, to those who have been sanctified in Christ Jesus, saints by calling, with all who in every place call on the name of our Lord Jesus Christ, their LORD and ours."* 1 Corinthians 1:2 NASB

> *"to all who are beloved of God in Rome, called as saints: Grace to you and peace from God our Father and the LORD Jesus Christ."* Romans 1:7 NASB

> *"and He who searches the hearts knows what the mind of the Spirit is, because He intercedes for the saints according to the will of God."* Romans 8:27 NASB

A saint is a person who is acknowledged as virtuous or holy. It's a title of honor, of recognition, of respect. The Catholic Church and even society at large have upheld certain individuals as being saints for centuries. St. Patrick of Ireland was born in Roman Britain and was captured by Irish pirates when he was a teenager and taken to Ireland as a prisoner. Later after escaping prison, he went back to Ireland and began to preach and teach and convert the people there to Catholicism. St. Francis of Assisi was a saint in France who founded the Franciscan Order. Then there's St. Mary the Virgin, the mother of Jesus, believed by many to be the greatest of all the saints. And there's even St. Nicolas of Greece whose legendary habit of secret gift-giving gave rise to the traditional model of Santa Clause. There are many, many people whose lives held such virtue that they were given the title "saint" by the Catholic Church. Yet these men and women were often recognized or at least canonized as "saints" after their deaths. The legend of their lives seems to still hold great sway on society today. It's from St. Patrick that we get St. Patrick's Day. It's from St. Nicolas that we have Santa Clause. And it's from St. Valentine that we celebrate Valentine's Day just to name a few. What an honor to be officially declared a "saint" by the council of man; however, One much, much greater than a religious organization has made this declaration over you in the council of heaven! Through Jesus Christ you have been sanctified, made holy and you are now called a saint by God!

My friend, you are not the labels the enemy has tried to peg you with. You are not even the outcome of your choices or your actions since Christ has made you a new creation. You are a saint! You are a person of virtue of holiness. "Therefore, come out from them and be separate, says the LORD..." (2 Corinthians 6:17 NIV). You don't have to earn your way into sainthood in the Kingdom of God! There's nothing you could do to be declared virtuous enough, holy enough to be considered a saint in God's eyes. Nor do you have to wait for a group of individuals to classify you as such. Faith alone in Jesus Christ has made you a saint to God!

Can I tell you; Satan wants you to consider yourself a mess-up, a failure, a piece of trash, just a sinner? If you only think of yourself in these terms then it is much easier for him to convince you to associate with and permit mess-ups in your life, failures in your life, trash in your life, and sin in your life. Oh well, I lied again, it's okay because I'm just a liar anyway. Oops, I sinned again, but that's okay, God understands because I'm just a sinner. No! Stop it right now! Jesus has made you a saint. He has made you holy, virtuous. Yes, you are saved by grace and not by your works, how good and virtuous they may or may not be. Yes, if you confess your sins, He is faithful and just to forgive you and cleanse you from all unrighteousness. Yet because of Christ, you are not identified by sin anymore, so you are not a sinner! The blood of Jesus has cleansed you, has sanctified you, and has identified you as a saint! According to 1 Thessalonians 5:5, you are not a child of darkness anymore; you are a child of light, a child of the day! The LORD your God Who has saved you, Who has redeemed you, Who has made you and set you apart for Himself is holy; therefore, be holy!

Father,

> I thank You for making me a saint through Jesus. I thank You that because of Christ I am not associated with sin anymore, with darkness anymore; rather, I am associated with light, Your light! Forgive me, LORD, for tolerating any sin in my life when that is not who I am anymore. Help me Holy Spirit to remember that I am called a saint by God, that He has officially declared me to be holy and virtuous because of Jesus. Help me to come out from among this world and be separate, to be what You have called me to be for my citizenship is in heaven and it is from there that I am eagerly awaiting my Savior, the LORD Jesus Christ! Only Your goodness, Your virtue, Your love, Your power could make me a saint and for that I am so thankful. May it be so in my life in Jesus's name, amen!

Day 45: I Am the Head!

> *"The LORD will make you the head, not the tail. If you pay attention to the commands of the LORD you God that I give you this day and carefully follow them, you will always be at the top, never at the bottom."* Deuteronomy 28:13 NIV
>
> *"The Son is the image of the invisible God, the firstborn over all creation. For in him all things were created: things in heaven and on earth, visible and invisible, whether thrones or powers or rulers or authorities; all things have been created through him and for him. He is before all things, and in him all things hold together. And he is the head of the body, the church; he is the beginning and the firstborn from among the dead, so that in everything he might have the supremacy."* Colossians 1:15-18 NIV

The LORD has made you the head and not the tail! Look at the Scripture above from Colossians. Jesus is the image of the invisible God. If you want to know what God is like, what He looks like, what His character is, look to Jesus! He is the firstborn over all creation for in Him all things were created. You were created in Him! You are made a new creation in Him! It's all because of Jesus! Everything created in heaven and on earth, everything that is visible and invisible, all powers, rulers, and authorities have been established through Him and for Him and He is the head of them all! Nothing is greater than Jesus! No authority could exalt itself above that of the authority of Jesus for He established all authorities and He holds supremacy over them all. Jesus is before all things and in Him all things hold together! My friend, if you are in Him, if you have been born again by the confession of your sin and your faith in Him, then you are being held together. This is incredible news! Satan is a liar! The enemy cannot destroy you; he cannot tear you apart, and he cannot unravel you. According to the Word of God, you are not falling apart because in Jesus you are being held together! Jesus is the head of the body of

Christ, the head of the church, He is over it all; even death, even the grave, in everything He has the supremacy!

And guess what, my friend? According to Ephesians 2:6, God has raised you up with Christ and you are now seated with Him in heavenly places! In Christ, you are now at the top, never again to be at the bottom! Spiritually you have great power, great authority, and great influence because of Jesus! You are not some weak, unassuming, powerless individual so don't let the enemy trample you under his feet. You are not meant to be at the bottom, you are not meant to be the tail just following the lead of your current life situations. You are not meant to be dragged around through this life. Jesus has made you the head. He has put you in a position of leadership in the spiritual realm. In Him, you now have the power, the authority, the influence to change things, to create things, to abolish things, to establish God's will on earth as it is in heaven. Your words are that powerful. Your prayers are that impactful. Jesus said in Matthew 18:18, that whatever you bind on earth will be bound in heaven and whatever you lose on earth will be loosed in heaven. And Jesus also said in Matthew 17:20 that if you have faith as small as a mustard seed you can say to this mountain "move from here to there" and it will move; nothing will be impossible for you!

My friend, Satan does not want you to pray. He doesn't want you to know God's Word because God's Word is God's will. He doesn't want you to know how to pray effectively and fervently because the fervent prayer of a righteous person is powerful and effective! Friend, Jesus has made you righteous, so your prayers are powerful and effective! The enemy will do anything possible to keep your mouth shut. Don't let the enemy bully you out of praying! He has no authority over you for you are the head and not the tail. You are at the top and not the bottom! It's time to rise up in Jesus's name!

Father,

> I thank You for Jesus. I thank You that in Him I am at the top and not the bottom, that I am the head and not the tail anymore. I thank You that it pleased You to have all Your fullness dwell in Jesus and to reconcile all things to Yourself through His shed blood. I thank You that in Christ I am seated in the heavenlies and that my prayers are now powerful and effective. Forgive me LORD for not praying often, for not praying fervently. Forgive me for not knowing

Your Word which is Your will so that I can pray effectively. Help me Holy Spirit, to open my mouth in the authority that Jesus has given me and establish the will of God on earth as it is in heaven. Give me courage, boldness in the name of Jesus, amen.

Day 46: I Am Rescued!

"For he (God) has rescued us from the dominion of darkness and brought us into the kingdom of the Son he loves, in whom we have redemption, the forgiveness of sins." Colossians 1:13-14 NIV

"As for you, you were dead in your transgressions and sins, in which you used to live when you followed the ways of this world and the ruler of the kingdom of the air, the spirit who is now at work in those who are disobedient. All of us also lived among them at one time, gratifying the cravings of our flesh and following its desires and thoughts. Like the rest, we were by nature deserving of wrath. But because of his great love for us, God, who is rich in mercy, made us alive with Christ and seated us with him in the heavenly realms in Christ Jesus, in order that in the coming ages he might show the incomparable riches of his grace, expressed in his kindness to us in Christ Jesus." Ephesians 2:1-7 NIV

Perhaps it's hard to appreciate all that God has done through Jesus when there's little knowledge of all that God has done through Jesus. Yet the Word of God is replete with evidence of the good things Christ has accomplished. For one, God has rescued you from the dominion of darkness and brought you into the kingdom of Jesus! Before Jesus, the testimony of your life was that darkness had power over you, authority over you, control over you. You were dominated by darkness. Maybe that's an unsympathetic way of putting it, but that's what the Bible says. The Word of God according to 2 Timothy 3:16 is

God-breathed and is useful for teaching, rebuking, correcting, and training in righteousness. It's hard to read the Word of God without it getting all up in your business. In the Scripture above in Ephesians, Paul describes how you were once dead in your transgressions and sins. This was your condition before Christ! But my friend, you have been rescued by God! In Christ, you have been rescued from the dominion of darkness, released from the power of sin! In Christ, you have been rescued from death and brought to life! God rescued you, saved you, set you free through Jesus!

Why did God come to your rescue? According to the Scripture above in Ephesians it was because of His great love for you! Satan is a master manipulator. He is always twisting truths into lies and making things appear a certain way despite their reality. 2 Corinthians 11:14 says that Satan masquerades as an angel of light. He gives a pretense of good, an appearance of what's right, an impersonation of truth to manipulate you, to deceive you. He doesn't want you to see God for who He really is so he crafts together a fabricated truth (which is another way of saying a lie) based on what you've been told and the events you have experienced in life that is completely contrary to the Word of God but feels so real that you accept his shenanigans as truth. Don't be deceived! Read God's Word, memorize God's Word, let the Word of God not just be written words on pages in your Bible, but let it be engraved and written on your heart. God's Word is truth and the more you know it, and the better you know it, the more easily you will recognize the crafty tales of the enemy as blatant lies.

Ephesians 2 describes God as being rich in mercy. "Who is a God like you, who pardons sin and forgives the transgression of the remnant of his inheritance? You do not stay angry forever but delight to show mercy." (Micah 7:18 NIV). The LORD enjoys showing mercy! He is wealthy, affluent, loaded with mercy! This is excellent news! Your need to be forgiven, your need to be shown kindness and grace could never exceed the amount of mercy God has for you! It brings Him joy to show you kindness. Why would we run from Him? Who is a God like Him? No one! In His mercy, He has rescued you. Because of His great kindness, He has brought you into the kingdom of the Son He loves. Out of His incredible love for you, He has made you alive in Christ and seated you with Jesus in heavenly realms. Who does that? God does! In all the earth, in all the heavens there is no one like our God! Praise His great name forever!

Father,

I thank You for rescuing me from darkness, for setting me free from the dominion of sin. Thank You for You great love and mercy that has brought me into the kingdom of Jesus. I am amazed that You delight in showing me mercy, that You enjoy being kind to me. Wow! There is no one like You, LORD. You are so good and today I just want to praise You. I praise You for who You are for You are merciful, faithful, righteous, and so incredibly good. I praise You for what You have done for me. You have rescued me from death and made me alive in Christ. You have raised me out of darkness and seated me in heavenly places with Jesus. You truly are an awesome God and today my heart is full, thank You LORD!

Day 47: I Am Accepted!

"May the God who gives endurance and encouragement give you the same attitude of mind toward each other that Christ Jesus had, so that with one mind and one voice you may glorify the God and Father of our LORD Jesus Christ. Accept one another, then, just as Christ accepted you, in order to bring praise to God." Romans 15:5-7 NIV

"Praise be to the God and Father of our LORD Jesus Christ, who has blessed us in the heavenly realms with every spiritual blessing in Christ. For he chose us in him before the creation of the world to be holy and blameless in his sight." Ephesians 1:3-4 NIV

"Remember the former things, those of long ago; I am God, and there is no other; I am God, and there is none like me. I make known the end from the beginning, from ancient times, what is still to come. I say, 'My purpose will stand, and I will do all that I please." Isaiah 46:9-10 NIV

You are accepted in Christ! You are acknowledged, received, established by God through Jesus! Look at the Scripture above in Romans. Paul writes to the church of God in Rome about having the same attitude towards one another as Christ has towards them. There was division and conflict between those who were Jews and the new Gentile followers of Jesus in the church at Rome. Specifically, after being taught for centuries that those who don't follow the Jewish customs and laws of purification are unclean and not fit to enter into the Temple, it was difficult for these Jewish believers to accept that the Gentile believers were just as sanctified and made holy through Jesus as they were. So, Paul encourages them to accept one another just as they have been accepted by Christ in order to bring praise to God. Rejection in the body of Christ doesn't bring praise to God, acceptance does! This doesn't mean that we should accept sin or compromise in our lives because God absolutely does not accept these things, but we should accept one another as brothers and sisters in Christ not counting other's sins against them when Christ has removed their sin and accepted them as His own. If Christ considers someone worth accepting, then you should too! Christ's acceptance of you brings praise to God. Whose praise does it bring. Your praise! Apart from Christ you are rejected by God because of your sin. But Jesus who had no sin became the acceptable sacrifice for sin and canceled the written record of wrongs against you. He nailed that record to the Cross no longer to be counted against you so that you are now accepted by God who gave you Jesus to begin with. That should result in you praising His great name!

In addition to this, God gives you endurance and encouragement. You might not think you can make it anymore. Maybe you're tired, or weary, or ready to throw in the towel. Don't give up! Run to the One who gives you stamina to keep going! Jesus says, "Come to me, all you who are weary and burdened, and I will give you rest." (Matthew 11:28 NIV). Not only so, God gives you encouragement, support, backup. "But you, LORD, are a shield around me; you are my glory, the one who holds my head high." (Psalm 3:3 NIV). No one else can keep your head lifted, but God sure can. He chose you in Him before the creation of the world. That is incredible! Long before you were ever born, God wanted you, preferred you, desired you, and made a way for you to be accepted by Him through Jesus! Look at the above Scripture in Isaiah and remember the former things, what the LORD has done for you. He wanted you long before anyone else ever wanted you. He preferred you to be His child, to be a part of His family and made this available to you through Jesus. To reject Him is to reject His love, His acceptance, His preference for us. Rejecting God is rejecting the very things we need the most. Why would we do that? He is God and there is no other! There is no one like Him who knows the end from the beginning. Don't let the enemy whisper lies of rejection, of being unwanted, undesired to you because this is not who you are in Christ! In Jesus you are accepted by God! You are not an outcast when Jesus has brought you near to God. You are near, you are close, you are received; thank you Jesus!

Father,

> I thank You for accepting me in Christ. I thank You that I am not rejected, unwanted, or an outcast; but that Jesus has brought me near, and You have received me. I am so humbled, so grateful. Holy Spirit, would You help me to view others with the appropriate heart? Help me to accept others just as I have been accepted by God. Give me endurance today, the stamina to keep going. Lift my head and encourage me, LORD, for I need You desperately. I praise You for acknowledging me as Your very own. May I have the same attitude as Christ today in Jesus's name, amen.

Day 48: I Am a Citizen of Heaven

"But our citizenship is in heaven. And we eagerly await a Savior from there, the LORD Jesus Christ," Philippians 3:20 NIV

"If you belonged to the world, it would love you as its own. As it is, you do not belong to the world, but I have chosen you out of the world. That is why the world hates you." John 15:19 NIV

"in which you used to live when you followed the ways of this world and of the ruler of the kingdom of the air, the spirit who is now at work in those who are disobedient." Ephesians 2:2 NIV

In Christ, you are a citizen of Heaven! You now have nationality and legal residency in Heaven! If your national citizenship was in question, the proper documentation would silence all doubt and prove you to be a legal citizen of the nation in which you reside. Open your Bible; it is the proper documentation to silence the enemy. A citizen is someone who legally belongs to a country and has the rights and protection of that country. As a citizen of Heaven, you no longer belong to this world, you belong to Heaven! You have the rights and the protection of Heaven! Citizens also adopt the culture and practices of the nation and kingdom to which they belong. Everyone is born into the kingdom of this world of which Satan rules. Ephesians 2:2 links following the ways of the world with following Satan, the ruler of the kingdom of the air, a spirit who works in those who are disobedient. Satan's kingdom enslaves its citizens as Romans 6:16 suggests. Those who don't know Christ live only for this world and the pleasures they can find for themselves. Yet when we are born again by faith in Jesus Christ, we are born into the Kingdom of Heaven. As a citizen of Heaven, you should no longer continue to follow the ways of this world but should adopt the culture and practices of the Kingdom of Heaven since that is now your eternal residency.

God has given you the power and the privilege of exiting the world's flawed value system and living for eternity. "Do not love the world or anything in the world. If anyone loves the world, love for the Father is not in them. For everything in the world—the lust of the flesh, the lust of the eyes, and the pride of life—comes not from the Father but from the world. The world and its desires pass away, but whoever does the will of God lives forever." (1 John 2:15-17 NIV). When you were adopted into the family of God, you became a citizen of an eternal kingdom where your Father is the King. Your focus should now turn towards eternal things and storing up treasure in Heaven where you will reside forever. You are no longer a citizen of this world; you are a citizen of Heaven and an ambassador to this earth as 2 Corinthians 5:20 says, imploring everyone on Christ's behalf to be reconciled to God and become fellow heavenly citizens with you.

Can I encourage you to lift your head up today and set your heart and mind on things above, not on earthly things? Satan will try to discourage you and distract you and cause you to focus only on the things of this world, this life. Yes, you live in this world, but only as a foreigner and stranger now. This is not all there is! You are a citizen of Heaven! Your residency is there not here which helps give proper perspective to daily life. Be encouraged, be encouraged, be encouraged; your citizenship in Heaven has brought about your protection from Heaven. In the United States citizens are protected by their government and the Constitution even when they are traveling to another country. Even though you are visiting another country, legally you are still a citizen of the United States and have the protection of your rights as an American citizen. Though you are in this world still, you are absolutely a citizen of Heaven and are covered and protected by the governing laws of the Kingdom of Heaven which is a greater kingdom by far. 1 John 4:4 tells you that you have overcome because the One Who is in you and the Kingdom that He represents is greater than the one who is in this world and the kingdom he stands for. You belong to a Kingdom of Light, a Kingdom of Victory, and a Kingdom that will last forever! Praise God, you belong to the Kingdom of Heaven!

Father,

> I thank You for making me a citizen of Heaven through Jesus. I thank You that my residency, my nationality is in Heaven with You not here in this world. Holy Spirit, would You help me to remember that I am a citizen of Heaven? Would you help me to have the proper perspective towards this life and the things of this life? I don't want to store all my treasures here when this world and the things of this world will pass away. I choose to set my heart and mind on things above today. Help me Holy Spirit in Jesus's name, amen.

Day 49: I Am Bold as a Lion

"Let us therefore come boldly unto the throne of grace that we may obtain mercy and find grace to help in time of need." Hebrews 4:16 NKJV

"Therefore I (Jesus) tell you, whatever you ask for in prayer, believe that you have received it, and it will be yours." Mark 11:24 NIV

> *"And I (Jesus) will do whatever you ask in my name, so that the Father may be glorified in the Son."* John 14:13 NIV

> *"The wicked flee though no one pursues, but the righteous are as bold as a lion."* Proverbs 28:1 NIV

If you are confident in something you are sure of it, certain about it, convinced of it, and secure in it. We teach our kids to be confident in their self, to believe in themselves and that isn't necessarily a bad thing. However, Psalm 118:8 says that it is better to trust in the LORD than to put confidence in man. Why? Because man is weak, man tends to fail. Placing your confidence, your certainty, your security in something so fallible makes for a bumpy ride in life; it sets you up for some major disappointments. But putting your confidence, your trust, your reliance upon Jesus Christ Who is the same yesterday, today, and forever enables even the weakest individual to be as bold as a lion in the LORD. "For the Spirit God gave us does not make us timid, but gives us power, love, and self-discipline." (2 Timothy 1:7 NIV). God's Spirit doesn't make you fearful, shy, or nervous! If the LORD has set His seal of ownership upon you, the Spirit of the Living God, then your prayers, your attitude in Christ should be bold, courageous, and audacious. You can do anything in Him because He is the One Who can do all things! His Spirit gives you power! His Spirit gives you love! His Spirit gives you self-discipline! Again, it has nothing to do with your personality, your abilities, or who you are in and of yourself. It has everything to do with who God is, His character and His abilities! Because of Jesus you don't have to approach God's throne of grace timidly, nervously, shyly; you can come boldly!

Lions are symbols of strength and courage. They are one of the largest big cats, second only to the tiger. However, while the tiger tends to mostly be a solitary creature, lions travel together in prides giving them a unique strength and protection. They are considered the king of the jungle with virtually no natural predators. Lions, the loudest of all big cats, roar to communicate their position to other prides and animals. And lions are 6 times more sensitive to light than humans giving them distinct advantage over prey while hunting at night. I don't believe it's a coincidence that the Bible calls Jesus the Lion of the tribe of Judah in Revelation 5:5. And guess what? According to the above Scripture in Proverbs, the righteous are as bold as a lion. Jesus has made you righteous; therefore, you are as bold as a lion! You are identified with Jesus, identified with strength and courage. You are not meant to be a solitary creature; you are meant to be a part of a pride, to find protection and strength with other lions. You virtually have no enemies because who in their right mind would take on a group of lions? Even in the darkest of nights, God has given you vision and sensitivity to light so that you are still victorious in Him. "Arise, shine, for your light has come, and the glory of the LORD rises upon you. See, darkness covers the earth and thick darkness is over the peoples, but the LORD rises upon you and his glory appears over you" (Isaiah 60:1-2 NIV). And in Christ, you have a position of authority, so when the enemy tries to lurk around you and your pride, maybe you need to roar and remind him of your position in Christ.

The lions' biggest threat besides humans is the hyena, a creature of far lesser strength that occasionally attacks and kills a lion, usually a cub, who has wandered away from the pride. Lions and hyenas occupy the same geographic territory and rely upon the same prey as food, so they have developed a competitive relationship. Hyenas also travel together in packs and although they cannot compare individually to a lion's strength and size, a group of hyenas can take down a lone lion or use teamwork to intimidate a lion away from its kill. Hyenas are considered scavengers and thieves, often using intimidation and other tactics of trickery to overcome their prey. Does that not sound altogether like the people of God and the enemy of our souls? Yet the Spirit of God has not made you timid, weak, unassuming; He has given you power! In Christ, Satan is not your equal! You are the overcomer, you are the victor, you are more than a conqueror! Jesus is the Lion of the tribe of Judah! All strength is His! All power is His! All confidence, all boldness is His! And praise God, my friend, you are in Him!

Father,

> I thank You for Jesus. I thank You that He is the Lion of the Tribe of Judah. He is the Victor, the Conqueror, the Overcomer and that in Him, so am I! Holy Spirit, would you fill me with courage today, boldness today? Fill me with love and self-discipline and power. In Christ, I am not weak or timid or nervous or shy. I am mighty, I am bold, I am confident because nothing is impossible with You, LORD. When it comes to the things of God, make me as bold as a lion in Jesus's name, amen.

Day 50: I Am Remembered!

"He who overcomes shall be clothed in white garments, and I will not blot out his name from the Book of Life; but I will confess his name before My Father and before His angels..." Revelation 3:5 NKJV

"But one has testified somewhere, saying, 'What is man, that you remember him? Or the son of man, that you are concerned about him?'" Hebrews 2:6 NASB

"Can a woman forget her nursing child and have no compassion on the son of her womb? Even these may forget, but I (God) will not forget you. 'Behold, I have inscribed you on the palms of My hands;" Isaiah 49:15-16 NASB

Have you ever been forgotten, overlooked; ignored? You've been in the same class all year and the teacher still has a hard time remembering your name. You're the most athletic one in the group but you're still the last one picked because you're the least popular. You seemed to have been continuously ignored for a job opportunity or promotion. It happens and it's not that big of a deal if it's an occasional thing, but if it's a perpetual state of being for you then there's more of a sting and hurt involved. We all desire to belong, to be known, to be seen. The great news is that in Christ, you do belong; you are known, and seen. Revelation 3:5 says that the one who overcomes this world, this life and makes it to Heaven will be clothed in white garments; Jesus will not erase their name from the book of life but will confess their name before the Father and His angels. You know what this screams to me? Jesus will not forget you! He will not only remember you; He will confess your name before the Father and an innumerable array of angels. You won't be forgotten on this day; you won't be ignored or overlooked. According to Revelation 2:17, you will be given a white stone written upon which is a new name, a name that Jesus will give you, a name that He knows you by. I don't know what this name will be for you or for me, but I have a feeling it will be something special between us and our LORD, something deeply personal and we will recognize it immediately. How incredibly humbling and honoring to be known by Jesus; to be seen, to be remembered, to be loved!

You are not forgotten, my friend! You are not just another number to Him, a statistic, a nameless face, or a faceless name. You are not excluded, unnoticed, or disregarded by God. The Bible says in Matthew 10:30 that even the very hairs of your head are all numbered. And the beginning of Psalm 139 talks about how the LORD has searched you and known you. He knows when you sit and when you rise; He perceives your thoughts from afar. He can discern your going out and your lying down. He is familiar with all your ways. Before you even speak a word, He knows it completely! Later on, in that same chapter it talks about how vast the sum of thoughts God has about you, they exceed the number of grains of sand on the face of the whole planet! Don't listen to Satan! God sees you; God knows you; God remembers you!

Who are you that God would remember you? Who are you that He would concern Himself about you? You are His child! Jesus has identified you as belonging to the Father! You are His. How could He ever forget you when He has inscribed you on the very palms of His hands? He has chosen you from your mother's womb and in response to you spending your life choosing Him, He will confess your name before the Father!

Father,

> I thank You for remembering me, for knowing me, for seeing me. I thank You for thinking about me so much and so often. I am amazed that You would concern Yourself with me, but I am so grateful that You do. Holy Spirit, would You encourage my heart with this truth today? Help me to grasp that I am not nor will I ever be forgotten by God. Let it be so LORD in Jesus' name, amen.

Day 51: I Am Brave!

> *"The LORD is my light and my salvation—so why should I be afraid? The LORD is my fortress, protecting me from danger, so why should I tremble? When evil people come to devour me, when my enemies and foes attack me, they will stumble and fall. Though a mighty army surrounds me, my heart will not be afraid. Even if I am attacked, I will remain confident."* Psalm 27:1-3 NLT
>
> *"So do not fear, for I (God) am with you; do not be dismayed, for I am your God. I will strengthen you* 41:10 NIV
>
> *"He (God) gives strength to the weary and increases the power of the weak."* Isaiah 40:29 NIV

Can I tell you that in Christ you can do things that would seem completely ridiculous for you to do in and of yourself? Why is that? Because God gives strength to the weary and increases the power of the weak. It's what He does. It's who He is! He is strength! He is power! If He is with you, you have His strength, His power despite your own weaknesses. That is awesome! The Bible is full of accounts of weak people whom God made brave in Him. The story of Gideon is one of those people. We find his story in Judges 6 and 7 where we see the Israelites suffering terribly at the hands of the Midianites. The Word of God describes how the people of Midian would come down in swarms like locusts to devour and destroy the crops of Israel. It was impossible to count them, or their camels and they invaded the land to ravage it. The Israelites prepared shelters for themselves in mountain clefts and hid out in caves. The power of Midian was so oppressive, and they impoverished Israel so greatly that the Israelites cried out to God for help. And in response, God sends an angel to an oak tree in Ophrah that belonged to Joash the Abiezrite, where his son Gideon was threshing wheat in a winepress to keep it from the Midianites. Gideon and his family weren't leaders in Israel; they weren't out rallying the people together or strategizing how to defeat the enemy. No, the Bible says that Gideon was hiding from the enemy, trying to just survive basically. But when the angel of the LORD appeared to Gideon, the first thing he says is, "the LORD is with you, mighty warrior." (Judges 6:12 NIV). My friend, I pray God's Spirit and His Word would speak to you today. You are a mighty warrior! Even if you feel more like a coward, even if you are in a state of currently hiding from the enemy. God is calling you out! He loves to call things that are not as though they are because He sees what things really are. And in Him, you really are a mighty warrior!

Gideon responds to the angel by saying, "Pardon me, my lord..." and then proceeds to question how God has been with Israel when they have suffered so much at the hands of Midian. Gideon initially only sees the problem, he only sees his circumstances, he sees the enemy, and this is exactly what he relays to the angel as if God doesn't know about all of this already. In response the LORD turns to Gideon and says, "Go in the strength you have and save Israel out of Midian's hands. Am I not sending you?" (Judges 6:14 NIV). Wow! You know what this says to me? God is raising you up, God is sending you out! Regardless to your circumstances, your problems, or the havoc the enemy may be causing in your life. God has made you His mighty warrior! Again, Gideon responds, "Pardon me, my lord, but how can I save Israel? My clan is the weakest in Manasseh, and I am the least in my family." (Judges 6:15 NIV). The LORD answers, "I will be with you, and you will strike down all the Midianites, leaving none alive." (Judges 6:16 NIV). My friend, it doesn't matter to God how weak you or everyone else may think you are. He has promised you victory over the enemy not based on how mighty you are but based on how mighty He is. What makes you a mighty warrior is the fact that He is with you! And if He is with you, you will strike down the enemy! I encourage you to read the rest of Gideon's story in Judges 6-7, how God gives a unique military strategy to Gideon on how to defeat the enemy and how God gives victory to Israel through Gideon. Yet as you read about Gideon one thing that becomes quite apparent is that he wasn't a military conqueror to begin with, he didn't even think of himself as a very brave or strong person. He considered himself the least of his whole family. But God chose him. God made him brave, and God used him to accomplish something Gideon could in no way have accomplished on his own simply because God was with him. Let it be so with you too, my friend! God is with you! He is your fortress, your help! He is upholding you with His righteous right hand! In Him, you are brave, you are a mighty warrior!

Father,

I thank You for Your strength, for Your power. No one is greater than You and You absolutely have no equal. I thank You that I am a mighty warrior in You. I am not defeated, I am not overcome, and I will not be afraid because You are with me. Holy Spirit, would You make me brave, make me courageous, make me fearless. I believe that with You I can do all things so be with me LORD in Jesus's name, amen.

Day 52: I Am Secure!

"He (God) will also keep you firm to the end, so that you will be blameless on the day of our LORD Jesus Christ." 1 Corinthians 1:8 NIV

"Be on your guard; stand firm in the faith; be courageous; be strong..." 1 Corinthians 16:13 NIV

"Let us hold fast the confession of our hope without wavering, for He (God) who promised is faithful." Hebrews 10:23 NASB

"But resist him (Satan), firm in your faith, knowing that the same experiences of suffering are being accomplished by your brethren who are in the world." 1 Peter 5:9 NASB

In Christ, you are firm, solid, and secure! God can keep you firm to the very end, unshakable! Hebrews 12:28 says that you have received a Kingdom that cannot be shaken. God is not surprised, stunned, dazed, traumatized, or taken back. He is sure. He is secure. He is absolute. Nothing or no one can shake Him! In the Bible we are encouraged repeatedly to stand firm in our faith, to have a faith that cannot be shaken. How is that possible when life is so unpredictable? Can I tell you that holding fast to the confession of your hope without wavering is possible because God who promised is faithful!

Just as the sun rises every morning and sets every evening, so God faithfully watches over His Word to perform it. Heaven and earth may pass away, but the Word of God will never pass away.

You are kept safe in Christ's love. "Though the mountains be shaken, and the hills be removed, yet my unfailing love for you will not be shaken nor my covenant of peace be removed,' says the LORD who has compassion on you." (Isaiah 54:10 NIV). You are secure because your God is secure! His love for you is unfailing, enduring, unshaken. Your faith in Him can be unwavering because He is always faithful! He has always been and will always be faithful! Satan will do his best to disprove this to you, to cause you to question, to doubt God and His character. Satan will try his hardest to shake you, but the LORD, your God, is unshakable! If you are in Christ, you are being kept firm, you are solid and though the enemy may try to shake you, you will not be destroyed, you will not unravel, you will not fall to pieces. Look at Paul's testimony, "We are hard pressed on every side, but not crushed; perplexed, but not in despair; persecuted, but not abandoned; struck down, but not destroyed." (2 Corinthians 4:8-9 NIV). My friend, according to the Word of God, the enemy may press in hard on you, he may even surround you from every side, but he cannot crush you! You may be perplexed and confused by this life, but you do not have to live in despair. Even if you are persecuted, God will not abandon you. And even if the enemy strikes you down, you go ahead and get back up because Satan cannot destroy you!

In 2 Kings 6 beginning in verse 8 we learn that the king of Aram was at war with Israel. The king would strategize ways to defeat or attack the king of Israel, but God would send warnings to Israel's king by way of the prophet Elijah. The Bible says this scenario happened several times until the king of Aram was enraged and thought that one of his officers was a traitor. Yet when he confronts his officers about this matter, they inform him that the prophet Elijah tells the king of Israel the very words the king speaks in his bedroom. So, the king of Aram sends a strong force of men at night to Dotham, where Elijah is, and surrounds the city. When Elijah's servant wakes up early the next morning and goes out, he sees that they are surrounded by an army of horses and chariots. They are surrounded by the enemy. He cries out to Elijah, "Oh no, my lord! What shall we do?" (2 Kings 6:15 NIV). And the prophet replies "Don't be afraid, those who are with us are more than those who are with them." (2 Kings 6:16 NIV). Then Elijah prays that God would open the eyes of his servant so that he may see, and the servant's eyes are opened, and he sees the hills full of horses and chariots of fire all around Elijah. Oh friend, I pray that the LORD would open your eyes today so that you could see how you are not just surrounded by the enemy, you are surrounded by an innumerable company of warring angels! Those who are with you are more than those who are against you! Here are two men, men of God at that, without a single weapon surrounded by a great military force with no possible route of escape. Yet Elijah wasn't shaken, he wasn't afraid. He prays and the LORD strikes the enemy with blindness until they are led out of the city. God did not abandon Elijah and his servant to the enemy, and He will not abandon you either! Open your eyes and see that the LORD of hosts is with you! Open your mouth and cry out to the One who is always faithful, the One who can keep you firm, solid, secure to the very end!

Father,

> I thank You that you are faithful. I can trust You; I can place my full faith in You because You are secure, You are unshakable, You are always faithful. Would You forgive me for not being more confident in Who You are? Forgive me for wavering in my faith, forgive me for not doing my part in standing firm against the enemy. Holy Spirit, would You give me eyes to see that those who are with me are more than those who are against me? I will not fear for You are with me. Let it be so, LORD, in Jesus's name, amen.

Day 53: I Am the Light of the World

> *"You are the light of the world. A town built on a hill cannot be hidden. Neither do people light a lamp and put it under a bowl. Instead they put it on its stand, and it gives light to everyone in the house. In the same way, let your light shine before others, that they may see your good deeds and glorify your Father in heaven."* Matthew 5:14-16 NIV

> *"You are all children of the light and children of the day. We do not belong to the night or to the darkness."* 1 Thessalonians 5:5 NIV

> *"The city (new Jerusalem) does not need the sun or the moon to shine on it, for the glory of God gives it light, and the Lamb is its lamp."* Revelation 21:23 NIV

You are the light of the world, a city on a hill! In Christ, you are not meant to be hidden, lurking somewhere in the shadows, playing it safe in the corner. No way! You are meant to give light to everyone, to shine before others so that they may see your good deeds and glorify your Father in heaven. "We now have this light shining in our hearts, but we ourselves are like fragile clay jars containing this great treasure. This makes it clear that our great power is from God, not from ourselves." (2 Corinthians 4:7 NLT). In Christ, you are a carrier of God's presence, God's glory! You bring the light of Christ with you everywhere! Matthew 5 is the beginning of Jesus's sermon on the Mount, a famous collection of sayings and teachings of Jesus which He presented at a certain location, the Mount of Olives, a mountain ridge east of the old city of Jerusalem. The sermon is the longest continuous section of Jesus speaking found in the New Testament and has been widely quoted from for thousands of years. It includes some of the best-known teachings of Jesus such as the beatitudes and the LORD's Prayer. However, it is here that Jesus commissions us to shine for Him!

What does it mean to let your light shine, to not put it under a bowl, but to put it on its stand and be a city on a hill? It means don't hide the love of Christ, don't hide your joy, your peace, your relationship with Jesus. Let the whole world see that you are a new creation in Him, that you have been transformed, made whole, cleansed. May the world look at your life, your actions, your words and be pointed towards Jesus. Satan wants you to hide, my friend. He wants you to be afraid of rejection, to be afraid of being different, to be afraid to speak up when you know that you should. He'll use loneliness to intimidate you, to mock you, to ridicule you. He knows that you're a light! He can't stop you from being a light, so he'll do his best to convince you to hide so that your light isn't shinning on anyone and becomes virtually ineffective. Did you know that Jesus called Himself the Light of the World in John 8:12? People were drawn to Jesus! Everywhere He went crowds followed Him, people just wanted to hear what He had to say, they pressed in to touch the

One who could heal them, Who could free them. He brought light, clarity, direction, illumination with Him wherever He went. And guess what? He has called you the light of the world too!

In the book of Jonah, we find the story of Jonah, a prophet of Israel whom God sends to the Assyrian capital of Nineveh with a message of destruction. Yet the Bible says that Jonah tries to run away from the LORD and faces some dire circumstances as a result until he comes to the realization that he can't run from the LORD. It's unclear as to why Jonah runs. Is he afraid of the people of Nineveh, is he afraid of God, or is he fearful of the task the LORD gave to him? Whatever the case may be, it is apparent that Jonah disobeys the voice of the LORD. However, the Bible describes Nineveh as a very wicked city, a very dark place. So, God tells Jonah to go there and bring a message that will ultimately bring clarity, bring light to the people of Nineveh even though it was a message of destruction. Sometimes you're so lost in darkness you don't even realize how lost you are until you are about to lose everything. Thus, was the condition of Nineveh. After Jonah finds himself in some pretty incredible circumstances, he decides to obey God's direction and tell the people of Nineveh of their impending destruction. And the Bible says that when Nineveh heard this message, they repented of their wickedness and God relented about their decreed destruction and chooses to show mercy to the city instead. Can I tell you that light brings clarity; it opens eyes, and unveils what is veiled? Light exposes things even when those things aren't necessarily good. This revelation gives an opportunity for grace, for mercy, for love, for an encounter with Jesus that changes everything. It's all because of the Light, because of Jesus who is the Light of the World and because of you since He has made you the light of the world also. It's time to shine!

Father,

> I thank You for the light of Christ. That Jesus brings clarity, illumination to the dark and with that clearness He brings opportunities for His grace, His mercy, His love to be received. Let it be so in my life LORD. And I thank You for making me a light in this world, a city on a hill. Holy Spirit, would You give me courage and boldness to shine for Jesus? Help me not to hide my light, to hide God's presence, His glory from others. Help me not to be afraid of rejection or failure or humiliation. I don't want to run from You LORD.

I want to shine for You. So, I invite You to make me Your lamp, Your light today in Jesus's name, amen.

Day 54: I Am Set Apart!

"You have been set apart as holy to the LORD your God, and he has chosen you from all the nations of the earth to be his own special treasure." Deuteronomy 14:2 NLT

"You can be sure of this: the LORD set apart the godly for himself. The LORD will answer when I call to him." Psalm 4:3 NLT

"Do not conform to the pattern of this world but be transformed by the renewing of your mind. Then you will be able to test and approve what God's will is—his good, pleasing and perfect will." Romans 12:2 NIV

"Therefore, come out from them and be separate, says the LORD. Touch no unclean thing, and I will receive you." 2 Corinthians 6:17 NIV

In Christ, you are set apart, you are unique, you are disconnected from darkness, from sin, from evil. This makes you different! This flies in the face of a culture of assimilation, of trying to "fit in", being a part of the popular crowd, and being like everyone else in order to be accepted. Christ has already accepted you! There's no need to try and be accepted anymore! We all desire to be liked, but in Christ, the pressure is off. We don't need to "fit in" anymore; rather, we've now been called to stand out! Listen to these amazing words, "Arise, shine, for your light has come, and the glory of the LORD rises upon you. See, darkness covers the earth and thick darkness is over the peoples, but the LORD rises upon you and his glory appears over you. Nations will come to your light, and kings to the brightness of your dawn." (Isaiah 60:1-3 NIV). My friend, darkness covers the earth and thick darkness is over the peoples. That darkness wants you to be a part of it, to fit into it, it will readily accept you as one of its own. But God has called you the light of the world! What is the purpose of light except to bring illumination and clarity? The very nature of light is to shine! By design, by nature, light is intended to stand out! You are meant to shine, to stand out so that people might be drawn to the brightness of your dawn, so that those in darkness might be drawn to the light of Christ in you!

Look at the life of Daniel in the Bible. Here is an exile of Israel from Judah now living in Babylon, a very wicked, a very dark nation to God. Yet Daniel was a light there. He was different, he was set apart, and although he adapted to the culture around him by undergoing the training provided by the king, when it came time to either "fit in" to the darkness around him or continue to honor God even if doing so made him different, he chose to be different, to be a light. I encourage you to read Daniel chapter six where we see this dynamic unfold to the point that Daniel was thrown into a den of lions as a result. Yet God protected him and shone through him and at the end of the story King Darius' eyes are lifted upward and he acknowledges the God of Daniel as the living God who endures forever. That is the power of light, of being set apart in Christ!

Satan wants you to conform to the pattern of this world. He doesn't want you to be transformed by the renewing of your mind, so he'll try endlessly to fill your mind with anything other than the truths of God's Word. He doesn't want you to come out from the darkness around you and be separate. He wants you to be like everyone else, to act like everybody else, look like everyone else. He'll intimidate you with loneliness, with fear, with rejection because he knows that Christ has made you a light and light is different than the darkness. Satan doesn't want your difference to make a difference! Far be it for light to "fit into" the darkness. How is that even possible? My friend, it's time to shine, to rejoice in the fact that Christ has set you apart for Himself. You don't have to be unsettled by the threat of loneliness. Yes, you may feel lonely from to time, but you are in no way alone! That is a lie, my friend, because your acceptance of Jesus has grafted you into the family of God. You are a child of God and guess what? You are not an only child! The world may not always receive you; they may even reject you, but it's okay because you are not of this world anyway. You are a citizen of heaven and an ambassador here. Diplomats and representatives of nations are not always received well by foreign nations, but the blood of Jesus has granted you admittance and welcome into the Kingdom of God, a greater kingdom by far! Thank you, Jesus, for setting me apart!

Father,

> I thank You for receiving me through Jesus. That I am not alone but that You have made me a part of Your family, a part of Your Kingdom. I thank You for making me a light, for setting me apart, and calling me to stand out for Your glory. Would You forgive me for trying so hard to "fit in" here when doing so contradicts my nature as a light. Holy Spirit help me to renew my mind in Christ, to not conform to this world, to not fade into the thick darkness around me. Rather, may the glory of the LORD rise upon me so that people would be drawn to the brightness of my dawn in Christ. Let it be so in Jesus's name.

Day 55: I Am Christ's Friend

"My command is this: love each other as I have loved you. Greater love has no one than this: to lay down one's life for one's friends. You are my friends if you do what I command. I no longer call you servants, because a servant does not know his master's business. Instead, I have called you friends, for everything that I learned from my Father I have made known to you." John 15:12-15 NIV

"…I am with you always, to the end of the age." Matthew 28:20 NLT

"And the Scripture was fulfilled that says, 'Abraham believed God, and it was counted to him as righteousness'—and he was called a friend of God." James 2:23 ESV

If Jesus is your LORD and Savior, then He is absolutely your master. Sin no longer rules over you. Jesus rules over you. Sin no longer has the authority in your life. Jesus is the authority in your life. You are no longer a slave to sin; you have become a servant of the LORD. You don't have to follow Jesus; you get to follow Him; it is your pleasure to do so. Micah 7:18 says that God delights to show mercy; it pleased Him to forgive you, He enjoys being kind and understanding to you. What master is like Him? No one! For He so loved the world, He so loved everyone, He so loved you that He gave His only begotten Son. That whoever believes in Him should have eternal life. God didn't have to give us Jesus, He chose to out of His great love for us. His goal for us is not enslavement, His goal is freedom. Sin masters us with fear, with shame; with pain. Jesus masters us with love, with freedom. There is a huge difference!

Yet in Christ, the dynamic of our relationship with God goes to a whole new level. Look at the above verses from John 15. They seem too good to be true, but Jesus spoke them, so they are truth. Jesus declares there to be no greater love than when someone lays down their life for their friends. This is exactly what Jesus did for you! He chose to lay down His life for you. He considered you a friend! In fact, Jesus says in the Scripture up above that we are His friends if we do what He commands. You aren't a servant if you do what He commands. No, Jesus considers you a friend. He says in John 14:15 that if you love Him, you will keep His commands, you will do what He says. Obedience isn't obligatory, it isn't your duty, it isn't what makes you a good servant. To Jesus, it is proof of your love for Him, your trust in Him. It's what makes you a friend. Wow! He goes on to say that He no longer calls you just a servant because servants don't know their master's business. Instead He calls you a friend because everything Jesus learned from the Father, He has made known to you. You know what this says to me? You are not an outsider! The blood of Jesus has brought you near! You are not just a servant who doesn't know the affairs of your master. Jesus has revealed to you the heart of the Father. That is intimacy, that is trust; that is friendship!

"The secret of the LORD is with them that fear him; and he will show them his covenant." (Psalm 25:14 NIV). The Hebrew word for "secret" here is symmachus primarily meaning "couch" implying the confidential talk of those sitting on it. Consider that for a moment. What master sits on the couch and confides in you, shares secrets with you, reveals mysteries to you? Jesus does! Yes, He is your Master, but amazingly enough He considers you His friend. That is incredible! Don't let Satan convince you that you're a nobody, that you're not worth friendship, that no one considers you trustworthy enough to share secrets with because Jesus does! You are worth friendship to Jesus. According to the Bible, He laid His life down not for His servants but for His friends. He wanted to bring you close, He wanted to reveal His heart to you, He wanted to share His secrets with you. Satan is a liar! Companionship with Christ is not for the elite or just for the apostles and disciples of old. It is for you! In Christ, you have been invited to sit on the couch and share sweet friendship with the Master. How cool!

Father,

> I thank You for Jesus. Thank You for considering me a friend, for bringing me close to You, and for sharing Your business with me. I am so humbled and amazed to be invited into such intimate fellowship with You, LORD. Forgive me for not enjoying our relationship more, for not talking to You, for not listening to You, for choosing to stay at a distance when Christ has brought me near. Today, I just want to sit on the couch with You Jesus. To share my heart with You and to have You share Yours with me. What a privilege! What an honor to be Your friend! Let it be so in my life in Jesus's name, amen.

Day 56: I Am Blessed

> *"But blessed is the one who trusts in the LORD, whose confidence is in him. They will be like a tree planted by the water that sends out its roots by the stream. It does not fear when heat comes; its leaves are always green. It has no worries in a year of drought and never fails to bear fruit."* Jeremiah 17:7-8 NIV

> *"The LORD bless you and keep you; the LORD make his face shine upon you and be gracious to you; the LORD turn his face toward you and give you peace."* Numbers 6:24-26 NIV

"Taste and see that the LORD is good; blessed is the one who takes refuge in him." Psalm 34:8 NIV

You are blessed, my friend! According to Deuteronomy 28, you are blessed in the city and blessed in the country. You are blessed when you come in and blessed when you go out. Your basket and kneading trough are blessed; your work, your labor is blessed. The fruit of your womb is blessed; your children, your legacy, your heritage is blessed. You are blessed! I know some people believe this is a part of the Old Testament and therefore isn't applicable to us anymore. It is a blessing reserved only for the children of Israel; however, this is the blessing promised to those who kept the covenant God gave Moses and the Israelites. The LORD is a covenant-keeping God. The covenant He gave to Abraham was to Abraham and his descendants. And guess what? Galatians 3:7 says that those who have faith are children of Abraham! Your faith in Jesus Christ grafts you in as a descendent of Abraham, making you a recipient of God's covenant-promises even those in the Old Testament. That is awesome!

My friend, you are blessed; made holy, consecrated. You are favored, you are preferred! It's not that you are better than everyone else. No way! "Do nothing out of selfish ambition or vain concept, but in humility to value others above ourselves." (Philippians 2:3 NIV). Your status of "blessed" has less to do with you personally and more to do with the presence of God, the hand of God upon you. Look at the Scripture above in Jeremiah. It says that the one who trusts in God, who puts his confidence in the LORD is blessed. It has nothing to do with how confident you are in yourself, but how confident you are in the One who holds your very life in His hands. If your security is in the LORD, then you will be like a tree planted by the water whose roots are by the stream. You have no fear of heat or drought because your trust is in the One who has the power to send rain and makes rivers stream forth in the desert. These kinds of people's leaves are always green, and they are always bearing fruit regardless to what's going on around them. They have no worries because they trust in God who blesses them.

In Numbers 22 we find the children of Israel traveling to the plains of Moab and camped out along the Jordan River across from Jericho. Balak, the king of Moab had seen all that Israel had done to the Ammonites and all of Moab becomes afraid because there were so many people in Israel. So Balak sends for Balaam, the diviner, to put a curse on the children of Israel. Moab wrongfully assumes that the enemy's curse might somehow undo the blessing and favor of God in order to bring about defeat. This tells me that even the enemy recognized that God was with Israel. The enemy recognized the blessing and sought to remove it with a curse. Yet as the story unfolds, we see that this is not how it works at all. Every time Balaam opened his mouth to curse Israel, God filled his mouth with a blessing instead, infuriating king Balak. Can I tell you that God has decreed his favor, his blessing, his approval over you and the enemy cannot undo that no matter how hard he tries? You are so blessed that the LORD can cause even your enemies to bless you! Being blessed is not synonymous with being wealthy. That is an ungodly belief through and through. Rather you are blessed because God through His Word has declared you to be through Jesus Christ. Heed the words above: take refuge in Him and be blessed!

Father,

> I ask You to bless me, to keep me, to cause Your face to shine upon me. Would You be gracious to me, turn your face towards me, and give me peace? I thank You for blessing me, for making me a blessing. Thank You for choosing me, for approving of me through Christ and for causing even my enemies to bless me. Let it be so in my life in Jesus's name, amen.

Day 57: I Am a Champion

"But thanks be to God, who always leads us as captives in Christ's triumphal procession and uses us to spread the aroma of the knowledge of him everywhere." 2 Corinthians 2:14 NIV

"But thanks be to God, who gives us the victory through our LORD Jesus Christ." 1 Corinthians 15:57 ESV

"The horse is prepared for the day of battle, but victory belongs to the LORD." Proverbs 21:31 NLT

In Exodus 17, Amalek comes to fight against Israel at Rephidim. The Israelites had recently left Egypt via the miraculous parting of the Red Sea and had set out from the Desert of Sin traveling place to place as the LORD commanded. They set up camp at Rephidim, but there was no water there for the people to drink, so the whole community began to quarrel with Moses. This is when the LORD told Moses to strike the rock at Horeb and water would come out of it for the people to drink. However, in response to the Amalekites' attack, Moses tells Joshua to choose some of Israel's men and go out to fight the enemy. Moses informs Joshua that he will stand on top of the hill with the staff of God in his hands. During this battle, Moses, Aaron, and Hur go to the top of the hill. If Moses held up his hands, the Israelites prevailed. Yet whenever he lowered his hands in exhaustion and fatigue, the Amalekites triumphed. When Moses' hands grew tired, Aaron and Hur took a stone and put it under him so that Moses could sit down. Then they each held up one of his hands so that his hands remained steady until sunset. Thus, Joshua overcame the Amalekite army with the sword. In response to this victory, Moses builds an altar to the LORD and calls it "the LORD is my banner."

It's interesting that still to this day when a nation enters battle with another nation, somewhere someone has set up that nation's flag indicating these men, this army, this territory belongs to a certain country. That flag is a standard, a sign, a banner to the enemy designating ownership and authority that if ignored or breeched brings about dire consequences. Did you know that one of the names of God is Jehovah-Nissi, the LORD our Banner? Like Moses, we lift our hands up; we raise our Flag, our Standard, our Banner. We exalt the name of the LORD as a sign to the enemy that he is in territory that does not belong to him anymore! Oh friend, hear me for a minute. You belong to the LORD Almighty! Your home, your family, your life belongs to the LORD since you have made Jesus your LORD and Savior. The enemy of your soul is not welcome there anymore! He has no right there anymore! So, raise up your Banner, your Flag; lift the name of Jesus and declare to the enemy that your family, your house, your life is restricted territory to him. It belongs to the LORD Almighty and the enemy must get out in the name of Jesus!

You are a champion, my friend! You are not defeated. You are not a loser. God will lead you always in Christ's triumphal procession. Jesus conquered the enemy by His death and resurrection. That cannot be erased. That cannot be overturned. That cannot be undone. Satan must submit to the authority, to the Lordship of Jesus Christ. He has no choice. It's not an option for him, so you make him submit to Jesus at your house, in your life, with your family.

Christ has made you the champion! He's done the work you could not do and when you lift His name, exalt His name, you are raising up a banner against the enemy. May it be so in your life in Jesus's name!

Father,

I thank You for Jesus. I thank You that You are the Champion and that in Christ, I am a champion too. I thank You that you are Jehovah-Nissi, the LORD my banner. You are my banner of conquest, of triumph, of victory. There is no standard that could compete with the standard of the LORD! So, I praise Your name today. I lift the name of the LORD Almighty. I exalt the name of Jesus who leads me always in His triumphal procession. I declare to the enemy today that he has no right in my home, in my family, in my life! He must get out in Jesus's name, amen!

Day 58: I Am a Child of the Day

"But you, brothers and sisters, are not in darkness...You are all children of the light and children of the day. We do not belong to the night or to the darkness. So then, let us not be like others, who are asleep, but let us be awake and sober. For those who sleep, sleep at night, and those who get drunk, get drunk at night. But since we belong to the day, let us be sober, putting on faith and love as a breastplate, and the hope of salvation as a helmet. For God did not appoint us to suffer wrath but to receive salvation through our LORD Jesus Christ. He died for us so that, whether we are awake or asleep, we may live together with him. Therefore encourage one another and build each other, just as in fact you are doing." 1Thessalonians 5:4-11 NIV

You are a child of the day! You are not a child of the night, a child of darkness anymore. You belong to the light. You belong to the day! Look at the Scripture up above. Paul encourages the church at Thessalonica to wake up, to be alert, to be sober since they are in Christ and are now children of the day, children of light. He says that those who sleep, sleep at night and sin seems to be more rampart in the darkness rather than in the light. Ephesians 5 sounds a similar note when it says, "For you were once darkness, but now you are light in the LORD. Live as children of light (for the fruit of the light consists in all goodness, righteousness and truth) and find out what pleases the LORD. Have nothing to do with the fruitless deeds of darkness, but rather expose them. It is shameful to even mention what the disobedient do in secret. But everything exposed by the light becomes visible—and everything that is illuminated becomes a light. This is why it is said: 'Wake up, sleeper, rise from the dead, and Christ will shine on you." (Ephesians 5:8-14 NIV).

It's time to wake up, my friend! It is not normal to sleep all night and still sleep all day too. No! The day is for being awake, for being clear-headed, for being alert, for putting on faith and love and hope. It's time to live as a child of light in all goodness, righteousness, and truth. Have nothing to do with the fruitless deeds of darkness, but rather expose them. In the light, in the day it's much easier to see things for what they really are. To see yourself how you really are. Whereas the darkness tends to hide things, light exposes things. Light brings visibility. As a child of the day now living in the light of Jesus Christ, the Holy Spirit will begin to expose things, shine on things, show you things you might not have seen before. Why? His goal is not to humiliate you or to condemn you. No, His goal is to make you a light! Whereas you seemed to have no problem with certain secret compromises in your life before, now they deeply grieve you. What happened? You've come into the day; you are a child of the day and you no longer want to have anything to do with the fruitless deeds of darkness; praise God!

It's interesting to note that according to Ephesians 5, everything that is illuminated becomes a light. You don't have to fear exposure with God! He doesn't illuminate something in your life to shame you. That's what the devil does! Rather, the Bible says that the very things the LORD illuminates to you, He can make those a light for others. Oh friend, hear me out for a second. Satan wants to embarrass you. He wants you to hide, to fear exposure, to run from the light. He uses that area of secrecy in your life as an anvil hanging over your head. He constantly threatens to drop that thing like a bomb on you and completely ruin your relationships, your reputation, your life. Oh, no one can ever find out. I'd be the laughingstock of the community, the laughingstock of my family. I'd be so humiliated. But can I tell you Satan wants you to keep those things in the dark, keep them a secret, to hide them even from the LORD because if it isn't exposed it still has power over you. He doesn't want you to enjoy the light, to enjoy the day. He wants you to be afraid of it, to be so afraid of exposure that you'll stay in the darkness. But nothing is hidden from the LORD! "Nothing in all creation is hidden from God's sight. Everything is uncovered and laid bare before the eyes of him to whom we must give account." (Hebrews 4:13 NIV). He is Light and there are no shadowy places to hide from in His presence. That isn't a bad thing, it is so, so good! He loves you! He loves you enough to expose sin in your life. He loves you enough to confront you when you're wrong. He loves you enough to shine His light on you and make you His child. Stop hiding, my friend! It's time to come into the light, to live in the day. It's time for exposure, for illumination, for clarity. God doesn't want to embarrass you. He wants to free you and use you to help free others! "Search me, oh God, and know my heart; try me and know my thoughts. See if there be any wicked way in me and lead me in the way everlasting." (Psalm 139:23-24 NIV).

Father,

> I thank You for calling me out of the darkness into the light. Thank You for making me a child of the day and not of the night anymore. Holy Spirit help me to be alert, to be clear-minded, to be awake today. I trust Your heart towards me that You don't want to humiliate me, but to free me. So, I willingly bring every area of my life into the light today. I don't want to hide from You or try to keep any secrets from You since You know it all anyway. Rather, I want to enjoy the light, enjoy the day. I invite you Holy Spirit to search my heart and to know my thoughts. Bring to my attention any area of my life that is wicked, that isn't pleasing to God so that I might repent of it and turn away from it. And please, Holy Spirit, lead me in the way everlasting today in Jesus's name, amen.

Day 59: I Am Fierce

> *"For you (God) have girded me with strength for battle; you have subdued under me those who rose up against me."* Psalm 18:39 NASB

> *"Through you (God) we will push back our adversaries; through your name we will trample down those who rise up against us."* Psalm 44:4 NASB

> *"For everyone born of God overcomes the world. This is the victory that has overcome the world, even our faith."* 1 John 5:4 NIV

In Christ, you are an overcomer, a victor. Jesus has crowned you with success, with triumph over the enemy. And this position in Christ makes you not just another warrior, but a mighty warrior. You are not just a conqueror, but you are more than a conqueror! You are fierce, vicious, and brutal to the enemy because the LORD your God has girded you with strength for battle and He has subdued under you those who have revolted against you. The LORD is your defender, your protector but He has also given you authority to push back the adversary and to trample down the enemy through His great name! My friend, it's time to go on the offensive. It's time to rise in the power of the name of Jesus and foil every scheme of the enemy, every plan of destruction in your life, in your family, in your city, in your nation. You have been born of God and you overcome this world! The LORD has given you victory by your faith. It's time to be fierce in the LORD!

"Therefore I (God) will shake the heavens, and the earth shall remove out of her place, in the wrath of the LORD of hosts, and in the day of his fierce anger." (Isaiah 13:13 KJV). In addition to this, "For this gird you with sackcloth, lament and howl; for the fierce anger of the LORD is not turned back from us." (Jeremiah 4:8 KJV). These and several other instances in the Bible use the word "fierce" in description of our God. He is Jehovah-Saboath, the LORD of hosts! He is the God of an innumerable array of warring angels. He is mighty. He is fierce! Who could stand against Him? Who could stop the LORD Almighty! And guess what? If Jesus is your LORD and Savior, then this God of uncontainable power is for you! Thus, Paul asks, "...if God is for us, who can be against us?" (Romans 8:31 NIV).

Listen to this declaration from Psalm 112, "Praise the LORD. Blessed are those who fear the LORD, who find great delight in his commands. Their children will be mighty in the land; the generation of the upright will be blessed...Even in darkness light dawns for the upright...Surely the righteous will never be shaken; they will be remembered forever...Their hearts are secure, they will have no fear; in the end they will look in triumph on their foes." (Psalm 112:1-2,4,6,8 NIV). My friend, can I encourage you to praise the LORD today? Because you fear the LORD, because you find great delight in His Word, in His commands you are blessed! You are mighty in the land; your children will be mighty on the earth! You are a part of the generation of the upright; you are blessed! Even in darkness, light dawns for you! In Christ, you are righteous. Jesus has made you the righteousness of God; therefore, you will never be shaken; never forgotten! Your heart is secure; you have no fear! In the end, you will look in triumph on your enemy! Lift your head up today, my friend. Lift your eyes to the hills. Where does your help come from? Your help comes from the LORD Almighty, the Maker of heaven and earth!

Father,

> I acknowledge You as the LORD of hosts. You are mighty. You are strong. You are victorious in battle. Who can stand against You, LORD? I thank You for girding me with strength, for subduing the enemy under my feet. I thank You that in Your name I can push back the adversary and trample down the enemy. Would You forgive me for playing it safe, for acting the victim when You have made me the victor in Christ? Holy Spirit, I invite You to make me fierce in the LORD. May the Spirit of the Living God rise in me today and gird me with strength, with boldness, with fierceness against the enemy in Jesus's name, amen.

Day 60: I Am Grafted into God's Family

> "...if the root is holy, so are the branches. If some of the branches have been broken off, and you, though a wild olive shoot, have been grafted in among the others and now share in the nourishing sap from the olive root, do not consider yourself to be superior to those other branches. If you do, consider this: you do not support the root, but the root supports you...After all, if you were cut out of an olive tree that is wild by nature, and contrary to nature were grafted into a cultivated olive tree, how much more readily will these, the natural branches, be grafted into their own olive tree!!" Romans 11:16-18, 24 NIV

Grafting is a horticultural technique where tissues of plants are joined, usually trees, to continue their growth together. A branch of a selected, desired tree is grafted into the stock or root system of another type. A cleft is made in the stock of a tree and a desired branch is placed in this cut. A nurseryman will bind this branch or secure this branch by wrapping it tightly and firmly, and then will remove the binding once he notices growth. If done successfully, the tissues of the desired branch and that of the root system will form a connection. The grafted in branch will absorb nourishment, strength, and life from the already well-established root system and will thereby flourish. According to the Scripture up above in Romans, you were a branch of an olive tree that was wild by nature and because of your faith in Jesus you have now been grafted into a cultivated olive tree, the family of God. God's family is cultivated; refined, sophisticated. It is well-established. The family of God isn't dying. It isn't broken or failing. It is thriving! Why? Because the root system of Jesus Christ runs deep. It cannot be uprooted or destroyed! The nourishing sap of Christ's blood makes dead things live again and absolutely binds us together! If the root is holy, so are the branches!

Can I tell you that you are a desired branch in God's family? God wanted you to be a part of His family. He cut you out of another wild, dying tree and grafted you into Him. In Christ, your tissue is now connected to the tissue of

God; you are one with Him and His family. You share in the nourishing sap and now it's time to grow and with that kind of root system as your base, the sky is truly the limit. Grafting is a tedious, lengthy process, but it's the term the Bible uses to describe your connection with God and His family. And the enemy cannot destroy the root system you have been grafted into. If you stay connected to that root system, you will bear fruit and thrive! Jesus sounded a similar note, "I am the vine, you are the branches: he who abides in me and I in him, he bears much fruit, for apart from me you can do nothing." (John 15:5 NIV).

Where the enemy sees a dead, decaying, rotted branch that has wild roots; God sees life. He sees the fruit you will bear in Him as His child. He sees you as a part of His family. He selected you. He desired you so He provided Christ to graft you in. You are in, my friend! Heed Paul's words in Romans and don't think yourself superior to the other branches. It's not you who supports the root, but the root is supporting you! What kind of tree someone came from is irrelevant now because in Christ we are all a part of the same root system? Thank You, Jesus!

Father,

> I thank You for grafting me into Your family, for selecting me, for desiring me, for making a way through Jesus for me to be a part of You. Forgive me for thinking myself superior in any way since it is You who is the One supporting me and not the other way around. Holy Spirit, would You help me to grow, to bear fruit, to be a productive part of this tree. Apart from You I can do nothing, so please I invite You to help me, to teach me, to give me strength today in Jesus's name, amen.

Day 61: I Am Alive in Christ

"But because of his great love for us, God, who is rich in mercy, made us alive with Christ even when we were dead in

transgressions—it is by grace you have been saved." Ephesians 2:4-5 NIV

"When you were dead in your sins and in the uncircumcision of your flesh, God made you alive with Christ. He forgave us all our sins." Colossians 2:13 NIV

"For as in Adam all die, so in Christ all will be made alive." 1 Corinthians 15:22 NIV

You are alive, my friend! I'm not sure if you realize it or not, but you are made up of three parts: body, soul, and spirit. Your body is the physical part of you. It's the part that eats, sleeps, works. It's the part of you that everyone sees. But God hasn't just given you a physical body; He has also given you a soul: your mind, will, and emotions. This is the part of you that thinks, that feels emotionally, your personality, your charm, and your strength of character. It isn't as visible as your physical body, but it's also something that people pick up on when they're around you especially if they are around you consistently. Almost all living things have a physical body and a soul per God's design, but there is something that sets you a part. God has given you a spirit. "Then God said, 'Let Us make man in Our image, according to Our likeness; and let them rule over the fish of the sea and over the birds of the sky and over the cattle and over all the earth, and over every creeping thing that creeps on the earth.' God created man in His own image, in the image of God He created him; male and female He created them." (Genesis 1:26-27 NIV). According to the Bible, mankind is distinct from the rest of creation, including animals, in that we are made in the image of God. And just as God is made up of three parts: Father, Son, and Holy Spirit; so, we are made up of three parts too. "Now may the God of peace Himself sanctify you entirely; and may your spirit and soul and body be preserved complete, without blame at the coming of our Lord Jesus Christ." (1 Thessalonians 5:23 NIV).

The spirit is the part of Adam and Eve that died at the fall of man. God said to them, "...you must not eat fruit from the tree that is in the middle of the garden, and you must not touch it, or you will die." (Genesis 2:17 NIV). They disobeyed. They sinned and their spirits died for as according to Romans 6:23 the wages, the penalty, the result of sin is death. Death physically entered the world as a result of sin, but spiritual separation from God happened immediately. Adam and Eve went from walking with God in the cool of the day to hiding from Him and being banished from the Garden of Eden. They lost that intimate aspect of their relationship with God and so we did too. But because of God's great love for us and because He is so rich in mercy, He made us alive with Christ and saved us by His grace. Jesus died so that your spirit could come to life, so that your spirit could be reconnected with God's Spirit, so that you could walk with Him in the cool of the day every day and for all eternity. Though outwardly you may still be wasting away, yet inwardly in your spirit you are being renewed day by day (2 Corinthians 4:16). How is that even possible? Because God has made you alive with Jesus! There is no separation. There is no disconnect from God's Spirit anymore! According to Galatians 2:20, if Jesus is your LORD and Savior, then you have been crucified with Christ, you died with Christ. You no longer live, but Christ lives in you! That is incredible!

You are alive, my friend! You have been brought to newness of life! Just as Lazarus was called out of the grave by Jesus in John 11, so He has brought you life in your spirit. Jesus said of Himself, "...I am the resurrection and the life. The one who believes in me will live, even though they die; and whoever lives by believing in me will never die. Do you believe this?" (John 11:25-26 NIV). The One who is the resurrection and the life has resurrected your spirit and given you life forevermore. Thank God who is rich, affluent, wealthy in mercy for making you alive in Christ!

Father,

> Thank You for Your mercy. Thank You for bringing me to newness of life in Jesus. I thank You that I am not dead anymore, but I am fully alive in Christ. Holy Spirit, would You help me to know this full well, to understand that Christ lives in me? I want to walk in the cool of the day with You LORD, to enjoy closeness of relationship with You. Forgive me for acting "dead" when You have made me alive. By the authority of God's infallible Word, I declare today that I am alive and well in Jesus's name, amen.

Day 62: I Am an Heir of God and Co-heir with Christ

"Now if we are children, then we are heirs—heirs of God and co-heirs with Christ, if indeed we share in his sufferings in order that we may also share in his glory." Romans 8:17 NIV

"If anyone does attack you, it will not be my doing; whoever attacks you will surrender to you...no weapon forged against you will prevail, and you will refute every tongue that accuses you. This is the heritage of the servants of the LORD, and this is their vindication from me,' declares the LORD." Isaiah 54:15, 17 NIV

"In him (Christ) we have obtained an inheritance, having been predestined according to the purpose of him who works all things according to the counsel of his will, so that we who were the first to hope in Christ might be to the praise of his glory. In him you also, when you heard the word of truth, the gospel of your salvation, and believed in him, were sealed with the promised Holy Spirit, who is the guarantee of our inheritance until we acquire possession of it, to the praise of his glory." Ephesians 1:11-14 NIV

In Christ, you are a child of God and this absolutely makes you an heir, a legal inheritor, benefactor, recipient of the LORD. Your position as a child does not just indicate the place you hold in the heart of your Father, but it is also a lawful, official, binding declaration that identifies you as a recipient of all that God has for you. This is awesome! You are an heir of God and a co-heir with Christ. You are seated with Christ in the heavenly realm. You aren't stuck in some dark corner, powerless, afraid; intimidated. You have been lifted with Christ and are now seated in a place of honor, a place of authority, a place of glory with Jesus; because of Jesus! Jesus conquered your enemy for you! You now have an inheritance of victory, my friend! The enemy who attacks you will end up surrendering to you because you are an heir of God. Make him surrender! No weapon that the enemy could form against you will prevail and you can refute every tongue that rises to accuse you because of your heritage of triumph from the LORD. God sealed your position as one of His heirs with the promised Holy Spirit, the guarantee of your inheritance in Him. Praise God for a legacy of victory!

In Genesis 25 we see the account of Jacob and Esau, twin sons of Isaac. While Rebekah was pregnant, she hears a prophetic word from the LORD informing her that two nations were in her womb, that one would be stronger than the other, and that the older would serve the younger. When it came time for her to deliver, the first child to be born was red and hairy and was named Esau. The second to be born came out grasping the heel of his older brother and was given the name Jacob. The Bible says that as the boys grew up, Esau became a skillful hunter while Jacob was content to stay at home. Isaac who had a taste for wild game loved Esau while Rebekah loved Jacob. Once when Jacob was cooking some stew, Esau came in from the open country famished and asked Jacob for some stew. Jacob convinces Esau to first give him his birthright in exchange for a bowl of stew and because Esau was so hungry, he promises his inheritance to Jacob. The Bible says that Esau despised his birthright; he didn't value it, love it, cherish it. Esau was the firstborn; he had the birthright and legally would receive a double portion of whatever was passed down from his father. He sold that inheritance for some stew. In Biblical times fathers would bless their children especially before the father's death, but birthrights were binding, official and reserved for the firstborn son. It was his inheritance; a double portion reserved just for him.

Well, the Bible describes Jesus in Colossians1:15 as being the firstborn over all creation. He holds the birthright; a double portion inheritance from God. Jesus has been exalted and seated at the right hand of the throne of God. He has inherited victory over the enemy, power over death, hell, and the grave. He has inherited glory. And my friend, you have been seated with Christ! You are a co-heir with Christ! You have inherited victory. You have inherited life forevermore. You have inherited glory! Shut the front door Satan! I am a benefactor of the LORD! I am an heir of God and my heritage in Him cannot be absolved and I will not let it be ignored in Jesus's name!

Father,

I thank You for making me an heir of God and a co-heir with Christ. Thank You for giving me an inheritance of victory. I am not defeated! I am not overcome! Rather, You have seated me with Christ in the heavenlies. Praise Your holy name! Help me Holy Spirit, to walk in the position that I have been given in Christ and to make the enemy adhere to all that I have been given in Christ. Let it be so in my life in Jesus's name, amen.

Day 63: I Am a Member of the Body of Christ

"For just as we have many members in one body and all the members do not have the same function, so we, who are many, are one body in Christ, and individually members one of another." Romans 12:4-5 NIV

"For even as the body is one and yet has many members, and all the members of the body, though they are many, are one body, so also is Christ. For by one Spirit we were all baptized into one body, whether Jews or Greeks, whether slaves or free, and we were all made to drink of one Spirit. For the body is not one member, but many....But God has so composed the body, giving more abundant honor to that member which lacked, so that there may be no division in the body, but that the members may have the same care for one another. And if one member suffers, all the members suffer with it; if one member is honored, all the members rejoice with it. Now you are Christ's body, and individually members of it." 1 Corinthians 12:12-14, 24-27 NIV

The Bible describes the church as the Body of Christ. Church is not a building you go to worship or even just the congregation that gathers there occasionally, to do so. No, the Bible teaches that if you have made Jesus your LORD and Savior then you have become a part of His church, you are now a member of His body. The church is not a building. It is a living, breathing organism. It is no accident that God used the analogy of a body to describe your function as a member in it. Why do we have physical bodies? They are the vehicles that get us where we need to go, that accomplish what we need to accomplish. Without legs, we couldn't walk. Without eyes, we couldn't see. Without a mouth, we couldn't talk and so forth. And just as our own physical bodies are made up of many parts and all of them work together for a common good, so the body of Christ is made up of many members, working together to accomplish God's purposes on earth.

When Jesus was physically here, He had a body just like us. He walked, talked, ate, breathed just like us. The incomprehensible, uncontainable God of the cosmos chose to be confined by a physical body, limited by a physical body for thirty-three years so that He could accomplish the purpose He came for. Yet after Jesus's resurrection, He ascends into Heaven and encourages His followers that it's better for Him to go to the Father so that He can send the promised Holy Spirit. According to the Scripture up above in 1 Corinthians, it is this Spirit we receive when we make Jesus our LORD that baptizes us into one body. You are individually a member of Christ's body. By the Spirit of God, you are now a part of the vehicle the LORD has chosen to carry out His purposes on earth. How cool! You are not insignificant! You are not some useless member! You are not alone! In Christ, God has made you an important part of a world-wide body of believers in Jesus. An individual member of a physical body cannot function in isolation. It needs connection to the rest of the body. So, God has designed His body, made up of individual members, to be connected to one another and thereby thrive. Stay connected, my friend!

In 1 Kings 19 we read about the prophet Elijah who had just put the prophets of Baal, of the devil, to the sword. The king of Israel, Ahab, tells his wife Jezebel everything that Elijah had done so Jezebel sends a messenger to Elijah to tell him that she's going to kill him by the following day. Just like the enemy, she wanted to manipulate him out of doing what God had called him to do, she wanted to intimidate him, threaten him, scare him and that's exactly what she did. The Bible says Elijah was afraid and he runs for his life. He even comes to a point in his running away where he tells the LORD that he's had enough, that God can just go ahead and take his life. Eventually he finds himself hiding out in a cave and when God confronts him, Elijah tells the LORD that he's the only prophet left in Israel and they are trying to kill him too. God instructs him to go back the way he came and to anoint Jehu the son of Nimshi as King over Israel and to anoint Elisha son of Shaphat as the prophet who would succeed him. So, Elijah finds Elisha and throws his cloak around him and Elisha becomes his servant. Here is the prophet of God, someone who was anointed, someone who heard God's voice, enjoyed close fellowship with the LORD, experienced incredible victories and favor now intimidated by the enemy, hiding in a cave, and convinced that he's the only one left serving God. In response the LORD sends him to find Elisha, another prophet, someone he could teach, he could mentor, someone who would go with him and be his servant. The LORD showed Elijah that he wasn't alone. Elisha received a double portion of Elijah's anointing. He did more miracles than his mentor ever did. Can you imagine the outcome of Elisha's life if Elijah had stayed hidden in that cave; if he had let the enemy intimidate and isolate him? God also told Elijah to go and anoint Jehu as the king of Israel. Ahab was the current king and he and his wife Jezebel were very wicked leaders. Can you imagine the outcome for the whole nation of Israel if Elijah hadn't gone and anointed another king, appointed another king, commissioned someone else to lead God's people? My friend, you are not on your own! You are not the only one serving Jesus! God has a purpose for you! You are a member of the Body of Christ! You are needed! Be a functioning member!

Father,

> I thank You for making me a part of the Body of Christ. Thank You that I am significant, that I am needed, that You have given me honor and purpose as a member of Christ's Body. Holy Spirit, would You help me to know that I am not alone. I can't thrive and accomplish Your purposes in isolation. I need to be connected to the rest of the body. Help me, Holy Spirit. Call me out of the cave, out of hiding, out of isolation and into the larger purposes You have. I want to be a part. In Christ, I am a part in Jesus's name, amen.

⥷⥸

Day 64: I Am a Warrior

> *"Finally, be strong in the LORD and in his mighty power. Put on the full armor of God, so that you can take your stand against the devil's schemes. For our struggle is not against flesh and blood, but against the rulers, against the authorities, against the powers of this dark world and against the spiritual forces of evil in the heavenly realms. Therefore, put on the full armor of God, so that when the day of evil comes, you may be able to stand your ground, and after you have done everything, to stand. Stand firm then, with the belt of truth buckled around your waist, with the breastplate of righteousness in place, and with your feet fitted with the readiness that comes from the gospel of peace. In addition to all this, take up the shield of faith, with which you can extinguish all the flaming arrows of the evil one. Take the helmet of salvation and the sword of the Spirit, which is the word of God. And pray in the Spirit on all occasions with all kinds of prayers and requests. With this in mind, be alert and always keep on praying for all the LORD's people."* Ephesians 6:10-18 NIV

In Christ, you have been equipped for warfare and positioned to be a mighty warrior in the Kingdom of God. Jesus has already secured your victory over the darkness, He's exalted you above the enemy, and He has prepared you with everything you need in order to be strong in the LORD. The Scripture up above emphasizes the importance of putting on the full armor of God so that you can take your stand against the devil's schemes. The enemy has schemes for you, plans of destruction for you and your life, strategies to overcome you, to defeat you. According to the Word of God, Satan has come to kill, steal, and destroy you (John 10:10). However, in Christ you can stand your ground and make the enemy adhere to the victory that is yours in Jesus.

In Ephesians, Paul encourages the believers living there to stand firm against the rulers, the authorities, the powers of this dark world. My friend, it's time for you to stand firm! It's not enough to sit this one out or to just take a flimsy stand at your house and in your life. Satan hates God and since you are now associated with Him, Satan hates you too. Yet you have the mighty power of the LORD on your side, so firmly without yielding in any way, shape, or form take a stand against the enemy. James 4:7 says that if you resist, refuse to go along with, stand firm against the devil he will flee from you. Satan won't just leave you alone, he won't just walk away. No, the Bible says he will run! He will high tail it out of there because of the mighty power of the LORD. If God is for you, not even Satan can successfully be against you. Thank You, Jesus!

You are a warrior, my friend, but a warrior who goes into combat without his/her armor is not a fully prepared warrior. So, put on the full armor of the LORD. Put on the belt of truth; be girded with the truth of God's Word. If you are fixed with truth, you won't be tossed back and forth by the waves of people in their deceitful scheming; you won't easily fall for the enemy and his lies. The Bible describes Satan as the father of lies in John 8:44. There is no truth in him, yet he is cunning and crafty in the way he presents lies to trick you into believing them. So, it is especially important to be rooted, established, and girded with truth every day. Put on the breastplate of righteousness. Jesus has made you the righteousness of God. It is this righteousness that you have received through faith in Him that protects your heart and soul from evil. Living righteously, according to His Word, also protects your heart. This breastplate of righteousness is held in place by the belt of truth. Without truth, our righteousness becomes based on our own attempts to impress God which leads to legalism or self-condemnation. But if we see ourselves as "in Christ" we realize that His righteousness has been credited to our account. This breastplate of righteousness guards out hearts and keeps them pure. These hearts that according to Jeremiah 17:9 are deceitful above all things and beyond cure. Oh, how we need a breastplate of righteousness! We also fit out feet with the readiness that comes from the gospel of peace. What is the gospel of peace? The message of Jesus Christ. This imagery is comparable to that of a runner who is ready to run with perseverance the race marked out for him (Hebrews 12:1). Any runner will tell you that if your shoes don't "fit" you aren't going to be able to endure the race very long. But your feet have been fitted, customized, especially designed to carry the message of Jesus Christ and to have that message keep you on course to finish this race and receive the prize reserved for you. You have the shield of faith to extinguish all the flaming arrows of the evil one. Satan is shooting fiery darts at you all the time, but your faith in God puts those flaming arrows out, your faith protects you, and it is your shield. You have the helmet of salvation to protect your mind, to seal your ears from absorbing the lies of the enemy and instead giving you ears to hear what the Spirit of God is saying to you. And you have the sword of the Spirit which is the Word of God to cut the enemy down. Jesus modeled how to do this well when He was tempted by Satan in the desert in Matthew 4. There are many resources that go into detail about the armor of God. It is a fascinating study. However, Paul ends these verses by encouraging the Ephesians to pray in the Spirit, with all kinds of prayers, be alert, and always keep on praying. You are a mighty warrior in the LORD. He has given you incredible armor to help you stand firm against the enemy. Put it on, my friend. In Christ, you are the victor!

Father,

Thank You for making me a warrior fully prepared for battle and crowned with victory in Jesus. Thank You that I can stand firm in Your mighty power and not just my own. Holy Spirit help me today to put on the full armor of God and to take a stand at my house, with my family, in my life against the enemy. I am more than a conqueror in Christ. Let it be so in my life in Jesus's name, amen.

Day 65: I Am Cared for by God

"Casting all your care upon him (God), for he cares for you." 1 Peter 5:7 NKJV

"He will not allow your foot to slip; he who keeps you will not slumber." Psalm 121:3 NASB

"What is man that you (God) take thought of him, and the son of man that you care for him?" Psalm 8:4 NASB

> *"So he (prodigal son) got up and came to his father. But while he was still a long way off, his father saw him and felt compassion for him, and ran and embraced him and kissed him."* Luke 15:20 NIV

God cares about you! I know that seems like such a novel, elementary idea, but please consider this truth for a moment. The infinite, all-powerful, uncontainable Creator of the cosmos Who fashioned the Earth by the words of His mouth cares for you. Let's put that in perspective for a second. The closest star to planet Earth is the famous Betelgeuse (aka beetle juice). Astrologers believe Betelgeuse is the ninth brightest star in the solar system. It is considered the largest of the terrestrial planets of the inner solar system; larger than Mercury, Venus, and Mars. Well, Betelgeuse is about 1,180 times larger than the sun and a rough approximation of how many times our planet could fit inside this ninth largest star in the solar system is 2 quadrillion times! I don't even know how to write that number. That is how big our God is! And that same God cares about you! Wow!

Don't let Satan lie to you, my friend! What is man that God would even take thought of him, that God would care for him? You are His son/daughter! The Bible says that this same God knows the number of hairs on your head. He is a good, good Father! Paul encourages us in 1 Peter to cast all our cares upon God because He cares so much for us. And when you consider just how big, how vast, how awesome our God is, you realize that He is well able to handle all your cares.

God cares for you, my friend! It may not seem possible, but He does! He runs to you, embraces you, and kisses you! This God whose words are so powerful that He spoke and all the solar system in its vast array was created, a solar system so complex, so immeasurable that astrologers and scientists still can't quite figure it out or discover it all. That God is your Father and He runs to you! That is remarkable! Tell Satan to shut his pie hole because your Father is awesome, and He cares about you!

Father,

> Thank You for caring for me, for concerning Yourself with me. Who am I that you would think of me, that you would be mindful of me, that you would care about me? Remarkably You do! You are familiar with all my ways. You even know

how many hairs I have on my head. I'm so amazed by You. Thank You for considering me worth caring about. Thank You for running to me, for embracing me, for kissing me. I am welcome with You. I am at home with You. You are such a good, good Father and today I just want to praise You for who You are in Jesus's name, amen.

Day 66: I Am Called

"And we know that in all things God works for the good of those who love him, who have been called according to his purpose." Romans 8:28 NIV

"I press on toward the goal to win the prize for which God has called me heavenward in Christ Jesus." Philippians 3:14 NIV

"There is one body and one Spirit, just as you were called to one hope when you were called." Ephesians 4:4 NIV

"But just as he who called you is holy, so be holy in all you do; for it is written: "Be holy, because I am holy." 1 Peter 1:15-16 NIV

If you call to someone you cry out to them, you yell, shout, or holler to get their attention. Mother's call their kids inside for dinner, a teacher calls his/her class to attention to give instruction, or an employer calls a meeting with all his/her employees. The implication from being called regardless to the tone or volume of voice being used in doing so is a sense of urgency. The one being summoned realizes the importance and necessity of what they are being called to. Children understand that they need to come inside immediately when their mother calls them. A class recognizes the need to pay attention when their teacher calls them, so they don't miss important instruction. And employees appreciate the magnitude of an employer calling a meeting with them. At least, that is the hope in all these scenarios. There is a dynamic of respect for the authority of the one doing the calling. If that respect is somehow missing, the one being called cares very little about responding and the urgency of the call is ignored. This leads to some serious issues. In like manner, you have been called by God! He has cried out to you. He has brought you to attention. You are called!

What does it mean to be called? What have you been called to? There are many instances in the Bible that refer to this, a few of which are mentioned above. God has called you heavenward in Christ Jesus. You are called to one hope, you have been called according to God's purpose, and since the One who called you is holy, you should be holy as well. You aren't just asked or suggested these things. You are called to them. There is urgency, a summons, a need associated with being called. Let me put it this way: the ultimate authority, God, has cried out to you. He has invited you, beckoned you, made His appeal to you to lift your heart and mind heavenward since you are now in Christ Jesus. Friend, please, set your heart on things above where Christ is seated at the right hand of God. Set your mind on things above, not on earthly things for you died and your life is now hidden with Christ in God. You are not of your own purpose anymore. You have been called according to God's purpose. Maybe you feel unqualified to be called in any way, shape, or form by the LORD. That is a lie! God always sees you at your full potential. He sees you at your best because Christ lives in you. That's why it so easy for Him to call things that are not as though they are because He sees you as you truly are, as He created you to be. It's time to rise, my friend; to ignore the call of the enemy and to adhere instead to the call of God.

In 1 Samuel 3, Samuel was just a boy ministering before the LORD under Eli, the priest. The Bible says that in those days the word of the LORD was rare, there were not many visions. I doubt it had less to do with God's unwillingness to speak and more to do with man's unwillingness to listen. Regardless, one night the LORD called to Samuel and Samuel gets up and runs to Eli thinking Eli had summoned him but is discredited and told to go back to bed. This happens three more times before Eli, the priest of God, one who should probably have known God's voice or how to listen to the LORD, yet it took several times before even he realizes that the LORD was calling Samuel. So, he finally gives Samuel some instructions should the LORD call to him again. This time when God calls to Samuel, he says, "Speak, for your servant is listening." (1 Samuel 3:10 NIV). And God reveals to Samuel some incredible information. My friend, in the same way, God has called you! Maybe you feel like you've missed the call somehow, you've had your opportunity and it passed you by. No way! It took Samuel a few times to figure it out and guess what? God kept calling him! He wants to speak to you. He is not hidden from you. He has given you His Word, His Spirit, He has called you! I pray you would sense the urgency; you would know that your Father, the Great I AM, has cried out to you, has invited you to commune with Him. How awesome!

Father,

> I thank You that I am called, that You have invited me to be in relationship with You, that You have cried out to me. Forgive me for ignoring Your voice, for disregarding Your call. Holy Spirit, would You give me ears to hear what You are saying and a heart that is willing to listen, to yield, to fellowship with You. Like Samuel, I invite You to speak for Your servant is listening. I want to know Your voice well, to recognize Your voice, Your call on my life. Let it be so LORD in Jesus's name, amen.

Day 67: I Am Known

> *"You have searched me, LORD, and you know me. You know when I sit and when I rise; you perceive my thoughts from afar. You discern my going out and my lying down; you are familiar with all my ways. Before a word is on my tongue you, LORD, know it completely. You hem me in behind and before, and you lay your hand upon me. Such knowledge is too wonderful for me, too lofty for me to attain. Where can I go from your Spirit? Where can I flee from your presence? If I go up to the heavens, you are there; if I make my bed in the depths, you are there. If I rise on the wings of the dawn, if I settle on the far side of the sea, even there your hand will guide me, your right hand will hold me fast. If I say, 'surely the darkness will hide me and the light become night around me,' even the darkness will not be dark*

> *to you; the night will shine like the day, for darkness is as light to you. For you created my inmost being; you knit me together in my mother's womb. I praise you because I am fearfully and wonderfully made; your works are wonderful; I know that full well. My frame was not hidden from you when I was made in the secret place, when I was woven together in the depths of the earth. Your eyes saw my unformed body; all the days ordained for me were written in your book before one of them came to be. How precious to me are your thoughts, God! How vast is the sum of them! Were I to count them, they would outnumber the grains of sand—when I awake, I am still with you."* Psalm 139:1-18 NIV

You are known! If you doubt that in any way, please reread the Scripture above from Psalm. Read it a gazillion times if you need to because the Word of God clearly and beautifully declares you to be known by God! He knows when you sit and when you rise. He can perceive your thoughts from afar. He knows what you are thinking! Maybe you think that's a little scary, but in all honesty it's incredibly comforting. He knows what's on your mind, what's in your heart. He understands you fully! He knows when you go out and when you lay down. He is familiar with all your ways. Those little quirks and unexplainable tendencies you have are recognizable to Him. Before a word is even on your tongue, He knows it completely. Where could you go from God's Spirit? If you were to ascend to the highest height in its entire splendor, He would be there. And even if you were to descend into the lowest depth, the Bible says that He would still be there. You are never alone! If you somehow feel as though you are completely lost in the darkness, surrounded by darkness, the Bible says that the darkness is as light to the LORD. There's no darkness that could hide you from Him. He can always find you, my friend.

He created your inmost being. He thought of you, imagined you, knit you together in your mother's womb. Your frame wasn't hidden from Him even as you were being made in that secret place. You had value to God before you were ever born! He saw your unformed body and all the days meant for you were written in His book before even one of them came to be. When people look at you now what do they typically look at first? Your body! Man looks at the outward appearance, but God looks at the heart. Yet the LORD seen you before you even had a body! He deemed you worthy of His attention long before your body was ever formed. Look in the mirror and contemplate that one for a second. That is incredible! The Bible says that He thinks about you more than anyone else could possibly think of you. His thoughts about you exceed the number of grains of sand on the whole earth. Just to put that in perspective a little bit, consider this: if you were on the beach somewhere and you scooped up a handful of sand, you would hold in your hand approximately 400,000 grains of sand! Now multiply that by the number of grains of sand on the planet and God's thoughts about you surpass that number. That is unfathomable! Satan has no right to tell you that you are forgotten, that you are insignificant, that God doesn't care about you, see you, or know you. Are you kidding me? Psalm 139 blows those lies right out of the water! God knows you, my friend! He doesn't just know you like an architect knows his work. He knows you like a Father knows His child. In fact, He knows you better than any earthly father could even possibly know their own child because He is both your Creator and your Father. He is a good, good Father, the very best!

Father,

> Thank You for knowing me so well. I'm amazed at how well You know me. Would You forgive me for doubting Your love, Your care, Your knowledge of me, and Your heart? Inscribe the truth of Psalm 139 upon my heart forever. May I never forget that I am known by You in Jesus's name, amen!

Day 68: I Am United with God

"But he who is joined to the LORD becomes one spirit with him." 1 Corinthians 6:17 ESV

"For this reason, a man shall leave his father and mother and shall be joined to his wife, and the two shall become one flesh. This mystery is great; but I am speaking with reference to Christ and the church." Ephesians 5:31-32 NIV

> *"However, you are not in the flesh but in the Spirit, if indeed the Spirit of God dwells in you. But if anyone does not have the Spirit of Christ, he does not belong to Him. If Christ is in you, though the body is dead because of sin, yet the spirit is alive because of righteousness. But if the Spirit of Him who raised Jesus from the dead dwells in you, He who raised Christ Jesus from the dead will also give life to your mortal bodies through His Spirit who dwells in you."* Romans 8:9-11 NIV

You have become one spirit with the LORD! The Bible says that just as a man leaves his mother and father and becomes one flesh with his wife which is a profound mystery, but this type of unity is an example of how Christ is united with the church. That is incredible! How do two separate, individual lives and persons become so joined, so combined and cohesive that they become as if they were one? Seems impossible, yet it isn't! You don't just have a relationship with the LORD, you are joined to Him; you are one with Him. The Spirit of God dwells in you indicating that you truly do belong to Christ. In fact, marriage between a man and a woman was created by God as a representation of the relationship He has with us in Christ. You belong to Him like a husband and wife belong to each other. You aren't classified as a servant belonging to his/her master. You aren't a piece of property to the LORD. Servants aren't typically aware of their master's affairs. That knowledge is reserved for close friends. Yet God doesn't just invite you to know His business, He invites you to know His heart. The Bible describes your relationship with the LORD with much more familiarity and closeness. The only human relationship that even comes close to this type of unity is that of a husband and wife. Wow!

You aren't disconnected. You aren't on the outside looking in. You aren't the third wheel here. You don't have to be envious of anyone else's relationship with God because what He has for you is uniquely for you. You are united with God! You are the object of His desire, of His love. He already knows everything there is to know about you, but He bids you to know Him that way. He isn't hiding from you. He has revealed Himself to you through Jesus, through His Word, by His Spirit. What other God is like Him? No One!

The whole book of Hosea in the Bible is about God asking the prophet Hosea to marry a woman who was a prostitute, a woman who repeatedly was unfaithful to him, a woman who did not have her husband's heart as a picture of God's relationship with the children of Israel. Hosea had to go retrieve Gomer out of her prostitution even after they were married because she ran away from him. He had to forgive her, love her sacrificially, be patient with her, show her so much grace, and choose to see her as she could be if she only knew how fully she was loved. The LORD says, "…I will show my love to the one I called 'not my loved one.' I will say to those called 'not my people,' 'you are my people,' and they will say, 'you are my God.'" (Hosea 2:23 NIV). God has chosen to show you His love, to call you His very own. He didn't have to be united to you, He decided to be. He sees you as you could be if you only knew how fully you were loved and He invites you to live from that place, from that security, from that knowledge by letting you know His heart. Why in the world would God who absolutely is self-sustaining, who doesn't need a single thing from a single person, who doesn't require to be united to anything or anyone choose to do such a thing? Because He is that good, because His heart for you, His heart towards you is that good! Satan is a liar, my friend! God is not against you. He takes no delight in your pain. He doesn't relish in your failures. Satan does that! The LORD is not unattainable or out of your reach. He has given you His Spirit and you are now united with Him, and what God has brought together let not any man, not even Satan himself, separate in Jesus's name!

Father,

> I thank You for causing Your Spirit to dwell with me, for uniting me to You through Your Spirit. I thank You that I am brought near to You through Christ's blood, that I am close to You, united to You, one with You. How awesome! I am so amazed by Your goodness, by Your love, by Your heart. Forgive me for ever questioning or doubting who You are and help me Holy Spirit to know the Father's heart, to belong to Christ, to have the kind of relationship and union with God that a husband and wife have with each other. I want to know You fully LORD, so I invite You to reveal Yourself to me in Jesus's name, amen.

Day 69: I Am Covered!

> *"He (God) will cover you with his feathers, and under his wings you will find refuge; his faithfulness will be your shield and rampart."* Psalm 91:4 NIV
>
> *"For you bless the righteous, O LORD; you cover him with favor as with a shield."* Psalm 5:12 NIV
>
> *"Then I (God) passed by you and saw you, and behold, you were at the time for love; so I spread my skirt over you and covered your nakedness I also swore to you and entered into a covenant with you so that you became mine,' declares the LORD God."* Ezekiel 16:8 NIV

You are covered, my friend! God covers you with His feathers and under His wings you will find refuge, shelter, protection. His faithfulness is your shield and rampart. It is the fortification and barricade you have against the enemy. Being uncovered denotes shame, fear, a sense of exposure, of danger. To go into battle uncovered is terrifying. To live life exposed is equally horrifying. Yet you don't have to fear being uncovered because His faithfulness keeps you safe. Not only so, He has covered you with His favor as with a shield. This is awesome! He favors you. He supports you. He helps you. It isn't just something He does for you occasionally, if He feels like it or if you deserve it. No, the Bible says He covers you with His favor, with His support, with His help like a shield covers you in battle. You are surrounded by His favor. You are enclosed by His help. You are shielded with His support. You are covered!

In Ezekiel 16 we see the nation of Israel compared to a woman coming of age to be married. In verse 6 we see Israel likened to an unwanted baby thrown out and despised, but the LORD chose Israel and made her live. He took care of her, nourished her, and watched her grow. Then in verse 8 the Bible says that when God noticed that she was old enough for marriage, He spread the corner of His garment over her and covered her nakedness. He entered a covenant with her like that of a marriage and she became His. A similar phrasing is found in Ruth 3 when Ruth goes to Boaz, her kinsman-redeemer and asks him to spread his garment over her. She asks him to marry her. You go, girl! Ha! This whole scenario is symbolic of Christ's relationship to us. He is our kinsman-redeemer. This phrasing implies a dynamic of relationship like that of marriage between a husband and a wife. Yet I don't think it's an accident that the Bible uses the word "cover" in reference to this relationship. In Biblical times a woman who wasn't married was considered "uncovered." She was outside of her father's house, she was unprotected. Life was very dangerous for her. Marriage provided security, a covering, protection for her physically as well as economically. Well, in Christ, you have been covered as well. He has spread His garment over you, entered a covenant relationship with you, and His faithfulness is your covering, your security, your protection. You are covered!

In Genesis 3 we find the account of the fall of man where Adam and Eve sinned and tried to hide from God as a result. The Bible says that once they sinned, they realized they were physically naked, and they were ashamed so they knit together fig leaves as a covering. It's almost as if they tried to cover their own shame, their own guilt, their own sin, but their covering was completely inadequate. Fig leaves were not very durable, they only covered part of their bodies and not all of it, and even as such they didn't cover them very well. They had on these coverings and they were still trying to hide from God. Yet the Bible says in Genesis 3:21 that the LORD made garments for Adam and Eve made of animal skin and completely clothed them with these garments. We aren't provided a lot of details about this, but it's apparent that Adam and Eve went from inadequately covering themselves to completely being clothed by God. My friend, in Christ you are sufficiently covered, you are fully clothed! Your guilt, your shame, your weakness; it's all covered! You are fully clothed in Christ! This is excellent news! Christ has covered your sin with His blood. You don't have to fear nakedness, exposure, guilt, or shame because in Christ you are completely covered! Thank You, Jesus!

Father,

> I thank You for covering me with Your favor as with a shield. Thank You for protecting me, for Your faithfulness to me and to the covenant that You have made with me. Your faithfulness is like a wall around me, keeping me safe from the enemy. It's not about me. It's all about Who You are!

I praise You today for covering my sin in Christ and for clothing me with righteousness instead. I stand before You fully clothed, unashamed, and without any guilt because of Jesus. Guilt, shame, it's all from Satan and I don't receive it. Instead I run to You, the One Who can free me, to cover me, to clothe me in Him. Let it be so in my life in Jesus's name, amen.

Day 70: I Am Fearless

"For God has not given us a spirit of fear, but of power and of love and of a sound mind." 2 Timothy 1:7 NIV

"Have I not commanded you? Be strong and courageous. Do not be afraid; do not be discouraged, for the LORD your God will be with you wherever you go." Joshua 1:9 NIV

"The LORD is my light and my salvation—whom shall I fear? The LORD is the stronghold of my life—of whom shall I be afraid? Psalm 27:1 NIV

"When I am afraid, I put my trust in you. In God, whose word I praise—in God I trust and am not afraid. What can mere mortals do to me?" Psalm 56:3-4 NIV

God has not given you a spirit of fear! Fear isn't from Him; He has no part in it. Fear is a spirit according to the Bible and if it isn't from God then we know that it's from the enemy. Fear is crippling, paralyzing, it inhibits the growth of faith in your life. It is entirely from Satan and God has nothing to do with it. Rather the Bible says that the LORD has given to each one of us a measure of faith (Romans 12:3) and that faith is so powerful that even if it could be measured and all of your faith amounted to was something the size of a tiny mustard seed, you could command mountains to move out of their places (Matthew 17:20). Contemplate that one for a second. This tells me that even though fear is powerful, faith has always been and will always be more powerful! Why? Because God is all-powerful, and He has given you a measure of faith. Oh friend, this is good stuff. Yes, Jesus got onto His disciples for having "little faith" especially after all of the miracles and teaching they had received from Him. It's apparent that He expected them to grow up in their faith, to learn to trust Him more, believe in Him more, but the initial quantity of their faith wasn't as important as what they chose to do with it. You see, God has given you a measure of faith and the Bible compares your faith to a seed. Seeds are small and the mustard seed is one of the smallest, but when planted seeds grow into bigger, greater, more fruitful things. Thus, is the expectation of the faith that God has given you. Don't let Satan taunt you on how small your faith is; rather, plant it and watch it grow to the glory of God.

Not only so, the Holy Spirit is a Spirit of power, a Spirit of love, a Spirit of clarity and understanding. The enemy often through fear tries to make you feel weak, unloved, and terribly confused. Fear will make a crazy person out of you! But the Holy Spirit brings power, love, and revelation. The Holy Spirit of the living God makes you fearless! Has not God commanded you to be strong and courageous? You don't have to be afraid or discouraged for the LORD, your God, will be with you wherever you go! Fear is a terrorist from the enemy of your soul. Treat it as such. Don't entertain, welcome, or play games with a terrorist from the enemy. Don't let the enemy make you afraid when God, through Christ, has made you fearless!

Hebrews chapter 11 is often described as being the "hall of faith" in the Bible. It lists numerous individuals from the Word of God who through faith accomplished some rather remarkable things. I'm sure these men and women experienced fear or at least had opportunities for fear to stop them, but they were ultimately confident in what they hoped for and sure of what they could not see. The incredible thing is that the measure of their faith isn't classified or compared to one another. We tend to compare everything even in the church; even when it comes to our faith. But it doesn't go into detail on how Moses only had faith the size of a mustard seed and Abraham had faith the size of a peach seed. How big the seed was, how big their faith was isn't relevant to the message being communicated here in Hebrews. Regardless to how big or small their faith in God was, the important thing here is that they had faith and they chose to plant that faith in God, and God showed up for them. My friend, God has given you a measure of faith! You can be in the" hall of faith" too because God has given you what it takes to trust Him, to believe in Him. He has given you faith. Don't discredit yourself or let the enemy discredit you. You may not consider yourself a superhero in the faith, but your faith isn't what is powerful in and of itself; rather, the One you have chosen to put your faith in IS powerful. Regardless to whether you put your faith in Him or not, God has always been and will always be powerful.

In Christ, you have been set free from the tyranny of fear. You no longer must tolerate the intimidation of fear in your life. The spirit of fear must leave at the mere whisper of the name of Jesus because you have received instead the Spirit of God. According to Romans 8:15, the Spirit you have received doesn't make you a slave so that you must fear again. The Holy Spirit makes you a son/daughter! You are a child of God. The most powerful Entity in the whole universe is now your Father. What in the world do you have to be afraid of? You are fearless!

Father,

> I thank You for giving to me a measure of faith. You are so powerful, so great, so awesome. You can do anything, and I can place even the tiniest amount of confidence and assurance in You because You've given me that ability. Would You help me to exercise that ability? Holy Spirit help me to be fearless for You are a Spirit of power, of love, of clarity and revelation. I need these things desperately. Today I choose to be strong and courageous because You are with me wherever I go. Let it be so LORD, in Jesus's name, amen.

Day 71: I Am God's Workmanship

"For we are his workmanship, created in Christ Jesus for good works, which God prepared beforehand, that we should walk in them." Ephesians 2:10 ESV

"I praise you, for I am fearfully and wonderfully made. Wonderful are your works; my soul knows it very well." Psalm 139:14 ESV

> *"And I am sure of this, that he who began a good work in you will bring it to completion at the day of Jesus Christ."*
> Philippians 1:6 ESV

You are God's workmanship, His design, His handiwork; His masterpiece. He didn't just form you and fashion you in your mother's womb. He created you in Christ Jesus for good works. That means that when you gave your life to Jesus, when you made Him your LORD and Savior, God completely created a whole new you for the good works which He prepared beforehand that you should walk in those. He has good things that He has created you to do and accomplish, things He appointed you to even while you were being made in that secret place. Yet sin has always hindered those plans and purposes from coming to fruition, but when you gave your life to Jesus, God recreated you so that you could accomplish those good works. How awesome is that!

And you can be sure of this: He that began a good work in you will bring it to completion! You know what this says to me? God's workmanship isn't half-hearted, it isn't poorly designed, or haphazardly thrown together. God doesn't abandon His workmanship; He doesn't start something and never finish it. He never gives up on His work! Oh friend, hear me out for a minute. Satan is a liar! You are not good for nothing. God has created you for good things! You aren't given up on or forgotten about. God will never walk away from you or suddenly decide that He's done with you. You are His handiwork and He has promised to carry out His work in you until that work is complete at the day of Jesus Christ. He doesn't make something good then just put it on the shelf to collect dust. No way! He has created you for good works, for a purpose, for a reason; to accomplish something. Others may throw in the towel, they may walk away, they may decide that there's no hope for you, that you'll never change but this is not the stance of the One who began His good work in you. He is with you at the starting line and to be sure He will be there when you cross the finish line, yet unlike so many others, God will also be with you every leg of the race in-between. You are His workmanship and He is faithful to His work.

Consider the life of the apostle Paul in the Bible. Here is one of the greatest leaders of the early church, one who is responsible for writing a good portion of the New Testament, a true pioneer of the faith. People have read his words, studied his life, and followed his example for centuries yet his life before encountering Christ was a bit uncanny. His name was Saul, he was a religious leader, he was devout, learned, a true leader but in the worst way.

His name in Hebrew meant "asked for" or "inquired of God" almost as if he was God's gift to the world. There was an air of arrogance and superiority about him. He strongly opposed Christianity, believed it to be heresy and was so passionately against it that he approved the killing of those who confessed to be Christians. In fact, he led the persecution of the Christian faith at the time. Acts chapter 9 describes Saul's journey to Damascus and how he had a supernatural encounter with Jesus that changed his life forever by humbling him before the LORD. Here God changes his name to Paul, meaning "small" or "humble". Paul became God's workmanship, completely recreated in Christ Jesus for the good works that God had prepared for him. God sends him out to preach the Gospel, to share the message of Jesus Christ with the gentiles, the very thing he so adamantly opposed to begin with. In fact, the other apostles and leaders of the early church were skeptical and afraid of him in the beginning. They thought his conversion may be a hoax, a trap, a ruse to find them out and resist them. It was hard for the other believers to see the good work that God had started, but the LORD sends Barnabas, a trusted leader among the group, to vouch for Paul.

God certainly created Paul from the beginning and had a purpose for him, good works in store for him. And to be sure, Paul persecuting the early church was not a part of those good works, but when Paul encounters Jesus he is completely recreated for the good works that God had prepared for him. That is the transforming power of Jesus! Maybe the enemy has tried to tell you that God couldn't use you for anything good; that your past is too messy, it's too bad, you've made too many mistakes. Can I tell you Paul was a murderer? This guy who is revered as being one of the greatest leaders of the early church, who God used to write a good portion of the Bible, and whose ministry to the gentiles brought about the message of Jesus Christ being spread to regions and people who were initially thought to be unworthy of that message. Paul's ministry led to you and I hearing and receiving the message of Jesus since we are also considered gentiles. This guy who God used for so many good works was a murderer to begin with. He was proud; arrogant. Paul had a past, a track record, a reputation that stood against him from time to time. Yet his reputation in Christ was greater. God's work prevailed in his life. May it be so for you too! Don't listen to the enemy! Your reputation in Christ is greater than any reputation you had for evil. You are God's workmanship and you are created for good works!

Father,

I thank You for the good works You have planned for me. I thank You that I am Your workmanship, I am Your creation, Your design and You are faithful to Your work. I thank You that Your plans are to prosper me and not to harm me, to give me a future and a hope. Help me Holy Spirit to accomplish the good things that God has created me for. I trust that the good work You have begun in me will be carried out to completion. You won't give up on me, You won't quit, You won't stop using me for good. Thank You, Jesus. Let it be so in my life in Jesus's name.

Day 72: I Have the Mind of Christ

"For who knows a person's thoughts except their own spirit within them? In the same way no one knows the thoughts of God except the Spirit of God. What we have received is not the spirit of the world, but the Spirit who is from God, so that we may understand what God has freely given us…For, 'who has known the mind of the Lord to instruct him?' But we have the mind of Christ." 1 Corinthians 2:11-12,16 NIV

"Do not conform to the pattern of this world but be transformed by the renewing of your mind. Then you will be able to test and approve what God's will is—his good, pleasing and perfect will." Romans 12:2 NIV

"Do not be anxious about anything, but in every situation, by prayer and petition, with thanksgiving, present your requests to God. And the peace of God, which transcends all understanding, will guard your hearts and your minds in Christ Jesus. Finally, brothers and sisters, whatever is true, whatever is noble,

> *whatever is right, whatever is pure, whatever is lovely, whatever is admirable—if anything is excellent or praiseworthy—think about such things."* Philippians 4:6-8 NIV

You have the mind of Christ! Look at the Scripture up above in 1 Corinthians. It questions who could know a person's thoughts except their spirit within them. No one can read your mind or know your thoughts except you, your spirit within you. If you are alive then no other person has your spirit (let's hope not anyway ha) so if you want someone to know what you are thinking about; you must communicate it to them somehow. In like manner, no one knows the thoughts of God except the Spirit of God. However, when you accepted Jesus as your LORD and Savior, you received God's Spirit so that you might understand what God has freely given you, so that you might know God's thoughts. God can communicate His thoughts directly to you through His Spirit. How cool is that? None of us could ever figure God out since His ways and thoughts are so much higher than ours (Isaiah 55:9), but according to the Bible we do have the mind of Christ. God has given us His Spirit, the very One who knows God's thoughts so that we might know His thoughts too. What other Creator, what other Ruler, what other Deity wants you to know His thoughts? God does! By His Spirit, He has given you the mind of Christ.

You can choose what you think about; to be aware of what you think about. God has given you control of your mind. By His Spirit, God will reveal His thoughts to you in your mind, but you have the right and responsibility to discern whether those thoughts are from God or not and you have the choice of whether to receive them or reject them. The enemy of your soul will also put his thoughts into your mind, but since you are now in Christ, Satan has no right to your mind anymore except what you legally forfeit to him. He can send thoughts to your mind, but you have the power to think on them or not. He can't make you think his thoughts. He can't force you to. He does not have that power or that authority anymore. God absolutely has that power and authority but chooses not to exercise it; rather, He has delegated that power and authority to YOU. So, it's imperative that you are aware of your own thoughts and that you discern what is from God and what isn't. "The mind governed by the flesh is death, but the mind governed by the Spirit is life and peace." (Romans 8:6 NIV). You are not a robot and God does not treat you as such. He does not preprogram you, control you, or manipulate you in any way, not even in the privacy of your mind. Jesus tells us to love the LORD with all of our heart, our soul, and our mind. To God, submitting your mind to the Lordship of Jesus Christ is an act of love. Wow! He has given you reign of your own thoughts, but He provides guidelines and instructions to help you have the mind of Christ. The Scripture above in Philippians tells us not to be anxious about anything but to pray about everything and the peace of God will guard and protect our hearts and minds in Christ Jesus. Yet the next verse is also connected to the previous ones when it informs us on what to think about. Our thoughts should be true, noble, right, pure, lovely, admirable, praiseworthy, and excellent. Test your thoughts and make them align to the parameters of the Bible. Those parameters are straightforward, but training your brain requires discipline, work, and practice. You are not a slave to whatever comes into your mind! God has given you discernment and the ability to take your thoughts captive to Christ.

Paul says, "...we take captive every thought to make it obedient to Christ." (2 Corinthians 10:5 NIV). You don't have to let your mind go, to let your thoughts race ahead of you. You are not subject to whatever thoughts pop into your head. God has given you the ability to take your thoughts captive and to make them obedient to Him. This means you have the power to stop your train of thought, to test what you are thinking about and where it is coming from, and to choose whether you will accept those thoughts in your mind or not. Satan wants to conform you to the pattern of this world. How does he do that? Through your mind, your thoughts! He wants you to feel powerless over your own thoughts. He wants you to be a slave to whatever garbage he tries to put into your head. He wants you to feel out of control in the area of your mind. Why? Because he wants to be in control of what you think about! He knows that if he has your mind, then he has your life since the Bible says that as a man thinks in his heart, so is he (Proverbs 23:7). However, Satan is in foreign territory now. He is trespassing, intruding, invading terrain that he does not rule over anymore. You have the ability and the opportunity to be transformed by the renewing of your mind. You have the power to take every thought captive; to take every thought as prisoner, to take them into custody and decide if they should be locked up or go free. God has given YOU control and just like every other area of your life; you can choose to submit even your thoughts to the Lordship of Jesus Christ. And to do, according to the Bible, is an act of your love for God. You can renew your mind. You can repair it, restore it, heal it with the Word of God. God has given you His Spirit to reveal to you His thoughts. You have the mind of Christ!

Father,

> I thank You for giving me Your Spirit, for revealing Your thoughts to me by Your Spirit. Would You help me to know Your voice, to discern Your Spirit, and to control my mind? Forgive me for being so lax in the area of my thoughts. I choose to submit even my thoughts to the Lordship of Jesus Christ. Help me, Holy Spirit. And even if my mind feels broken, out of control, or just run down; I choose today to renew my mind with Your Word. I am not a crazy person. I have the mind of Christ. Let it be so in my life LORD in Jesus's name, amen.

Day 73: I Am the Aroma of Christ

> *"But thanks be to God, who always leads us as captives in Christ's triumphal procession and uses us to spread the aroma of the knowledge of him everywhere. For we are to God the pleasing aroma of Christ among those who are being saved and those who are perishing. To the one we are an aroma that brings death; to the other, an aroma that brings life..."* 2 Corinthians 2:14-16 NIV

> *"The priest is to burn all of it on the altar. It is a burnt offering, a food offering, an aroma pleasing to the LORD."* Leviticus 1:9 NIV

You are to God the pleasing aroma of Christ. You even smell like Jesus and God uses you to spread this aroma of the knowledge of Him everywhere! Some people love the fragrance of Jesus all over you. They are drawn to Jesus in your presence because you carry the aroma of hope, of life, of grace; of Jesus. Others find the aroma of Jesus a stench in their nostrils. They hate the smell, the reminder of their sinfulness, the confrontation of the cross of Jesus

Christ, the presence of the Holy Spirit with you. They despise it, run from it, are afraid of it. But God enjoys, is pleased with, and delights in the way you smell! What in the world?

On sixteen different occasions in the book of Leviticus, an "aroma" is mentioned as something that pleases the LORD and the aroma of a sacrifice is specifically important to God. The smell of a sacrifice represented the substitute atonement for sin; a picture, an aroma of Jesus. The very first mention of God smelling an aroma of a burnt offering is found in Genesis 8:21. After the flood and after leaving the ark, Noah offers a burnt offering of clean animals and birds to God as a sacrifice, as a means of worship, as a satisfaction of God's righteous requirements and the Bible says that God was pleased with the aroma. Afterwards God promises never to destroy the earth again with a flood. A pleasing aroma is also mentioned in connection with the various offerings of tabernacle worship in Leviticus. Leviticus 1:9 and 13 emphasize the substitute atonement for sin as an aroma that pleased the LORD. The same is true in Leviticus 2 regarding the grain offering and in Leviticus 23 with a much larger sacrifice done yearly at the Feast of Weeks. Ephesians 5:2 describes Jesus as being the final sacrifice for sin, an offering that is eternally pleasing to God. God's righteous requirements were met in Jesus and as Galatians 2:20 denotes you were crucified with Christ and it's no longer you who lives anymore but Christ lives in you. And if He lives in you then you absolutely are a pleasing aroma to God since Jesus is a pleasing aroma to God.

Even those who worship false gods often burn incense as a way to please those gods, to win their approval, to gain their attention and favor. It's all about worship, producing a sweet smell. So too when you worship Jesus, lift the name of Jesus, live for Jesus you are producing a sweet aroma that is pleasing to God. "Therefore, I urge you, brothers and sisters, in view of God's mercy, to offer your bodies as a living sacrifice, holy and pleasing to God—this is your true and proper worship." (Romans 12:1 NIV). In fact, according to the Bible you have become that sweet fragrance, your life is a living sacrifice, a life-long act of worship. You are the aroma of Christ!

My friend, one of the reasons Satan hates you so much is because you smell like Jesus. You remind him of Jesus. He can't stand the aroma of Jesus! That aroma is to him the smell of defeat, of being overpowered, of being crushed. But to God, Jesus is your atonement; He is the sacrifice that has covered your sins. Jesus pleases the Father. A life surrendered to Him is pleasing to Him. You carry with you the sweet perfume of Jesus and God has sent you to spread that aroma of the knowledge of Him everywhere. How awesome! You are the aroma of Christ!

Father,

I thank You for making me the aroma of Christ and that You are pleased by this. I am a sweet perfume to You, You delight in the way I smell because of Jesus. This is so bizarre but so awesome! Help me Holy Spirit to continue to be an aroma pleasing to the LORD. I want to carry the knowledge of You everywhere I go, to spread the fragrance of You everywhere I go. Let it be so LORD in Jesus's name, amen.

Day 74: I Am Far from Oppression

"You will be firmly established in righteousness: you will be far from oppression, for you will not fear, and from terror, for it will not come near you." Isaiah 54:14 AMP

"We know that anyone born of God does not continue to sin; the One who was born of God keeps them safe, and the evil one cannot harm them." 1 John 5:18 NIV

"The LORD is a stronghold for the oppressed. A stronghold in times of trouble." Psalm 9:9 ESV

If you are oppressed you are kept down by something, dominated by something, afflicted in some way. Oppression gives the mental image of being sat on by an elephant, a person who carries the weight of the world on their shoulders, someone who is just weighed down. If you are being oppressed it's hard to function, all the extra weight you're carrying around makes you tired quicker. It's even hard to breathe sometimes. The enemy uses oppression to push you down, little by little to pile as much cares up on top of you so eventually you'll give out and be crushed. But Jesus says to you, "Come to me all you who are weary and burdened and I will give you rest." (Matthew 11:28 NIV). You are also encouraged in 1 Peter 5:7 to cast all your cares, all those things that are piling up on you, upon Him because He cares so much for you. In Christ, you are far from oppression! At every opportunity something comes to keep you down, to dominate you, to afflict you in some way you can cast that off of you and onto Jesus. How do you do that? Through prayer. Philippians 4:6 tells us that prayer removes our anxiety about things, prayer gives us peace about things, prayer is the vehicle by which we cast off our cares upon God.

My friend, can I tell you that Jesus did not just die upon the cross for your salvation. He didn't die on the cross so that you could continue to be weighed down, so that you could be oppressed by the enemy all your life. No! The cross of Jesus Christ doesn't just secure your eternal victory, it provides you victory now, for your life today! You are more than a conqueror right now. You are far from oppression at this very moment because the One who is in you is greater than the one who is in this world! You are admonished in Scripture to cast, to shed, to throw your cares off you and onto God. He's God, He can handle your cares, but He doesn't pry them from the death-grip you have on them. You must shed them, to throw them off. It's up to you. You are free from fear, from terror because the LORD, your God is with you, He is fighting your battles for you!

In 2 Kings 19 we find Hezekiah, the current king of Israel, had just received a letter from the enemy, the king of Assyria. This letter openly defied the God of Israel, mocked the king and his people, and threatened destruction. It was absolutely a letter of oppression from the enemy. The Bible says that when King Hezekiah heard these words, he tore his clothes and put on sackcloth and went into the Temple to pray. Rather than carry the load of this care himself, Hezekiah rightly decides to cast this thing at the feet of God through prayer. The Bible says that he spread the letter out before the LORD almost as if he was saying, "Here God, read this. This is what the enemy is saying!" The prophet Isaiah is sent to the king to inform him that God has heard his prayer and the prophet gives a word from the LORD about the whole situation. Then it says, "That night the angel of the LORD went out and put to death a hundred and eighty-five thousand in the Assyrian camp. When the people got up the next morning—there were all the dead bodies!" (2 Kings 19:35 NIV).

My friend, God is fighting your battles for you! When you cast those cares on Him, when you pray, He gives you rest and peace and while you are sleeping, He goes out and destroys the enemy for you so that when you wake up in the morning you already have the victory! How awesome is that! Your God is Jehovah-Saboath, the LORD of hosts, the God of an innumerable array of warring angels. According to the Scripture above in 2 Kings, just one of God's angels put to death one hundred and eighty-five thousand of the enemy. Our God is mighty. He is awesome! Don't listen to the enemy! The odds are in your favor. There are more with you than there are those against you because God is on your side. Oppression is kept far from you! The evil one cannot touch you. He has no right to touch you. He would be a fool to touch you because you belong to God and God has given you the victory in Jesus!

Father,

> I thank You for Jesus. Thank You for the victory that I have in Him. Oppression is kept far from me, I am kept safe in Him, because of Him. You are mighty God. You are so awesome. The enemy cannot defeat you, will never defeat you, is a fool to even try, and I thank You that You have given me the opportunity and the privilege of casting my cares, my troubles, my problems upon You. I thank You for rest, for peace. I thank You for fighting my battles for me, that there are more with me than there are those against me because You are with me. You are the LORD Almighty so today I run to You. I throw off my cares on You because You care for me. Thank You Jesus! Let oppression be kept far from me in Jesus's name, amen.

Day 75: I Am Not Enough Unless He Comes

> *"Not that we are sufficient in ourselves to claim anything as coming from us, but our sufficiency is from God, who has made us sufficient to be ministers of a new covenant, not of the letter*

> *but of the Spirit. For the letter kills, but the Spirit gives life."* 2 Corinthians 3:5-6 NIV

> *"But he (God) said to me, 'My grace is sufficient for you, for my power is made perfect in weakness.' Therefore, I will boast all the more gladly of my weaknesses, so that the power of Christ may rest upon me."* 2 Corinthians 12:9 NIV

> *"But now, this is what the LORD says—... "Do not fear, for I have redeemed you; I have summoned you by name; you are mine. When you pass through the waters, I will be with you; and when you pass through the rivers, they will not sweep over you. When you walk through the fire, you will not be burned; the flames will not set you ablaze. For I am the LORD your God, the Holy One of Israel, your Savior;...Since you are precious and honored in my sight, and because I love you, I will give people in exchange for you, nations in exchange for your life." Isaiah* 43:1-2, 4 NIV

According to the first verse above from 2 Corinthians in and of yourself you aren't enough, you aren't adequate; yet your adequacy, your sufficiency isn't rooted in you, it comes from God. You are a minister of the new covenant; a minister of the Spirit and that Spirit gives life. That Spirit makes you enough! You know what this says to me? Your weaknesses, your failures, the things about you that you may consider disqualifiers, those things others may exclude you because of; they don't matter to God. I don't mean that He doesn't care about your inadequacies, but He doesn't look at them the same way that you and everyone else look at them. The Bible says that His grace is enough for you for His power is made perfect in weakness. God doesn't see weaknesses as setbacks or reasons for exclusion. He sees them as opportunities to display His power, His sufficiency, His grace! In Christ, because of Christ, you will never not be good enough! Say what! How is that even possible? The grace of Jesus Christ is sufficient for you. You may not be enough, but your God is enough.

In Exodus chapter 3 Moses is taking care of his father-in-law's sheep and goats and in doing so one day comes to Mount Sinai. Here the angel of the LORD appears to him as a flame coming from the middle of a bush. Moses sees that the bush was on fire but isn't burning up and thinking the whole thing to be a little strange, he goes closer to see what's going on. And when he does, God speaks to him. The LORD instructs Moses to take off his sandals for the ground he was standing on was holy then He begins to tell Moses that He has heard the cries of His people and seen their distress at the hand of the Egyptians. He then says that He is sending Moses to the king of Egypt so that Moses can lead God's people out of the country. How does Moses reply? "I am nobody. How can I go to the king and bring the Israelites out of Egypt?" (Exodus 3:11 NIV). Moses didn't think he was adequate, good enough for the job God was giving him, he considered himself a nobody, but God answers, "I will be with you..." This is the key, my friend. This is the truth that completely unglues the enemy's tactic of exclusion. You see, the enemy specializes in pointing out your inadequacies and it's not hard to find people who seem to be experts in everything you're not good at. And since you know yourself better than anyone else, I'm sure it's easy for you to identify your own weaknesses as well. But even if you feel like a nobody, even if you feel completely inadequate, insufficient; God's response to you is, "I will be with you!" And because He is with you, your weaknesses, your insufficiencies, your inadequacies become nothing!

Moses continues his conversation with God by asking the LORD who he should tell the Israelites has sent him and God says, "...You must tell them: The One who is called I AM has sent me to you." (Exodus 3:14 NIV). The Hebrew word for "I AM" here is YHWH (Yahweh), the most holy written name of God in the Hebrew language according to the Jews. I don't think it's an accident that God identified Himself as "I AM" to Moses especially when Moses was feeling totally insufficient for the task at hand. My friend, God IS. He has always been and will always be, and He is self-sustaining, completely adequate all by Himself! Your weaknesses can't alter Who He is. Rather, He is so sufficient, so adequate, so abounding with competence that He is able to make you strong in your weaknesses, completely competent in your incompetency; He is able to make you enough even in those areas that you feel like a complete nobody. How does He do that? Because He, the Great I AM, is with you! Oh friend, let that bless your socks off for a minute. The next time Satan reminds you of all your weaknesses, of all your inadequacies, of all the reasons why you are not good enough; you remind him that the Great I AM is your Father and He is with you! You may not be enough, but the One who is with you will always be enough! Sufficiency is Who God is. It's what He does. He brings sufficiency with Him wherever He goes, and that same God is with you! Hallelujah!

Father,

> I thank You for Who You are. You are the Great I AM! You are completely adequate, self-sustaining, competent, and enough all by Yourself. No one and nothing could ever change that. And because of Your grace, because You are with me, I can do all things! You make up for everything that I am not. You are that awesome, that good and You are my Father. You are with me. Help me Holy Spirit to focus on Who God is and the truth that He is with me rather than focusing on my weaknesses or everything that I am not. I invite You, the Great I AM, to be with me today in Jesus's name, amen.

Day 76: I Am Full!

> *"and to know the love of Christ which surpasses knowledge, that you may be filled up to all the fullness of God."* Ephesians 3:19 NIV
>
> *"For from His fullness we have all received, grace upon grace."* John 1:16 ESV
>
> *"Then Jesus declared, 'I am the bread of life. Whoever comes to me will never go hungry, and whoever believes in me will never be thirsty."* John 6:35 NIV
>
> *"Blessed are those who hunger and thirst for righteousness, for they will be filled."* Matthew 5:6 NIV

In Christ, you are full; you are satisfied. There is no lack, no need, no emptiness that Jesus does not fill. You are full! Jesus said of Himself in John 6:35 that He is the Bread of Life. He likened Himself to bread, bread that was always available, always fresh, able to always keep you full. There's a picture of this in the Old Testament as well. Exodus 25:30 talks about the bread of the Presence or the showbread; special bread that was always present on a table in the tabernacle and later on in the temple as well. Leviticus 24:5-7 describes this bread: it was made of fine flour, baked in 12 loaves, arranged in two piles of six loaves each on a table of pure gold, covered with frankincense, and served as a memorial food offering to the LORD. The bread was only eaten by Aaron and his sons in a holy place and was set out every Sabbath day. This bread was baked fresh every Friday, set out every Sabbath, and replenished weekly so that it was always fresh. It was an invitation of God's presence, a request to have God come and dine with Aaron and his sons and ultimately with all of Israel since the priests were Israel's representatives before God and there were 12 loaves, one for each of the tribes of Israel. God gave these special ordinances to the people of Israel to ensure the fullness of His presence. Jesus is the Bread of Life! He is the fullness of God and He is yours! Whereas the priests in the Old Testament set out the bread of the Presence every week as an invitation for God to come and be with them; Jesus is the Bread and He now invites YOU to come to Him! If you have Jesus, you will never be hungry! He is the Bread of Life and always keeps you full!

Did you know that you can have as much as God as you want? Sounds too good to be true, but the Bible promises in James 4:8 that if you draw near to God, He will draw near to you. You know what this says to me? You can never have too much of God! You'll never be too hungry for Him that He isn't able and willing to satisfy you. You can draw as close to Him as you want. You can feast on the bread of His presence as much as you desire because He is the Bread of Life. He is always fresh, always available, always filling. You are not too needy for Him. He is not turned off by your desperation for Him. He brings fullness with Him wherever He goes. He is your fullness! How awesome!

In 1 Kings 17 we find the prophet Elijah directed by God to leave the place he was at and to go to the Kerith Ravine east of the Jordan River and stay there until God directs him otherwise. God instructs Elijah to drink from the brook and promises to supply him every day with food through the ravens. So, Elijah does what God directs him to do and just as the LORD promised, the ravens brought Elijah bread and meat every morning and every evening for quite some time. It's interesting to note that God chose to use the ravens to bring Elijah food every day. Ravens are one of the most restless birds in all creation. They rarely travel to the same location twice. They are wanderers and yet the LORD chose them to go to the same location every day, twice a day for an extended period just to supply Elijah with food to eat. The LORD is faithful! He brings you His fullness!

Eventually the brook dried up since there was no rain and when this happened, God directs Elijah to go to Zarephath and stay there for He had told a widow there to supply Elijah with food. So, Elijah goes and when he arrives, he sees a widow there gathering sticks. He asks her to bring him some water and a piece of bread. The widow responds by saying that she has no bread, but only a handful of flour in a jar and a little olive oil. She informs him that she's out gathering some sticks so she can go home, cook a meal for her and her son, eat and die. This woman and her son were in that desperate of a situation. She had no bread, or at least she thought that way! But the prophet tells her not to be afraid, to go home and do as she has said, but to first make him a loaf of bread. He promises that the flour will not be used up and the oil will not run dry. He basically informs her that she already has everything she needs to make bread! And he promises that bread, those supplies will not run out. Wow! She goes and does what Elijah says and the Bible tells us in verse 15 that there was food every day for Elijah and for the woman and her family. My friend, your God IS fullness! Jesus is the Bread of Life! Maybe like the widow, your situation seems rather bleak and the enemy is telling you that you have no bread, that God isn't there, that He isn't present with you. Can I tell you, the widow had everything she needed to make bread already? The flour and olive oil wouldn't satisfy her, but if she started with the little that she had, she would see and hold in her hand the tangible evidence of bread, of nourishment, of life. And God had promised to faithfully replenish her supply. May it be with you too! May you see God's presence with you even in your darkest moments and may you realize that even if God somehow seems far away that you have everything you need to invite Him back. Jesus is the Bread, He is the tangible evidence of God's presence, He is nourishment and life and if you but whisper His name, He is there. Satan is a liar! You are full because you have Jesus!

Father,

> I thank You for Jesus! I thank You that He is the Bread of Life, that He is fullness, and that my hunger is satisfied in Him; only Him. Oh, I need You more and more. I can't get enough of You, Jesus. I thank You that if I draw near to You, the Bible says that You will draw near to me. So, I come near

to You today asking You to fill me again. In You, I am full, I am satisfied, I lack nothing. Thank You, Jesus!

Day 77: I Am Understood

"For we do not have a high priest who is unable to empathize with our weaknesses, but we have one who has been tempted in every way, just as we are—yet he did not sin. Let us then approach God's throne of grace with confidence, so that we may receive mercy and find grace to help us in our time of need." Hebrews 4:15-16 NIV

"...you have searched me, LORD, and you know me." Psalm 139:1 NIV

You are understood. Someone "gets" you even if you don't "get" yourself! Sigh. Isn't that great news? What a relief! All of us want to be understood, to have someone see our hearts, appreciate what makes us tick, value why we are the way we are. God designed us with that need, the most basic emotional need of all human beings: the need to be understood. Yet why would He create you with a need that is not fully met in Him? He wouldn't. He didn't! The Bible says in Psalm 139 that He is familiar with all your ways, that He perceives your thoughts from afar. He knows what you're thinking about before you even know what you're thinking about. He's God. He's all-knowing, but what sets the Living God apart from all other religious claims is the fact that He is also all-understanding. How do I know? Because of Jesus!

In Luke 22 we find Jesus in the Garden of Gethsemane. Moments before His betrayal and the events that were surely to ensue, Jesus prays to God asking Him to remove this cup from Him. He asked God to save Him from what He was about to go through, to deliver Him from the need to go to the Cross, to find some other way to reconcile the world to Him. Yet even considering all Jesus was about to endure, He prays that God's will would be done as oppose to His own. Wow! Jesus surrendered His will to the Father.

A surrendering of your will to God brings peace. You have the power to surrender your will, what you want, what you think is best to God. And to be sure, this is not always easy to do, but Jesus modeled this well. The Bible says that He was in anguish, torment, distress. He was praying earnestly, sincerely, intently with everything He had. He was sweating drops of blood! Perhaps you can identify with being in distress and crying out to God with everything you have, but I doubt any of us have experienced the extent of anguish that Jesus felt that caused His body to literally sweat drops of blood. That's some intense emotional pain! Yet after He surrenders His will to the Father, God sends an angel from heaven to strengthen Him.

Oh friend, you do not have a high priest, a leader, a Savior, a God who is unable to empathize with your weaknesses. Rather, you have One who understands, One Who identifies with your weaknesses because according to Hebrews 4:15, He was tempted in every way just like you, yet was without sin. You have a God Who "gets" you. He didn't just create you and knows you as one of His works. He isn't just your Father who now knows you intimately as His child. He is your friend, a trusted confidant because He chose to walk where you walk. He understands not just because He's God and He knows everything, but because He personally experienced it first-hand Himself even though He didn't have to. That's love. That's goodness. That's incredible! How dare Satan ever tell you that you don't matter to God or that God doesn't understand! Tell Satan to shut his big, fat, ugly mouth because nothing could be further from the truth! He understands much more than you realize. He doesn't just know what's going on; He empathizes with you about what's going on. You have His heart! He knows your pain; personally, thoroughly, to a greater extent than you could ever imagine. That's why the Bible says in Psalm 34:18 that He is near to the brokenhearted. His heart is soft towards you especially when you feel broken, crushed, hurt. He is not disgusted, repulsed, turned away from your pain. He is tender to it. He is near! What other god is like Him? No one! You are understood, my friend! Jesus will always be proof that God understands you!

Father,

> I thank You for being such an awesome God. You amaze me and astound me. I'm blown away by Your goodness, by Your love, by Your heart. Thank You for understanding me, for "getting" me, for knowing me so well. Thank You for not just

having knowledge about me, but for truly understanding me because of Jesus. Holy Spirit, help me to remember that God is with me, is near me, empathizes with me. I can run to You, LORD, because You understand what I'm going through, what I'm feeling. May You always have my heart. Let it be so LORD in Jesus's name, amen.

Day 78: I Am Christ's Ambassador

"We are therefore Christ's ambassadors, as though God were making his appeal through us. We implore you on Christ's behalf: Be reconciled to God." 2 Corinthians 5:20 NIV

"Therefore, be imitators of God, as beloved children. And walk in love, as Christ loved us and gave himself up for us, a fragrant offering and sacrifice to God." Ephesians 5:1-2 NIV

You are Christ's ambassador, His representative, His spokesperson. Jesus isn't physically on the earth anymore. Romans 8:34 tells us that Jesus died, rose to life, and is now at the right hand of God interceding for us. Jesus is in heaven. Yet before Jesus ascends into heaven, He tells His disciples in John 14:16-17 that He will ask the Father to give them another advocate, another supporter, another helper to be with them forever, the Holy Spirit of the Living God. Jesus says that the world cannot accept the Holy Spirit because the world doesn't see Him or know Him, but Jesus says you will know the Holy Spirit for He lives with you and will be in you. You have God's Spirit with you, and He is in you helping you to represent Christ, to imitate God, to walk in love so that when others look at you they see an accurate picture of Jesus.

An ambassador from the United States is often formally addressed in relation to his/her title as an ambassador. For example, if the representative's name is Bob Smith, the representative would be addressed even in casual conversations, even in foreign lands, as "Ambassador Smith". His being an ambassador seems to go beyond just a job title or what he does for a living and translates into his identity. He doesn't just identify himself by that title.

Proper social etiquette requires others to identify him by that title as well. He is an ambassador, a representative, a spokesperson for the United States. When those from another country look at him, listen to him, they are seeing and hearing an accurate picture of the American people. At least, this is the hope. The same is true for you, my friend.

When you made Jesus your LORD and Savior, your citizenship translated into heaven. Your nationality is now in heaven with Jesus, but He has officially made you His ambassador, His representative here. Representing Him isn't just something He's told you to do. It isn't just your duty or your job. Being His representative is part of who you are in Him! It's your identity! And the currency, the proper social etiquette for representing Christ in this world is His love. Ephesians 5 encourages you to imitate God as a child would imitate their mother/father and to walk in love as Christ loved you and gave Himself up for you. Because the Holy Spirit is now in you, Jesus can love other people through you. How cool is that! It's Christ's love through you that connects people to Jesus. Jesus loved you enough to give up His life for you so that now you can show your love for Him by giving up your life to let Him love other people through you. Wow! The love of Christ in you makes you an accurate representative of Jesus!

In Acts 8 an angel of the LORD tells Philip, one of the leaders of the early church, to go to the south towards a road that goes from Jerusalem to Gaza. Not knowing exactly why, Philip obeys and finds an Ethiopian eunuch, a court official of the Ethiopian queen Candace who oversaw all her treasure. This eunuch had come to Jerusalem to worship and was returning, sitting in his chariot, reading the prophet Isaiah, but didn't understand what he was reading. So, the Spirit tells Philip to go and join this man in his chariot. Philip runs to him and hears him reading the prophet Isaiah and simply asks the man if he understands what he's reading. The Holy Spirit told Philip to go to this eunuch! That's what the Spirit does. He's with you, He's in you, He talks to you! And the Bible says that upon hearing this from the Spirit, Philip runs to the man. He obeys quickly, earnestly, he catches a glimpse of God's heart for this eunuch and races to him. Only love causes you to run towards someone! The man basically says no, that he doesn't understand what he's reading then he invites Philip to come, sit with him, and explain the Scriptures to him. Philip does and upon hearing the good news of Jesus Christ, the eunuch decides to get baptized, so Philip baptizes him. Philip was Jesus's representative that day to this Ethiopian eunuch, a man who needed direction, clarity, help. God saw him sitting in his chariot, a wealthy man, but one who was lost and searching for answers and probably frustrated. So, God sends him Philip to represent Him so that by the Holy Spirit, that eunuch could have an encounter with Jesus. My friend, there are people everywhere in need of an encounter with Jesus and God has decided to make YOU His representative, His ambassador. He has decided to send you! And the fact that God could use such a fragile jar of clay to showcase His treasure, His power absolutely brings glory to His name. Praise God, you are His ambassador!

Father,

> I thank You for making me Your representative, Your ambassador. What a privilege, what an honor! Thank You for choosing to house the treasure of Your power in my fragile, clay jar to show Your glory. If You can speak through a donkey, You can surely use me! Thank You Jesus! Would You help me Holy Spirit to represent Christ well, to showcase His love to this world? Give me Your eyes for people LORD, Your heart, let me be Your hands and Your feet. May it all be to the praise and glory of Your great name in Jesus's name, amen.

Day 79: I Overflow with Hope

"Praise be to the God and Father of our LORD Jesus Christ! In his great mercy he has given us new birth into a living hope through the resurrection of Jesus Christ from the dead, and into an inheritance that can never perish, spoil, or fade. This inheritance is kept in heaven for you, who through faith are shielded by God's power until the coming of the salvation that is ready to be revealed in the last time." 1 Peter 1:3-5 NIV

"You will be secure, because there is hope; you will look about you and take your rest in safety. You will lie down, with no

> *one to make you afraid, and many will court your favor."* Job 11:18-19 NIV

> *"May the God of hope fill you with all joy and peace as you trust in him, so that you may overflow with hope by the power of the Holy Spirit."* Romans 15:13 NIV

There is hope. You have hope. Jesus is hope! God is a god of hope! The message of Jesus Christ is not gloom, doom, and despair; it is a message of hope! There is expectancy, something to look forward to, and anticipation with God. In His great mercy, He has given you new birth into a living hope through Jesus. You now have an inheritance that can never perish, spoil, or fade, but is kept safe in heaven for you. Through Jesus, you have been born again into a living hope. Hallelujah! My friend, Satan is so, so negative. Have you noticed how negative he is? Every word, every scheme, everything he does and represents is so unconstructive and depressing. He brings negativity, darkness, disaster, and despair with him everywhere he goes. He has nothing to do with hope. In fact, he tries very hard to convince you that there is no hope. But I pray that the God of hope would fill you with all joy and all peace as you trust in Him, so that you may overflow with hope by the power of the Holy Spirit. You are secure, unshaken, safe, protected because there is hope! And there is hope because there is Jesus!

When Jesus walked this earth, He brought hope with Him to seemingly hopeless situations. Just His presence, His touch, His word caused possibility to spring up in the middle of impossible circumstances. When Jesus walked into a room, a life, a location every hopeless situation ceased to exist. Why? Because He is hope! In John 11 we find the familiar story of Lazarus, a friend of Jesus who was very sick and dies as a result. Verse 17 tells us that when Jesus arrived in Bethany, He finds that Lazarus had already been in the tomb for four days. Lazarus wasn't still on his sick bed; he was already dead. There was no heartbeat, no breath, seemingly no opportunity for him to get well. And it wasn't as if he had just died either. The Bible says that he had been in the tomb, in the grave for four days. That's 96 hours! That's a long time for the stench of death to set in, for there to be no sign of life, no possibility of healing. I'm sure Lazarus' sisters, Mary and Martha, were hit with the finality of the whole thing. Their brother was dead. He was gone. How could there be hope for anything different? Then Jesus shows up! Martha goes out to meet Jesus and says, "LORD, if you had been here, my brother would not have died."

(John 11:21 NIV). She knew that Jesus had the power to heal her brother, but Lazarus was dead; what could be done now? Jesus tells Martha, "Your brother will rise again," (John 11:23 NIV), and Martha assumes He is talking about in the resurrection at the last day. Martha certainly had that assurance, but Jesus completely takes hope to a whole new level when He says, "I am the resurrection and the life. The one who believes in me will live, even though they die, and whoever lives by believing in me will never die. Do you believe this?" (John 11:25 NIV). After this conversation with Martha, Jesus goes on to raise Lazarus from the dead in the sight of all who had gathered there.

My friend, I don't know what you're going through or how hopeless your situation may feel to you. I know life is hard so I am in no way downplaying what has happened or what may be happening right now. But regardless to how "dead", how hopeless things may be for you, I invite Jesus to show up, to walk into the room with you. Jesus is the resurrection and the life! He is hope! Resurrection, life, hope come with Him wherever He goes because that's Who He is! Hopeless situations come to an end in His presence because He is hope! He is life! He revitalizes, refreshes, restores, resurrects because that's Who He is! Though something may be impossible for you, impossible with man; nothing is impossible with God!

Father,

> I thank You for Jesus. I thank You that He is the resurrection and the life. I thank You that He is hope, that I have hope because You are a God of hope! Nothing is impossible with You, LORD! I'm sorry for being so negative, for having such a pessimistic outlook on things. I don't want to be like Satan. I want to be like You. So, help me Holy Spirit to overflow with hope by Your power. Jesus, I invite You to walk into my room, my situation, my life because I know that every hopeless situation ceases to exist in Your presence. May it be so in my life in Jesus's name, amen.

⤙⤚

Day 80: I Am Necessary

"For the body does not consist of one member but of many." 1 Corinthians 12:14 ESV

"Are not two sparrows sold for a penny? And not one of them will fall to the ground apart from your Father. But even the hairs of your head are all numbered. Fear not, therefore; you are of more value than many sparrows." Matthew 10:29-31 NIV

You are necessary! Let's be real: God doesn't need you in order to be God. He isn't reliant upon you. He doesn't depend upon you for anything. He is God; completely self-sufficient, but He does choose you. He chooses to love you. He chooses to use you, but you absolutely have a say in the matter. You don't have to love Him, serve Him, listen to Him, or obey Him. You aren't being forced, coerced, or manipulated into God's will or plan for your life. If you decide to do your own thing apart from God, He will let you and He'll find some other way to accomplish the purposes He created your life to accomplish. He's God. He can do anything. He isn't dependent upon anyone. That shouldn't be offensive or make you feel excluded; rather, it absolutely relieves you of the pressure of handling everything yourself. You will never be as good as God at being God because you were never intended to be in that role. He is good at being God all by Himself.

With that being said, you are necessary, indispensable, irreplaceable. How do I know? Because you are the only you that has ever existed or will ever exist. You're it. There is no other! There wasn't another you in a previous life that was somehow recreated with your body nor will your soul take residence in another life-form after you die. The Bible says, "It's appointed unto man once to die and after that to face judgment." (Hebrews 9:27 KJV). There's only one of you, my friend; just one. And maybe that doesn't seem like a big deal but consider this for a moment. You are made up of billions and billions of tiny cells. Each cell has its own size and shape and is suited for a job in your body. Within every cell are strands of DNA. Your cells read this DNA code to determine what they should do. Your DNA contains all the information needed to build your body, to give you the appearance that you have, to broadcast your personality to the world. You receive your DNA from your parents who received it from their parents and so forth back to the very beginning of your lineage. So, the prediction of which combination of genes will transpire in a prospective child is virtually impossible.

God designed you fearfully, wonderfully, meticulously in such a way that there has never been another person who looks exactly like you, acts exactly like you, has your identical personality nor will there ever be. You are that original! There are approximately 7 billion people on the planet right now not counting all those who have lived previously or who will live long after you are gone. None of them are you! That makes you irreplaceable, valuable, and necessary!

In Exodus 2 Moses is born in Egypt and is hidden for three months by his parents; his parents who were Israelite slaves. Pharaoh had recently told the midwives to put all the Israelite boys born to death since the Hebrew slave population was getting too big. Pharaoh feared they might rally together and revolt and there would be too many of them for him to stop. These were the conditions Moses was born into; a situation in which more people wanted him dead than those who wanted him alive. Yet his mom saw that he was a fine child, so she hides him. I'm not sure how she managed to do that, but when she couldn't hide him any longer, she places him in a basket and sends him down the Nile River and follows him to see where he would end up. Turns out, Moses is found by Pharaoh's daughter and is raised in Pharaoh's house as royalty. This Moses was the one who would later be sent by God to lead His people out of Egypt, out of slavery, to the Promised Land. Seems like quite a few coincidences or random occurrences to me. God created Moses and chose to use him to lead His people out of slavery even though Moses wasn't eloquent of speech, he was just another slave, who grew up under a guise of royalty and experienced a crisis of identity when the only family he knew kicked him out of the country. To be sure if Moses would have refused to do what God asked him to, God would have rose up another or found some other way to lead His people out of Egypt. His purposes weren't contingent upon Moses, but that doesn't mean that Moses wasn't necessary. God could have accomplished His purposes some other way, but there was no other Moses. The same is true for you, my friend. God doesn't necessarily need you to be God, but that doesn't mean that you aren't necessary. You absolutely are because there isn't another YOU!

Father,

I thank You for being so awesome, so big, so vast. You don't need me to be God, but you absolutely choose me. Thank You for creating me fearfully and wonderfully as the original self that I am. Only You could do that! Help me Holy Spirit to know that I am necessary simply because I am the only me that there has ever been or will ever be. May all the purposes You have created me for come to pass in my life in Jesus's name, amen.

Day 81: I Am Born of God!

"No one who is born of God will continue to sin, because God's seed remains in them; they cannot go on sinning, because they have been born of God." 1 John 5:18 NIV

"For everyone born of God overcomes the world. This is the victory that has overcome the world, even our faith." 1 John 5:4 NIV

"But as many as received him, to them gave he power to become the sons of God, even to them that believe on his name: which were born, not of blood, nor of the will of the flesh, nor of the will of man, but of God." John 1:12-13 NIV

You are born of God; not just of the will of the flesh or the will of man, but of God because He wanted you as His child. Think about that for a second. God in His great mercy provided Jesus so that you might be born of Him. You are not trash, junk, the black sheep of the family, or some unwanted life to God. God is many things, but 1 John says, "...God is love." (1 John 4:8 NIV). You have been born of Him; therefore, you are born of love.

Your faith in Jesus Christ, believing on His name has given you the power to become a child of God. You are born of God and you don't continue to willfully sin because God's seed remains in you. That is a holy, righteous, set-apart seed. You have been born of God and you overcome the world, you overcome sin, you overcome the enemy. You are born of something greater, something better, something much more remarkable than anything you could find in the richest royalty of this world. You are born of God! Revelation gives us a glimpse of the New Jerusalem's splendor, "The twelve gates were twelve pearls, each gate made of a single pearl. The great street of the city was of gold, as pure as transparent glass." (Revelation 21:21 NIV). Pearls are a sign of wealth, they are valuable, they are precious, and the most expensive ones have few to no blemishes. It might cost you roughly $20,000 to buy a pearl bracelet made with freshwater pearls. Yet in the New Jerusalem described in the Bible, the twelve gates of the city are made of pearls. Pearls must be incredibly plentiful because the Word of God says that each gate is made from a SINGLE pearl. Wow! Not only so, but the streets in that great city are also paved in gold as pure as transparent glass. This tells me that there must be a lot of gold to have enough to pave all the streets with it. Yet God isn't somehow hoarding the wealth in heaven. No way! He's sharing it with you, with me, with everyone in heaven! He's so bountiful, so gracious, so full of love and goodness and mercy He has paved the streets He walks on, the streets you will one day walk on with Him with pure gold. How awesome! God is rich, my friend! "The silver is mine and the gold is mine, declares the LORD Almighty." (Haggai 2:8 NIV). It all belongs to God and you have been born of Him! You are born of wealth, born of royalty, born of class, of importance. You are born of mercy, born of grace, born of love. You are born of God! Satan should be afraid. He should be very afraid because you are born of the greatest, most powerful, living God that has ever been and will ever be. You are born of God and you will overcome this world, you will overcome the enemy! You will inherit glory and hear your Father say, "well done."

Jesus told a parable in Matthew 25 of a man going on a long journey that called his servants and entrusted his wealth to them. To one he gave five bags of gold, to another he gave two bags, and to still another he gave one bag according to their ability. While the master was on his journey, the servant with five bags went at once and put his money to work and gained five more bags. The one with two bags did likewise and gained two more bags. But the servant with one bag went and dug a hole in the ground and hid his master's money. The Bible says that a long time later the master returns to settle accounts with his servants. He reprimands the servant who did nothing with the money his master gave to him; but to each of the ones who put their master's money to work he says, "Well done, good and faithful servant! You have been faithful with a few things; I will put you in charge of many things. Come and share in your master's happiness!" (Matthew 25:23 NIV). There are many applications of this parable, but one thing that is evident is that the master in this story is a picture of God. And God says to those servants who were faithful to steward, to share what He had given them, "Well done." In other words, the master said, "I'm proud of you." How incredible to hear God, your Father, your Creator, the One who holds the universe in His hands tell you that He's proud of you. That is awesome! Oh, how I long to hear those words from Him one day!

Father,

> I thank You that I am born of You because of Jesus. Thank You for being my Father. I thank You that because I am Your child I am born of wealth, of royalty, of mercy, of love. I am born of God. Holy Spirit help me to remember who I am in Christ. May my ears be sealed to hear only Your voice, Your song being sung over me. I am born of You, God, and I will overcome in Jesus's name, amen.

Day 82: I Am Empowered!

> *"But you will receive power when the Holy Spirit comes on you; and you will be my witnesses in Jerusalem, and in all Judea and Samaria, and to the ends of the earth."* Acts 1:8 NIV

> *"Flesh gives birth to flesh, but the Spirit gives birth to spirit. You should not be surprised at my saying, 'you must be born again.' The wind blows wherever it pleases. You hear its sound, but you cannot tell where it comes from or where it is going. So it is with everyone born of the Spirit."* John 3:6-8 NIV

> *"When the day of Pentecost came, they were all together in one place. Suddenly a sound like the blowing of a violent wind came*

> *from heaven and filled the whole house where they were sitting. They saw what seemed to be tongues of fire that separated and came to rest on each of them. All of them were filled with the Holy Spirit and began to speak in other tongues as the Spirit enabled them."* Acts 2:1-4 NIV

You have received, you will receive POWER when the Holy Spirit comes on you. You are not weak, afraid, timid, puny, or pathetic. Not if the Holy Spirit is on you. You are empowered! God is powerful. He is mighty, strong; nothing can stand against Him. He speaks and things are established; created. His words are powerful. Everything you see, all of creation was made because He spoke it into existence. "For he (God) spoke, and it came to be; he commanded, and it stood firm." (Psalm 33:9 NIV). There are over three trillion trees in the world today; that is roughly 400 trees for every human. And each tree is unique, original even among its own kind. The amazing thing is that before the advent of agriculture, the earth had twice as many trees as it does today. That is A LOT of trees! God spoke and boom the earth was covered in trees; trees of different types and shapes and sizes; trees that varied greatly even among the same family. Trees created to withstand and flourish in the environment in which they were established. That is detailed, that is powerful, that is awesome! And God did this for all His creation. Oh friend, we so underestimate the grandeur of our God. He is powerful! Just a word changes everything! His presence changes everything! His Spirit brings power!

The Bible references the Spirit of the LORD coming upon many different people at many different times. In Judges 14:6 the Spirit of the LORD came upon David with power when he was still very young, out tending his father's sheep and he tears a lion apart with his bare hands. What? In 1 Samuel 10:6, Samuel prophesies to Saul that the Spirit of the LORD will come upon Saul in power and he will join with the procession of prophets and prophesy with them and he will be changed into a different man. The Spirit of the LORD came upon Ezekiel in Ezekiel 37 and he finds himself in the middle of a valley of dry bones, a valley that was soon to become the birthing place of a mighty army. The Holy Spirit came upon Mary in Luke 1:35 with power and she conceives the holy One, Jesus inside of her womb. Say what? The Spirit of the LORD came upon Othniel in Judges 3:10 so that he became Israel's judge and overpowered the enemy. The Spirit of the LORD is powerful! All throughout the Bible, people found themselves in difficult places, impossible situations, they were ordinary, weak, frail human beings just like the rest of us. Then the Spirit of the LORD would come upon them and amazing, unexplainable, powerful things would happen as a result. What was the difference; what changed? The Spirit of the LORD came!

My friend, I don't know what the facts of your life may be telling you right now. Maybe the facts say that a lion is standing in front of you, poised to take you out. You have no weapon, nothing on your person to protect yourself, to stop this lion that by all logical accounts is stronger and more powerful than you. Maybe the facts say that you're too young, too old, too unlearned, too inexperienced to have anything extraordinary happen in your life. Maybe the facts say that the enemy has come against you, surrounded you, attacked you, and invaded your territory with a strong force. Maybe the facts say that this whole thing is just a bit too risky; a risk of your safety, your reputation, your life. Maybe the facts say that you're in the middle of a valley of dry bones; a valley of death, of hopelessness, of loss. Maybe the facts say that your title, your identity, your job description doesn't include being a prophet, that you don't have the training, the background, the pedigree to hear from God and prophesy. That it's reserved for certain people, the few, the chosen, the elect, but not you. Maybe the facts say that you're already well into your life, you're already established, you already have a good thing going for you. You're not sure you can change or even if you want to change. Regardless to what the facts are saying, the truth says that the Spirit of the LORD brings you power! In all the instances referenced above, when the Spirit of God came upon these people everything changed! By the Spirit of the LORD you can rip that lion apart with your bare hands; limb by limb, tear that thing apart! By the Spirit of the LORD you can say "yes" to what God wants to accomplish in your life regardless to how crazy it sounds or appears; regardless to what it costs you! By the Spirit of the LORD you, the unlikeliest of candidates, can join with the procession of prophets and prophesy! By the Spirit of God, you can be a changed man, a changed woman; you'll never be the same again! By the Spirit of the LORD you can go out against the enemy and overpower him! By the Spirit of the LORD you can risk it all for Jesus! By the Spirit of the LORD you can prophesy to those dry bones and watch as God breathes His breath and transforms a lifeless assortment of bones into a mighty army of warriors. May the Spirit of the LORD come upon you today in power! I hear the sound like the blowing of a mighty wind. I don't know where it comes from or where it is going, but when it comes, everything changes. Hallelujah, you are empowered!

Father,

I thank You for Your Spirit, for Your power, for Your word. You are an awesome God, a powerful God, an uncontainable God. Forgive me, LORD, for all the ways I have shrunk You down to fit inside of my understanding when you blow my understanding right out the window. Spirit of God, come. Like these people in the Bible who had Your Spirit come on them in power, I invite You to come upon me. I want more, LORD. More of You. Blow my mind. Speak a word. Show up suddenly, like a mighty wind and change everything. You are God whether I give you permission to be or not, yet here I am surrendering to You. Come, LORD, in Jesus's name, amen.

Day 83: I Am a Doer of the Word

"Do not merely listen to word, and so deceive yourselves. Do what it says. Anyone who listens to the word but does not do what it says is like someone who looks at his face in a mirror and, after looking at himself, goes away and immediately forgets what he looks like. But whoever looks intently into the perfect law that gives freedom and continues in it—not forgetting what they have heard, but doing it—they will be blessed in what they do." James 1:22-25 NIV

"What good is it, my brothers and sisters, if someone claims to have faith but has no deeds? Can such faith save them? Suppose a brother or a sister is without clothes and daily food. If one of you says to them, 'Go in peace, keep warm and well fed,' but does nothing about their physical needs, what good is it? In the same way, faith by itself, if it is not accompanied by action, is dead." James 2:14-17 NIV

If you want to turn your life upside down, read the book of James in the Bible every day for like a month. It's full of those "all up in your face" kind of messages. This first Scripture reference from James admonishes you to be a doer of the word and not just a hearer only. There are a lot of "hearers of the Word". With all the technology available at our fingertips, people have access to church services and sermons twenty-four-seven. However, James says that anyone who listens to the Word of God but doesn't do what it says is like someone who after looking at his face in a mirror, walks away and immediately forgets what he looks like. This tells me that the Bible is comparable to a mirror. What is the purpose of a mirror except to give us an accurate reflection of what we look like? Yet if you're looking in a mirror and then walk away and you can't seem to remember what you were wearing or if you had brushed your hair or you can't seem to tell if the person staring back at you is actually you or someone else then something is either wrong with you or wrong with your mirror. The Bible requires you to investigate it intently and to do what it says for you to better grasp who you really are.

Not only so, but this second Scripture referenced from James claims that faith without works, without action is dead. That's a bold statement to make, but the example the Bible gives for this is brilliant. If someone comes to you without any clothes or food to eat and all you do is pray for them or tell them to go in peace and keep warm and well fed but you've done nothing to feed them or clothe them, then what good is your faith, your prayer, your blessing? Talk about getting all up in your face real fast! A few verses later in James 2 says, "You believe that there is one God. Good! Even the demons believe that--and shudder." (James 2:19 NIV). According to the Bible, it is not enough just to believe in God. What are you doing as a result? Faith is best spelled r, i, s, k because faith, real faith, the kind of faith that sets you apart from the demons requires action. Whew. Take a breath. I told you the book of James doesn't mess around. I'm guessing James was one of those "radical" kinds of Christians.

In Matthew 25 beginning in verse 31, Jesus talks about separating the sheep from the goats at the end of the age. The sheep, His sheep will go on His right and all the goats, all those who don't know Him will go on His left. The King, Jesus, will say to those on His right, "Come, you who are blessed by my Father; take your inheritance, the kingdom prepared for you since the creation of the world. For I was hungry and you gave me something to eat, I was thirsty and you gave me something to drink, I was a stranger and you invited me in, I needed clothes and you clothed me, I was sick and you looked after me, I was in prison and you came to visit me." (Matthew 25:34-36 NIV). The righteous will answer in essence, "LORD, when did we see you in these conditions and do these things for you?" And Jesus will answer, "Whatever you did for one of the least of these brothers and sisters of mine, you did for me." (Matthew 25:40 NIV). Wow! It takes risk to love people who may not be able to love you very well in return. It takes risk to give what you have to someone who could never repay you. It takes risk to invite someone in, a stranger into your home, your family, your life. It takes risk to stop and notice people, to care for them and their needs especially when they don't look like you, smell like you, or sit in the same social circles as you do. But the Bible says, Jesus said that whatever you do for others in this way, you do for Him. That is risky! That is powerful! It takes risk to be a doer of the Word!

Father,

> Thank You for Your Word that is alive and active and sharper than any double-edged sword. Help me, Holy Spirit, to be a doer of the Word and not just a hearer only. I don't want to walk away from Your Word and immediately forget what I look like. Rather, I want to look intently into Your Word even if what I see reflected in myself is kind of ugly so that Your Word can transform me. Give me Your eyes for people, Your heart in Jesus's name, amen.

Day 84: I Am Renewed

> *"Therefore, we do not lose heart. Though outwardly we are wasting away, yet inwardly we are being renewed day by day."* 2 Corinthians 4:16 NIV

> *"I pray that out of his glorious riches he may strengthen you with power through his Spirit in your inner being,"* Ephesians 3:16 NIV

> *"but they who wait for the LORD shall renew their strength; they shall mount up with wings like eagles; they shall run and not be weary; they shall walk and not faint."* Isaiah 40:31 NIV

You are being renewed by the power of the Holy Spirit in your inner being. And this renewal is happening day by day. Isn't that awesome? Outwardly you might still be wasting away. That's life, but don't lose heart because inwardly you are being renewed, rehabilitated; improved every single day. Isaiah promises that those who wait upon the LORD will renew their strength. They will mount up with wings like eagles. They will run and not grow weary. They will walk and not faint. You don't have to be discouraged. You don't have to be weary. Jesus invites you in Matthew 11:28 to come to Him if you are weary and burdened and He will give you rest. You can exchange your strength for the strength of the LORD. You can trade in your run down, tired, drained strength for that of the LORD's. That is awesome!

There's a "tired" that has little to do with how much physical rest you've had and is more a deep weariness of the heart, the soul. A feeling of being zapped, drained, discouraged, defeated. Maybe the enemy has been telling you just how wore out you are. Maybe you've been serving the LORD for a long time and you're just tired. Maybe you feel like no one notices the good that you've been doing or trying to do. The Bible encourages us, "Let us not become weary in doing good, for at the proper time we will reap a harvest if we do not give up." (Galatians 6:9 NIV). Don't give up, my friend! You will reap a harvest! You will renew your strength! You will soar with the eagles! You will have your inner being strengthened by the power of the Holy Spirit! Come to Jesus and you will find rest!

In Ezekiel 43, we find that Ezekiel has been communing with a heavenly messenger from God, an angel. He sees a vision of a temple and the angel goes with him to measure the temple. For several chapters, Ezekiel is doing the behind-the-scenes job of measuring walls and altars and outer courts. Then in chapter 43, the glory of God comes. His voice was like the roar of rushing waters to Ezekiel and the land was radiant with His glory. The glory of God enters the temple and fills it and Ezekiel goes from conversing with one of God's messengers to speaking directly with God, Himself. The Bible says that God's glory suddenly showed up and filled the temple so much so that Ezekiel ends up on his face in God's presence. My friend, God is good at suddenly showing up, abruptly, unexpectedly, rapidly filling us with His glory. What if Ezekiel hadn't been willing to measure the temple, hadn't been faithful in what God had given him to do? I wonder if Ezekiel would have missed God's glory suddenly showing up in the temple if he wasn't already ministering in the temple. There is strength in God's presence; hope, encouragement, refreshment, renewal. Don't let the enemy discourage you. Don't give up when it comes to living for Jesus. Stay faithful. Stay in the temple and wait for God's glory to suddenly appear. "In the last days, God says, I will pour out my Spirit on all people. Your sons and daughters will prophesy, your young men will see visions, your old men will dream dreams." (Acts 2:17 NIV).

Father,

> I thank You for Your Spirit. Thank You for renewal, for strength, for refreshing me with Your presence. Thank You that I am being renewed day by day. I invite You to come LORD. Let Your glory suddenly show up at my house, at my church, at my job, among my family. Strengthen me today, Holy Spirit. Renew me and refresh me in a tangible, evident way I pray in Jesus's name, amen.

Day 85: I Am Full of Joy

> *"The prospect of the righteous is joy, but the hopes of the wicked come to nothing."* Proverbs 10:28 NIV

> *"Though you have not seen him (God), you love him; and even though you do not see him now, you believe in him and are filled with an inexpressible and glorious joy, for you are receiving the end result of your faith, the salvation of your souls."* 1 Peter 1:8-9 NIV

> *"I tell you that in the same way there will be more rejoicing in heaven over one sinner who repents than over ninety-nine righteous persons who do not need to repent."* Luke 15:7 NIV

You have been given joy! You are full of joy! I understand; life isn't always that joyful. There certainly are joyful moments for sure, but the whole of it can be rather difficult sometimes. Your happiness may come and go, but the joy you have should always remain. Though you have never seen God, you've decided to love Him because He first loved you. And even though you don't see Him right now, you believe in Him. You are receiving the result of your faith which is the salvation of your soul. This should fill you with an inexpressible and glorious joy. Did you catch that? That's where your joy comes from. It isn't contingent upon how many followers you have on social media. It has nothing to do with how much money you have in your bank account or what you do for a living. Your joy isn't wrapped up in finding the next thrill or accomplishing something you've always wanted to accomplish. All these things can bring you enjoyment, but your true joy is found in the reality that you have received the end result of your faith; God in His amazing grace has saved your soul!

We've already established that Jesus has made you the righteousness of God and the verse above in Proverbs says that the prospect, the outlook, the viewpoint of the righteous is joy. My friend, can I ask you what is your outlook on life? What does your view of things tend to be? If you are a child of God, then your prospect according to the Bible should be joy. Satan is always trying to distract you from the things of God. He's always trying to keep your mind down here instead of on things above. He wants your view to be pessimistic, negative, and cynical just like his. Yet God's presence brings joy. One of the fruits of the Spirit listed in Galatians 5:22-23 is joy. One of the byproducts of walking closely with the LORD is joy. I'm guessing there's going to be a lot of joy in heaven. In fact, the Bible says in the Scripture listed above from Luke that there's more rejoicing in heaven over one sinner who repents. Heaven throws a party whenever one person gives their life to Jesus. Heaven is a place of rejoicing; a place of joy. Why? Because God's presence is there!

In Nehemiah chapter 8, the children of Israel had recently returned from captivity to rebuild their city. Ezra, the teacher of the Law gathered the people together in one place and began to read from the book of the Law of Moses. Upon hearing the Word of God, the people responded by worshiping and praising the LORD. Verse six says that they bowed down and worshiped the LORD with their faces to the ground. That's the power of the Word of God, the presence of God. It often pierces our hearts and brings us to a position of humility before the LORD. Then in verse ten Nehemiah commemorates the day as being holy and he tells the people not to grieve for the joy of the

LORD is their strength. My friend, life is too difficult to make happiness anything but fleeting. Yet there are some truths that life cannot alter, that the enemy cannot change. You have received the salvation of your soul! That is reason enough to have an inexpressible, glorious joy every single day. So, if you feel down today. If the enemy is taunting you with depression or despair or discouragement, then let me encourage you that the joy of the LORD is your strength! Your joy comes from the salvation of your soul and that joy gives you power. May you have a prospect of joy!

Father,

> I thank You for the salvation of my soul through Jesus. I thank You that for this reason alone I have an inexpressible, glorious joy. Forgive me for not having an outlook of joy. Forgive me for being so negative and pessimistic when I have received the result of my faith. Holy Spirit, come and fill me with joy. Let it spring up like a well deep inside of me, the joy of Your presence, and may it ever be my strength in Jesus's name, amen.

Day 86: I Am a Partaker of the Divine Nature

> *"His (God) divine power has granted to us all things that pertain to life and godliness, through the knowledge of him who called us to his own glory and excellence, by which he has granted to us his precious and very great promises, so that through them you may become partakers of the divine nature, having escaped from the corruption that is in the world because of sinful desire."*
> 2 Peter1:3-4 ESV

God has divine power! And from that He has granted you all things that pertain to life and godliness. Pause right there for a second. Everything that is relevant to giving you life and to making you godly is from Him. The LORD wants you to thrive, He wants you to truly live, not just exist and He wants you to be holy like Him. The more in relationship with Him you are, the more alive you will become and the more holy you will be. Holiness is not following a set of rules and guidelines without fault. It has little to do with duty and obligation and more to do with relationship, with desiring God and being close to Him more than you desire anything else. The LORD has granted you His precious and very great promises that through them you may become a partaker of the divine nature. You were meant to participate in the divine nature, to act like, to live like someone who's already in heaven even though you're still here on earth; to have the character of a person who lives in the glory of God's presence every single day, where sin isn't even an option anymore because it is so contrary to your nature. How is that even possible? Because God has given you His precious and very great promises!

You were made for ever-increasing glory! "And we all, who with unveiled faces contemplate the Lord's glory, are being transformed into his image with ever-increasing glory, which comes from the Lord, who is the Spirit." (2 Corinthians 3:18 NIV). As you think on, ponder, consider, reflect upon, chew over the LORD's glory you are being transformed into His image. That's what His glory does. It transforms you, changes you, makes you more and more a partaker of His nature because anything contrary to His nature can't endure the power of His glory. And it's all done with ever-increasing glory which comes from the LORD who is the Spirit. God's glory doesn't run out, doesn't diminish, or decrease in any way. It is limitless, measureless, always increasing. His glory is awesome; a taste of His glory leaves you with an appetite for more of that glory. That's Who He is. That's what you've been called to so don't settle, my friend, for where you are right now. Don't let the enemy convince you to be complacent with how close you are to God, that you have your whole life to get more serious about God. That is a lie! James 4:14 asks what is your life? You are a mist that appears for a little while then vanishes. Your life is like a mist that is here today and gone tomorrow so if there's ever a time to draw close to God, it's right now!

In 1 Kings 19 we find the prophet Elijah had just fled from Queen Jezebel and finds himself hiding out in a cave. When he's questioned by the LORD as to what he's doing there, Elijah says how he's the only one left who's trying to serve God and that they're trying to kill him too. In response to this, God tells Elijah to go out and stand on the mountainside for the LORD's presence is about to pass by. Notice that God's answer for feeling alone, for feeling defeated, for dealing with the threat of the enemy is to get in His presence.

So, Elijah goes and stands on the mountainside and a great and powerful wind tears the mountain apart and shatters the rocks, but the Bible says that the LORD wasn't in the wind. Then there was an earthquake, but God wasn't in the earthquake and there was also a fire, but the LORD wasn't in the fire either. Finally, after the fire there was a gentle whisper and when Elijah heard it, he pulls his cloak over his face and goes out to stand at the mouth of the cave. My friend, God doesn't always show up in the way that you think He's going to. He doesn't always speak in the manner you might be expecting. Maybe you're expecting some grand sign from God or lightening to come down from heaven and not that God doesn't perform signs or confirm His spoken word, but He is more interested in those who will take the time to listen to that gentle whisper, to trust that still, quiet voice. God cares more about revealing His glory to you in your heart rather than putting on a show for your entertainment. Jesus said in John 10:27, that His sheep listen to His voice. God's presence, His glory, His voice, it's everywhere. He's always speaking, He's always there, His nature and character is always worthy to be praised. Thankfully, in Christ you have been made a partaker of the divine nature. Who you are is now hidden with Him. How cool!

Father,

> I thank You for making me a participant of the divine nature. I thank You that my character is now wrapped up with You. I'm not the same anymore. You have changed me, transformed me by Your glory. I thank You that I am made for ever-increasing glory. Take me from glory to glory, LORD. Holy Spirit, help me to know Your voice, listen to Your voice and not just be interested in the show of Your glory. I'm interested in the relationship, the intimacy with You that ushers in more of Your presence. Let it be so LORD, in Jesus's name, amen.

Day 87: I Am the Bride of Christ

"Husbands love your wives, as Christ loved the church and gave himself up for her, that he might sanctify her, having cleansed her by the washing of water with the word, so that he might present the church to himself, in splendor, without spot or wrinkle or any such thing, that she might be holy and without blemish." Ephesians 5:25-27 NIV

"Let us rejoice and exult and give him the glory, for the marriage of the Lamb has come, and his Bride has made herself ready; it was granted her to clothe herself with fine linen, bright and pure—for the fine linen is the righteous deeds of the saints. And the angel said to me, 'write this: blessed are those who are invited to the marriage supper of the Lamb.' And he said to me, 'these are the true words of God." Revelation 19:7-9 ESV

There is an incredible imagery in the Bible of Christ as the Bridegroom and the church as His Bride. You are compared to a bride, a bride that Christ gave Himself up for, a bride He has sanctified and cleansed by the washing of water with the word, a bride that He is presenting to Himself in splendor, without spot or wrinkle or any such thing; a bride that is holy and without blemish. You are His bride. Wow! There is a major assault on the power of this imagery since there is such an attack on the institution of marriage and what it means to be a bride. Most of us don't like being equated to a bride because the whole picture is just so feminine. Yet marriage and brides; they're all God's idea. "For this reason, a man will leave his father and mother and be united to his wife and the two will become one flesh." (Ephesians 5:31 NIV). "He who finds a wife finds what is good and receives favor from the LORD." (Proverbs 18:22 NIV). Apparently, according to the Bible, brides are a good thing and a sign of favor from the LORD.

Regardless, God seems to celebrate, take great delight in, and rejoice over marriages. In fact, the whole thing is so important to Him that it is one of the central ways that He relates to us. Your marriage was gifted to you by

God as a picture of His relationship with you. Interesting huh? Yet there is a culmination of this whole imagery that reaches its climax in heaven at the marriage supper of the Lamb. Revelation describes this event as a celebratory occasion; a time of feasting, of rejoicing, of joy; a great and elaborate party exclusively planned and thrown in honor of the Bridegroom and His Bride finally being together for all eternity. There is coming a day when Christ will honor you as His Bride, a day when all of heaven will celebrate who you are in Him. Revelation declares that the Bride has made herself ready, that she is adorned in fine linen bright and pure. You are going to shine on this day, my friend! The glory-meter in heaven is going to go off the charts because Christ has made you bright and pure. You are going to bring a special glory to heaven because of the glory the Bridegroom's love has given you. Jesus has made you worthy to be His bride, worthy to be the object of His desire, worthy to be the one He declares His faithfulness to for all eternity, worthy to be the one He has pledged Himself to; the one He has chosen.

My friend, if today you feel "less than" in some way. If you feel like you're not worthy, you're not anyone's chosen one, that no one considers you worthy of being faithful to. If the enemy is telling you that you don't matter or that you're just a nobody. Can I remind you that you are the Bride of Christ! The imagery of you being Christ's Bride is significant, it's important, it's relevant because this terminology declares you to be in a position of honor; a position of love! All of heaven will celebrate you (the church) one day in the greatest, most elaborate party you've ever heard tell of. Why would all of heaven go through such trouble? Why put on such a display? Because Jesus, your Bridegroom, celebrates you being His bride! The Bible could have called you His helpmate, His servant, His handmaiden, His anything, but no! The Bible calls you His Bride!!! Why? Because you, my friend, have His heart! So, if Satan is taunting you in any way today remind him of the marriage supper of the Lamb and specifically remind him that he isn't invited! I have a feeling that the only thing you will care about on this day is your Bridegroom, Jesus!

Father,

> I thank You for Jesus. I thank You that I am the Bride of Christ, that I belong to You, that I am looking forward to the marriage supper of the Lamb. I thank You that Jesus has made me worthy to be His Bride. Help me Holy Spirit to glimpse the Bridegroom's heart for me in that He has

arranged a day in Heaven reserved especially for celebrating our relationship, the relationship He has with His church. You are so, so good and I love you so much! Thank You Jesus!

Day 88: I Am Anointed

"But you have an anointing from the Holy One, and all of you know the truth." 1 John 2:20 NIV

"But the anointing you have received from him (Jesus) abides in you, and you have no need that anyone should teach you. But as his anointing teaches you about everything, and is true, and is no lie—just as it has taught you, abide in him." John 2:27 ESV

"Now it is God who makes both us and you stand firm in Christ. He anointed us, set his seal of ownership on us, and put his Spirit in our hearts as a deposit, guaranteeing what is to come." 2 Corinthians 1:21-22 NIV

You have an anointing from the Holy One! This anointing abides in you, given to you by Jesus, and His anointing teaches you about everything. There is no lie in this anointing; rather, it is true and teaches all truth. And this anointing helps you to abide in Jesus. God is the One who makes you stand firm in Christ. He anointed you! He set His seal of ownership upon you. He put His Spirit in your heart as a deposit, guaranteeing what is to come. You have been anointed by God!

All throughout the Old Testament, certain individuals were anointed to perform specific roles. For example, both the high priests and the kings over Israel were both anointed. In many ways, being anointed was a rite of inauguration into that office. It was a means of appointment, of assignment, of designation that implied the LORD's backing. On more than one instance David found King Saul at his mercy and after being unjustly put on the run by the king, David would ask, "Who can lay a hand on the LORD's anointed and be guiltless?" (1 Samuel 26:9 NIV). David thought it no light matter that Saul had been anointed as the king of Israel. It wasn't just a ceremonial anointing that appointed Saul as the king. It was much more significant than that. In fact, it was so significant that David left it in the LORD's hands rather than mess with it himself. Being anointed was no ordinary thing. In similar fashion, the high priest and his decedents as well as the tabernacle and all its furnishings were anointed as a means of consecration. God gave the recipe for this anointing oil found in Exodus 30:23-24 and the people were strictly forbidden from reproducing the oil for personal use. It was made up of myrrh, cinnamon, and other natural ingredients, mostly ingredients that put off a sweet fragrance. In Exodus 29 when Aaron and his sons were anointed as high priests, the anointing oil was to be poured on his head. This sweet-smelling oil would run down to his beard and the collar of his robe. The evidence of the high priest's anointing was all over his face, you could see the anointing and you could smell it too!

My friend, there was nothing particularly powerful about the oil itself used in the Old Testament for anointing. The ingredients used weren't somehow holy, they didn't magically make you holy and set apart to God. Rather, it's what this anointing represented, the presence of God, the approval of God, the assignment of God. Unlike what we find in the Old Testament, your anointing doesn't come from a bottle, it comes from the Holy One Himself, His Spirit poured out upon you, running down your face, consecrating you to the LORD. You are the LORD's anointed! It is implied that if the enemy messes with you they also mess with the position and title you have been anointed for, a position given to you by God.

In Matthew 26, Jesus is in Bethany in the home of Simon the leper. The crucifixion is drawing near and here Jesus is in the house of a social outcast, a leper, an untouchable human being by all societal accounts, yet what and whom God values often flies in the face of what we tend to place value upon. While He's there, a woman comes to Him with an alabaster jar of very expensive perfume which she pours on His head as He's reclining at the table. The disciples were indignant at such a waste of very expensive perfume, but Jesus defends this precious woman by declaring what she has done a very beautiful thing for she had anointed His body for burial. I wonder if she understood exactly what she was doing or if her love led to such extravagant worship, she was willing to get a little undone, to offer up the best that she had, to suffer ridicule because of the value she placed upon Jesus. I also wonder how the disciples missed this value! They had been with Jesus almost nonstop for three years. They had listened to His teachings, witnessed countless miracles in His presence, yet here they were concerned only about the cost of this woman's worship. Why didn't any of them step up to anoint Jesus's body for burial? They were His closest friends! I wonder if this woman felt a little self-conscious at first, a little foolish pouring out probably her most expensive commodity upon Jesus while judgmental eyes stared a whole in her back. I wonder what brought her to that place, what gave her the courage, the boldness to go to Jesus in the first place; what motivated her to take such risk. I wonder what made her so radical even in the presence of a bunch of people who probably should have been a little more drastic than her. I wonder if she thought at all about the rest of the people in the room or if her heart was completely fixed upon her Savior. Yet while everyone else was criticizing her, Jesus was moved by the beauty of her love for Him. I wonder what Jesus was thinking as that sweet perfume ran down His face to His beard and the collar of His robe. I wonder if it brought back to His remembrance all the times the high priests were anointed in like fashion throughout Israel's history. I wonder if it pained Him to consider that He was about to suffer and die for a world He was born into that did not seem to receive Him. I wonder how often He recalled the value of this moment throughout the treacherous moments that were to follow as those He loved just as much as He loved this sweet woman chose instead to slap Him and spit in His face. I wonder if everyone in that house wished they'd done something to honor Jesus after their lack of honor was brought glaringly to the forefront by some woman's brazen actions. I wonder if she expected at all to be honored in return by Jesus, if she had the slightest inkling that her love for Jesus was about to cause her reputation with God to skyrocket. I wonder if she ever missed her alabaster box or if it all seemed worth it just to look for a moment in the face of the One who would take her place and save her soul. Oh, I wonder so much about this story. Regardless, the anointing wasn't lost on Jesus. He is the Holy One and you, my friend, have been anointed by Him!

Father,

> I thank You for anointing me, for setting Your seal of ownership upon me, for putting Your Spirit in my heart. I have been consecrated. I have been appointed by Jesus. Help me, Holy Spirit. Pour out fresh anointing on me today for I am the LORD's anointed. Let it be so in Jesus's name, amen.

Day 89: I Am God's House

"But Christ is faithful as the Son over God's house. And we are his house, if indeed we hold firmly to our confidence and the hope in which we glory." Hebrews 3:6 NIV

"You yourselves like living stones are being built up as a spiritual house, to be a holy priesthood, to offer spiritual sacrifices acceptable to God through Jesus Christ" 1 Peter 2:5 NIV

"For no one can lay a foundation other than that which is laid, which is Jesus Christ." 1 Corinthians 3:11 NIV

You are God's house, built upon the foundation of Jesus Christ. You are steady, unmovable, held firmly to your confidence in God and the hope that you have in Him, a hope that causes you to glory, to triumph, to succeed. You are a living stone being built into a spiritual house. Even Jesus was compared to a stone. "Now to you who believe, this stone is precious. But to those who do not believe, 'the stone the builders rejected has become the cornerstone." (1 Peter 2:7 NIV). Jesus is known as the stone the builders rejected, unfit material for building, unwanted, not considered worth constructing anything upon. Yet this very stone that was rejected, Jesus, has become the cornerstone. Not just a piece of the house, but the foundation. Jesus is faithful as the Son over God's house and YOU are His house. That's cool!

What is the purpose of a house? At its most basic function, a house provides shelter and protection. It is a place you go to feel at home, a place of rest; a place of safety. There is a universal rule of hospitality widely upheld especially in other cultures. This rule gives preeminence to strangers and passers-by. It causes you to open your home to the traveler, to the one just passing through to provide them momentary shelter, safety, protection; a place of rest and refreshment. It values the sojourner and recognizes that we all have found ourselves in need of hospitality at various points in our life. "Don't forget to show hospitality to strangers, for by so doing some people have shown hospitality to angels without knowing it." (Hebrews 13:2 NIV). Wow!

Did you know that this is who you are? Who God has made you to be? You are God's house! You should be the place people could go to in order to find rest, to find shelter, to find safety; to find hospitality. Strangers, sojourners, those who are lost and weary, even angels should find you a place of respite; a place of relief for YOU are God's house. Yes, the church is considered God's house, but the building itself is just a product of functionality. You, yourself, the people who make up the church, that is truly God's house!

In Matthew 7, Jesus tells a parable about a wise and a foolish builder. He says that everyone who hears His words and puts them into practice is like a wise man who built his house on the rock. The rain came down, the winds blew and beat against that house, yet it did not fall because its foundation was on the rock. Jesus goes on to say that everyone who hears His words but doesn't put them into practice is like a foolish builder who built his house on the sand. The rain came down, the winds blew and beat against that house and it fell with a great crash because its foundation was just sand. The implication of the parable is the importance of the stability of our foundation. Regardless to the grandeur of what is built, if the foundation is weak, what is built on it simply will not endure. My friend, Jesus is your foundation. He is the Rock! And you are God's house! When people are lost and tired and in need of some love can they come to you? Can God open His home and invite strangers in so that He can minister to them, refresh them, bless them? Do people find God's house a place of welcome or a place of judgment and exclusivity? Do people think of God's house as the safest, most hospitable place to go because of their experience with you or do you keep the place on firm lock-down? My friend, God honors the rules of hospitality. The Bible says that He stands at the door and knocks. He's God, He doesn't have to knock, but He does. Why? Because He honors hospitality! He doesn't need a house, a place to dwell, rather; He's chosen you to be the place people can go to find Him. Think about that for a second. He has entrusted you to be His house, you to be His shelter for people, you to be a place of welcome, of love, of refreshment; a place where the stranger and the angel are treated the same. What kind of house are you? The Bible doesn't say that you are His mansion; part of gated community. You aren't His business office where everyone is evaluated based on their usefulness to you or to God. Nor are you His tent, part of a nomadic tribe for Jesus kind of thing. No, the Bible says that you are His house! My friend, God has a house and it looks a lot like you!

Father,

> I thank You for making me Your house, built upon the foundation of Jesus Christ. I don't have to fear the wind and the rain and the storm because my foundation is solid, it's enduring. Would You forgive me for not being a place people can run to? For not being a safe place, a shelter for the stranger, for the traveler, for even the angels. You have made me Your house and I haven't been very hospitable. Forgive me, LORD. Holy Spirit give me Your eyes for people, Your heart towards them. May I roll out the welcome mat for everyone You send my way so that people might be refreshed in God's house. Let it be in Jesus's name, amen.

Day 90: I Will Do Even Greater Works Than Jesus

> *"Very truly I tell you, whoever believes in me will do the works I have been doing, and they will do even greater things than these, because I am going to the Father. And I will do whatever you ask in my name, so that the Father may be glorified in the Son. You may ask me for anything in my name, and I will do it."* John 14:12-14 NIV

> *"For we are God's handiwork, created in Christ Jesus to do good works, which God prepared in advance for us to do."* Ephesians 2:10 NIV

You were created for good works, greater works than that of Jesus. What? How is that possible? Do you even live like that is possible? Look at what Jesus said in the Scripture above from John. He said that whoever believes in Him will do the works that He has been doing. "Whoever," that means whoever; anyone regardless to their title, their personality, their socio-economic status, their training, their degree, their family background, the color of their skin, or what language they speak. Whoever qualifies everyone who believes in Jesus! All it takes is belief in Jesus. What did Jesus do? He preached the gospel, He healed the sick, He cast out demons, He brought the dead back to life; He ministered to people everywhere He went. According to Jesus, if you believe in Him and don't just say that you believe in Him, you should be doing these things too. Healing the sick, casting out demons, resurrecting the dead, preaching the Good News is the product of believing in Jesus. What? How many of us believe that and really live like we believe that? Yet Jesus went on to say that whoever believes in Him will do even greater things than these because He is going to the Father. You were meant for greater things! Jesus said He would do whatever you ask in His name so that the Father may be glorified through Him. You can ask Jesus for anything in His name and He will do it! That's what the Bible says! My friend, what are you asking, what are you praying, what are you doing? You should be asking, praying, doing greater things than Jesus!

If this is what the Bible says, if this is what Jesus promised then what is the problem? Why aren't we seeing greater things happening? It must be our lack of belief! I don't mean to get all up in your business, but the ONLY qualifier Jesus put on that statement from John is us believing. We must not believe Jesus. We don't believe we're able to do what He did let alone anything greater. We've beat ourselves down so much and allowed the enemy to absolutely lie to us for so long that the truth sounds a little bit ridiculous to us. It may sound ridiculous and if you tell people that you believe Jesus can heal them or set them free from demonic oppression or bring the dead back to life again, people are going to look at you like you're a little bit ridiculous. It's not reasonable at all, but it's what the Bible says; greater things!

In Matthew 8:16 it says that many who were demon-possessed were brought to Jesus and He drove the spirits out and with a word He healed all the sick. In Matthew 4:23 Jesus went throughout Galilee teaching in their synagogues, proclaiming the good news of the Kingdom, and healing every disease and sickness among the people. In Matthew 12:15, a large crowd follows Jesus and the Bible says He healed all the sick that were among them. In Matthew 9, Jesus is in Capernaum teaching and four men bring their friend who was paralyzed and couldn't walk to Jesus. The crowd was surrounding Jesus and these men couldn't get close to Him, so they cut a hole in the roof and lowered their friend down on his mat to Jesus. Jesus forgives this man of all his sins and completely heals his body. The paralyzed man takes up his mat and walks. This mat that he laid on for so long; that was a sign to many that he was indeed paralyzed; a sign of his weakness of his ailment of his limitations was now the banner of victory, of healing, and of praise in his life. What happened? Jesus healed him! In Luke 8 a woman who had been suffering with an issue of blood for TWELVE years, who had been bleeding and was considered unclean because of this issue, who had spent all she had on medical bills and doctor's visits trying to get well presses through the crowds in the streets behind Jesus and touches just the hem of His garment. The Bible says that when she did this, immediately the issue of blood was healed. Just a touch of the outer fringes of Christ's garment and immediately this woman found the healing she had so desperately been looking to find for so long. Just a touch and immediately the last twelve years of her life was redeemed in an instant! In Mark 8, Jesus is in Bethsaida and some people bring to him a blind man. Jesus leads the blind man outside the village, spits in the guys' eyes, puts His hands on him and asks the man if he sees anything. The blind man says that he sees people like trees walking around so Jesus puts His hands on the man's eyes again and his eyes were opened, his sight was restored, and he could see clearly. These are just some of the works Jesus did. In many instances the Bible says that all the sick who were present were healed. All of them, with varying degrees of sickness, from just a cold to terminal cancers, all of them, every disease, every sickness was healed with just a word. Wow! Can you imagine? This is what Jesus did and the Bible says that you will do even greater things than this because Jesus has gone to the Father. My friend, is anyone healed when you pray for them? Are you even praying for anyone to be healed? Are people cutting holes in your roof to get you to pray for them? Is anyone pressing in just to touch the hem of your clothes so that they'll be healed? This was normal for Jesus. Why is it so bizarre for us? Friend, what are you doing that is greater? Whoever believes in Jesus will do greater things to the glory of the Father. It has nothing to do with you and everything to do with Jesus, with glorifying the Father! Let it be so in Jesus's name!

Father,

> I thank You for all that Jesus did. I thank You that Jesus has the power to heal the sick, raise the dead, cast out demons, and preach the good news. And I thank You that I will do even greater things than these because Jesus is at Your right hand praying for me. Forgive me for not asking, for not praying, for not doing, for not believing. Help me

Holy Spirit to live like I believe this so the Father might be glorified in Jesus's name, amen.

Day 91: I Am Qualified

"And giving joyful thanks to the Father, who has qualified you to share in the inheritance of his holy people in the kingdom of light." Colossians 1:12 NIV

"It's not that we think we are qualified to do anything on our own. Our qualification comes from God." 2 Corinthians 3:5 NLT

"But God has chosen the foolish things of the world to shame the wise, and God has chosen the weak things of the world to shame the things which are strong, and the base things of the world and the despised God has chosen, the things that are not, so that he may nullify the things that are, so that no man may boast before God." 1 Corinthians 1:27-29 NIV

You are qualified to share in the inheritance of God's holy people. Your faith in Jesus has qualified you to be a part of the Kingdom of Light. You are qualified to live for Jesus. You are qualified to serve your family, your community, your world. You are qualified to preach the Gospel. You are qualified to pray for people to be healed, to be free, and to be saved. God has qualified YOU! Your education level isn't a factor. Your age, your gender, your popularity level, your job description, or your tenure in the Kingdom doesn't factor into your qualification. God considers you skilled, trained, capable, competent, and experienced. The blood of Jesus has made you enough! So if the enemy tells you that you're just too foolish, too stupid to be used of God; that you're too weak, too unassuming; that you're no one important, that you're at the bottom of the social standing ladder; that people don't really like you; that society considers you one of the "despised" ones because you can't work or you require care from others or you have a "history", a record against you.

The Bible says that God has chosen the foolish things to shame the wise. He's chosen the weak things of the world to shame the strong. God has chosen the base things, the despised things, the things that are not, that no one thinks is good for anything to nullify the things that are. If you feel unqualified to be used of God that is a good indication that God has chosen you! He looks for the ones no one else seems to even see, He asks you to do things that require you to lean on Him because His glory, His presence, who He is shines even brighter under such circumstances. His goal isn't to glorify your name, but to draw you closer to Him. And the inheritance reserved for God's people, for His children; you are qualified to share in it!

In Isaiah chapter six we find that King Uzziah had just died. This was a king of Israel who sought the LORD during most of his reign, but because of his fame and success, he eventually becomes proud and this pride leads to his downfall. King Uzziah enters the Temple to burn incense on the altar, something he was not permitted to do, something God had not qualified him to do. Yet King Uzziah's pride made him think that he was the one who qualified himself rather than God and this caused him to sin. The king was struck with leprosy from that moment on and eventually dies as indicated in Isaiah chapter six. In the year that the king dies, Isaiah sees the LORD high and exalted, seated on a throne and the train of His robe fills the Temple. Above Him were two seraphim, mighty angels with six wings each that were calling to each, "Holy, holy, holy is the LORD Almighty. The whole earth is full of His glory." (Isaiah 6:3 NIV). And the Bible says that at the sound of these angels' voices, the whole Temple shook and was filled with smoke. Isaiah responds to all this by saying, "Woe to me! I am ruined! For I am a man of unclean lips, and I live among a people of unclean lips, and my eyes have seen the King, the LORD Almighty." (Isaiah 6:5 NIV). Isaiah didn't think himself qualified to see the LORD Almighty, but one of the seraphim flies over to him with a live coal in his hand that he had taken with tongs from the altar and he touches Isaiah's mouth with it. The angel says, "See, this has touched your lips; your guilt is taken away and your sin atoned for." (Isaiah 6:7 NIV). And after this the LORD talks directly with Isaiah, commissioning him, qualifying him, and promising to fill his lips with God's words to speak to the people. Wow! What a contrast between King Uzziah's experience in the Temple and Isaiah's experience with God. One was proud, the other was humble. One thought himself beyond reproach, uncorrectable and was struck with leprosy as a result. The other is aware of how undone he is, how unworthy he is to be in God's presence, how unclean his lips are to converse with the LORD Almighty. Yet God heals his lips, purifies them, and fills them with His words. The LORD qualified Isaiah to be His mouthpiece, to speak to Israel on God's behalf, and to show Isaiah glimpses of the coming Messiah. Isaiah wasn't a king like Uzziah, but God chose him and entrusted him with several prophesies about Jesus. Isaiah chapter nine is one of these prophesies about the birth of Jesus, a r prophesy that is referenced a lot in Christmas songs and cards and plays. "For to us a child is born, to us a son is given, and the government will be on His shoulders. And he will be called Wonderful Counselor, Mighty God, Everlasting Father, Prince of Peace. Of the greatness of His government and peace, there will be no end." (Isaiah 9:6-7a NIV). God qualified Isaiah to hear such words and to share such words even though Isaiah lived many, many years before Jesus was ever born. Isaiah cried out, "Woe is me!" in God's presence but he also responded to God, "Here I am, LORD, send me!" (Isaiah 6:8 NIV). He may not have thought himself qualified, but his humility and boldness qualified him. In like manner, you may not think yourself experienced enough, capable enough, eligible enough to converse with God. Maybe in your grief, in your loss you keep going to the Temple, you keep being faithful to show up for God. And just maybe this is the day the LORD will decide to fill the Temple with the train of His robe. Maybe today is the day that started out like any other, but God is about to shake up the Temple with His presence. Just maybe today you'll see God's mighty angels or better yet, you'll hear God asking, "Whom shall I send… who will go for Us?" (Isaiah 6:8 NIV). Maybe today is the day you say, "Here I am, LORD, send me!"

Father,

> I thank You for Jesus. I thank You that He has qualified me to share in the inheritance of Your holy people. I am not excluded. I am a part of the Kingdom of Light. LORD, who am I to be in Your presence, to hear Your voice, to see Your glory? Like Isaiah, I cry out woe is me! But in similar fashion I also respond like Isaiah responded by saying, here I am, LORD, send me! If You're going to talk to someone, talk to me. If You're going to show Your glory to someone, show me. If You're going to send someone, send me LORD! I praise You for choosing the foolish, the weak, the base things of this world to shame everything the world values.

I don't put my confidence in my intelligence, my strength, my popularity, or my success. My confidence is in You alone for with You all things are possible. Let it be in Jesus's name, amen.

Day 92: I Am a Builder

"He is the one we proclaim, admonishing and teaching everyone with all wisdom, so that we may present everyone fully mature in Christ." Colossians 1:28 NIV

"Not giving up meeting together, as some are in the habit of doing, but encouraging one another—and all the more as you see the Day approaching." Hebrews 10:25 NIV

"Do not let any unwholesome talk come out of your mouths, but only what is helpful for building others up according to their needs, that it may benefit those who listen." Ephesians 4:29 NIV

"Therefore encourage one another and build each other up, just as in fact you are doing." 1 Thessalonians 5:1 NIV

You are a builder! You are meant to build Christ in others, to encourage one another, to construct, to put together, to assemble others according to their needs. You are not meant for destruction. You aren't meant to tear down, to demolish, to destroy. That's what the enemy does! Rather, Jesus has made you a master builder. He's called you, commissioned you to help build Christ in others. This seems so simple; yet, it is incredibly difficult for us. Can I tell you it is easy to put others down? It's easy to criticize, to tear someone else apart, to find something you don't like about someone. No one is perfect. Everyone has weaknesses, faults, or things about them that may not mesh well with you. That's life. That's human nature. It takes no intelligence whatsoever, no heart, and no effort to point out and bring to attention what's wrong with people. But it does take some brains, some compassion, and some intentionality to recognize what someone else needs and build them up accordingly. Building others up requires you to pay attention to someone other than yourself. It requires some discernment, some courage, and some love to speak life when all you see is death, to speak hope when what you really feel is despair, to speak the truth even when the lie seems more believable. God has given you an amazing tool for building, for creating, for constructing; He's given you a tongue. He's given you words that hold the power of life and death in them. This tongue that is such a constructive tool for you can also be a major source of destruction if used incorrectly. "With the tongue we praise our LORD and Father, and with it we curse human beings, who have been made in God's likeness." (James 3:9 NIV). Jesus, have mercy on us!

How do I build people up? What do I say? This is where knowing God's Word is incredibly helpful. You can't go wrong when you speak what the Bible says over people. Instead of just trying to say something nice which gets hard to do when people are being ugly and mean or you're upset and frustrated, you can speak the Truth. Your emotions and feelings about people may ebb and flow, but God's Word remains true regardless to how you feel and regardless to what is going on in someone's life. If someone is having a hard time believing they can do something, you can remind them that they can do ALL things through Christ who gives them strength. If someone feels small and intimidated, you can encourage them that the One who is in them is greater than he that is in this world. If someone is just beat down and discouraged, you can tell them that the LORD is a shield around them, He is their glory, and the One who lifts their head high. The Word of God builds us up so when we speak it over ourselves and each other, we are helping to build Christ in that person. You may feel silly doing it. People may look at you like you're crazy because we're so accustomed to criticism and being critical and most of us keep our walls up rather high for this very reason. But I'm telling you, life and death is in the power of your tongue and those who love it will eat its fruit. If you love life, you'll eat the fruit of life that comes out of your mouth. Are you enjoying the fruit that you're eating that comes out of your mouth or are you choking on your own words? What kind of fruit are you eating?

Jesus sounded a similar note in Luke 6 when He said that no good tree bears bad fruit and no bad tree bears good fruit. He went on to say that each tree is recognized by its own fruit. Jesus said that a good man brings good things out of the good stored up in his heart and an evil man brings evil things out of the evil stored up in his heart. He ends this dialogue by saying that the mouth speaks what the heart is full of. Wow! What mostly comes out of your mouth is a direct indication of what's in your heart. That's what Jesus said! I understand we all mess up and say stupid things from time to time, but if what you say is mostly good then that's a good sign that what's in your heart is good. Yet if what you say is mostly evil, mostly critical and negative and bad then that is also an accurate warning that what's in your heart is evil. According to Jesus, your words are an express outlet, a window for what's in your heart. God, help us! Pay attention to what you're saying and what your words are saying about your heart. And let God use that tool He has given you to create and construct so you can build Christ in others. With the Holy Spirit's help, you can do it!

Father,

> I thank You for my tongue, for the ability You have given me to create, to build, to encourage others. I thank You that the power of life is in my words. Forgive me for being so lax in this area of my life. Forgive me for not paying attention to what people need to hear and to what I'm saying. Forgive me for not paying attention to what my words are saying about the condition of my heart. Help me, Holy Spirit. Help me to be aware. Help me to speak God's Word over people. Help me to bring forth good out of the good that is stored up in me. I need Your help, so please help me to build Christ in others in Jesus's name, amen.

Day 93: I Am in Christ's Hand

"I (Jesus) give them eternal life, and they shall never perish; no one will snatch them out of my hand." John 10:28 NIV

"See I (God) have engraved you on the palms of my hands; your walls are ever before me." Isaiah 49:16 NIV

> *"Which of all these does not know that the hand of the LORD has done this? In his hand is the life of every creature and the breath of all mankind."* Job 12:9-10 NIV

> *"Fear not, for I (God) am with you; be not dismayed for I am your God; I will strengthen you, I will help you, I will uphold you with my righteous right hand."* Isaiah 41:10 NIV

Your life, your very breath is in the hand of God. I know that tends to be a cliché statement, but it's what the Bible says. The life of every creature and the breath of all mankind are in God's hand. How could He forget you? He has engraved you, stamped you, and fixed you on the palms of His hands! If you're wondering where you are to God, where you stand with Him. If the enemy is trying to tell you that you don't mean anything to God, you tell Satan that he's a big, fat liar because God has you carved on the palms of His hands. God can't do anything without seeing your name engraved on His hand! Jesus said Himself that He is the One who gives you eternal life. You will never perish and no one, not even Satan will snatch you out of His hand. God's hand is mighty. It is strong! "The strong right arm of the LORD is raised in triumph. The strong right arm of the LORD has done glorious things!" (Psalm 118:16 NIV). "Your (God) arm is endowed with power; your hand is strong, your right hand exalted. Righteousness and justice are the foundation of your throne; love and faithfulness go before you. Blessed are those who have learned to acclaim you, who walk in the light of your presence, LORD." (Psalm 89:13-15 NIV). The hand of the LORD is strong. It is mighty. No one is going to man-handle you out of God's hand! And the Bible says that God's hand is exalted. It is lifted in triumph. My friend, you are in that hand; therefore, you are lifted in triumph! Hallelujah! Take a praise break. Come on, somebody!

The LORD tells you through His Word to fear not for He is with you. He tells you not to be dismayed, distressed, distraught, or disappointed for He is your God. He will strengthen you. He will help you. He will uphold you with His righteous right hand. That hand is righteous. It is good. It is honorable. It is just. That hand never fails. It never loses. It never mishandles anything or anyone. You can trust the hand of God! He's got you in His hand. His mighty, strong, triumphant, and righteous hand. God is not fickle. He will never just drop you like you're hot. He is faithful! If the Bible says that you are engraved upon the palm of His hand then you can rest in the knowledge that the very hands that hold all of creation, that right hand that upholds the righteous and crushes the enemy, that hand that is exalted and lifted high, that hand, His hand has got you!

In Exodus 15, Moses and his sister Miriam comprise a song to the LORD that all of Israel sings to commemorate God's incredible act of parting the Red Sea and leading Israel out of Egypt with a mighty hand. Most of us are familiar with the story of Pharaoh's pursuit of the Israelites in the desert after he had decided to let them go. It took ten plagues, ten acts of God, including one devastating loss of all the firstborn males in Egypt to get Pharaoh's attention and ultimately convince him to let the Israelites go free. Yet Pharaoh changes his mind after the fact and pursues the Israelites with a convoy of soldiers. Here comes the enemy with horses, chariots, weapons, and trained soldiers to attack and overtake a group of slaves with lots of women and children and cattle trekking through the desert and at a roadblock with the Red Sea stretched out in front of them. There appears even to the Israelites to be no possible way of escape, but God has Moses stretch out his staff over the waters and the sea parts so that Israel can walk through on dry ground. Can you imagine? I wonder what those men and women and children and even animals were thinking as they walked through on dry ground with walls of water on each side of them. I wonder how long it took all of them to walk through to the other side, if they ever feared the waters were going to just come crashing back over them, or if they could see sharks and whales and fish swimming in the water on either side of them. I think I might have passed out if I looked over and seen a killer whale swimming right next to me. Yet God parts the sea long enough for every person, every piece of livestock and supply wagon, every lagging child, every single Israelite to make it through to the other side safely before He releases the water to go back to the way it was. I'm not sure what Pharaoh and his men were thinking as they witnessed this event, but they were audacious or stupid enough to go into the waters in pursuit only to have God shatter them as the waves crashed back to their original position. Part of the song commemorating this event says, "Your right hand, LORD, was majestic in power. Your right hand, LORD, shattered the enemy." (Exodus 15:6 NIV). Can I tell you, friend, God doesn't just defeat the enemy, He shatters him! Sometimes like Pharaoh the enemy is stubborn, he doesn't relent, he keeps pursuing even when the odds are clearly against him, even when God shows up mightily to defend you, to rescue you. Out of foolishness and denial, the enemy somehow keeps pursuing. But you are in God's hand and that hand is mighty, it is triumphant, it is righteous, and that hand completely shatters the enemy! There is coming a day when the enemy will be completely, eternally, absolutely, irreversibly shattered by the right hand of God. Hallelujah!

Father,

> I thank You for Your righteous, Your mighty, Your triumphant right hand. I thank You that I am in Christ's hand and no one can ever snatch me out of it. I thank You that I am engraved on the very palms of Your hands. I am lifted in triumph over the enemy because Your right hand is exalted, Your right hand shatters the enemy and I am in that hand. Thank You Jesus!

Day 94: I Am Healed

> *"He (Jesus) himself bore our sins, in his body on the cross, so that we might die to sin and live for righteousness, by his wounds you have been healed."* 1 Peter 2:24 NIV

> *"But he (Jesus) was pierced for our transgressions, he was crushed for our iniquities; the punishment that brought us peace was on him, and by his wounds we are healed."* Isaiah 53:5 NIV

> *"Praise the LORD, O my soul, and forget not all his benefits— who forgives all your sins and heals all your diseases."* Psalm 103:2-3 NIV

You are healed! Jesus has healed you! Jesus was pierced for our transgressions, for our wrongdoing, for our disobedience; for our offense. The Bible says that while Jesus was on the cross, "...one of the soldiers pierced Jesus' side with a spear, bringing a sudden flow of blood and water." (John 19:34 NIV). Someone took a spear and pierced, stabbed, punctured, sliced open Jesus's side while He was hanging on the cross, lifeless, already dead. The Jewish leaders did not want the bodies left on the cross during the Sabbath so they asked Pilate if the men's legs could be broken and the bodies taken down. So, the other two men who were crucified with Jesus had their legs broken before they were taken down from their crosses. But when the soldiers got to Jesus, He was already dead; He had already given up His Spirit, so one of the soldiers pierces His side instead with a spear. I guess the soldier was trying to see if Jesus was dead or not, but the Bible says that SUDDENLY a flow of blood and water came out of Jesus's side. Not one of His bones was broken and they did in fact look upon the one that they had pierced. 1 John 5:6-8 says, "This is the one who came by water and blood—Jesus Christ. He did not come by water only, but by water and blood. And it is the Spirit who testifies, because the Spirit is the truth. For there are three that testify: the Spirit, the water, and the blood; and the three are in agreement." (1 John 5:6-8 NIV).

My friend, Jesus was pierced for your transgressions. That piercing brought out of Him a sudden flow of water and blood. Water purifies, water cleanses, water refreshes, and water heals. And the blood of Jesus covers your sins, brings atonement, and gives you forgiveness. The Bible goes on to say in Isaiah that Jesus was crushed for our iniquities, for our wickedness, for our evil, for our sins. "Yet it was the LORD's will to crush him (Jesus) and cause him to suffer, and though the LORD makes his life an offering for sin, he will see his offspring and prolong his days, and the will of the LORD will prosper in his hand." (Isaiah 53:10 NIV). It was the LORD's will to crush Jesus. Say what? Man did not crush Him, Satan did not crush Him, sin did not crush Him. God did! And why did He crush Jesus? For our iniquities! Jesus's life was made an offering for sin and through that, God has seen His offspring, His children, His will prosper in Christ's hand. Wow! The punishment that Jesus endured brought us peace and by His wounds we ARE healed. Jesus has wounds! In both of His hands, in both of His feet there is a wound from where they drove nails through His body in order to nail Him to the cross. There is a wound on His side from where the soldier pierced His side after He had died upon the cross.

Before Jesus's crucifixion, He was sentenced by Pilate to be flogged, scourged, hands and feet bound, tied to a post with back bared, and whipped by a Roman soldier. Jewish law denotes in Deuteronomy 25:3 that criminals should not receive more than 40 lashes, so the Jews would only give criminals 39 lashes. Paul references this "five times I received from the Jews the forty lashes minus one." (2 Corinthians 11:24 NIV). The Bible says in Isaiah that by Jesus's stripes, by the lashes that were made in His back when He was flogged, by His wounds, you are healed! His body was crushed and beaten and pierced not only for your sins, but also so your body could be whole and healed. And one day you will receive a "glorified body", a body that is healthy and whole, free from death and decay and aging, free from sickness and germs and pain; a body that you will have and enjoy for all eternity because Jesus's body was crushed and pierced and wounded. That body is ONLY available to you because of Jesus. Thank You Jesus!

His wounds show that He really is who He says He is. He really is the same Christ that was crucified. Those wounds are the evidence that He was crucified on the cross, that He died, and they pierced His side, and that He rose again since He's alive and still bears those wounds. Oh friend, those wounds are reasons to praise Him, reasons to fall on your face and thank Him. Those wounds declare Him to be LORD and Savior. They are signs of His power over sin, His power over death, His power over hell, His power over sickness, His power over the enemy. They are tangible reminders of His great love for YOU! Imagine every time you look at Jesus in heaven, you are going to be reminded of how much He loves you. Every time He reaches out His hand to you, every time He pulls you close to His side, it will be impossible for you to ignore the fact that God so loved the world that He gave His only begotten Son. Every time you see those wounds, you'll be overwhelmingly reminded that Jesus considers YOU a friend! Wow! You may have never seen JESUS, never seen those wounds, or felt them physically with your own hands. But there is coming a day when you will undoubtedly, undeniably, without question behold Jesus, the Lamb of God, wounds and all, not suffering, not hanging on a cross somewhere or still recovering from His wounds. No, you will see Jesus high and exalted and those wounds will humble you to your knees. Oh God, thank You!

Father,

> I thank You for Jesus. I thank You that He was pierced, He was crushed, He was wounded for me! Because of Jesus, I am forgiven, I am healed, I will receive a glorified body one day. It's all because of Jesus! He didn't have to go through all that He went through, but He loved me that much. I am so humbled, so grateful. Holy Spirit help me to remember those wounds. Forgive me for treating Your wounds Jesus like such a light and ordinary thing when what You did is

beyond extraordinary. Forgive me for doubting Your love, for questioning Your heart, for disbelieving that I am Your friend when the evidence is in Your wounds. Oh LORD, I'm so undeserving, but I am so thankful. I am whole, I am healthy, I am well, I am forgiven, I am free and it's all because of You, Jesus. Praise Your name forever!

Day 95: I Am Seen

"When the LORD saw that Leah was not loved, he enabled her to conceive, but Rachel remained childless." Genesis 29:31 NIV

"The LORD said, 'I have indeed seen the misery of my people in Egypt. I have heard them crying out because of their slave drivers, and I am concerned about their suffering." Exodus 3:7 NIV

"She (Hagar) gave this name to the LORD who spoke to her: 'You are the God who sees me,' for she said, 'I have now seen the One who sees me." Genesis 16:13 NIV

God sees you! He notices you. The LORD doesn't just watch your life because He's God and He sees and knows everything; rather, He notices you because He considers you worth noticing. He sees you because He cares about you. You are never off His radar! There are so many examples of this in the Bible. For instance, in the verse above from Exodus it says that the LORD saw the misery of His people in Egypt. He heard their cries. He was concerned about their suffering. He saw them and sends Moses to deliver them out of bondage. In Genesis 29, Leah is one of the wives of Jacob. The Bible says that Jacob loved Rachel and worked seven years in order to gain Rachel as his wife. But when the time came for him to receive his wife, his father-in-law, Laban, tricks him and gives Jacob his other daughter Leah instead, so that when Jacob wakes up the next morning, the morning after his wedding night, he finds that he's just consummated his marriage with the wrong sister. Talk about some family drama! Jacob confronts his father-in-law only to be told that it isn't customary for the younger daughter, Rachel, to marry before the older one, Leah. So, Jacob agrees to work seven MORE years in order to receive Rachel as his wife. After fourteen years these two sisters end up married to the same man. Yet the Bible is clear that Jacob loved Rachel but didn't love Leah. And in Genesis 29:31 it says that the LORD saw that Leah was not loved. God saw Leah. It's implied that He cared about her and what she was going through.

And earlier in Genesis, we find the story of Abraham and his wife Sarah. God gave to Abraham a promise that He would make Abraham into a great nation, too numerous to count; however, there was a problem. Abraham didn't have any children; his wife was barren. For many, many years he and Sarah saw no fulfillment to this promise to the point that they began to get impatient and Sarah suggests that Abraham should conceive a child through her handmaiden, Hagar. So, she gives her handmaiden to Abraham and Hagar conceives a child and immediately conflict begins to develop between Sarah and Hagar. Sarah begins to mistreat her handmaiden because Hagar despised her, and the Bible says that for this reason Hagar runs away. Hagar finds herself in the middle of the desert by a spring and the angel of the LORD appears to her. The angel tells her to go back to her mistress and to submit to her. And the angel assures Hagar that her decedents will be increased and will be too numerous to count. After this encounter with the LORD she says to God, "You are the God who sees me for I have seen the One who sees me." (Genesis 16:13 NIV). Hagar was touched by the fact that God saw her. He cared about her and what she was going through. She had seen the One who had always seen her.

My friend, the LORD sees you! You are not invisible to Him. He is not indifferent towards you. He sees what you are going through. He cares about you. He loves you! Hagar was just a handmaiden. She was a woman amid a society that didn't value women very much and she was a slave. She was the victim of some pretty horrible circumstances, pregnant with a child that really wasn't her idea, and mistreated by her mistress for this very reason. She was just being used for her ability to conceive and have a baby. That's it. That's all her life amounted to in the eyes of Sarah and even Abraham since he went along with the whole ordeal. These were some messy circumstances; yet, God saw Hagar in the middle of it all! In the middle of her mess, a mess that she wasn't solely responsible for creating herself, a mess that others had sort of thrown her into, even though no one else seemed to see her, the Bible says that the LORD saw her. Oh, my friend, I don't know what you're going through or how messy is your mess. Maybe like Hagar you feel like you are the victim of some pretty horrible circumstances. But can I tell you that regardless to where you are and how you feel right now, God does in fact see you? Satan is lying to you if he has told you anything otherwise. So today I pray that you would see the One who sees you! May you see His heart for you, may you glimpse His goodness; may you notice the One who has always noticed you!

Father,

> I thank You for seeing me, for noticing me, for caring about me. I am not invisible to You. You know what I'm going through and more than that, You actually care about what I'm going through. Holy Spirit, would You help me today to see the One who sees me. You are a good God, a good Father. You are the very best. I praise You for valuing me, for considering me worth noticing, worth seeing, worth caring about. You are the God who sees me. Thank You Jesus!

Day 96: I Am Holy

> *"Praise be to the God and Father of our LORD Jesus Christ, who has blessed us in the heavenly realms with every spiritual blessing in Christ. For he chose us in him before the creation of the world to be holy and blameless in his sight."* Ephesians 1:3-4 NIV
>
> *"For it is written, 'be holy, because I (God) am holy."* 1 Peter 1:16 NIV
>
> *"You are to be holy to me because I, the LORD, am holy, and I have set you apart from the nations to be my own."* Leviticus 20:26 NIV

You are holy. Christ has made you holy; blameless in God's sight! You are not trash, garbage, just a mess-up, or this dirty, despised thing. No! You are holy, sacred, and set apart! Most of us have no problem adhering to the truth that God is holy. His Word is holy, His Spirit is holy, and holiness is part of who He is. In comparison to Him, we cannot compare. Yet the Bible says that God chose us to be holy and blameless in His sight. He has set us apart as His very own. I think holiness has gotten a bad rap because we've somehow disconnected it from relationship with God and made it more to be about our behavior and our actions. It's become more a legalistic thing about what you can and cannot do, what you can and cannot get away with, when you being holy has more to do with the closeness of your relationship to God. Nearness to God brings about holiness. And the blood of Jesus has brought you near to God. Christ has taken away the written record of wrongs against you. Through Jesus your sins are not just forgiven, they are removed, absolved, completely done away with. That's the miracle of Jesus! God doesn't look at you and see sin. He looks at you and sees the blood of Jesus! He sees you as holy and blameless in His sight!

My friend stop letting Satan label you as a failure or a sinner or a loser or a reject or whatever title he has tried to label you with. Stop going along with his shenanigans; his lies! If you are in Christ, God doesn't see you as a failure. He doesn't look at you and see a loser or a reject. No way! According to the Bible, He sees you as holy and blameless in His sight! You have been brought near to Him and He is holy. When Isaiah saw the LORD in Isaiah 6:3 and later on when John sees the LORD in Revelation 4:8, both these men indicated that they saw and heard angels crying out to God, "Holy, holy, holy is the LORD God Almighty!" In the presence of God, amid His holiness, both these guys end up on their faces. The angels know that God is holy. He is so holy that they can't help but cry out and declare Him to be holy. In Deuteronomy 4:24 and in Hebrews 12:29 our God is called a consuming fire. The attribute of Him being holy is intense, it is powerful, it is consuming; it is like a fire. When you are in the middle of a fire, you know that you're in the middle of a fire. The intensity of the heat, the fire is impossible to ignore. Naturally, humans are not immune to fire, so we are trained and taught to get out, to run away, to put a fire out and rightly so. However, there is an attribute of fire that is intended to purify. Certain metals are put in the fire to burn off all the impurities and blemishes. Only the fire is intense and hot enough to get rid of these impurities. And though the fire doesn't chemically change the metals in any way, these metals come out of the fire more refined, more valuable, purer than when they went in. Oh, friend thus is our God. He is a consuming fire! You cannot ignore fire. In His presence, you cannot ignore the fact that He is holy. His holiness is consuming, it is overwhelming; it is intense. When you see Him in all His glory, you will join with the angels in crying out, "Holy, holy, holy is the LORD God Almighty!"

In 1 Kings 18, the prophet Elijah goes before Ahab the king of Israel in the middle of a severe famine and drought. This was something that Elijah had forewarned the King about because of his wickedness and his worship of Baal, yet Ahab did not listen, so Elijah prayed and for three and a half years it did not rain on the land. This was the third year when Elijah came before the King again and Ahab addresses him as being a "troubler of Israel." Ahab wanted to assign blame to Elijah, to make this whole mess Elijah's fault instead of acknowledging the true God of Israel. Elijah tells King Ahab to summon all the people and have them meet him on Mount Carmel. And he tells Ahab to bring the four hundred and fifty prophets of Baal and the four hundred prophets of Asherah who eat at the Queen Jezebel's table. So, Ahab assembles the people on Mount Carmel and Elijah says to the people, "How long will you waiver between two opinions? If the LORD is God, follow Him; but if Baal is god, follow him." (1 Kings 18:21 NIV). The people say nothing in reply, so Elijah gets two bulls and he prepares one to be offered as a sacrifice to the LORD and he instructs the prophets of Baal to prepare the other bull and offer it to their god. Elijah says, "you call on the name of your god, and I will call on the name of the LORD. The God who answers by fire—He is God." (1 Kings 18:24 NIV). The prophets of Baal go first. They prepare their bull, they cry out to Baal, they dance and shout, they even go so far as to cut themselves with swords trying to get Baal's attention. They do all this from the morning until the time for the evening sacrifice, but nothing happens. There was no fire. So Elijah prepares his bull, puts it on the wood and has four large jars of water poured on the bull, the stones he had arranged, and the soil three times so that the bull was soaking wet and all the excess water ran down and filled the trench he had dug around the bull. This whole thing was wet and would be difficult to catch fire considering how wet it was. At the time of the evening sacrifice Elijah steps forward and prays to the LORD. In verse 38 it says that fire from heaven fell and consumed the wood, the stones and the soil, and licked up ALL the water in the trench. When all the people saw this, they fell on their faces and cried out, "the LORD, He is God—the LORD, He is God!" (1 Kings 18:39 NIV). My friend, the LORD is holy. He is a consuming fire. He is God and when His presence comes, when His fire falls, people end up on their faces acknowledging Him as the One, true God. Yet in Christ you are found to be holy and blameless in His sight. Because of Jesus, you can now approach His throne of grace with confidence and when you do, I have a feeling you will join with all the angels in crying out to Him, "Holy, holy, holy is the LORD God Almighty…the whole earth is full of His glory!"

Father,

> You are so holy, so awesome, so majestic, so pure. You are a consuming fire! How could I be in Your presence? How could I endure in the presence of such a holy God?!? Thank You Jesus for making me holy and blameless in God's sight! So today, I come before Your throne with confidence and in absolute humility I cry out holy, holy, holy is the LORD God Almighty! You are holy! The whole earth is full of Your glory LORD. And I thank You for Jesus, for doing the seemingly impossible in making me holy and blameless in Your sight. His blood has brought me near to a holy God. Thank you, Jesus!

Day 97: I Am Confident

"Am I now trying to win the approval of human beings, or of God? Or am I trying to please people? If I were still trying to please people, I would not be a servant of Christ." Galatians 1:10 NIV

"For the LORD will be your confidence and will keep your foot from being caught." Proverbs 3:26 ESV

"In the fear of the LORD there is strong confidence, and his children will have refuge." Proverbs 14:26 NASB

> *"This is the confidence which we have before him (God); that if we ask anything according to his will, he hears us."*
> 1 John 5:14 NIV

The LORD is your confidence. He will be your confidence, your assurance, your reliance, your poise. It doesn't matter how confident you are in yourself, in your own abilities, in your own skill, your own strength, or intelligence. Eventually confidence, reliance, assurance in self will fail you. None of us are completely self-reliant. None of us have it all together all by ourselves all the time. However, there is a God who IS self-reliant, self-sustaining. He never fails, never waivers, never changes. He has always been God. He will always be God. It's fine to have confidence, but as a follower of Christ, your confidence goes beyond self and rests more in Jesus. The Bible says in Proverbs 14:26 that in the fear of the LORD there is STRONG confidence. Acknowledgement of God, humility before the LORD, submitting to the authority of Jesus Christ produces strong confidence in your life. Boy, does that fly in the face of the culture of this world! We are taught to live for what feels good, that there are no absolutes; everything is relative, and what we believe is not as important as the sincerity of our belief. But the Bible teaches that those who fear the LORD have a strong confidence. Why? How? Is it because they, themselves are so stinking awesome? No! It's because those who fear the LORD rely on the LORD, they acknowledge the LORD, they trust in the LORD, and who He is never fails!

My friend, can I tell you that you can have the strongest, healthiest confidence in the world because your confidence isn't in something temporary, something seen, something broken, and finite. Instead, your assurance, your reliance is upon the God who does not change like shifting shadows, who He is remains the same yesterday, today, and forever! He is everlasting. He is eternal. He is perfect. He is infinite. He is endless, limitless, enduring, unending! He is a healer, a provider, and a deliverer! His very nature is fullness, freedom, love, goodness, and life! Who He was from before the beginning of the world is who He is at this very moment and who He will be when all is said and done. Since His identity is so secure and unchanging, so too is your identity in Him! When it comes to your confidence, don't let the enemy make it about you. He wants you to only rely upon yourself. He wants you to either feel like you don't need God because you have it all together anyway or he wants you to feel like you can't do anything. Either option is a trap because if you are in Christ then your confidence isn't about you, it's about the LORD. And since you fear Him, you have a strong confidence, an unshakable confidence, and an assurance not because you are so great but because your God is so great!

You can have confidence before the LORD that if you ask anything according to His will, His Word, you can know that He hears you. Wow! Your prayers are not aimless; they aren't a waste of time, too much work, or something that you are too busy for. The Bible says that you can be confident before Him. You can know and trust that He hears you when you pray if you pray according to His will; according to His Word. Isn't that awesome?

In Joshua chapter 2 we find the Israelites are about to go in and attack the city of Jericho, the first city on their quest to inherit the land promised to them by God. Yet beforehand Joshua secretly sends two spies from Shittim to go look over the land. So, these spies went and entered the house of a prostitute named Rahab. The King of Jericho was informed about these spies so he sends a message to Rahab for her to bring the spies out, yet she had hidden them in her house and sends the king's messengers on a wild-goose chase instead, pursuing two men that had never even left the city. It says that before the two spies went to sleep that night, Rahab goes to them and says, "I know that the LORD has given you this land and that a great fear of you has fallen on us..." (Joshua 2:8 NIV). She "knew" that the LORD had given the land of Jericho to the Israelites. She wasn't an Israelite. She was one of the so-called "enemies". She certainly didn't have much of a reputation with Israel. She lived in Jericho, the city to be destroyed. And she was a prostitute. She didn't even have a very good reputation among her own people. Yet she said that she "knew" God had given the land to Israel. She was confident of it, confident in the LORD. She had only heard of what the LORD had done for Israel and based on what she had heard she says to these spies, "the LORD your God is God in heaven above and on the earth below." (Joshua 2:11 NIV). She's so confident in who God is, she has the audacity to ask the spies, two men who should have been her enemies to save her and her family and that's exactly what happened. My friend, the LORD is God in heaven above and on the earth below. For this very reason, you can be 100% confident, assured, in Him!

Father,

> I thank You for who You are. You are God. You are awesome, mighty, you have always been, and you will always be. I can have a strong confidence because I fear You, I trust

You, I humble myself before You. Forgive me for making this all about me, when it is entirely about You. I need You, Holy Spirit. Please fill me with a strong confidence today, a confidence rooted in who God is and who I am in Christ in Jesus's name, amen.

Day 98: I Am Connected

"For I am convinced that neither death nor life, neither angels nor demons, neither the present nor the future, nor any powers, neither height nor depth, nor anything else in creation, will be able to separate us from the love of God that is in Christ Jesus our Lord." Romans 8:38-39 NIV

"I (Jesus) am the vine; you are the branches. If you remain in me and I in you, you will bear much fruit; apart from me you can do nothing." John 15:5 NIV

"So, in Christ we, though many, form one body, and each member belongs to all the others." Romans 12:5 NIV

You are connected, attached, joined to the LORD and to other believers. That's what the Bible says. There is nothing in all of creation that can separate you from the love of God! Your past can't separate you. What's going on in your life right now or what might be going on in the future can't separate you. There's no demon strong enough to separate you from God's love. No angel can separate you. No living soul has the power to separate you from God's love. Not even death itself can separate you. God's love is that powerful, that enduring, and that cohesive. His love has joined you to Him. You are not disconnected, not cut off, and not isolated. According to the Bible, you belong to God and you belong to other believers. My friend, you belong! You are connected! Things that are attached and joined to other things must be severed in order to be separated. Severing is painful; it's dangerous and it isn't necessary in this case. Jesus is the vine and you are the branches. If you remain in Him and He remains in you, you will bear much fruit. But apart from Him, separated from Jesus, you can do nothing.

1 Corinthians 6:17 says that whoever is united to the LORD is one with Him in Spirit. Shut the front door! You aren't just connected to God; you are so united with Him that you are one with Him in Spirit. My friend, the Holy Spirit of the Living God is always with you, always near you. You don't have to do anything crazy to get His attention. You don't have to scream, yell, say 47 Hail Mary's, do a back flip, or will yourself into His presence. He is less impressed by what you say or do and more attuned with what's in your heart. A heartfelt request for Him to come and boom He's there to empower, to refresh, to love, to minister, to heal, to transform, to give peace; to do what only He does so well. He's with you, He's attentive to you even in the middle of the night when everyone else is asleep, even when you've burnt all your bridges with everyone else. He's there; loving you, correcting you, ministering to you, listening to you, talking to you, available to you. Why would you ignore someone, not talk to someone, not listen to someone like that?

In Luke chapter 4 we find Jesus full of the Holy Spirit and led by the Spirit into the wilderness where for forty days He was tempted by the devil. Jesus was physically by Himself. None of the disciples were with Him and He was fasting. The Bible says that He ate nothing during those days so that at the end of them, He was hungry. Jesus knows what it's like to be hungry. Not just I skipped breakfast so I'm ready to chow down for lunch kind of hungry, but a I haven't eaten anything for forty days kind of hungry. That's some intense hunger! It was during all of this that the devil tempts Jesus three distinct times. Each time Jesus resists, He talks out loud to Satan, and dismantles the enemy's schemes by referencing what the Word of God says. My friend, when all else fails, God's Word will never fail! When you're in the middle of an attack, when everyone else has abandoned you, when you're alone and tired and hungry and vulnerable, that's when you absolutely need to default to the truth of the Bible. Not to your feelings, not popular opinion, not your thoughts, not even your heart. No, Jesus modeled the anchor as being God's Word! And Jesus spoke the Word! What you say matters and the enemy listens to what you have to say. So, speak God's Word!

If you feel like Satan is down your throat all the time, after you all the time, run to Jesus, learn from Jesus; the One who overcame! Luke says that after this whole episode with the devil, Jesus returns to Galilee in the power of the Spirit. Did you notice that Jesus was full of the Holy Spirit before this whole assault in the wilderness by the devil? Jesus was led into the wilderness by the Spirit and the Bible says that He came out of the wilderness in the power of the Holy Spirit. At every juncture, regardless to the highs and lows Jesus experienced physically, whether He was preaching and teaching and performing miracles surrounded by people, or He was all by Himself in the middle of nowhere, hungry, and vulnerable. Through it all, He stayed connected to God's Spirit. My friend, you are not alone! Even when you are physically all by yourself, you still aren't alone because you are connected to the Spirit of God! Tell Satan to back off right now in the name of Jesus for you are joined to, united to, and attached to the Great I AM!

Father,

> I thank You for joining me to You by Your Spirit. I am not disconnected. I am not alone. I am attached to You, the King of all kings and the LORD of all lords. Holy Spirit help me to grasp just how awesome this truth is in my life. Help me to lean on God's Word, to default to the Word of God all the time and especially when I feel the most vulnerable to the enemy. I am victorious in Christ. I stand as more than a conqueror because of Jesus. Thank You Jesus!

Day 99: I Overcome!

> *"And they overcame him (the enemy) by the blood of the Lamb and by the word of their testimony, and they did not love their lives to the death."* Revelation 12:11 NKJV

> *"Consider it pure joy, my brothers and sisters, whenever you face trials of any kind, because you know that the testing of your faith produces perseverance. Let perseverance finish its work so that you may be mature and complete, not lacking anything."* James 1:2-4 NIV

You overcome! Jesus overcame! He overcame death, hell, and the grave. He overcame sickness, sin, betrayal. Jesus overcame every attack of the enemy. He overcame being mocked, being beaten, being persecuted. He overcame every trial. He overcame every strategy against His life. He overcame the controversy surrounding His conception, the whispers, the sneers, the judgment. He overcame the plot of King Herod to kill Him by killing all the boys in Bethlehem who were 2 years old and under. He overcame the hate, the injustice, the irrationality of the whole thing. He overcame the wilderness, He overcame temptation; He overcame the anguish of the Garden of Gethsemane. He overcame being so emotionally distraught that His body sweated drops of blood. He overcame loneliness, fatigue, He overcame being stabbed in the back by a close friend; He overcame the agony of the cross. Jesus overcame the tomb, He overcame death. No one killed Jesus. He gave up His spirit. He was raised to life by the power of the Holy Spirit. Jesus overcame this world, this life, and is now seated in glory at the right hand of God. Jesus is an overcomer and in Him, so are you!

In the book of Revelation there are seven extraordinary promises for those who overcome; for those who endure to the end; for those who never give up. Oh, friend, don't give up! I know life is hard sometimes. I know the darkness can be so thick and prevalent and it's hard to press on. But if you would just hang on. If you would just keep going. If you'll just keep enduring to the end. The rewards are coming. This life really isn't all there is. Hang on, dear friend, hang on.

Can I tell you Jesus's life was hard? "Consider him (Jesus) who endured such opposition from sinners, so that you will not grow weary and lose heart. In your struggle against sin, you have not yet resisted to the point of shedding your blood." (Hebrews 12:3-4 NIV). Jesus understands the struggle. Jesus understands suffering. He walked through it deeply. But more than that, Jesus overcame! And He has set you up to overcome also; in Him, because of Him! One day you will receive the sweet rewards of overcoming, rewards given to you by Jesus, the ultimate overcomer; rewards that will pale in comparison to being in the presence of the One who overcame! You truly can do all things through Christ who gives you strength, through Jesus who is an overcomer and who gives you the power to overcome also. Don't give up! Overcome in Jesus's name!!

Father,

> I thank You for Jesus. I thank You that Jesus overcame and that in Him, because of Him, in His strength I can overcome too. Help me Jesus! Holy Spirit remind me of all the promises Jesus has reserved for those who overcome. May those promise preserve my life in Jesus's name, amen!

Day 100: I Will Not Shrink Back

> *"The Spirit clearly says that in later times some will abandon the faith and follow deceiving spirits and things taught by demons. Such teachings come through hypocritical liars, whose consciences have been seared as with a hot iron."* 1 Timothy 4:1-2 NIV

> *"But my righteous one will live by faith. And I take no pleasure in the one who shrinks back. But we do not belong to those who shrink back and are destroyed, but to those who have faith and are saved."* Hebrews 10:38-39 NIV

You do not belong to those who shrink back! You are not of those who pull away, who give up, or who back down. You do not retreat. You do not recoil. You do not draw back. You are not a victim of this life, a victim to other people's poor choices, or a victim of your own shortcomings. Christ has made you a victor! "Be alert and of sober mind. Your enemy the devil prowls around like a roaring lion looking for someone to devour." (1 Peter 5:8 NIV). Stop listening to the enemy! Don't let him prowl around at your house. Don't let him devour you or your children or your family! Know his voice and shut him up whenever he opens his mouth. John 8:44 says that Satan is the father of lies and that there is no truth in him. Whenever he speaks, whatever he speaks is a lie. It is deceptive; always! So, don't listen to him. Don't reason with him, and don't just try to tune him out. Tell him to shut up and get out in Jesus's name! You are not of those who abandon their faith because, according to the Bible, those who have faith are saved!

In 1 Samuel chapter 14 we find the children of Israel dealing with their enemy, the Philistines. They were in the middle of a battle, a stand-still, the calm before the storm. Saul had just recently become king and was still trying to figure out how to lead the people and throughout this whole ordeal we see a lot of insecurity in this newly appointed leader. Because of the threat of the enemy and the failure of the king (1 Samuel 13), the people end up hiding out in caves. However, Jonathan, the son of King Saul, gets tired of waiting around and one day says to his armor-bearer, "Come, let us go over to the Philistine garrison on the other side." (1 Samuel 14:6 NIV). So, Jonathan and the young man who carried his armor go over to the Philistine garrison, the stronghold of the enemy where numerous soldiers are camped out. Here are two men audacious enough to take on seemingly insurmountable odds. How would two guys defeat a whole camp of enemy soldiers? Yet Jonathan says, "It may be that the LORD will work for us, for nothing can hinder the LORD saving by many or by few." (1 Samuel 14:6 NIV). Oh, I love this! Jonathan wasn't about to shrink back from the enemy. He wasn't about to waiver like his father. He was bold enough, sure enough in the LORD to step out in faith. He trusted that this whole battle was the LORD's not his anyway. He believed that the LORD would save regardless if many went up to fight or just a few. The numbers really didn't matter! Jonathan's idea, his plan seems so crazy, completely ridiculous, but his armor-bearer didn't try to talk him out of it, nor did he blindly follow him out of duty and obligation. Jonathan's armor-bearer says in response, "Do all that is in your heart. Do as you wish. Behold, I am with you heart and soul." (1 Samuel 14:7 NIV). Jonathan didn't have to go up against the enemy all by himself. Yes, he had the LORD, but the LORD made sure that Jonathan also had his armor-bearer.

Jonathan devises a plan, a ruse, a strategy to test and see if the LORD had given them victory and when the scenario works out favorably towards them, they end up attacking and securing the Philistine garrison. Israel, out of fear of the enemy, had hidden out in caves and crags and holes in the ground. Yet Jonathan and his armor-bearer come out of hiding and show themselves to the enemy and when they do, the enemy is so surprised, one of the Philistines invites Jonathan and his armor-bearer up into their camp. Jonathan and his armor-bearer end up striking down twenty men and this initial attack sends a panic throughout the entire enemy camp, a panic that causes the Philistines to flee, a panic that ignites courage and faith throughout the Israelite camp to motivate them to pursue and overtake the rest of the Philistines. I wonder what would have been the outcome if Jonathan and his armor-bearer had shrunk back, if they had played it safe, if they had been content to stay hidden. Instead they had faith, they took a risk; they trusted the LORD and saved the whole company of Israel. You are not of those who shrink back and are destroyed. Nor are you alone! Who is an armor-bearer in your life? Who has your back in prayer? Who will go with you, fight with you? Who is with you heart and soul? Thank God for armor-bearers! You are of those who have faith and are saved! Let it be in Jesus's name!

Father,

> I thank You for giving me faith. for making me a part of those who have faith and are saved. Would you help me, Holy Spirit, to have courage, to not shrink back? I don't want to be destroyed. I don't want to be devoured by the enemy. I don't want to be deceived. Forgive me for being so apathetic. Forgive me for remaining an infant in my faith when You have always intended for me to grow up. Help me, Holy Spirit. Send me an armor-bearer, LORD. Let me be an armor-bearer to someone else. By the power of the Holy Spirit I will not shrink back in Jesus's name, amen!

Day 101: I Am Beyond Compare

"We do not dare classify or compare ourselves with some who commend themselves. When they measure themselves by themselves and compare themselves with themselves, they are not wise." 2 Corinthians 10:12 NIV

"Now Abel kept flocks, and Cain worked the soil. In the course of time Cain brought some of the fruits of the soil as an offering to the LORD. And Abel also brought an offering—fat portions from some of the firstborn of his flock. The LORD looked with favor on Abel and his offering, but on Cain and his offering he

did not look with favor. So Cain was very angry and his face was downcast." Genesis 4:2-5 NIV

Have you noticed that we tend to compare everything even in the church, even amongst the family of God? We compare our appearances, our personalities, our incomes, our children, our talents, our jobs, and even our posts on social media. Nothing seems to be off limits when it comes to comparison. Everything seems to be a competition. Our stance, our view, our perspective often only goes as far as how things relate to us. Yet this mindset sets you up for failure. It's not as innocent as you might initially believe. In 2 Corinthians 10, Paul refuses to compare his ministry to anyone else's. In fact, he says in the verse mentioned above that those who compare themselves are not wise! Why? What's the big deal? Comparison is based on your perception; what you see, how you feel, what you think and not always truth. Remember Satan is the father of lies so he loves this kind of stuff. And comparison only sets you up to have one of two reactions. When you compare yourself to someone else in any way you will either come out of the whole thing feeling superior to that person in that area or feeling inferior. You will either think yourself better than that individual or you will think that they are better than you and both views affect your heart in a negative way. Romans 12:3 encourages you not to think more highly of yourself than you ought, but to think soberly according to the measure of faith God has given to you. Like it or not, comparison is a trap, a trap from the enemy and you are beyond this trap; beyond comparison!

Did you know that Satan compared himself to God? The Bible describes Satan in Isaiah 14:12 as Lucifer, a beautiful angel in heaven, an angel that according to Ezekiel 28:14-15 was anointed and blameless until unrighteousness was found in him. "You (Lucifer) said in your heart, 'I will ascend to heaven; above the stars of God I will set my throne on high; I will sit on the mount of assembly in the far reaches of the north, I will ascend above the heights of the clouds; I will make myself like the Most High." (Isaiah 14:13-14 NIV). Satan compared himself to God and thought himself equal to God, like God, even superior to God. His comparison led to pride entering his heart. It led to him believing something about himself that is not true. He believed that he was just as good as God, better than God, and this pride, this lie got him thrown out of heaven. Wow! Can I tell you that comparison is from Satan? He was the first one who compared himself since the fall of Satan happened sometime after the creation of the angels, before the foundation of the world, and the temptation of Adam and Eve in the

Garden of Eden. Comparison is Satan's idea! He's the one who is behind it! He wants you to compare yourself with others, to even compare yourself to God. He wants you to think yourself better than everyone else, superior to everyone else even God. He doesn't want you to recognize your need for God. Or he wants you to think yourself the lowest of the low, to think that God is somehow holding out on you. In fact, the very first temptation was about comparison to a certain degree. Satan tempted Adam and Eve with being like God. He tempted them with being able to know everything that God knows. Satan has always tried to be like God. "He (the antichrist) will oppose and will exalt himself over everything that is called God or is worshipped, so that he sets himself up in God's temple, proclaiming himself to be God." (2 Thessalonians 2:4 NIV). But Satan is not God, you're not God. Only God is God! I'm telling you friend; comparison is a deadly trap!

In Genesis chapter 4 we find that Adam and Eve bore two sons, Cain who was a tiller of the ground and Abel who was a shepherd. The Bible says that in the course of time Cain brought an offering of the fruit of the ground to the LORD and Abel also brought an offering of the firstborn of his flocks and their fat. Verse four says that the LORD favored Abel and his offering but that He did not favor Cain and his offering. At first this whole scenario just doesn't seem fair. Why would God favor one over the other? It's about the sincerity of your gift, not what you give right? Well, there is a principle of firsts in the Bible indicating that the first thing received is the first thing offered and this first offering is an offering of faith that blesses the rest. We see this in the tithe, the first fruits, the redemption of the firstborn of Israel, and even Jesus is called the firstborn over all creation (Colossians 1:15). In the case of Cain and Abel, the Bible indicates that Abel offered the firstborn of his flocks, but it doesn't say that Cain offered his first fruits. It just says that Cain brought some of the fruit of the ground as an offering to the LORD. This could have been the reason why Abel's offering was more favored than Cain's. Regardless, verse five says that because of this Cain was very angry and his countenance fell. Why would Cain be angry over an offering that he brought to the LORD? Even if the LORD corrected him over not offering the first of his fruits, what does that have to do with his brother, and why would that make him angry, angry enough to kill? Offerings are for the LORD, to the LORD. They are between you and the LORD, not anyone else. Why do you give an offering? The focus is intended to be on the LORD. It's all for Him! The LORD said to Cain, "Why are you angry? And why has your countenance fallen? If you do well, will you not be accepted? And if you do not do well, sin lies at the door. And its desire is for you, but you should rule over it." (Genesis 4:6 NIV). I'm sure God knew what was in Cain's heart. I'm sure He recognized the familiar pattern of comparison that led to Satan being cast out of heaven, and it appears that He was trying to bring it to Cain's attention. Yet Cain didn't respond. He's painfully quiet. Then the Bible says that while Abel and Cain were in the field, Cain revolted against his brother and killed him. What led to Cain getting so angry that he would kill his own brother? God didn't incite him to kill! I wonder what lies the enemy whispered and what lies Cain believed that brought him to take such drastic measures. And all of this was supposedly over an offering to the LORD!

My friend, comparison is no joke! God didn't want Cain to compare himself. God doesn't correct you by comparing you with someone else. He doesn't measure you against anyone else. He measures you by the standard of the Law, the Ten Commandments, and since none of us can keep the whole Law, Jesus redeemed us from the curse of the Law by becoming a curse for us! God's standard is Jesus! The only thing that matters is Jesus! It's all about Jesus! Stop comparing!!! It is a trap, a trap from the enemy! There was no comparing before Satan and there will be no comparing in heaven. We will genuinely rejoice in each other's rewards because it will all be for Jesus anyway! Revelation 4:10 says that we will lay our crowns at His throne. You are beyond compare because you are not unaware of the enemy's schemes. In Christ, there is no comparison!

Father,

> I thank You for Jesus. I thank You for redeeming me from the curse of the Law through Jesus. Would You help me to remember that it's all about Jesus? Forgive me for comparing myself: my talents, my stuff, my personality, my appearance to others. Forgive me for thinking more highly of myself than I ought. Forgive me for thinking that You are holding out on me in some way. Holy Spirit help me to recognize the trap of comparison and to avoid it altogether. I choose to humble myself before You because You are God and I am not. You will always be God and I will never be. I choose to pray for others rather than compare myself to them because I want to have Your heart, Your eyes for others. Help me

Jesus to live a life beyond compare because I am in You in Jesus's name, amen.

Day 102: I Am In Christ

"But if Christ is in you, though the body is dead because of sin, yet the spirit is alive because of righteousness." Romans 8:10 NASB

"I am crucified with Christ; and it is no longer I who live, but it is Christ who lives in me." Galatians 2:20 NIV

"To them God willed to make known what are the riches of the glory of this mystery among the Gentiles: which is Christ in you, the hope of glory." Colossians 1:27 NIV

You are in, my friend! You aren't on the outside. You aren't a reject, an outcast, or a nobody. You are in! And you're not just in the group, in the know, or in the how. You are in Christ! Christ is in you! That's what the Bible says. Because Christ is in you, your spirit is alive. Because you have been crucified with Christ, He really does live in you. Because Christ is in you, you carry the hope of glory with you wherever you go. Why would you be downcast when the hope of glory resides in you!

Did you know that Jesus prayed for you some 2,000 years ago while He was here on the earth? John 17 records Jesus's prayer for His disciples and for all believers, including you! Jesus prayed that you would be one with Him and the Father just as They are one with each other so that the world may believe that God sent Jesus. Verse 24 says that the Father loved Jesus from before the foundation of the world. And verse 26 says that the whole point of Jesus declaring the Father's name is so that the love that the Father has for Jesus may be in you, so that Christ may be in you! Colossians 3:3 says that your life is now hidden with Christ. You are not excluded! There are no exceptions to the rule. Being in Christ doesn't apply to everyone else but you. It is for you!

In Luke chapter 23 Jesus is being led to the cross to be crucified and the Bible says in verse 32 that there were two others, criminals, who were led with

Jesus to be put to death. One criminal was hung on the right hand of Jesus and one was hung on the left. Jesus was at the center. Those in the crowd mocked Jesus. They sneered; they made fun of Him and said, "If You are the King of the Jews, save Yourself." (Luke 23:37 NIV). The Bible says that one of these criminals that were hung with Jesus joined with the crowd and mocked Him. But the other criminal rebuked this man saying, "Do you not even fear God, seeing you are under the same condemnation?" (Luke 23:40 NIV). He goes on to say that those two criminals were receiving the due reward for their deeds, but that Jesus had done nothing wrong. He recognized that they were guilty; deserving of punishment, but that Jesus was innocent. Then he says to Jesus, "LORD, remember me when You come into Your Kingdom." (Luke 23:42 NIV). While the rest of the crowd and even the other criminal were mocking, snickering, jesting about the King of the Jews; this guy from his heart calls Jesus "LORD" and asks Jesus to remember him. He was just a criminal, the scum of the earth to most everyone else. Who knows what he did to end up being crucified on a cross, but it's apparent that the value of his life in the eyes of the crowd was minimal. Jesus chose not to save Himself from the cross so that He could save this guy who no one thought was worth saving. Regardless to what brought both these criminals to the cross, it's clear that God loved them enough, valued them enough to let them meet Jesus, the Savior of the world, before they died. One mocked, one ridiculed, one rejected who Jesus was. But the other believed and asks simply to be remembered. And Jesus responds, "Assuredly, I say to you, today you will be with Me in Paradise." (Luke 23:43 NIV). And for the last few hours of this man's life, he was in Christ. I can't wait to meet this guy in heaven and hear his testimony firsthand because I have a hunch that he was more alive hanging on a cross to be crucified than he had ever been in his life. Jesus was bloody and broken and by all appearances defeated, hanging on a cross and completely humiliated in front of a crowd of people He loved beyond words. Where most everyone else saw a fraud, a fake, a phony; this criminal saw a Savior, he saw a King, he saw love rather than nails keeping Jesus on that cross. And a few hours later he saw Jesus in the glory of heaven! Jesus is the hope of glory. He is the anticipation, the expectation of beauty, of wonder, of splendor, of brilliance; of heaven. And that hope of glory is in you because Jesus is in you! Hallelujah!

Father,

> I thank You for Jesus. I thank You that I am in Christ and that Christ is in me. I no longer live, but Christ lives in me. The hope of glory is in me. My spirit is alive. It can never be put to death because Christ is in me and He conquered the grave. Holy Spirit reveal to me just how significant is this truth. May I walk in the spirit and not in the flesh. May I know today that I carry the hope of glory, I carry Jesus with me everywhere I go. Let it be LORD, in Jesus's name, amen.

Day 103: I Am Refreshed

> *"He (God) restores my soul. He leads me in paths of righteousness for His name's sake." Psalm 23:3 ESV*

> *"Be not wise in your own eyes; fear the LORD and turn away from evil. It will be healing to your flesh and refreshment to your bones."* Proverbs 3:7-8 ESV

> *"For I (God) will satisfy the weary soul, and every languishing soul I will replenish."* Jeremiah 31:25 ESV

> *"A generous person will prosper; whoever refreshes others will be refreshed."* Proverbs 11:25 NIV

You are refreshed. You will be refreshed! God's Word, His Spirit invigorates, revives, and re-energizes. According to the Bible, fearing the LORD and turning away from evil heals your flesh and refreshes your bones. It is to the benefit of your health to follow Jesus! God will satisfy, He will keep happy the weary, worn out, exhausted soul. And He will replenish, refill every languishing, decaying, suffering soul. That's what God's Word says. Your soul is your mind, will, and emotions. It's the part of you that thinks, reasons, and feels. So if your soul is just tired today; beyond tired, you're completely exhausted in your mind, in your will, in your emotions, go to the One who will refresh you, who will satisfy you, who will keep you happy. No one else can keep you happy. People can make you happy, but they can also make you unhappy. Yet God is the only One who doesn't just make you happy, but He's able to keep you happy! If you feel like your soul is suffering, fading away; your mind and your emotions are in some serious pain, run to the One who will replenish you, who will fill you up again with His presence, His love, His goodness, with who He is! Life can be hard. The enemy often tries to just wear you down. My friend, God does not expect or even want you to do it all yourself or to figure it all out. He is God. You are not. Philippians 4:6 tells you not to be anxious about anything! Don't dwell on it, don't think obsessively about it, and don't get worried over it. Instead pray. I know that sounds so "churchy", but the Bible promises that the peace of God will guard and protect your heart and mind in relation to whatever you pray about. So, pray about everything! Prayer is your security; it is your defense against anxiety! You can cast, throw your cares upon the One who is well able to handle all your cares because He cares for you! And if you just don't know what else to do, here's a novel idea from Proverbs 11: refresh someone else! The Bible says that those who refresh, restore, and replenish others will be refreshed!

In 2 Kings chapter 5, Naaman, a Syrian commander, was a great and honorable man, a man of valor, but he was a leper. And the Bible says that there was a young girl from Israel who worked for Naaman's wife and this girl tells her mistress about the Prophet Elisha. She says that the prophet would heal Naaman. So Naaman goes to the King of Syria who sends him to the King of Israel who thinks the Syrian King is trying to pick a quarrel with him by asking him to heal someone; something that the King can't figure out, something he doesn't think he can handle, something that was impossible to him. Elisha hears that the King was in distress, so he requests Naaman to be sent to him. Naaman shows up at Elisha's house with his horse and chariot, in all his greatness, his importance, his authority. Elisha doesn't even talk to the man; he simply sends a message to Naaman for him to go wash in the Jordan River seven times and he will be restored. Elisha doesn't engage Naaman in his superiority complex. Rather, he asks him to do something that would require him to humble himself, something incredibly simple: wash and be clean. Naaman becomes furious that Elisha didn't even come out to talk to him or touch him or anything. He thinks the Jordan River isn't good enough of a river for him to wash in. He had expected something more, something better; something different. Naaman was a great man and he was expecting something great, to be treated in accordance to how great he thought he was. He was in a rage over the whole ordeal. But his servants come to him and say, "...if the prophet had told you to do something great, would you not have done it? How much more then, when he says to you, 'wash and be clean?" (2 Kings 5:13 NIV). I want to high-five these servants because their words are like a physical shaking, a slap in the face; a call for Naaman to get a grip. Thank God for those who help us to get a grip! So Naaman goes and dips himself in the Jordan River seven times according to what Elisha had said and the Bible says that his flesh was restored like the flesh of a little child. My friend, God has restored you. He will restore you. Maybe you feel like Naaman in the sense that your mind and your emotions are just numb like leprosy numbs the nerves in the skin. Maybe the weariness, the exhaustion of your soul is equivalent to the debilitating condition of being a leper like Naaman. It's destroying you. No matter how "great" you are, or you try to be, you feel like you're still wasting away emotionally, in your mind. I hear the Spirit of the LORD saying, "Wash and be clean." Humble yourself before the LORD and be refreshed! He is the One who refreshes your soul!

Father,

> Today I just need to be refreshed. I thank You for being the One who restores my soul. I can't figure it all out and I'm exhausted trying to. I can't do it all on my own, in my own strength; I need You. So, today I cast all these cares on You because You care for me. Holy Spirit, would You give me peace, the peace of God that surpasses all understanding to guard and protect my heart and my mind in Christ Jesus. Let God's peace be like a warring soldier standing guard to the door of my heart and my mind, keeping worry and anxiety out in Jesus's name. Come Holy Spirit and refresh me, revitalize me, re-energize me and give me strength. I invite You in. Be welcome here in Jesus's name, amen.

Day 104: I Am Not Forsaken

"Be strong and courageous. Do not be afraid or terrified because of them, for the LORD your God goes with you; he will never leave you nor forsake you." Deuteronomy 31:6 NIV

"Let your conduct be without covetousness; be content with such things as you have. For he himself has said, 'I will never leave you nor forsake you." Hebrews 13:5 NIV

"I (Jesus) will not leave you as orphans; I will come to you." John 14:18 NIV

You are not forsaken. You will never be forsaken! God doesn't turn His back on you, walk away from you, or abandon you. He is faithful! You can be strong and courageous because He is with you. You don't have to be afraid or terrified because He is with you. You can be content, happy, and thankful for what you have because He is with you. He has said that He would never leave you or forsake you! Where could you go from His presence? If you were to ascend to the heavens, He would be there. If you were to descend into the lowest depth, behold He is there. If you were to say that the darkness could somehow hide you from Him, He'd find you still because darkness is as light to Him. My friend, you are never forsaken!

In John chapter 11, a certain man, Lazarus was sick. I'm not sure exactly what his sickness was, but it was serious enough that his sisters, Mary and Martha, send word to Jesus saying, "LORD, behold he whom you love is sick." (John 11:3 NIV). Verse five says that Jesus loved Martha and Mary and Lazarus. But when Jesus learns that Lazarus is sick, He says that this sickness is not unto death but for the glory of God, so He stays two more days in the place where He was. I'm sure Jesus knew that He was going to raise Lazarus from the dead, but Lazarus didn't know this. I wonder what those two days were like for Lazarus. I wonder if he felt forsaken by Jesus; if he felt ignored or somehow not as important to Jesus as he thought he was. I wonder as he lay upon his sick bed facing death, if he ever felt like Jesus had abandoned him.

He knew the Healer. He was close to the One who had done miracle after miracle for everyone else. Where was *his* miracle? Why wouldn't Jesus come running to save him, to heal him, to rescue him from death? The answer to what ailed him was the One he loved, Jesus. What he needed was within his reach, within his circle of influence; Lazarus knew that Jesus loved him. Yet when he reached out to Jesus in his time of need, Jesus didn't come quickly, He didn't seem to make Lazarus a priority. Jesus had said that his sickness wasn't unto death and yet here Lazarus was getting worse and worse. He was dying. I wonder how many times Lazarus looked to the door just waiting for Jesus to walk through. How many times did he close his eyes and picture the Healer standing right there next to him? How many times did he will himself to hear Jesus's voice, knowing that if he just heard the Master's voice, this meant Jesus had come and everything was going to be okay? I wonder as the reality of his death was settling into his heart if he ever wished Jesus would have come just to be with him. Where was his Master, His healer; His friend? "Hope deferred makes the heart sick…" (Proverbs 13:12 NIV). Oh, can you relate at all?

Jesus says to His disciples one day, "Lazarus is dead…let us go to him." (John 11:14 NIV). So, when Jesus came to Bethany, He found that Lazarus had already been in the tomb for four days and that there was still a rather large crowd that had gathered to comfort Mary and Martha in their loss. Jesus speaks personally to both Mary and Martha and both these sisters say that if Jesus had come, their brother would not have died. They all knew and believed the obvious about Jesus; they knew He was the Healer; they knew He could do miracles, but they were about to have their minds blown as they witnessed Him as the Resurrection and the Life. When Jesus saw Mary weeping and all the Jews who had gathered there weeping over Lazarus, He groaned in His spirit and was troubled. And when He came to Lazarus' tomb, the Bible says that Jesus wept. Then He stands at the mouth of the tomb and calls out, "Lazarus, come forth! (John 11:43 NIV). "And he who had died came out bound hand and foot with grave clothes, and his face was wrapped with a cloth." (John 11:44 NIV). Jesus had him loosed and let go and oh the sweet reunion that must have transpired when that cloth came off Lazarus' face and he finally saw Jesus. I have a feeling that when Lazarus heard that voice, saw that face, he knew that he had never been forsaken. My friend, don't give up on Jesus! Even if it all seems impossible for you, even if it all appears to be over, you've been forsaken, abandoned by the One you thought loved you, even if you're in the tomb somewhere, things are beginning to really stink, it's dark and you feel absolutely hopeless. Jesus is calling for you to come forth, come out, live, and look upon the face of the One who has never forsaken you!

Father,

> I thank You for being with me. Because You are with me, I am strong, I am courageous, I am content, I am not afraid. I thank You for never leaving me, for never forsaking me. Would You help me to know that You are there, to trust that You are there, to feel today the nearness of Your presence with me? I need You. I need to see You, to hear Your voice. So come LORD Jesus, come Holy Spirit and simply be with me in Jesus's name, amen.

Day 105: I Am Transformed with Ever-Increasing Glory

> *"And we all, who with unveiled faces contemplate the LORD's glory, are being transformed into his image with ever-increasing glory, which comes from the LORD, who is the Spirit."* 2 Corinthians 3:18 NIV

> *"You will also be a crown of beauty in the hand of the LORD, and a royal diadem in the hand of your God."* Isaiah 62:3 NASB

> *"And one (angel) called out to another and said, 'Holy, holy, holy, is the LORD of hosts, the whole earth is full of his glory."* Isaiah 6:3 NIV

You are being transformed into God's image. His glory is changing you, making you into something you could never be on your own; His glory radiates on you, is evident upon you. And this is all happening with ever-increasing glory! Oh friend, the whole earth is full of God's glory. Creation itself points you to God. His glory, His magnificence, His splendor, His brilliance is uncontainable. It is awesome, fearsome, incredibly humbling. God's glory is bright; it illuminates; it shines. God was pleased to have all His fullness dwell in Jesus who is the radiance of God's glory and the exact representation of His being. God is full of glory and this glory shines, it's powerful; it transforms you into the likeness of God. The closer you get to God, the closer you come to His glory and the more you encounter the glory of God, the more you will become like Him. That's awesome!

In Exodus 34 Moses goes atop Mount Sinai to receive from the LORD the Ten Commandments engraved on two stone tablets by the finger of God. Moses spends forty days and nights on top of this mountain with the LORD. Forty days in God's presence. Forty days receiving from the LORD. Forty days communing with God in all His glory. After these forty days, Moses descends the mountain and returns to Israel's camp to deliver all that God had given to him, but the people notice that his face is shining. His countenance is physically glowing with the radiance of having been in God's presence. The glory of God is all over his face! Those forty days in God's glory changed Moses; transformed Moses. Verse 30 says that when everyone saw that Moses' face was glowing, they were afraid to come near him. They didn't understand the effect of being in God's presence. It scared them. It must have been a major issue or distraction because in verse 33 it says that Moses put a veil over his face to cover this glory.

My friend, God's glory is intense. It changes us. It's evident upon our lives. Maybe your face doesn't physically glow from being in God's presence (then again, maybe it does), but people should look at you and see the evidence of the glory of God on your life. Moses' face was transformed after being in God's glory. What has been transformed in you after encountering God's glory? No one encounters God and walks away the same. The very nature of the glory of God is transformative. Wow!

Can I tell you friend that you are being changed, shaped, and altered into God's image with ever-increasing glory? It's ever-increasing. This process is ever-increasing. God's glory is ever-increasing. God's glory doesn't hit a plateau at some point. You'll never reach a certain quota when it comes to the glory of God. You'll never walk away from being in His presence and not be different in some way, not be more like Him. That's what His glory does. There's an amazing attribute about the glory of God. Once you have experienced it, once you've had a taste of it, your appetite for it increases. You just want more! You cannot separate God from His glory nor would it be wise to even want to because it is this glory, His glory that is transforming you into something that you could never be apart from Him. His glory is making you like Jesus!

> Oh Jesus, show me Your glory! Rain down Your glory on me! I want to just be in Your presence today. I want to have an encounter with Your glory. Jesus, let me radiate with the evidence of having been with You. More glory LORD. More of You than I've ever experienced. I want more. I'm asking for more. Change me. Get out of me all that You need to. I want people to see You when they look at me. Let it be so in Jesus's name, amen.

Day 106: Jesus is Not Ashamed of Me!

> *"Both the one who makes people holy and those who are made holy are of the same family. So, Jesus is not ashamed to call them brothers and sisters. He says, 'I will declare your name to my brothers and sisters; in the assembly I will sing your praises."* Hebrews 2:11-12 NIV

> *"Whoever acknowledges me (Jesus) before others, I will also acknowledge before my Father in heaven."* Matthew 10:32 NIV

Jesus is not ashamed of you. He's not embarrassed by you. He is proud to have you associated with Him. He considers you family! He's the One who makes you holy. You and Jesus are family. You belong to each other, so Jesus is not ashamed to call you a brother/sister. Think about that for a second. Have you ever had someone consider you family that weren't your biological family? They took you in, loved you as if you had always belonged to them, included you, and trusted you; made a place in their life, a place in their heart, a place in their home, a place in their family for you. Wow! This is what Jesus has done for you, my friend. He considers you a brother/sister. He calls you a brother/sister!

My friend, maybe you've never had a brother/sister, but you've always wanted one. You've wanted someone to share your life with, someone who would be there for you, someone to be close to, to have as a support, and someone you could count on. Maybe you've looked for this type of person within your own family, but it's just not reciprocated. Or maybe you've tried to find a friend who might stick close like a brother/sister, but no one seems to stick with you for long. Or maybe you are blessed with lots of brothers/sisters whether biological or otherwise. Regardless, can I tell you that Jesus is this person for you! Jesus considers you this person for Him! He identifies you as His family, His brother; His sister. In fact, Proverbs 18:24 says that Jesus sticks closer than any brother. He is not ashamed of you!

In 2 Samuel 10, David thought to show kindness to Hanun son of Nahash because of the relationship he had with Hanun's father, so he sent a delegation to express his sympathy to Hanun on the passing of his father. However, the commanders of the Ammonites suspected David was sending men to spy out the land in order to overthrow it, so they took David's men shaved them, cut off their garments and sent them away ashamed and humiliated. When Hanun realized that what he had done had made him and his people obnoxious to David, Hanun hires chariots and charioteers from the Arameans to muster together with his own army in order to move out for battle against David. David sends Joab and his entire army out to meet this threat and Joab quickly realizes that there are battle lines in front of him and behind him. He is surrounded. So, he selects some of his best troops in Israel and deploys them against the Arameans and puts the rest of the men under the command of his brother Abishai to fight against the Ammonites. Then Joab tells his brother, "if the Arameans are too strong for me, then come and rescue me…but if the Ammonites are too strong for you, I will come and rescue you." (2 Samuel 10:11 NIV). With this strategy in mind they each march out boldly against their enemies and each enemy group flees enough so that the Arameans were not willing to help the Ammonites anymore.

Abishai and his brother Joab had each other's back. If the enemy appeared to be too strong for one, the other had promised to come and help. The enemy wasn't just messing with each of these brothers individually. To Joab and Abishai, it was a family matter. They were family. They looked out for each other. They helped each other and because of this, the enemy became no match for them even though the enemy had formed an alliance against them. Oh friend, Jesus, the One who considers you a brother/sister, He has already defeated your enemy. He has already conquered, destroyed, and dismantled every coalition, every weapon that the enemy could ever form against you. Jesus has your back! Jesus is your help! You may be no match for Satan yourself, but Satan is no match for Jesus! Lift your eyes to the hills. Where does your help come from? Your help comes from the LORD, the Maker of Heaven and Earth!

Father,

> I thank You for Jesus. I thank You that You are not ashamed of me, not ashamed to call me a brother/sister. You have taken me in; we are family. Thank You Jesus! The battle may be too much for me, but You are my help Jesus. You have given me victory already, Jesus. Let it be so in my life, LORD. Holy Spirit remind me today that I belong to Jesus! In Your name I pray, amen.

Day 107: I Broadcast God's Praises

> *"But you are a chosen people, a royal priesthood, a holy nation, God's special possession, that you may declare the praises of him (God) who called you out of darkness into his wonderful light."* 2 Peter 2:9 NIV

> *"I will praise you, LORD my God, with all my heart; I will glorify your name forever."* Psalm 86:12 NIV

> *"My mouth is filled with your praise, declaring your splendor all day long."* Psalm 71:8 NIV

You show forth the praises of God. You broadcast His goodness, His faithfulness, His love; who He is to the world around you. He has called you out of darkness into His wonderful light. Through Jesus, He has freed you from the enslavement of sin, He has canceled the written record of wrongs against you; He has given you His Spirit as a deposit guaranteeing your inheritance from the LORD. He has made you to be more than a conqueror through Christ, He has surrounded you with His favor as with a shield; He has given you His Spirit not to make you a slave, but to bring about your adoption into His family, to make you a son/daughter. Your life, your heart is a display of praise to God. Considering who He is, of what He has done for you, how could you not praise Him?

My friend, I know life is rough sometimes. Things happen; unexplainable, unexpected, just flat out bad things happen not because God isn't good, but because we live in a fallen world, a world full of the effects of sin; a world groaning as in the pains of childbirth right up to the present time. Sometimes it's hard to praise God, to be thankful, to worship the LORD amid the mess you might be in. It's hard, but it's not impossible. Can I tell you; the enemy doesn't want your mouth to be filled with praises to God? He doesn't want you to declare God's splendor all day long. Why? Because praising God changes your heart, your perspective, your attitude. Praising the LORD causes you to lift your head up to the hills from whence your help comes from. It causes you to remember all that God has done, to recall who God is and when you dwell on who He is, your joy increases, your faith increases; your hope increases, and your problems decrease. Satan would rather you complain. He'd rather you talk about how big and bad your situation is. He'd rather fill your mouth with words of defeat and discouragement. Satan wants you to forget that God has pardoned all your iniquities, that He has healed all your diseases, that God has redeemed your life from the pit, that He has crowned you with loving-kindness and compassion; that He has renewed your youth like the eagles. Don't forget! There's power in your praise; victory comes when you praise the Victor!

In 2 Chronicles 20, a vast army of Moabites, Ammonites, and some of the Muenites came to wage war against Jehoshaphat and all of Judah. When Jehoshaphat was told of this enemy alliance and their plan to attack Judah, he was alarmed but resolved to inquire of the LORD, so he proclaims a time of fasting and prayer. Jehoshaphat stands up in front of all the people and just pours his heart out to God. He says, "…we have no power to face this vast army that is attacking us. We do not know what to do, but our eyes are on you." (2 Chronicles 20:12 NIV). Maybe you don't have the power to face what you are up against. Maybe you're alarmed at what the enemy has brought against you. Maybe you don't know what to do, but at some point, you've got to decide where you will fix your eyes. The next verse says that all of Judah, all the men and their wives, all the children and little ones stood before the

LORD. Then the Spirit of the LORD came! I don't know how long they stood there, how many there were all together, or how many tears were shed in the process, but they kept standing together; all of them, even the children and little ones until the Spirit of the LORD came. Oh friend, keep standing! Keep standing until the Spirit of God comes! Through Jahaziel the LORD tells Jehoshaphat and all of Judah not to be afraid or discouraged because of this vast army for the battle is not yours but God's. The LORD says, "You will not have to fight this battle. Take up your positions; stand firm and see the deliverance the LORD will give you." (2 Chronicles 20:17 NIV). In response, the people fall on their faces in worship. Some of them stand up and in a loud voice proclaim praise to God. Early the next morning, the people set out to face their enemy and Jehoshaphat, after consulting with the people, appoints a group of men to go out at the head of the army to sing and to praise the LORD. What kind of military strategy is this anyway? What good would a group of singing men do against the weapons of the enemy? It might not have been easy for these men to praise God; they were soldiers, not a choir. Maybe they felt a little silly. They were marching out to face something that was by all appearances going to be their defeat. How could they praise God and sing of His enduring love when things looked so dark, so impossible, but they did it anyway! And the Bible says in verse 22 that as they began to sing and to praise, the LORD set ambushes against Moab and Ammon and Mount Seir who were invading Judah and they were defeated! This enemy group that had allied themselves together against God's people, rose up against one another and helped to destroy each other so that when the men of Judah came to the place that overlooked the vast army, they saw only dead bodies. No one of the enemy had escaped! And there was so much plunder from this victory that it took Jehoshaphat and his men three whole days to collect it all.

Oh friend, there is power in your praise! There is victory in your praise! Praising God doesn't somehow change who God is. It is the appropriate response to who God already is! It's time to take up your position against the enemy; a position of victory; a position of triumph; a position of praise; a position you have been given because of Jesus. It's time to stand firm, to refuse to be discouraged out of your position in Christ and see the deliverance that the LORD will give you. It's time to fall on your face in worship, to stand up and in a loud voice proclaim the praises of God. Why? Because He is worthy! Sometimes the greatest strategy against the enemy is to sing and praise the LORD, to lift your voice and give thanks for God's enduring love! Oh friend, this situation for Israel was a death sentence and they knew it, but instead of moping around in gloom, doom, and despair they offered up to God a sacrifice of praise. And as soon as they began to sing and to praise, God confused the enemy, completely wiped out the enemy, and absolutely plundered the enemy. Let it be so with you too! May you return from the battle today rejoicing because God has fought your enemy for you!

Father,

> Today I just want to praise You. You have pardoned my sins, healed my diseases, redeemed my life from the pit; You have crowned me with loving-kindness and compassion and renewed my youth like the eagles. You are so worthy to be praised! I may not have the power to face what I'm up against today. I may not know what to do, but my eyes are on You. Today I choose to take my position, to stand firm against the enemy and see the deliverance that You will bring to me. Thank You for fighting my battles for me. Thank You for crushing the enemy on my behalf. I rejoice today because You have made me the victor in Christ. I broadcast Your praises LORD for You are so, so good. Let it be in Jesus's name, amen.

Day 108: I Am the Salt of the Earth

"You are the salt of the earth. But if the salt loses its saltiness, how can it be made salty again? It is no longer good for anything, except to be thrown out and trampled underfoot." Matthew 5:13 NIV

"Salt is good, but even if the salt becomes unsalty, with what will you make it salty again? Have salt in yourselves and be at peace with one another." Mark 9:50 NASB

> *"On the second day you shall offer a male goat without blemish for sin offering, and they shall cleanse the altar as they cleansed it with the bull. When you have finished cleansing it, you shall present a young bull without blemish and a ram without blemish from the flock. You shall present them before the LORD, and the priests shall throw salt on them, and they shall offer them up as a burnt offering to the LORD."* Ezekiel 43:22-24

You are the salt of the earth. That's what Jesus said of you recorded in the Bible in Matthew, Mark, and Luke. What in the world does that phrase mean? Why would Jesus refer to you as salt? Salt has two distinct qualities about it. Salt is a preservative. We don't use it in this sense as much anymore, but before the development of refrigeration, salt was often used to preserve foods especially meats. Salt is a natural preservative, protecting foods from bacteria and decay. Considering this preservative quality of salt, you are also called the salt of the earth. One of your purposes on the earth is to preserve what is good, what is noble, what is right, what is pleasing to God; to help protect the earth from the devastating effects of evil and sin. Salt is also used to enhance flavor. Even the sacrifices offered in the Old Testament by the priests were sprinkled with salt. You are intended and expected to add "flavor" to this world. By the Holy Spirit, you bring taste, seasoning, and zest to the world around you.

Think about it. The love of Jesus in you causes you to act and react differently than the world. It causes you to serve, it causes you to pray for those who persecute you, to keep no record of wrongs, and to always protect, always trust, always hope, and always persevere. Because Jesus is in you, everything you do, everything you are a part of should be enhanced. A lot of people can sing, write, draw, work, serve, love, give, etc.; but having Jesus in you improves all of this and somehow makes singing, writing, drawing, working, serving, loving, giving, etc. so much better, go so much further. You enhance the world just like salt enhances the flavor of the food it is used on. People often notice when food has been salted or not and in like manner this world should notice the effect God's people have on it. When the rapture of the church takes place (1 Corinthians 15:51-53), the earth should notice and miss us because of the positive effect God's people have on the earth, an effect that will be noticeable and missed when it is suddenly taken away. It was no accident that Jesus called you the salt of the earth.

Think of Daniel in the Bible, think of Shadrach, Meshach, and Abednego living in Babylon. Think of Paul and Peter and Stephen and all the apostles and early believers in the New Testament. Think of John the Baptist. Think of Queen Esther. Think of Joseph in the land of Egypt. All these people and so many more mentioned in the Bile were salt to the world around them. They preserved what was honorable, what was good, what was right, what was pleasing to the LORD in the lands they lived within even when those lands and countries were predominately hostile to the God of Israel. Not only so, but these men and women also added life, and flavor, and spice to the people they lived among. Daniel was one of the smartest people in the Kingdom of Babylon. He was able to interpret dreams and he was so honoring and respectful with the authorities that God had instituted in his life, that he was put in second command of the whole nation of Babylon. The same was true for Joseph in Egypt. Sold as a slave and seemingly forgotten about in prison for a crime he was falsely accused of committing, Joseph also could interpret dreams and he was excellent at planning and managing. Pharaoh ends up entrusting him with the responsibility of preserving Egypt during a time of sever famine. Esther found herself married to a king who was very rash and cruel and irrational, dealing with a powerful man in the kingdom, Haman, who was favored by the king but who also hated Esther's people and devised a plan to destroy all the Jews. Yet Esther uses her influence with the king for good, and God, largely through her, ends up saving all the Jewish people. These people weren't incredible or extraordinary in and of themselves. Rather, they belonged to the LORD, they had the LORD with them, and this made them different. This made them salt to the earth. Don't lose your saltiness, friend! The enemy is a liar. This world needs you! You are its salt. You are what preserves it, what gives it flavor and taste. It's not about you in and of yourself. It's about Jesus in you, the LORD with you. It's all because of Him and it's all for Him. Let it be in Jesus's' name!

Father,

> I thank You for making me the salt of the earth. You have made me to impact this world in a positive way. Help me, Holy Spirit, to do just that. I need Your help, Your guidance, Your leading to do things in Your strength and not my own, to follow You and not to lean on my own understanding. Help me never to lose my saltiness in Jesus's name, amen.

Day 109: I Look Up!

"But you, LORD, are a shield around me, my glory, the One who lifts my head high." Psalm 3:3 NIV

"Lift up your heads, you gates; be lifted up, you ancient doors that the King of glory may come in." Psalm 24:7 NIV

"But when these things begin to take place, straighten up and lift up your heads, because your redemption is drawing near." Luke 21:28 NIV

"I lift up my eyes to the hills—where does my help come from? My help comes from the LORD, the Maker of heaven and earth." Psalm 121:1 NIV

There are many joys, many pleasures in life, but life can sometimes be hard and well, full of trouble according to Job 14. There are so many things to deal with, so many unexpected issues that arise, so much of life that just doesn't make sense; that simply breaks your heart. Do you ever feel like things are just coming at you from all sides? Your job is stressful, relationships in your life need mending, and there are more bills than there is money coming in to cover them all. Or someone you love has received a gut-wrenching report from the doctors. The cares and concerns of life weigh on you, they push you down, maybe slowly but you surely feel the weight of them on your shoulders. Sigh. You're just exhausted. How are you supposed to deal with it all? It's just too much so your head droops in discouragement, in defeat, in despair. My friend, can I tell you that according to the Bible the LORD is a shield around you. He is your glory and the One who lifts your head high. "Cast your cares on the LORD and he will sustain you; he will never let the righteous be shaken." (Psalm 55:22 NIV). You may be hard-pressed on every side, but you're not crushed. You may be perplexed, but don't you dare give in to despair. You may be persecuted, but you are never abandoned. The enemy may have struck you down with this one, but you are not destroyed. Why? Because there is a treasure housed in your fragile jar of clay of a body and that treasure is the Hope of glory, Jesus, to show that this all-surpassing power to endure, to press on, to overcome is from God alone.

Lift your head, my friend, for the King of Glory is coming in. Lift your head, my friend, for your redemption is drawing near. Lift your eyes to the hills for your help is not here on this earth somewhere, your help isn't in any man, it isn't in anything of this world. Rather, lift your head up high for the LORD, the One from whom your help comes from is high and lifted. Lift your head up to the Maker of heaven and earth, the One who meets your needs according to His glorious riches in Christ, the One who owns the cattle on a thousand hillsides. Lift your head up to the One who saw your unformed body while you were yet hidden in that secret place, the One who knew all the days ordained for you before one of them came to be. My friend, the One who watches over your life does not slumber or sleep. Rather, He is your shade at your right hand. Lift your head up to the One who causes the sun not to harm you by day, or the moon by night. Lift your head up to the One who watches over your coming and going both now and forevermore. God has called you heavenward in Christ Jesus. Your prize is in heaven. Look up!

In Luke 21, the disciples asked Jesus what the sign of His coming and of the end of the age would be. Jesus answers by warning them of deception, of many who will come in His name claiming to be the "Messiah". He tells of wars and rumors of wars, of nation revolting against nation, and kingdom against kingdom. He says that there will be famines and earthquakes in various places, there will be an increase in persecution and that many will turn away from the faith. He tells of Jerusalem being surrounded by armies, and Matthew 24 expounds also on an influx of wickedness and how the love of most will grow cold. Yet Jesus says, "When these things begin to take place, stand up and lift up your heads, because your redemption is drawing near." (Luke 21:28 NIV). Amid these crazy, dreadful, frightening things Jesus warns to happen, when the only logical response seems to be to go hide somewhere, to look left and right frantically back and forth for help or a way out, or to hang your head in defeat. Jesus says during this junk to stand up and to lift your head! My friend, I don't know how crazy your life is right now. I don't know how hard-pressed you are, how frightened you are, or how dreadful things are looking for you. But in the middle of what appears to be a mess, in the middle of what seems to be too big, too hard, too much for you to handle; in the middle of dreadful, terrible news and circumstances can I encourage you to stand up and lift your head today for your redemption, your help, your glory, your LORD is coming! May the One who is your shield, who is your glory; may the LORD Almighty lift your head high today in Jesus's name!

Father,

I thank You for being a shield around me. Thank You for being the One who lifts my head high. I may be hard-pressed on every side, but by Your grace I am not crushed. I may be perplexed by this life, by what's happening around me, but I am not in despair. I may have been struck down, but I am not destroyed. Today I lift my eyes to the hills for I know where my help comes from. You are LORD, You are the Maker of heaven and earth, You are the One who sustains me. I lift my head up today and invite you the King of glory to come into my life, my situation, my problems and reign. Let all of Your glory completely transform my life, my situation, my problems in Jesus's name, amen.

Day 110: I Am Free from Accusation

"But now he has reconciled you by Christ's physical body through death to present you holy in his sight, without blemish and free from accusation." Colossians 1:22 NIV

"No weapon forged against you will prevail, and you will refute every tongue that accuses you. This is the heritage of the servants of the LORD, and this is their vindication from me, declares the LORD." Isaiah 54:17 NIV

"Then I heard a loud voice in heaven say: 'Now have come the salvation and the power and the kingdom of our God, and the authority of his Messiah. For the accuser of our brothers and sisters, who accuses them before our God day and night, has been hurled down." Revelation 12:10 NIV

The Bible calls Satan, your enemy, the accuser. He never stops looking for things to accuse you of before God. He blames you. He charges you, and he indicts you before the LORD both night and day. He never stops probing for a foothold in your life, searching for an open door to get in at your house; he's constantly trying to kill, steal, and destroy you. But the Bible says that God reconciled you to Himself through Christ. Because of Jesus, you are now holy and blameless in God's sight and you are free from accusation! Oh friend, you are a servant of the LORD and part of your inheritance, your heritage, what you have received in Christ is victory over the enemy both now and for all eternity. No weapon that Satan could form against you will prevail and you can refute, disprove every tongue, you can counter Satan's lying, accusing tongue that rises to accuse you. Jesus has freed you from accusation! Jesus has freed you from the charges that Satan could bring against you. His blood has covered and conquered your sin. Thank you, Jesus!

"My dear children, I write this to you so that you will not sin. But if anybody does sin, we have an advocate with the Father—Jesus Christ, the Righteous One. He is the atoning sacrifice for our sins, and not only for our sins but also for the sins of the whole world." (1 John 2:1-2 NIV). Satan may be the one who accuses you before God, but Jesus is your advocate! He is the One who supports you, who has your back before the Father, who believes in you, who advocates for you to God. Satan accuses you both night and day, but Jesus defends you both night and day! Jesus is praying for you, interceding for you; He is sitting at the right hand of God in a place of honor, of authority, of favor with God. This same Jesus is your advocate! My friend, there is coming a day when your accuser, when Satan will be hurled down, cast down out of God's presence. He won't be able to accuse you anymore! There will come a day when his lying, accusing tongue will be silenced forever! You need Jesus because Jesus is your Advocate, He is your victory, He is the Righteous One who frees you from accusation! Jesus is your Defender, your Conqueror, your victory over Satan now and forevermore!

In Jeremiah 37, Babylon's king Nebuchadnezzar appoints Zedekiah to be king of Judah in place of his nephew Jehoiachin who was overthrown and taken as a prisoner by Babylon after only three months of leadership. The Bible says that neither Zedekiah nor any of his attendants paid any attention to the words of the LORD spoken through Jeremiah the prophet. Yet at the threat of Babylon, the king asks Jeremiah who had been foretelling of Babylon's invasion of Judah to pray for him. Seems a little ironic. King Zedekiah sought support from Egypt, but the LORD through Jeremiah warned the king that Egypt would withdraw, and Babylon would attack and capture Judah. Yet with Egypt's current help, things still looked promising to the king and he refused to listen to the LORD. King Zedekiah was deceived. He was appointed by the King of Babylon, but he thought he could defeat the authority that had appointed him.

In verse 12 Jeremiah goes to the territory of Benjamin to receive his share of the property there. Yet when he reaches the Benjamin Gate the captain of the guard seizes him and arrests him and accuses him of deserting to the Babylonians. In verse 14 Jeremiah says, "That's not true!" But no one believes him. He's arrested, beaten, and thrown into a vaulted cell in a dungeon where he remained for a long time according to the Bible, until Babylon overthrew Judah and released Jeremiah. Jeremiah was falsely accused and turned on by his own people and by a king he loved, but was somehow rescued by a brutal, openly hostile king, Nebuchadnezzar. Talk about God preparing a table before you in the presence of your enemies. King Zedekiah didn't believe the word of the LORD and since Jeremiah so often told of Babylon's invasion of Judah, the King believed that Jeremiah was favorably disposed to Babylon. My friend, Satan is a liar and the father of lies. He is a deceiver because he, himself is deceived. He believes that he can be like God. He believes that he can overthrow the Kingdom of God. But he is deceived! Proverbs 6 says there are seven things the LORD hates, one of which is a lying tongue and a false witness that speaks lies. Satan is a false witness who speaks lies! There is no truth in him! King Zedekiah refused to listen to the truth. He believed a lie although God tried tirelessly to tell him otherwise. King Zedekiah was deceived, and he turned on the one through whom the message and warnings came, Jeremiah. But the Bible says that Babylon did invade and capture Judah, taking King Zedekiah as prisoner. 2 Kings 25:7 records the Babylonians killing all of King Zedekiah's sons before his eyes, then they gouged out his eyes, bound him with bronze shackles and took him as a prisoner to Babylon. He died as a prisoner in Babylon. What a high price deception cost him!

My friend, its' time to refute the lying, accusing tongue of your accuser! In Jesus, you are free from accusation. This is your inheritance from the LORD! God will hurl Satan down out of His presence one day, but Jesus is your Advocate now, because Jesus has freed you from accusation already, you can resist, refute your accuser right now. According to God's Word, he will flee from you. Praise God, you are free from accusation!

Father,

> I thank You for freeing me of all accusation through Jesus. I thank You that because of the blood of Jesus, I am holy and blameless in Your sight. Holy Spirit, would you seal my ears to hear only Your voice? I don't want to listen to the voice of my accuser for he is a liar and the father of lies. I don't want to be deceived. You are the truth, Jesus, so I run to You. Thank You for being my advocate, for praying for me, for defending me; for giving to me an inheritance of victory. Let it be so in Jesus's name, amen.

Day 111: I Am Sure

> *"Now faith is confidence in what we hope for and assurance about what we do not see."* Hebrews 11:1 NIV

> *"Because the Sovereign LORD helps me, I will not be disgraced. Therefore, have I set my face like a flint, and I know I will not be put to shame."* Isaiah 50:7 NIV

> *"Not only so, but we ourselves, who have the first fruits of the Spirit, groan inwardly as we wait eagerly for our adoption to sonship, the redemption of our bodies. For in this hope we were saved. But hope that is seen is no hope at all. Who hopes for what they already have? But if we hope for what we do not yet have, we wait for it patiently."* Romans 8:23-24 NIV

You are sure of what you hope for, certain about what you do not see. Because the sovereign LORD helps you, you will not be disgraced. You can set your face like a flint, knowing that you will not be put to shame. Flint is a hard, grey rock often flaked or ground in ancient times to make weapons and can also be used to ignite a spark and start a fire. In Ezekiel 3:9, the Israelites are living as exiles in Babylon and God raises Ezekiel, the priest, to be one of His prophets and speak to Israel on His behalf. In Ezekiel 3, God warns Ezekiel of how hard and stubborn the children of Israel are. In verse 6 God says, that if He had not sent Ezekiel, the Israelites would have listened to him. He goes on in verse 7 to say that the people of Israel will not listen to Ezekiel because they won't listen to God. That's how hardened and obstinate they are. Their refusal to listen to Ezekiel, to receive him had nothing to do with Ezekiel and everything to do with the hardness of their hearts before God. But the LORD says that He will make Ezekiel just as unyielding, "I will make your forehead like the hardest stone, harder than flint. Do not be afraid of them or terrified by them, though they are a rebellious people." (Ezekiel 3:9 NIV).

Being sure of what you hope for and certain about what you do not see is what the ancients were commended for. In Ezekiel 37, the Spirit of the LORD brought Ezekiel out and placed him in the middle of a valley full of dry bones. The LORD led Ezekiel back and forth among these bones and verse two says that these bones were very dry. These were bones that had been lifeless for a long time. They were brittle, fragile; not good for anything. This was a valley of death, of dreams lost, of hopelessness. But the LORD asks Ezekiel, "Can these bones live?" (Ezekiel 37:3 NIV). With a simple question the LORD releases the possibility of hope into what appears a completely hopeless situation and I love Ezekiel's response. He says, "Sovereign LORD, you alone know." (Ezekiel 37:3 NIV). Ezekiel doesn't dismiss the question or give God a piece of his mind about the matter; rather, with his response to the LORD he chooses to acknowledge that with God all things are possible. In verse four, the LORD tells Ezekiel to prophesy to those dry bones and tell them that the LORD will cause breath to enter them and they will come to life. The LORD will attach tendons to them, cause flesh to appear on them, and cover them with skin, then God will cause breath to enter them and they will come to life. Then those dry bones will know that the LORD is God. Sounds completely ridiculous, but Ezekiel obeys.

Oh friend, sometimes you must prophesy to the dry bones in your life. Sometimes you must call forth life, call forth breath, call forth destiny even when all you see before you are lifeless and brittle bones. As Ezekiel is prophesying to these bones, there was a noise, a rattling sound as the bones began to come together. Ezekiel looked and there appeared tendons and flesh on these bones and there before him lay a vast army that looked more alive than they once did, but still they were lifeless. They had no breath. The LORD has Ezekiel prophesy for the breath to come. "Come breath, from the four winds and breathe into these slain, that they may live." (Ezekiel 37:9 NIV).

And that's exactly what happened. These dry bones were a picture to Ezekiel of the children of Israel. Israel had said, "Our bones are dried up and our hope is gone; we are cut off," (Ezekiel 37:11 NIV). But the LORD responds that He will open the grave if He must and bring His people out. These people that were hardened and rebellious, that would not listen to Ezekiel because they would not listen to God; God would resurrect them! Don't lose hope! Never lose hope even when things look dead, completely hopeless in your life. Even when you feel broken and brittle and good for nothing, even when things haven't seemed to turn around for you in a very long time. There is still a reason to be sure of what you hope for and certain about what you do not see because God, your God, has the power to breathe life back into long dead things. He has the power to resurrect dreams and do the seemingly impossible. Ezekiel was sure of this; certain about it even before he seen the evidence in front of him.

My friend, you can be sure of what you hope for and certain about what you do not see because your faith is in Someone unseen, Someone eternal, Someone beyond confines, beyond limitations, beyond physical restraint or restriction. You don't have to be tossed back and forth and blown here and there by every wind of doctrine. You don't have to be double-minded and unstable in all that you do. You don't have to waiver, falter, or be deceived. Rather, you can set your face like a flint; the LORD can make you just as unyielding and strong in your faith as one of the hardest stones in creation. You can be sure; you can be confident because He is the Rock. He never fails. He does not change like shifting shadows and He makes you like a rock too. You are sure, you are unyielding; you are like flint. You may encounter hard things, but those hard things in life don't break you. They don't crush you. And there's an interesting quality about flint: when certain materials are struck against it, a spark forms and a fire starts. One of these materials is steel. Steel is strong, virtually indestructible. But when a piece of flint rock is struck by steel, a spark is released, and a fire starts. In the same way, those things in life that seem virtually indestructible to you, those things that are too strong, that seem to surely be your destruction. Don't let them crush you, friend. Instead let them ignite a spark and start a fire in your life!

Father,

> You are awesome, You are sovereign. Nothing is impossible with You. Holy Spirit help me to remember this. To default

to this truth rather than to what I see before me. Help me to be sure of what I hope for and certain about what I do not see in Jesus's name, amen.

Day 112: I Am Real

"As for you, the anointing you received from him remains in you, and you do not need anyone to teach you. But as his anointing teaches you about all things and as that anointing is real, not counterfeit—just as it has taught you, remain in him." 1 John 2:27 NIV

"When Simon saw that the Spirit was given at the laying on of the apostle's hands, he offered them money and said, 'Give me also this ability so that everyone on whom I lay my hands may receive the Holy Spirit.' Peter answered, 'May your money perish with you, because you thought you could buy the gift of God with money!" Acts 8:18-20 NIV

What you have is real. If you are born of God; the anointing you received from the LORD is real. It isn't counterfeit, fake, phony, or bogus. It can't be bought with money, imitated by man, or somehow replicated by the enemy. Any attempt at this may have an appearance of what is of the Spirit but will fall way short in comparison to the real thing. In 2 Corinthians 11, Paul talks about false apostles, deceitful workers who masquerade as apostles of Christ. And he says, "And no wonder, for Satan himself masquerades as an angel of light." (2 Corinthians 11:14 NIV). Darkness may try to impersonate light, and initially this may appear real and even confusing, but every ruse to imitate the authentic will eventually prove bogus. Why? Because darkness cannot be light, evil cannot be good; Satan cannot be God. To do so goes against their very natures.

In Acts chapter 8, there was a man, a sorcerer named Simon who had practiced sorcery for a long time. He boasted that he was someone great and all the people in the city of Samaria were amazed by the things he did. They gave him their attention and exclaimed, "This man is rightly called The Great Power of God." (Acts 8:10 NIV). This is a perfect example of darkness masquerading as light. However, in verse 12 it says that the people of Samaria believed Philip and the message he proclaimed about Jesus Christ and they were all baptized, both men and women. Even this sorcerer, Simon, believed and was baptized. According to the Word of God, afterward Simon followed Philip around everywhere because he was astonished at the signs and miracles he saw. This man was attracted to the power and to the acclimation that power brought. He seemed to be more interested in the signs and miracles; rather, than the God of those signs and miracles. In verse 14, the apostles Peter and John came to Samaria to pray for these new believers so that they might receive the Holy Spirit, the baptism of the Spirit as evidenced by speaking in tongues described in Acts 2. So, Peter and John placed their hands on these men and women, and they received the Holy Spirit. When Simon saw that the Spirit was given at the laying on of the apostles' hands, he offers them money and says, "Give me also this ability so that everyone I lay my hands on may receive the Holy Spirit."(Acts 8:19 NIV). It wasn't the reception of the Holy Spirit Simon was interested in. His proposal proves his heart was captivated by the power of performing miracles and signs and the attention those things brought. Whether those signs and miracles were real or simply counterfeit was irrelevant to Simon, and Peter firmly rebukes him in verse 20. Peter tells Simon that he has no part in this ministry because his heart isn't right before God and Simon needs to repent for even having such a thought! God, help us!

My friend, the fake, the phony; every impersonation of the real thing cannot compare, will never compare to what is really of the Spirit. Satan may try to impersonate God, but he will never be God. Darkness may attempt to personify light, but if you look closely it's still just darkness. And evil may give an initial appearance of good, but at its core it's still evil. Don't be deceived! God will not be mocked! What is born of the Spirit gives birth to Spirit and what is born of the flesh gives birth to flesh. And not every spirit is from God. That's why 1 John 4 admonishes you to test the spirits to see if they are from God or not. How do you do this? "By this you will know the Spirit of God: every spirit that confesses that Jesus Christ has come in the flesh is from God, and every spirit that does not confess Jesus is not from God. This is the spirit of antichrist…" (1 John 4:2-3 NIV). If you want to avoid the fake, stay in the real! If you only want the authentic experience of the Spirit, stay in God's presence. Flesh cannot give birth to the Spirit. We can pretend, but God is not a God of pretense; He is the One, True, Authentic God of all creation. There is nothing phony about Him.

Father,

> You are God; there simply is no other! Today, I just want to humble myself before You and confess that You are LORD. Forgive my heart for ever exalting another. Holy Spirit, give me wisdom, give me discernment to recognize what is truly of God and what isn't. May I never veer from the truth that Jesus Christ did in fact come in the flesh. To deny that He came is to deny the Good News of the Bible completely. I don't want any part in what's fake, what's phony, what's only a pretense of the real thing. I want You! I want what's real in Jesus's name, amen.

Day 113: I Am Equipped

> *"Devote yourselves to prayer, keeping alert in it with an attitude of thanksgiving."* Colossians 4:2 NASB
>
> *"But in your hearts revere Christ as LORD. Always be prepared to give an answer to everyone who asks you to give the reason for the hope that you have. But do this with gentleness and respect."* 1 Peter 3:15 NIV
>
> *"When you are brought before synagogues, rulers and authorities do not worry about how you will defend yourselves or what you will say, for the Holy Spirit will teach you at that time what you should say."* Luke 12:11-12 NIV

You are equipped, prepared; you are ready! The Word of God on several instances admonishes you to be alert. 1 Peter 5:8 tells you to be alert because your adversary, the devil, prowls around like a roaring lion just looking for someone to devour. You must be alert against the enemy. In Luke 12, you are told to be dressed in readiness for your Master because you do not know the exact hour He will return. In fact, Luke says that you are blessed if the Master finds you waiting for Him when He does return. If you know that Someone of great importance is coming to your house, but you don't know exactly the day or the hour that He will arrive; you'll more than likely have your house prepared and ready every day just in case today is the day He decides to come. Think of the embarrassment of Him showing up and your house is a complete disaster especially when you knew that He was coming! Thus, it is with Jesus and His return. Colossians instructs you to devote yourself to prayer and to stay alert while doing it by having an attitude of thanksgiving. And 1 Peter 3:15 encourages you to always be ready to give an answer to everyone who asks you to give a reason for the hope that you have, but to do this with gentleness and respect. It's clear that being alert, being prepared; being ready is in your best interests. Thankfully, God has equipped you; He has given you everything that you need to be prepared.

You're prepared against your adversary, the devil. You are equipped to defeat the enemy. Jesus conquered your enemy for you on the cross and He has made you to be more than a conqueror through Him. You don't just have the victory in Him, you way more than have the victory in Him. He's given you His Word that you might not be conformed to the pattern of this world, but that you might be transformed by the renewing of your mind. The Bible likens the Word of God to a weapon, the Sword of the Spirit (Ephesians 6:17) and a double-edged sword (Hebrews 4:12). You have a powerful weapon that the enemy cannot overcome. God has given you a family and this family of believers helps you to resist the enemy. "Resist him (Satan), standing firm in the faith, because you know that the family of believers throughout the world is undergoing the same kind of suffering." (1 Peter 5:9 NIV). You're not alone! You're not the only one going through what you're going through! The closer you get to other brothers and sisters in Christ, the more you realize that the enemy attacks us all in very similar ways. Connection with other believers exposes the tactics and plans of the enemy. No wonder he tries to isolate us so much! 2 Corinthians 2:11 says that we are not unaware of the enemy's schemes. God doesn't want you to be unaware. He's given you awareness through His Word, through connection with other believers. I'd say an isolated believer with no involvement or interest in the Word of God suffers the dangers of being completely unaware. You have been prepared and equipped for victory over your adversary, the devil. Thank You, Jesus!

Father,

> I thank You that I am no unaware of the enemy's schemes. I thank You for Your Word, for other believers that help me to resist the devil so that he might flee from me. I thank You that Jesus has made me to be more than a conqueror in Him. I am prepared with victory, with triumph, with everything that I need to overcome. Let it be LORD, in Jesus's name, amen!

Day 114: I Have Peace

> *"Do not be anxious about anything, but in every situation, by prayer and petition, with thanksgiving, present your requests to God. And the peace of God, which transcends all understanding, will guard your hearts and your minds in Christ Jesus."* Philippians 4:6-7 NIV
>
> *"You will keep in perfect peace those whose minds are steadfast, because they trust in you."* Isaiah 26:3 NIV
>
> *"Peace I (Jesus) leave with you; my peace I give you. I do not give to you as the world gives. Do not let your hearts be troubled and do not be afraid."* John 14:27 NIV

You have been given peace! Jesus has given you His peace. Not as the world gives. There are no strings attached, it isn't based on circumstances, and it cannot be explained away. The Bible teaches that you don't have to be anxious about anything! Rather, in every situation, by praying and petitioning God with thanksgiving, you can present your requests to the LORD. And when you do this, the peace of God which goes beyond all understanding, that exceeds all human reasoning, and transcends what's considered a logical response or way that you should be feeling based on your situation; this peace will guard and protect your heart and your mind in Christ Jesus. Peace is often equated with calm, with zero conflict, with doing nothing; with something that is almost weak and unassuming. But the peace of God is strong. It is mighty. It is a force to be reckoned with. Imagine it as a ninja warrior of sorts standing guard at your heart and your mind as you pray just karate-chopping and annihilating every anxious thought that tries to take residence with you. Maybe that's a juvenile picture, but the point is God's peace is powerful. The peace of God is more powerful than worry, than anxiety, than fear! God can keep you in perfect peace if your mind is steadfast, and you trust in Him.

My friend, you are not a mess, or, at least, you don't have to be! You're not crazy! 2 Timothy 5:7 says that God has given you a sound mind! Fear, worry, anxiety; the enemy uses these to rob your mind of its God-given soundness. Think about it. Have you noticed how your anxious thoughts seem to snowball? And the internal snowball of thoughts just keeps going. Before you know it, you feel frazzled, worried, your heart starts beating faster, you can't sleep at night, and you're fidgety; on the defensive. What is going on? The enemy is robbing you of your peace!

In Numbers 13 the children of Israel had escaped slavery in Egypt and endured forty years in the wilderness due to their disobedience but were now on the brink of entering the land promised to them by God, the land of Canaan, a land flowing with milk and honey. This was a land already inhabited, but God had promised to give Israel the land as a possession. It was His gift to them. He would take care of all the details, they need only trust in Him. So, the LORD tells Moses in Numbers 13 to send twelve men, one from each ancestral tribe of Israel, throughout the land to explore it. It's almost as if God wanted to give the people a preview of the gift, He had prepared for them. These men go throughout the land, exploring it for forty days then they return to report to the whole Israelite community. They tell of the richness of the land, that it is a land flowing with milk and honey, and they show the people the fruit of the land. They had cut off a branch bearing just one cluster of grapes and this fruit was so big and bountiful that two of them had to carry it on a pole between them. The land was a land of abundance, a land of provision, a land of more than enough. God was not only supplying their needs; He was giving to them more than they could possibly need. Yet the men who went to explore the land also reported that the people who lived there were powerful, and the cities they lived in were fortified and large. Before anxiety threatens to strike fear in the camp of Israel, one of the men, Caleb, speaks up and says, "We should go up and take possession of the land, for we can certainly do it." (Numbers 13:30 NIV). Caleb knew the land was promised to them by God. The land had giant fruit cultivated by giant people who lived in giant cities, but God has no problem slaying giants. The people had nothing to worry about. God was bigger than the enemy that stood in their way just as He was bigger than Pharaoh, bigger than the Red Sea, but instead of focusing on the greatness of God and His promise to them, they chose to exalt themselves and their own inadequacies. The other men who went to explore the land spread a bad report among the people. They say that there's no way Israel can go up to attack those living in Canaan for the enemy is stronger than Israel is. In verse 32 they say that the land they saw devours those living in it, that all the people they saw were of great size, that Israel seemed like grasshoppers in comparison to the enemy. This bad report spreads fear, worry, and anxiety among the whole camp of Israel. Numbers 14 shows that the Israelites begin to weep and grumble against Moses and Aaron. They cry out, "If only we had died in Egypt! Or in the wilderness!" (Numbers 14:2 NIV). They are so consumed with defeat; their minds are so confused by fear that they were ready to stone Moses and Aaron and Caleb and Joshua. They wanted to kill the very ones who were trying to remind them of the truth! Their worry, their fear, their anxiety and disbelief end up preventing them from ever seeing the Promised Land. What happened? Through fear, through worry, through anxiety and unbelief the enemy robbed Israel of their promise and prolonged the fulfillment of the promise for those who were faithful.

My friend, don't let the enemy rob you! Shut the front door in the face of that stuff! Don't let fear and anxiety trigger more fearful and anxious thoughts. Rather, let feeling anxious about something trigger you to pray about it! I wonder how the camp of Israel would have reacted if considering this bad report, they had stopped and prayed before their thoughts went south. The Word of God promises the peace of God to stand guard at the door of your heart and mind regarding those things you pray about. So, pray, my friend! Pray and pray again and again. Every time you start to feel worried about it, stop and pray. Don't be robbed of peace when Jesus has given you His peace! God's peace trumps anxiety every time! Let it be LORD, in Jesus's name!

Father,

> I thank You for peace. I thank You that Jesus is the Prince of peace. You have given me peace. Not as the world gives so that I am not troubled or afraid. Holy Spirit help me to

stop and pray when I feel anxious about something so that God's peace can come and guard my heart and mind in Christ Jesus. I'm not going to let Satan rob me anymore of the peace I have been given in Jesus. Forgive me Father. Help me, LORD in Jesus's name, amen.

Day 115: I Am Not a Victim

"But thanks be to God, who gives us victory through our LORD Jesus Christ." 1 Corinthians 15:57 NIV

"Some boast in chariots and some in horses, but we will boast in the name of the Lord our God. They have bowed down and fallen, but we have risen and stood upright." Psalm 20:7-8 NIV

"O give us help against the adversary, for deliverance by man is in vain. Through God we shall do valiantly, and it is he who will tread down our adversaries." Psalm 60:11-12 NASB

You are not a victim! You're not a victim of your past nor are you a victim of the family you were born into. You're not a victim of what's been done to you, your own poor choices, or the careless words others have spoken over you. Bad things may have happened to you; horrible, unjust, terrible things. And those things may have drastically impacted your heart and your life, but those things do not have to rule over you. They do not have to have power over you forever. You do not have to be subject to them for the rest of your life. How is that even possible? Because God has made you to be more than a conqueror through Jesus! Oh friend, it's not a cliché. It's the truth! Colossians 3:15 says to let the peace of Christ rule in your heart. Tragedy doesn't have to rule in your heart. Loss, brokenness, injustice, shame, defeat, deception, the failures of your past, or the hurt that has been inflicted upon you by others does not have to rule in your heart. These things are not your lord; they do not rule over your emotions, they do not have that power and authority over you. Jesus is your LORD!

Ephesians 1:22 tells us that God has put all things under the authority of Jesus and has made Jesus the head over all things for the benefit of the church. Nothing has supremacy over Jesus! Satan is a liar, my friend. Just because something has been passed down through your bloodline, just because something is hereditary or been a part of your family for generations does not mean that thing is doomed upon you. How? There is power in the blood! Alcoholism is under the blood! Addiction is under the blood! Sexual perversion is under the blood! Diabetes, heart failure, cancer; it's all under the blood! You have a new bloodline, a bloodline that is more powerful than that which you were born into naturally. A bloodline that sets you free from the law of sin and death, a bloodline that has brought you near to God; a bloodline that overcomes every time! You are now part of a bloodline of victory, a bloodline of wholeness, a bloodline of glory; a bloodline of honor because of Jesus. Oh friend, there is power in the blood! You overcome by the blood of the Lamb!

Oh friend, don't let the enemy convince you that you are a victim, that things will always be the way they've always been, that the only choice you have in this matter is to lie down and die. No, no, no! You are not a victim! In Jesus, you are more than a conqueror. In Christ, you are the victor, the winner; the champion! Go ahead and cry out to God. Go ahead and weep bitterly if you must, but don't you dare roll over on this one and give up. The LORD hears your prayers. The LORD sees your tears and I pray today the Holy Spirit of the living God would walk into the room with you wherever you are. I pray God's Spirit would lift your head high today because on your head is a crown; a crown of identity, of victory, of position, a crown given to you by Jesus. Victims may hang their heads, but victors wear their crowns. Thank You, Jesus, I am not a victim!

Father,

> I thank You that I am not a victim, that in Christ, I overcome; in Jesus, I am more than a conqueror. Holy Spirit, would You help me to remember this truth, to live this out daily. I don't want anything to rule over me but Jesus. I don't want anything to have supremacy in my heart but Jesus. Forgive me for believing myself to be a victim when Christ has set me free. Forgive me for exalting anything in my heart other

than Jesus. I cry out to You, LORD. I belong to You. Let it be in Jesus's name, amen.

Day 116: I Am Found

> *"Then Jesus told them this parable: 'suppose one of you has a hundred sheep and loses one of them. Doesn't he leave the ninety-nine in the open country and go after the lost sheep until he finds it? And when he finds it, he joyfully puts it on his shoulders and goes home. Then he calls his friends and neighbors together and says, 'rejoice with me; I have found my lost sheep."*
> Luke 15:3-6 NIV

> *"Or suppose a woman has ten silver coins and loses one. Doesn't she light a lamp, sweep the house and search carefully until she finds it? And when she finds it, she calls her friends and neighbors together and says, 'rejoice with me; I have found my lost coin.' In the same way, I tell you, there is rejoicing in the presence of the angels of God over one sinner who repents."*
> Luke 15:8-10 NIV

You are found! God has found you! You aren't some faceless name or nameless face to Him. The LORD has gone to great lengths to find you. He searches for you carefully, with great intent, with all His heart and He rejoices over you being found. How sweet! How awesome! In Luke 15 Jesus gives several parables or stories to illustrate this truth. One of these is the parable of the lost sheep. Jesus says that you are like a lost sheep, a sheep that God is willing to leave the ninety-nine others just to go after that one that is lost, to go after you. Oh friend, God values that one that is lost! "My sheep listen to my voice; I know them, and they follow me." (John 10:27 NIV). How could this sheep get lost if it was listening to the Shepherd's voice, if it was following the Shepherd? The fact that it is lost implies that it wasn't listening. It wasn't following. It wandered off on its own, but God still values that one sheep enough to leave all the rest and go after it, to search for it. My friend, you are worth going after to God! You are worth searching for even if it's your own fault that you got lost in the first place. God will still come after you. God values each one of His sheep! Jesus goes on in that parable to say that when that lost sheep is found, the Shepherd joyfully puts it on His shoulders and goes home. Then He calls all his friends and neighbors to have them rejoice with Him over that sheep being found. Oh friend, I don't know how lost you feel, how alone you feel, how abandoned you feel by the other ninety-nine sheep. But I do know that God has not abandoned you! God is looking for you and when He finds you, He doesn't scold you or reprimand you for wandering away. No, the Bible says, Jesus says that He joyfully puts you on His shoulders and carries you home.

Maybe today you feel like you just can't find your way back, your way home. You're tired, you're scared, and it doesn't seem like anyone is searching for you anymore. It doesn't seem like the other ninety-nine are concerned at all that you're gone. Maybe you want the Shepherd to find you, but you're afraid of what He'll think of you when He does. Maybe you don't have the strength to make it back to the ninety-nine. You don't just need someone to lead you and guide you back, you need someone to pick you up and carry you home. Maybe you thought the Shepherd's voice was just trying to control you, to limit you, to restrict you in some way; but now you realize the protection of that Voice, how being in the Shepherd's presence and care is where you truly belong. Oh friend, the Word of God says that He joyfully, happily, gladly puts you on His shoulders and carries you home. He loves to bring you back to Him! Thank you, Jesus! Oh friend, God values the one. He cares about the one. He rejoices over the one. He values you! He wants you; He searches for you. It's not enough to have the other ninety-nine sheep apart from you so He goes after you. He finds you! You add value to the rest and God recognizes that value even if you don't, even if no one else does. You're worth searching after. You're worth finding! Thank God you are found!

Father,

> I thank You for finding me, for searching for me, for valuing me enough to go after me. I praise Your name that I am not lost anymore. I am found! You have joyfully put me on Your shoulders and carried me home. You have turned the whole world upside down just looking for me. Thank You Jesus for finding me!

⊰⊱

Day 117: I Am an Answer

"The LORD God said, 'It is not good for man to be alone. I will make a helper suitable for him." Genesis 2:18 NIV

"But we have this treasure in jars of clay to show that this all-surpassing power is from God and not from us." 2 Corinthians 4:7 NIV

"Now an angel of the LORD said to Philip, 'Rise and go toward the south, to the road that goes down from Jerusalem to Gaza.' This is a desert place. And he rose and went. And there was an Ethiopian, a eunuch, a court official of Candace, queen of the Ethiopians, who was in charge of all her treasure. He had come to Jerusalem to worship, and was returning, seated in his chariot, and he was reading the prophet Isaiah. And the Spirit said to Philip, 'Go over and join this chariot.' So Philip ran to him…" Acts 8:26-30 NIV

You are an answer! God has made you to be an answer. You're not a problem, my friend. You may have problems, you may cause or have caused problems in your life, but you, yourself, are not a problem! Hang with me for a second. The very first problem recorded in the Bible is found in Genesis 2. God had created the earth, the sea; the land, the animals, and then he created Adam and gave Adam dominion. Adam had perfect fellowship with God (this was before sin entered the world), Adam lived in paradise, he was fulfilled in the task God had given to him, to name the animals and to rule over them, but Adam was alone. And being alone was a problem! So, in verse 18 God says that it isn't good for man to be alone and as a result God created Eve, a helper suitable for Adam. Eve was the answer for Adam's problem. She was created to be an answer. Oh friend, you too were created to be an answer! I don't know the circumstances that brought you into this world or the problems that were attributed to you as a result, but I do know that you, your life, is not a problem, has never been a problem! The Bible says that you were made in the image of God. You were crafted in the likeness of the One whose very nature is a solution. The Bible says that the LORD saw your unformed body while you were yet hidden in that secret place, that He knit you together in your mother's womb, fearfully, wonderfully whether that womb wanted you there or not, God wanted you there! God doesn't create problems; He creates answers! After Adam and Eve sinned, they certainly experienced some problems. They were banished from the Garden of Eden; they now had to deal with the aftermath of living in a world inhabited by sin. Yet when the LORD confronts Adam about what he had done (not what Eve had done), Adam responds, "The woman you put here with me—she gave me some fruit from the tree, and I ate it." (Genesis 3:12 NIV). He blames Eve. This woman that God had given to Adam as an answer was now a problem in the eyes of Adam because of sin, the deception of sin. Eve contributed to the problem, but she, herself, was never the problem. The serpent was; sin was! Eve was still an answer because God had created her to be an answer.

My friend, sin distorts the truth, clouds the truth, confuses the truth. Sin brings deception, accusation, and lots of problems. As a result, we tend to view people as our problems. Oh, if I just had a different boss, my life would be better. If my spouse was better to me, things would be so much better. If the people in my life would stop causing me so much trouble, my life would be great. Oh friend, people cause problems for sure, but people are not your problem! Ephesians 6:12 says that your struggle isn't against flesh and blood. It's against sin, it's against Satan and all the powers of this dark world. The problem is sin! But Jesus dealt with this problem on the cross! It amazes me that God often answers problems by sending a person. In the Scripture mentioned above in Acts, the Ethiopian eunuch had a problem: he was reading the prophet Isaiah, but he didn't understand it. Philip didn't know this to begin with. An angel tells him to go toward the south, to the road that goes down from Jerusalem to Gaza, the same road this Ethiopian eunuch was on. Philip isn't provided any more details than that, but he goes anyway. And when he gets to the eunuch's chariot, the Spirit of the LORD tells Philip to go over and join this chariot. The Bible says Philip ran to the chariot. He obeyed quickly, passionately even though he didn't know all the answers up front, and finds the eunuch needing the Scriptures explained to him. Philip walks this man through the Scriptures and then baptizes the eunuch. This eunuch wanted to know Jesus; he was returning from Jerusalem; he had gone to Jerusalem to worship. Why would an Ethiopian go to Jerusalem to worship? Only the Jews go to Jerusalem to worship. He wanted to know the God the

Jews worshiped. He was sitting in his chariot reading the prophet Isaiah for crying out loud. This was a man trying to learn about the one, true God, but he had a problem: he wasn't a Jew. He didn't understand the Scriptures. He hadn't heard the good news of Jesus. So, God sends Philip, a finite human being, to be this eunuch's answer. How awesome!

My friend, you may not have all the answers (none of us do), but you are an answer! You are just a jar of clay according to the Bible, but there's a treasure inside of you and that treasure is Jesus. He IS the answer! And Him being inside of you shows that this all-surpassing power is from God and not from you. Everywhere Jesus went on this earth there were problems: people were sick, people were dead, people were self-righteous and judgmental, people were demon-possessed, people were lost, people were blind, people were deceived; people were paralyzed; problems, problems, problems! These people weren't problems themselves, but they had problems. Sounds a little familiar doesn't it? All these problems proved to be no match for Jesus; Jesus is the answer! If your life is a mess because of sin, Jesus is the Savior. He is your answer. If you're sick; if you're in pain, Jesus is the Healer. He is your answer. If you're confused; deceived even, Jesus is the Truth. He is your answer! If you're dead in your sin; if you're dead in your body, Jesus is the Resurrection and the Life. He is your answer! If you're lost; if you don't know how to get to God, Jesus is the Way. He is your answer! My friend, Jesus is the answer and because He is your LORD and Savior, you carry the Answer with you wherever you go. What a treasure. Thank You, Jesus!

Father,

> I thank You that I am not a problem. You don't see me as a problem. You see me as an answer. You created me to be an answer. I thank You that other people are not my problem either. I don't wrestle against flesh and blood, I wrestle against sin, against darkness, against the enemy. Holy Spirit, would You help me to have the right perspective about myself and about others. Help me to view problems properly without identifying people by those problems even if those people contributed to the problem. The real problem is sin and Jesus is the answer! Holy Spirit help me to be an answer. Send me to be an answer because Jesus is the answer and I have Jesus. Let it be, LORD, in Jesus's name, amen.

Day 118: I Need the Rain!

"Drip down, O heavens, from above, and let the clouds pour down righteousness; let the earth open up and salvation bear fruit; and righteousness bear fruit with it. I, the LORD, have created it." Isaiah 45:8 NASB

"Now Elijah said to Ahab, 'Go up, eat and drink, for there is the sound of the roar of a heavy shower." 1 Kings 18:41 NIV

"For ground that drinks the rain which often falls on it and brings forth vegetation useful to those for whose sake it is also tilled, receives a blessing from God." Hebrews 6:7 NASB

"In the last days, God says, I will pour out my Spirit on all people. Your sons and your daughters will prophesy, your young men will see visions, your old men will dream dreams." Acts 2:17 NIV

The earth needs the rain. God designed the land to flourish as a result of being "watered" with the rains. We see the importance of rain throughout the Bible especially in terms of the land agriculturally. Rain is often synonymous with being blessed by God. "Are there any among the idols of the nations who give rain? Or can the heavens grant showers? Is it not You, O LORD our God? Therefore, we hope in You, for You are the One who has done all these things." (Jeremiah 14:22 NIV). And Psalm 147:8 makes it clear that it is God who provides rain for the earth. In Biblical times much of society was sustained by agriculture. Nations flourished based on the livelihood of what they could grow and what they could sell. So, the rains were a necessary part of this process. In Deuteronomy 28, Moses informs the children of Israel of several blessings and curses that were contingent upon their obedience or their disobedience to God. "The LORD will open the heavens, the storehouse of his bounty, to send rain on your land in its season and to bless all the work of your hands. You will lend to many nations but will borrow from none."

(Deuteronomy 28:12 NIV). A promise of rain; a timely rain provided in its season so that the land may flourish.

Rain; the land needs the rain. In its season, at the right time. Too much rain is a flood and not enough is a drought. Both are devastating to the land and the people who rely upon the land for their livelihood. But rain in its season is a blessing! All throughout the Bible Kingdom principles are conveyed in a horticultural context. Paul speaks of it. Jesus speaks of it. That's what made sense to the audience of that time. The people understood planting crops, relying upon the rain to water it, and harvesting those crops at the right time.

In 1 Kings 18 Israel was experiencing a 3-year drought. For 3 and half years it did not rain on the land. You can imagine the effect this had on the land and its crops and thus the livelihood of the people. In this third year the word of the LORD came to Elijah the prophet telling him to go to King Ahab (a very wicked and disobedient king) to tell him that God was sending rain to the land. God shows Himself as the One, True God in front of all the prophets of Baal on Mount Carmel. Considering what God had done here, the people of Israel end up on their faces in repentance. It is right after this that Elijah says to King Ahab, "Go, eat and drink, for there is the sound of a heavy rain." (1 Kings 18:41 NIV). It hadn't rained for a long time. The people hadn't heard a heavy rain for a long time, but now that the people had turned back to God, the rain was coming. Elijah goes atop Mount Carmel and bends down to the ground and puts his face between his knees. He humbles himself before the LORD, he bends down to the ground, but he's also still on his feet, ready for the rain to come. He tells his servant to go look toward the sea and the servant goes six times and returns six times with the same report, "there is nothing." Elijah keeps telling his servant to go back, to not give up, to keep looking for some sign that the rain is coming. Oh friend, don't give up! Keep going back. The rain IS coming! And on that seventh time, the servant returns in verse 44 and reports that a cloud the size of a man's hand is rising from the sea. When Elijah hears this, he immediately tells his servant to go tell King Ahab. The servant didn't see a rain cloud, or a storm cloud; he didn't hear a distant thunder. All he saw was a small cloud the size of a man's hand rising, but Elijah knew. He had faith. He took a risk that this cloud was the answer to his prayers. And in the meantime, that cloud grew and got darker and eventually the heavy rains fell. Oh friend, it's time to cry out to the God who answers by fire! It's time to cry out to the One who sends the rain in its season! It's time to have faith, to humble yourself before God, but to stay on your feet and be ready for what God is going to do. Can you hear a heavy rain? Don't underestimate that small cloud the size of a man's hand! Let it rain, LORD, let it rain!

Father,

> I thank You for the rain. I thank You that You are the One who sends rain on the land in its season and that this rain is a picture of refreshing, of blessing, of Your favor, of Your Spirit. I need the rain! We need the rain. So, LORD, let it rain. Shower down Your presence on me, in my life, at my house. Let it be LORD, in Jesus's name, amen.

Day 119: I Am Tested

> *"Count it all joy, my brothers, when you meet trials of various kinds, for you know that the testing of your faith produces perseverance. And let perseverance finish its work so that you may be mature and complete, not lacking anything."* James 1:2-4 ESV

> *"Dear friends, do not be surprised at the fiery ordeal that has come on you to test you, as though something strange were happening to you. But rejoice inasmuch as you participate in the sufferings of Christ, so that you may be overjoyed when his glory is revealed."* 1 Peter 2:12-13 NIV

> *"The crucible is for silver, and the furnace is for gold, and the LORD tests hearts."* Proverbs 17:3 NIV

Do you count it pure joy when you face trials of various kinds? I hardly do! What in the world does James mean? Are we supposed to enjoy being tested and rejoice in our sufferings as if this is what makes us a good Christian in the LORD's eyes? "For no one is cast off by the Lord forever. Though he brings grief, he will show compassion, so great is his unfailing love. For he does not willingly bring affliction or grief to anyone." (Lamentations 3:31-33 NIV). My friend, the LORD is not the source of your affliction, your suffering; your grief. Even if you are being persecuted because you're a follower of Jesus, He is not the One persecuting you. The Bible says in Matthew 5:12 that great is your reward in heaven over this. God doesn't want you to be persecuted. He wants you to be rewarded! He takes no delight in your suffering. He's not in heaven just waiting for you to mess up, doing His best to make you stumble and fall. The Bible says also in James 1 that God is not tempted by evil nor does He tempt anyone. Instead each person is tempted when they are dragged away by their own evil desire and enticed by the enemy. The LORD doesn't want you to fail. Satan does! Satan is the one who tempts you, who entices you, who tries to kill, steal, and destroy you. Rather Jesus came so that you may have life and have it more abundantly.

However, there is this quality about testing, about trials, about hardships that can develop perseverance and maturity in your faith. That's what the Bible says. The testing of your faith develops perseverance and perseverance when it has finished its work helps to make you mature and complete, not lacking anything. My friend, although God is not the source of your pain and He certainly doesn't enjoy your suffering in any way, shape, or form, He does care about your heart, your maturity; He doesn't want you to lack anything. And amazingly enough, the perseverance and maturity that is developed as a result of making it through a trial brings about this complete work in your faith. The LORD doesn't look at what man looks at. According to 1 Samuel 16:7, man looks at the outward appearance, but God looks at the heart. God cares about your heart. He tests your heart like silver is tested by the crucible and gold is tested by the furnace. The furnace and the crucible are instruments designed to remove the impurities in silver and gold. Testing is an instrument to remove the impurities in your own heart.

In Genesis 22, the Bible says that God tested Abraham by telling him to take his only son, the son whom he loved, Isaac, and to go to Moriah and to sacrifice him there as a burnt offering. Are you kidding me? This is Abraham's only son, the son through whom the promise of his descendants being as numerous as the stars would be fulfilled. Abraham had to wait a long time before Isaac was even conceived. Abraham wasn't in the prime of his life. He was old. It wouldn't be easy for him to just have another son. God had promised him life, blessings, legacy; this thing that was very, very good and now God wants him to give that up? It doesn't make a lick of sense, but verse 3 says that early the next morning Abraham got up and set out for the place that God had told him about with Isaac and two of his servants. Oh friend, God is trustworthy! You may not always understand Him because His ways and thoughts are so much higher than yours, but He has always been and will always be worthy of your trust. When they all reached the mountain, Abraham tells his servants to stay where they are and that he and Isaac will go to the mountain to worship then they will come back. Even in that statement Abraham prophesied that both he and Isaac would return. This blows my mind! Abraham trusted God. He trusted that God would provide another sacrifice, that God would raise Isaac from the dead if He had to, that regardless to what happened, they would both come back! As they went along together, Isaac spoke up and asked his father where the lamb was for the burnt offering and Abraham responded, "God Himself will provide the lamb for the burnt offering." (Genesis 22:8 NIV). Oh friend, Abraham trusted God's heart, God's intentions. You can tell from the way he chose to respond to the people who questioned him. He may not have known how, but he knew God would provide. I know sometimes life is hard and messy even when you feel like you've heard from the LORD and you're doing what God told you to do. And when things start looking questionable or people start asking you tough questions that it takes a lot of faith for you to even answer; sometimes you just got to keep holding on to what you already know! I don't know how God's going to provide, but I know He's going to provide because that's what the Bible says. I know this all seems crazy, it doesn't make a lot of sense right now, but I'm obeying the LORD, I'm holding onto His Word. When they reached the place, God had told him about, Abraham built the altar and bound Isaac and laid him on the altar. Can you imagine what Isaac was thinking? Nowhere does it say that Isaac fought Abraham or tried to escape. Isaac trusted his father just as Abraham trusted God. Abraham said that God would provide a lamb and Isaac trusted that would happen. Abraham takes the knife to slay his son when the angel of the LORD calls out to him in verse 11 and 12 and tells him not to lay a hand on the boy. The angel says, now I know that you fear God since you have not withheld your only son and Abraham looks up to see a ram caught in a thicket. Abraham sacrifices this ram as a burnt offering instead of his son and calls the mountain, "the LORD will provide." The LORD tested Abraham and this test proved that Abraham feared God.

Oh friend, I don't know what kind of test you might be in the middle of right now. I don't know the trials and hardships you've had to go through in this life, but I do know that God does not delight in your suffering. He is not the source of your pain even if He does test your heart. And I also know that those trials can develop perseverance in your faith and that perseverance can develop maturity until you are complete, not lacking anything. Abraham offering his son Isaac as a sacrifice foreshadows the Father offering His only begotten son, Jesus, as a sacrifice for the sins of the whole world. Can I tell you, friend, that although you may not understand right now and perhaps, you'll never understand this side of heaven, God understands; God knows! You can trust Him even in the test!

Father,

> I thank You that You are good, that You are God, that You are worthy of my trust even in the test. Help me, Holy Spirit, to listen to You, to learn from You, to have You reveal what's in my heart so that I don't need a test to do this. Help me to grow up easily, to mature easily; I don't want to lack anything. I need You, LORD. Please be near me in Jesus's name, amen.

⇜⇝

Day 120: I Am Sealed

"And you also were included in Christ when you heard the message of truth, the gospel of your salvation. When you believed, you were marked in him with a seal, the promised Holy Spirit." Ephesians 1:13 NIV

"Now it is God who makes both us and you stand firm in Christ. He anointed us, set his seal of ownership upon us, and put his Spirit in our hearts as a deposit, guaranteeing what is to come." 2 Corinthians 1:21-22 NIV

"Place me like a seal over your heart, like a seal on your arm; for love is as strong as death, its jealousy unyielding as

> *the grave. It burns like blazing fire, like a mighty flame."*
> Song of Solomon 8:6 NIV

When you believed, you were marked in Christ with a seal, the promised Holy Spirit. God has anointed you and set His seal of ownership upon you. He has put His Spirit in your heart as a deposit, guaranteeing what is to come. The Spirit you have received doesn't make you a slave again; rather, according to Romans 8:15, the Spirit of God has brought about your adoption to sonship. You aren't owned like a master owns a slave or like a person owns a piece of property. You belong to God like a child belongs to their father. The Spirit of God identifies you as a child of God. When God looks at that seal, His very own Spirit, He knows you are His. When other people recognize that seal, the Spirit of God on your life, they know you belong to God. The Spirit of God will testify with your own spirit that you are a child of God. You are marked in Christ. You are sealed with the Holy Spirit.

A seal in Biblical times was used to guarantee security and to indicate ownership. Ancient seals were often made with wax and embedded with the personalized imprint of their guarantor. A seal was only as good as its backer. In 1 Kings 21, Jezebel wrote letters to the nobles and elders of Naboth's city and sealed those letters with King Ahab's seal indicating that these letters came from the king even though they really came from Jezebel. In these letters Jezebel had arranged to have Naboth falsely accused and therefore stoned to death because Naboth had refused to sell his vineyard to the king. That vineyard was his inheritance from his ancestors and was legally his, but the king wanted to use it for a vegetable garden. The elders and nobles living in Jezreel did as Jezebel had said in her letters because they thought the letters came from the king. Those letters were marked with the king's seal and because of the authority and ownership that backed that seal, those nobles and elders carried out the orders to a "T." Oh friend, the enemy is crafty, he's cunning. He gives an appearance of light. He's very good at deceiving. Jezebel had authority but she didn't have the same authority as that of the king. Yet she used the king's authority as a ruse, she masqueraded under the guise of the king and misused the seal of the king to accomplish her own purposes. Yet later in 1 Kings 21, after Naboth was stoned to death, the word of the LORD comes to the prophet Elijah and God says in verse 23 that dogs will devour Jezebel by the wall of Jezreel. That's exactly what happened in 2 Kings 9! This queen that had used her authority and the authority of her husband to accomplish so much evil was violently killed in the city of Jezreel, the same city she had arranged to have Naboth falsely accused and stoned to death. This was not an accident! Yet when they went to retrieve Jezebel's body for burial, her flesh had been devoured by the dogs just as God had said would happen.

There was an authority and power that backed seals in the Bible, the authority and power of the king, an authority that could not be overturned by any man. But the authority that backs the Holy Spirit that you have been sealed with is greater than your situation, it's greater than all other authorities, it's greater than the plan of the enemy for your life! You are sealed with the promised Holy Spirit, but the One who backs this seal is of the greatest power and authority that has ever been or will ever be. God can change unchangeable circumstances! God's decree overturns all other decrees! He alone is God! God can overthrow a manmade seal, but man cannot overthrow God's seal! God has declared you to be His child because of Jesus and that truth is sealed with the precious Holy Spirit.

Oh friend, if Satan starts telling you that you don't belong, that God has abandoned you, that you aren't a real follower of Jesus, that God doesn't see you, or know you, or care about you, you tell him to look at the seal that you've been marked with; the promised Holy Spirit of the living God! The enemy cannot ignore that seal, he cannot undo the work of that seal, and he cannot revoke or overturn the authority backing that seal! You are God's child. You belong to God, and the Holy Spirit shows this ownership; demonstrates this authority in your heart. Who are you that the enemy would listen to you? Who are you that the powers of darkness would submit to what you say in the name of Jesus? You are a child of Almighty God! You are an heir of God and a co-heir with Christ! You are sealed with the promised Holy Spirit!

Father,

> I thank You for Jesus. I thank You that because of Jesus I am sealed with the precious Holy Spirit. I belong to You. The Holy Spirit declares me to be Your son/daughter. I thank You for the authority that backs this seal. That no one can overturn You, LORD; no one can supersede Your authority for You alone are the One, True God. Holy Spirit, thank You for showing that I belong to the King. I am of royal descent. I am not a slave; I am a son! Thank You LORD!

Day 121: I Am a Tree

"Blessed is the one who does not walk in step with the wicked or stand in the way that sinners take or sit in the company of mockers, but whose delight is in the law of the LORD, and who meditates on his law day and night. That person is like a tress planted by streams of water, which yields its fruit in season and whose leaf does not wither—whatever they do prospers." Psalm 1:1-3 NIV

"But blessed is the one who trusts in the LORD, whose confidence is in him. They will be like a tree planted by the water that sends out its roots by the stream. It does not fear when heat comes; its leaves are always green. It has no worries in a year of drought and never fails to bear fruit." Jeremiah 17:7-8 NIV

"The righteous will flourish like a palm tree, they will grow like a cedar of Lebanon; planted in the house of the LORD, they will flourish in the courts of our God. They will still bear fruit in old age, they will stay fresh and green, proclaiming, 'The LORD is upright; he is my Rock, and there is no wickedness in him." Psalm 92:12-15 NIV

The Bible compares you to a tree, not just any tree, but one that is planted by streams of water, that sends out its roots by the stream. Look at the Scripture above from Psalm 1. It says that you are considered blessed when you aren't walking in step with the wicked or standing in the way that sinners take or sitting in the company of mockers, but you are delighting in the law of the LORD and meditating on His law both night and day. This kind of person is like a tree planted by the water. If you are right by the water, then you will bear fruit in season regardless to how much rain you may or may not receive, regardless to your circumstances. Your leaf will not whither because you are right next to a source of water! Jeremiah says that the one who trusts in the LORD, whose confidence is in Him is also like a tree planted by the water.

That person does not fear the heat. Their leaves are always green even in the heat. This person has no worries even in a year of drought. They will still bear fruit because their roots are planted by the stream!

My friend, you have been given the Word of God. This Word that is living and active and sharper than any two-edged sword (Hebrews 4:12) should be your delight. You can read it. You can study it. You can meditate on it both day and night, you can speak it and it will never die on you, it will never be inactive in your life; it will never stop being like a two-edged sword. A two-edged sword cuts both ways. Its' sharp. It does a lot of damage to an aggressor, more damage than a single-edged sword could ever do. And Hebrews 4:12 also says that God's Word penetrates even to the point of dividing your soul and spirit, your joints and marrow; your thoughts and attitudes of your heart. That's a precise tool to be able to separate things that are so closely related. But God's Word is that precise, that sharp! And the Greek word used for two-edged sword here is the word "distomos" which literally translates into "two-mouthed." 2 Timothy 3:16 says that all Scripture is God-breathed. It all came out of God's mouth and that is powerful. God's Word is powerful. He speaks and things are established. Just read the account of creation in the beginning of Genesis. He said, "Let there be....," and there was! God's Word is powerful, but something happens when you begin to speak what God has already said out of your own mouth. It's like you're adding another blade, another edge, another mouth to that Sword and the Word of God you speak becomes the most powerful weapon imaginable, doing unthinkable damage to your aggressor, Satan. Wow!

Oh friend, it's time to know the Word, to love the Word, to speak the Word, to pray the Word over your home, your family, your children, your life. It's time to delight in God's Word. It is alive! It will mess with you, it will correct and teach and reprove you, but it is like a two-edged sword that destroys the enemy! The LORD wants you to flourish, to still bear fruit even in your old age; to stay fresh and green! How do you do that? Be planted by the stream!

In Daniel 4, King Nebuchadnezzar, the king of Babylon has a dream. He dreams about a tree in the middle of the land. Its height was enormous. The tree grew large and strong and its top touched the sky so that it was visible from the ends of the earth. Its leaves were beautiful, its fruit was abundant, and on it was food for all. Under it the wild animals found shelter, and the birds lived in its branches; from it every creature was fed. This was a magnificent tree, a beautiful tree; an incredible tree! Yet in this dream, Nebuchadnezzar hears a messenger from God say, "Cut down the tree and trim off its branches; strip off its leaves and scatter its fruit. Let the animals flee from under it and the birds from its branches." (Daniel 4:14 NIV). This messenger goes on to say that this mighty tree will be but a stump in the ground then the messenger foretells some humbling circumstances for Nebuchadnezzar. When the king wakes up, he sends for all the wise men to interpret this dream for him, but the magicians, the astrologers, the enchanters, and diviners couldn't interpret the king's dream. Daniel is brought before the king and when told about the dream, Daniel humbly tells Nebuchadnezzar that the great tree he saw in his dream is none other but king Nebuchadnezzar and that God is about to cut Nebuchadnezzar down. Daniel goes on to provide more details about this dream, but this great tree in the middle of the land that was so great and mighty and fruitful was about to be cut down to a stump. What was the problem with this tree; what was up with Nebuchadnezzar? It wasn't planted by the stream! Nebuchadnezzar's source wasn't the LORD. He was in the middle of the land, his source was himself. He thought his success was a result of his own power and for the glory of his own majesty when it was God who raised Nebuchadnezzar (Daniel 2:21). Oh friend, you can be a magnificent tree, a beautiful tree, an abundant tree, but don't you dare be planted in the middle of the land. Be planted by the stream, be planted in the house of the LORD, flourish in the courts of God! This is how you stay fresh and green because it is God who keeps you fresh and green, and this is how you keep from being cut down! Surely goodness and mercy will follow you all the days of your life and you will dwell in the house of the LORD forever!

Father,

> Would You make me like a tree planted by the streams? I want to flourish in Your courts. I want to be planted in Your house. I want to stay fresh and green. I want to yield fruit in season. Help me, Holy Spirit, to stay in the Word, to delight in the Word, to meditate on the Word, to speak the Word. May God's Word be a two-edged sword in my life. I don't want to whither. I don't want to be cut down. I want to flourish. Let it be LORD in Jesus's name, amen.

⤙⤚

Day 122: I Am Provided for

"And my God will meet all of your needs according to the riches of his glory in Christ Jesus." Philippians 4:19 NIV

"Therefore, I tell you, do not worry about your life, what you will eat or drink; or about your body, what you will wear. Is not life more than food, and the body more than clothes? Look at the birds of the air; they do not sow or reap or store away in barns, and yet your heavenly Father feeds them. Are you not much more valuable than they?" Matthew 6:25-26 NIV

"Let them give thanks to the LORD for his unfailing love and his wonderful deeds for mankind, for he satisfies the thirsty and fills the hungry with good things." Psalm 107:8-9 NIV

The LORD is your provider. The LORD revealed Himself to Moses in Exodus 3:14 as "I am that I am". He is! The very nature of His identity, His character is provision! It's His personality, not just what He does, but who He is. He is your supplier, your source, the One who meets your needs; all of them! There is nothing you could possibly need that He is not the answer for. What? According to the Bible, God meets your needs in agreement with the riches of His glory in Christ Jesus, not the riches of your glory or the riches of anyone else's glory, not even the riches of some organization or nation's glory. "All people are like grass, and all their glory is like the flowers of the field; the grass withers and the flowers fall." (1 Peter 1:24 NIV). But the Word of the LORD endures forever! Man's glory, like the flowers, is here today and gone tomorrow. It appears for a little while and then is no more, but God's glory is not like this. The glory of God is ever-increasing (2 Corinthians 3:18). That is richness, my friend! And He meets all your needs according to the riches of His ever-increasing glory! Wow!

The first mention of the LORD as provider is found in Genesis 22:14. After God had provided a ram as another sacrifice for Abraham in place of his son Isaac on the mountain, Abraham calls the name of that place, "the

LORD will provide." It's interesting to me that this first mention of the LORD as provider had nothing to do with food or drink or clothes or any of the things that we typically look to God for provision with, the things that we need daily. Rather this provision was about a substitute sacrifice, a picture, a foreshadowing of Jesus being provided as the atonement for our sins. God not only provides for your daily needs; He provides for your eternal ones. "He who did not spare his own Son, but gave him up for us all—how will he not also, along with him, graciously give us all things?" (Romans 8:32 NIV). My friend, God is your provider! How could you question His provision when He has given you Jesus? This God who did not spare even His own Son, how will He not also along with Jesus graciously give you what you need? It may not be in the way or time that you think or expect, but you can absolutely trust His provision. He knows what you need before you even ask (Matthew 6:8)! The LORD is faithful!

In Matthew 14 after Jesus hears of John the Baptist being beheaded by King Herod, He withdraws by boat privately to a solitary place. Jesus knows the pain and grief of losing someone close to Him. Yet when the crowds heard of Jesus leaving, they followed Him on foot from their towns. People were so hungry for Him. They just wanted to be around Him, listen to Him. He was the Healer, the Deliverer, the Truth, the Miracle-Worker. These people were a little desperate, desperate enough to walk for a long time on foot just to search for Jesus. In verse 14, the Bible says that when Jesus saw this large crowd, He had compassion on them and healed their sick. My friend, unlike most people, Jesus doesn't get sick of you, put off with you; He isn't annoyed by your neediness. He has compassion on you. He knows what you have need of and what you have need of is Him! As the evening approaches, Jesus's disciples tell Jesus to send the crowds away so that they can go get food. But Jesus says, "They don't need to go away. You give them something to eat." (Matthew 14:16 NIV). This crowd of people came to Jesus because of their neediness to begin with and now they were getting hungry and in need again. Maybe you feel like you're too needy for God. That you can't keep going back to Him; that somehow, He's going to cut you off eventually and send you away, but Jesus says that you don't need to be sent away from Him. He won't send you away. He is all that you need! This is where Jesus multiplies the five loaves of bread and two fish until they had all eaten and were satisfied. Not only that, but the disciples picked up twelve basketfuls of leftovers and the number of those that had eaten was about 5,000 men besides women and children. Scholars believe the number of the crowd more than likely consisted of approximately 15,000-20,000 people. That's A LOT of people to have eaten and been satisfied by five loaves of bread and two fish. This miracle is recorded in all four Gospels, and one of the disciples, Philip, declares, "it would take more than half a year's wages to buy enough bread for each one to have a bite." (John 6:7 NIV). Jesus more than accomplished what would have taken man half a year to barely accomplish! God is a provider. He is a God of more than enough. This is evidenced by the fact that the disciples collected twelve baskets FULL of leftovers. There were way more than the people needed! My friend, the LORD is your provider! He knows what you need before you even ask. And He meets all your needs according to the riches of HIS glory. You'll never be too needy for Him!

Father,

> I thank You that You are the LORD, my provider. I thank You that all my needs are met according to the riches of Your glory. I thank You that You don't send me away because all I need is found in You. You are worthy of my trust because You are faithful. Help me, Holy Spirit, to have faith in the Great I am, the LORD who will provide. Let it be in Jesus's name, amen.

Day 123: I Am Sung Over

"The LORD your God is with you, the Mighty Warrior who saves. He will take great delight in you; in his love he will no longer rebuke you but will rejoice over you with singing." Zephaniah 3:17 NIV

"I will sing to the LORD all my life; I will sing praise to my God as long as I live." Psalm 104:33 NIV

"I will be glad and rejoice in you; I will sing the praises of your name, O Most High." Psalm 9:2 NIV

> *"Shout for joy to the LORD, all the earth, burst into jubilant song with music."* Psalm 98:4 NIV

The LORD, your God is with you. He is not a God far off, out of reach, and impossible for you to be in relationship with. The blood of Jesus has brought you near to Him! Jesus is Immanuel, God with us! The good news of the Gospel isn't a religion given to you, a set of things you must do to get to God. No, the good news of the Gospel is what God did through Jesus to bring you close to Himself. He, the Word made flesh, came and dwelt among us. What other deity worshiped by man can even hold a flame to the One, True God! The LORD is a mighty warrior, One who doesn't war to destroy, but to save. Because of Jesus, the LORD takes great delight in you. In His love, expressed through Jesus, He doesn't rebuke you. Rather, the LORD rejoices over you with singing.

This passage in Zephaniah is about Jerusalem. It speaks of a future time when God has ended His judgment upon Israel; a period when all of Israel's enemies have been destroyed and Israel will enter a time of safety and blessing. The LORD is a mighty warrior who will save His people, who will save Israel. He will take great delight in this remnant that is saved and will rejoice over them with singing. Yet in Luke 15 in reading the parables of the lost sheep and the lost coin, we see rejoicing over the one that was found. In verse 7 and 10 the Bible says that there is more rejoicing, there is rejoicing in the presence of the angels over ONE sinner who repents. When there is joy, when there is rejoicing, there are shouts for joy; and where there are shouts for joy, there is singing! Why do we sing? According to the Bible, you sing because you're happy, you sing to celebrate, you sing to praise (Psalm 9:2); you sing to commemorate all that has been done. Read the song of Deborah in Judges 5, the song of Moses in Deuteronomy 32, and Miriam's song in Ezekiel 15. All these recorded songs in Scripture commemorated what the LORD had done. They were songs of victory, songs of praise, songs to remember the greatness and goodness of God in Israel's history. And it's amazing to think that heaven rejoices when you repent and follow Jesus. The angels in God's presence celebrate you being found, you being brought near to God, you being reconciled through Jesus. I have a feeling shouts for joy are part of this. I have a feeling there are songs being sung in honor of you being added to the family of God.

There are numerous Scriptures that denote people, all of creation singing to the LORD. "Sing to the LORD a new song; sing to the LORD all the earth. Sing to the LORD, bless His name..." (Psalm 96:1-2 NIV). "But let all who take refuge in you be glad, let them ever sing for joy..." (Psalm 5:11 NIV). In Isaiah 52:9 we see rejoicing and great shouts of joy being made over Jerusalem being redeemed and God comforting His people, Israel. "Praise the LORD all you Gentiles and let all the peoples praise Him." (Romans 15:11 NIV). There's a lot of singing, a lot of rejoicing, a lot of praise being directed towards God and rightly so for He is worthy of it! Considering who He is, of what He has done, how could we not sing to Him? Yet can I tell you friend that God sings over you. He rejoices over you with singing. Nowhere else in the Bible do we see God singing except over Israel when they are restored to Him as described in Zephaniah and we see all of heaven rejoicing over one sinner who repents. I don't think this is a coincidence. I think there's a correlation between you repenting and following Jesus and the LORD rejoicing over you with singing. Why would God sing if He wasn't happy, if He wasn't celebrating, commemorating what had been done through Jesus? What does God have to sing over? In Christ, He has you! The Bible doesn't say that He's rejoicing in His people, in who we are, in what we've done or accomplished because all that we are and all that we could do is because of Him and should be for Him anyway. No, He rejoices over you. He sings over you. His rejoicing is greater than you, larger than you, more than you, and above you. It isn't contingent upon you, but it is over you. Maybe you think God is too holy, too dignified to sing, to rejoice, to shout for joy. Yet when you read the story of the prodigal son in Luke 15 that Jesus told and you see a picture of Father God through the father of this parable, something catches in your throat when you see this father, your Father, running to his son to embrace him, to kiss him. God's position as King of the whole universe will never supersede the position that you hold in His heart. He runs to you! He made a way for you through Jesus! He rejoices over you being His child! He is happy that you belong to Him! Doesn't He just blow your mind? Praise God, He rejoices over you!

Father,

I thank You for Jesus. Thank You for making a way for me to know You, to be close to You through Jesus. Thank You for running to me even though I am so unworthy, You rejoice over me; You celebrate me being found. You are so good and today I just want to thank You, to praise You, to sing to You.

You are so holy, so righteous, so high and exalted. How could I be in Your presence? How could I know You as Father? Seems so impossible! But I thank You for Jesus. I praise You for Jesus. He is the way to You, His blood has brought me near to You. It's all because of Jesus. Praise His name forever!

Day 124: I Am Not a Spectator

"In all my prayers for all of you, I always pray with joy because of your partnership in the gospel from the first day until now." Philippians 1:4-5 NIV

"Let no one deceive you with empty words, for because of such things God's wrath comes on those who are disobedient. Therefore, do not be partners with them." Ephesians 5:6-7 NIV

"For we have become partakers of Christ, if we hold fast the beginning of our assurance firm until the end." Hebrews 3:14 NIV

"Do not merely listen to the word, and so deceive yourselves. Do what it says." James 1:22 NIV

"What does it profit, my brethren, if someone says he has faith but does not have works? Can faith save him? If a brother or sister is naked and destitute of daily food, and one of you says to them, 'Depart in peace, be warmed and filled,' but you do not give them the things which are needed for the body, what does it profit? Thus, also faith by itself, if it does not have works, is dead." James 2:14-26 NIV

You are not a spectator. You're not here for the show, to watch, to be entertained. You're not a customer in Christ. Jesus is not just another commodity to add to your life, nor are you merely a consumer of religious goods and services.

In order to have a healthy relationship with the LORD, you are required to participate. Following Jesus is more than just walking with your head down trying to mimic His every step and move, making sure your footsteps fit exactly in His so much so that you don't even see anyone else. Following Jesus does imply that He is the leader, but you're also walking with Him, He's the One who lifts your head high. You have become a partaker of Christ, a participant, not a spectator, an observer, or a critique.

Spectators don't do anything. They watch, they observe, they criticize what they don't like, and praise what they do like, but they aren't involved beyond this. In Philippians 1 Paul writes to the church at Philippi and tells them that in all his prayers for these believers he always prays with joy because of their partnership in the gospel from the very first day right up to the time Paul wrote the letter. What made Paul pray with joy for these Philippians? Their partnership in the gospel, a partnership that began the very first day! These believers weren't just hearers or spectators; they participated in helping to preach the gospel. They were involved with Paul and they kept participating. They didn't give up! My friend, it's time to start participating! It's time to do, to go, to be involved in what the LORD is doing. It's time for your faith to start profiting other people!

In Acts 6 we learn of a man named Stephen, a man full of God's grace and power who performed great signs and wonders among the people according to the Bible. Opposition arose among certain Jews of Cyrene and Alexandria and they began to argue with Stephen, but they could not stand up against the wisdom the Spirit gave Stephen as he spoke. So secretly these men persuaded some men to accuse Stephen of speaking blasphemous words against Moses and God. They stirred up the people with this false accusation enough so that Stephen was seized and brought before the Sanhedrin or the religious court. Verse 15 says that all who were sitting in the Sanhedrin looked intently at Stephen and they saw that his face was like the face of an angel. Stephen was innocent, even his accusers saw the face of an angel when they looked at him. That's intense, but sometimes spectators can't always see things clearly. Their perception is skewed because they only ever see things from one side, from one vantage point, the point of a third party and not a participant! Oh man, it's about to get real up in here.

When the high priest asked Stephen about the validity of these charges, Stephen begins to preach to the crowd using the law and Moses and Israel's history. This was a deeply personal message and Stephen says that these people, the ones privileged enough to receive the law that was given through angels, they had not obeyed the law. They had heard the law, but they weren't doing it. Stephen invites them to participate by telling them the truth of where they are. When the members of the Sanhedrin hear this, they were furious, absolutely consumed with rage. These guys are gnashing their teeth, probably foaming at the mouth, transforming into a bunch of animals over one man marked by the Spirit of God. But the Bible says in Acts 7:55 that Stephen remained full of the Holy Spirit throughout all of this and he looks up to heaven and sees the glory of God and Jesus standing at the right hand of God. Shut the front door!! Seems like an inopportune time for the heavens to open and God's glory to be revealed, yet the LORD doesn't always show up at the most convenient of times. While the rest of the religious leaders were furious, gnashing their teeth and ready to stone this "falsely accused blasphemer"; Stephen is having the time of his life in God's presence. Stephen is participating in God's glory being revealed even though the people around him are going crazy! My friend, don't let your circumstances or even what the people in your life are saying and doing keep you from enjoying the glory of God! Stephen is so excited he just tells the Sanhedrin flat out what he's seeing. Of course, they don't want to hear about God's glory at a time like that, so the Bible says they covered their ears, started yelling at the top of their voices, rushed towards Stephen, dragged him out of the city and stoned him to death. Even as Stephen is being murdered, he prays "LORD, do not hold this sin against them." (Acts7:60 NIV). Then he falls asleep which I think is an interesting way of putting it considering him being violently stoned to death. You'd think his death would have been brutal, agonizing even, yet the Bible says that he just falls asleep, a picture of unexplainable peace and protection; truly remarkable. And all those religious leaders who knew the law so well missed out on seeing God's glory. The heaven's opened up in their presence and this group of people were so furious with this man who was preaching truth to them that they didn't even notice Jesus had showed up on the scene. More than that, they didn't even want to hear about it. They covered their ears, they yelled at the top of their voices. These people had a chance to glimpse the glory of God, to see this Jesus that they had heard so much about standing at the right hand of God, but they didn't participate. In fact, they outright refused to participate. They were spectators to what Stephen was experiencing with God. And this made them want to kill him even more! Oh friend, it's dangerous to only be a spectator. There's so much you don't understand when you choose not to participate. Thank God you are not a spectator; you have become a partaker of Christ!

Father,

I thank You for making me a partaker of Christ, a participant in the gospel. I don't want to just observe or watch or just be a spectator when you have made me to get involved. Forgive me for criticizing, for looking to be entertained, for not understanding because I'm not participating. Help me Holy Spirit....I don't want to be a customer, I want to participate in the glory of God being revealed, not throw stones at those who are experiencing it firsthand. Give me wisdom, LORD. I need Your discernment. When the heavens open, I want to be looking up to You not around at everyone else and their reactions. I thank You that I am not a spectator, but a partaker of Christ in Jesus's name, amen.

Day 125: I Am Nothing Without Love

"Now you are the body of Christ and individually members of it. And God has appointed in the church first apostles, second prophets, third teachers, then miracles, then gifts of healing, helping, administering, and various kinds of tongues. Are all apostles? Are all prophets? Are all teachers? Do all work miracles? Do all possess gifts of healing? Do all speak with tongues? Do all interpret? But earnestly desire the higher gifts. And I will show you a still more excellent way." 1 Corinthians 12:27-31 NIV

"If I speak in the tongues of men and of angels, but have not love, I am a noisy gong or a clanging cymbal. And if I have prophetic powers, and understand all mysteries and all knowledge, and if I have all faith, so as to remove mountains, but have not love, I am nothing. If I give away all I have, and if I deliver up my body to be burned, but have not love, I gain nothing." 1 Corinthians 13:1-3 NIV

You are individually a member of the body of Christ, the church. And in the church, within the body, God has appointed various positions and gifts such as teaching, healing, helping, and administering so that when all work together, the body functions properly. Paul asks in 1 Corinthians if everyone works miracles, if everyone teaches, if everyone is an apostle? Everyone may not do every single one of these things, though the Scripture encourages you to earnestly desire the higher gifts. Gifts leave little room for pride because the whole premise of a gift is that it has been given to you. It wasn't yours to begin with. And these gifts of the Spirit are gifts that belong to the Spirit, not to any person. God give gifts and its okay to earnestly want the higher gifts. Yet the focus isn't on the gifts themselves because verse 31 of 1 Corinthians 12 says there is still a "more excellent way." 1 Corinthians 13 describes this way to be that of love and most of us have heard this passage of Scripture quoted quite a bit especially at weddings and things of that nature. This is appropriate, but the context of Scripture where Paul talks about love is in relation to the various gifts that make up the church and although these gifts are incredible and amazing and needed, the most excellent way is still love. You are nothing without love.

The Word of God says that even if you could speak in all the different languages of the earth so that you could converse with any man and you could speak in the tongues of the angels so that you could converse in a language that only heaven understands, but you don't have the love of Jesus, you don't show the love of Christ to anyone; you are the equivalent to a noisy gong or clanging cymbal. No matter how eloquent and intelligent your speech may be, if it is devoid of love people are not going to listen to you; rather, they may want you to shut up because to them you are a clanging cymbal. Wow! Help us, LORD. The Scripture from 1 Corinthians 13 also says that even if you have prophetic powers and you understand all mysteries. Even if you possess all this knowledge and you know everything because you have access to look up anything you don't know. Even if you have all this faith to believe God for crazy amazing things, but you don't have any love; you are nothing. Even if you were willing to be burned at the stake for your faith. Even if you gave away all that you had to the poor, to help those less fortunate than you, but you don't have any love, you gain nothing. It profits you nothing. All these things are awesome, commendable, and praiseworthy, but they are all meaningless without love. The most excellent way has always been and will always be love.

Father,

I thank You for Jesus. I thank You for spiritual gifts, for healings, for teaching, for miracles, for all the things Jesus modeled and I have access to through Him. Whatever you have for me LORD, that's what I want. I earnestly desire those higher gifts, but I don't want to be a clanging cymbal or a noisy gong. I don't want to be nothing, it all to be for nothing. I want to pursue love because the greatest of all hope, of all faith is love. Let it be in my life LORD. Help me, Holy Spirit in Jesus's name, amen.

Day 126: I Am Shown Mercy

"But because of his great love for us, God, who is rich in mercy, made us alive with Christ even when we were dead in transgressions—it is by grace you have been saved." Ephesians 2:4-5 NIV

"The steadfast love of the LORD never ceases; his mercies never come to an end; they are new every morning; great is your faithfulness." Lamentations 3:22-23 NIV

"Who is a God like you, who pardons sin and forgives the transgression of the remnant of his inheritance? You do not stay angry forever but delight to show mercy." Micah 7:18 NIV

Who delights in being compassionate, kind, understanding with you? Who enjoys forgiving you of your wrongs, your faults; your failures? Who takes pleasure in, is happy about, and finds joy in showing you mercy? God does! The LORD, your God, is rich in mercy. His love never ceases, and His mercies never come to an end. That's what the Bible says! You will never reach the end of God's mercy. Your wrongs could never outdo the extent of mercy that He has for you. Isn't that awesome! It's only when you refuse this mercy that you are in danger of being judged without it. In fact, even if you were to come close to exhausting His mercies for the day, those mercies are made new every morning. Who does that?! Romans 2:4 warns us not to show contempt for His kindness, forbearance, and patience because this kindness is intended to lead you towards repentance, not away from it. It is the kindness of God, not His sternness that is intended to lead you toward repentance. Romans 11:22 says that God is both kind and stern; stern to those who continue to disobey and kind to those who continue to trust in His kindness. Read the Bible in its entirety and you will glimpse the sternness of God. He is righteous, holy, and just. He judges sin when people fail to repent, and this is illustrated quite a lot throughout the Word of God. But even in these judgments we often see multiple provided warnings and opportunities for repentance. The Bible also broadcasts the infinite mercies of God. Just look at Jesus. It's only because of God's great love for you and because He is so rich in mercy that He provided Jesus. It is by grace you have been saved! He is faithful even in the area of being merciful. Just as the sun rises each morning to welcome a new day, so the LORD's mercies are made new each morning.

In Joshua chapter 6 the children of Israel had recently conquered the city of Jericho after marching around the city seven times for seven days, giving a loud shout on that seventh march until the walls of the city came crashing down. This was a victory that was credited to the LORD rather than to Israel's strength or military prowess. God had directed Israel to destroy the entire city, to burn the entire city, but to keep the silver and gold and bronze to put in the Temple of the LORD as a memorial and dedication to God, a reminder of His faithfulness. Yet in Joshua 7 we learn that Achan was unfaithful; he had taken some of these devoted things for himself and because of this God's anger burned against Israel. Israel's leader Joshua sends a smaller army out to conquer the city of Ai since it was not as strong a city as Jericho was, but what seemed like an easy victory turned out to be an embarrassing defeat. The Israelites were chased out of the city and Joshua tears his clothes and pleads with the LORD to understand why they were delivered to their enemies. In verse 11, God tells Joshua that Israel has sinned in keeping some of the devoted things for themselves. Therefore, they couldn't stand against their enemies.

The LORD tells Joshua to have the people consecrate themselves and that each tribe should be brought before the LORD, then the clan the LORD chooses should present themselves family by family, then man by man. Whoever is caught with the devoted things will be destroyed by fire along with all that belongs to him. Achan refused to repent, his sin was exposed and he and his whole family were judged. Over Achan Israel heaped a large pile of rocks and they called that place the "Valley of Achor" ever since, a memorial of sin, of judgment; a reminder of the trouble caused by disobedience to God. This was a valley of hopelessness. Yet Hosea 2:15 prophesies that the LORD will make this Valley of Achor, this place of death and this reminder of sin a door of hope for Israel. When the prophet Ezekiel is taken by the LORD to a valley of dry bones in Ezekiel 37, many scholars believe this valley could have been the Valley of Achor for the people had said that their bones were dry, and their hope was lost. What did the LORD do in this valley of dry bones? He breathed life back into that dead, dry assortment of bones and they became a mighty army! A picture of God's mercy, the reviving power of His Spirit, and how mercy triumphs over judgment. My friend, even if there's an area of your life that you feel is a reminder of your sin, of your disobedience, or your hopelessness; a desolate, broken, dry, lifeless place like the valley of Achor; a place where you chose to hide until you were forced to confess similar to what Achan did. I believe God wants to turn that place into a door of hope for you just like He did for Israel. Jesus is that door! Like the prophet Ezekiel, I hear a noise, a rattling sound as those dry bones come together again. May it be so in your life today in Jesus's name.

Father,

> I thank You for Jesus. I thank You that you delight in showing me mercy, that You enjoy forgiving me of my sin. What God is like You? Holy Spirit, would You help me not to show contempt for the kindness of God, but to understand and appreciate that it is His kindness that leads me to repentance. I praise You LORD for being rich in mercy, that Your mercies are new every morning. Help me to be merciful because mercy triumphs over judgment. And I invite You LORD to turn even those areas of brokenness and those reminders of sin and pain and judgment in my life into doors of hope for me in Jesus's name, amen.

Day 127: I Am Hosting a Dove

"And when he (Jesus) had been baptized, Jesus came up immediately from the water, and behold, the heavens were opened to him, and he saw the Spirit of God descending like a dove and alighting upon him. And suddenly a voice came from heaven saying, 'This is my beloved Son, in whom I am well pleased." Matthew 3:16-17 NKJV

"But you (disciples) will receive power when the Holy Spirit comes on you; and you will be my witnesses in Jerusalem, and in all Judea and Samaria, and to the ends of the earth." Acts 1:8 NIV

"John testified saying, 'I have seen the Spirit descending as a dove out of heaven, and he remained upon him (Jesus).' I did not recognize him, but he who sent me to baptize in water said to me, 'He upon whom you see the Spirit descending and remaining upon him, this is the one who baptizes in the Holy Spirit." John 1:32-33 NASB

In reading the Bible we learn that God is triune in nature. He is made up and is expressed in three persons: The Father, the Son, and the Holy Spirit. We see this from the get-go as man is being created by God. "Let us make man in our image, after our likeness…" (Genesis 1:2 NIV). God didn't use singular pronouns in making this declaration. He used plural ones because you are made in the image of a triune God, a God who consists of three persons in one. One of these persons is the Holy Spirit. Throughout the Bible we see references to the Spirit of the LORD. The Spirit of the LORD would come upon certain individuals and they could do things that they were otherwise incapable of doing. The Spirit of the LORD is all throughout the Word of God, yet before Jesus we see a broken relationship with the Holy Spirit just as we see a broken relationship with God. God's Spirit would come upon certain individuals at certain times for certain reasons, but the Spirit didn't seem to remain upon them. In John 14, before Jesus ascends to the Father, He promises to pray to the Father who will send another Comforter, the Spirit of Truth; the Holy Spirit of the living God that will abide with you forever!

Jesus tore the veil of separation through His death and resurrection so that you have direct access to God. Hebrews 4:16 says that you can now approach the throne of grace with confidence. The Bible says that you were once an enemy of God because of your friendship with the world, but when you accepted Jesus as your LORD and Savior, you received God's Spirit and that Spirit brought about your adoption to sonship. The Spirit of God has translated you from an enemy to a son! Enemies can't approach the throne of grace with confidence, but sons sure can! Praise God for His Spirit that has made you a son!

In Matthew 3 and in John 1 we read the account of Jesus being baptized by John the Baptist. An interesting thing happened when Jesus was baptized. The Bible says that the heavens were opened, and the Spirit of God descended in the form of a dove and remained upon Jesus Then a voice from heaven declared, "This is my beloved Son, in whom I am well pleased." (Matthew 3:17 NIV). The Word of God likens the Holy Spirit to different things throughout the Scriptures things such as wind, fire, and water and each of these paints a picture of what the Holy Spirit is like. He is like the wind; you can't see Him, but you can feel Him. Wind is not always predictable, you don't always know where it came from or where it is going, but wind is refreshing, it is powerful; the breath of God, the Spirit of God brings life. He is like fire in that He is all-consuming. He purifies, refines, He burns up the junk in your life that cannot endure in the presence of God. He helps to make you holy. And He is like water, like rain; He is refreshing, He cleanses; He renews. Yet in this description of the Spirit that descended upon Jesus, He is likened to a dove. Doves are symbols of peace and of purity, but they also require a lot of care to keep them around because they take flight easily. They can be startled easily then they take off and fly somewhere else. It's one thing for a dove to light on you; it's another thing altogether for a dove to remain upon you. How does one live in order to keep that dove from flying off? They must live with that dove always in mind, always conscious and aware of that dove, always sensitive to that dove so that it always remains with them. I don't believe it was an accident that the Spirit of God took the form of a dove when it descended upon Jesus. Friend, I think God is giving us a glimpse of what His Spirit is like, of what living in the Spirit, walking in the Spirit is like. We are admonished in Galatians 5 to walk in the Spirit so as not to gratify the desires of the flesh. And Romans 8:14 says that those who are led by the Spirit of God are the children of God. Oh friend, if you have Jesus, you certainly have His Spirit. Yet learning to walk in the Spirit, being led by the Spirit, yielding to the Spirit is like walking with a dove on your shoulder. Every move is made with that dove in mind, there is great sensitivity to that dove and if every move is made in relation to that dove, to the Holy Spirit, then you are absolutely being led by the Spirit. May it be in Jesus's name!

Father,

> I thank You for Your Spirit. I thank You that Your Spirit has brought about my adoption and made me a child of God. I can approach Your throne of grace with confidence because I am Your child. Thank You, Jesus! Holy Spirit, I know that I have You because You were given to me when I accepted Jesus as my Savior and made Him my LORD, but I want a deeper relationship with You. I want to walk in the Spirit, be led by the Spirit. I want to cultivate the kind of relationship with You that I see You had with Jesus in the Bible. I want to remain in You and You with me, to live with You always in mind. Forgive me for not being more sensitive to You. I don't want to just seek Your power without being sensitive to Your constant presence in my life. Let it be LORD in Jesus's name, amen.

Day 128: I Am Transformed

> *"Do not be conformed any longer to the pattern of this world but be transformed by the renewing of your mind. Then you will be able to test and approve what God's will is—his good, pleasing, and perfect will."* Romans 12:2 NIV

> *"And we all, with unveiled faces contemplate the Lord's glory, are being transformed into his image with ever-increasing glory, which comes from the LORD, who is the Spirit."* 2 Corinthians 3:18 NIV

> *"Moreover, I will give you a new heart and put a new spirit within you; and I will remove the heart of stone from your flesh and give you a heart of flesh."* Ezekiel 36:26 NASB

You are transformed. You are being transformed! Romans 12 tells you not to be conformed any longer to the pattern of this world, not to play the same games, obey the same rules, and follow all the same traditions of this world. Rather, you are admonished to renew your mind with the Word of God and doing this transforms you. God's Word has the power to change you, to completely renovate your life and it all starts with the way that you think. Wow! 2 Corinthians says that God's glory is transforming you into His image and that this is all happening with every-increasing glory. This transformative work comes from the LORD who is the Spirit. The Spirit of God in all His glory is transforming you, changing you, altering you into His image, making you more like the LORD. How is that possible? How can you be like the LORD Almighty? The Holy Spirit has the power to transform you! Only He can make you like God for He doesn't just know God, He is God. This is awesome!

You are not the same, my friend. God's Word changes your thinking, the way that you think; it restores and heals your mind. You don't have to be conformed to the patterns of success this world exalts, you don't have to be conformed to the patterns of over-sexualizing everything, you don't have to play the same game this world plays in its quest to get to the top, to have status and importance and value, to view everything through the lens of how it affects yourself. You are not a product of the environment you grew up in or the culture you live in daily. These things can affect you in a powerful way, but you don't have to be conformed to them regardless to how powerful they are. Why? Because you have the Word of God and this Word has more power. This God-breathed Word has the power to renew, to heal your mind; to completely transform you! Oh friend, do you really believe that? If you want to change your life; if you need to change your life, I challenge you to feast on God's Word, to let it change your thinking and totally transform your life because it will!

The LORD is excellent at transforming things. He can make something out of absolute nothingness. Just look at the account of creation. The land, the light, the seas, the animals they were all spoken into existence. They weren't created from something. They were created from nothing. God spoke and they were. Yet even in the creation of Adam, God took some dirt and transformed that dirt into a living, breathing, complex individual with eleven different major organ systems all functioning properly, beautifully, uniquely for the glory of God, it's Creator. Not only so, when the LORD created Eve, a helper suitable for Adam, He took one of Adam's ribs and transformed that bone that in and of itself has no life, no function outside of Adam's body, and transformed that bone into a whole other person; a person different from Adam but still a part of him. That's transformation! Look at the valley of dry bones in Ezekiel 37. God's breath transformed those lifeless, brittle bones into a mighty, thriving army. By the Spirit of the LORD, an unassuming shepherd boy, David, had the strength to physically tear apart a lion. The Spirit of the LORD transformed Gideon, a man that appeared content to hide from the enemy all his life with his family, into a great leader and a mighty warrior. It doesn't take long reading the Bible and you realize that God transforms things. Maybe all you have is dirt; all your life amounts to is a bunch of dirt, unglamorous, of little value, messy dirt. Maybe all you have is the leftovers from someone else; someone else's work, someone else's success, someone else's life. Maybe you're just a kid, maybe you're not very strong physically or what you do for a living doesn't qualify you to take out lions. Maybe you've been a coward; you're not a leader, you've hidden from everything all your life. Just maybe you don't have anything. Your life is such a mess you don't even have a good place to start. It all amounts to a bunch of nothing. It's okay because God transforms things! In the story of creation after each of His creations God saw all that He had made, and it was very good. My friend, God makes very good things out of nothing! His glory is transformative! His Word is transformative! My friend, it's time to stop focusing on what you don't have, talking about what you don't have, exalting what is lacking in your life and start realizing that even if you have nothing God is an expert at making good things out of nothing! Creation itself is a testament to this truth. All that you see was made by Him and for Him and without Him was nothing made that has been made. Thank God, you are being transformed and He who began His good work in you, will carry it out to completion. Hallelujah!

Father,

I thank You for Your Word. I thank You that I don't have to conform to the ways and thinking of this world, but that I can be transformed by the renewing of my mind. Help me Holy Spirit to do this. I don't want to be conformed to the patterns of thinking of this world for the mind of the flesh is death, it is hostile to God and that's not what I want at all. I thank You for transforming me with ever-increasing glory by Your Spirit LORD. Let it be in my life. I want to be more like You, so I freely give You all that I have even if it feels like nothing to me because You are the One who creates beautiful things, very good things out of nothing. I invite You to transform me into God's image, Holy Spirit in Jesus's name, amen.

Day 129: I Am Not a Judge

"Do not judge, or you too will be judged. For in the same way that you judge others, you will be judged, and with the same measure you use, it will be measured to you." Matthew 7:1-2 NIV

"Brothers and sisters do not slander one another. Anyone who speaks against a brother or sister or judges them speaks against the law and judges it. When you judge the law, you are not keeping it, but sitting in judgment on it. There is only one Lawgiver and Judge, the one who is able to save and destroy. But you—who are you to judge your neighbor?" James 4:11-12 NIV

"You, therefore, have no excuse, you who pass judgment on someone else, for at whatever point you judge another, you are condemning yourself, because you who pass judgment do the same things. Now we know that God's judgment against those who do such things is based on truth. So, when you, a

> *mere human being, pass judgment on them and yet do the same things, do you think you will escape God's judgment?"* Romans 2:1-3 NIV

There is only one Lawgiver and Judge and, my friend, it isn't you. Are you the one who makes the rules, who determines what's right and what's wrong, who sets the standards for everyone, who knows the mind and heart of all people? Are you able to save or destroy anyone eternally? In James, the Word of God says that when you judge a brother or sister, a fellow believer, you are judging the Law, that same Law that God gave to Moses, that Law that Jesus came to uphold and to fulfill; a Law that you are required to keep, but that you haven't kept. "For whoever keeps the whole law and yet stumbles at just one point is guilty of breaking all of it." (James 2:10 NIV). Yet when you evaluate the Law, when you criticize the Law, when you write a review of what you, the created, think about God, the Creator's Laws; you aren't keeping the Law; rather, you are sitting in judgment on it. But who are you to judge the perfect Law of God? Therefore, you have no excuse, you who pass judgment on someone else. In fact, when you choose to judge someone else, you are choosing to condemn yourself because you do the very same things that you criticize others for. I know this seems harsh, but it's what the Bible says!

God's judgments are based on truth. He alone sees and knows the heart of all people for He doesn't look at what man looks at. Man looks at the outward appearance, but God looks at the heart. He knows what's in your heart, where your heart is as well as where you are circumstantially. He sees the end from the beginning. His judgments are based on truth because He's the only One who can see and know a person's heart plus what's going on in their life at this very moment as well as what has happened in their past and what will take place in their future. You may know facts about someone; rock solid, very reliable, real facts. Yet it's impossible for you to see and know someone's heart unless they reveal it to you. And even if you know a person's past, how are you to know their future? How can you make judgments based on truth unless you know the truth, the whole truth? And can I tell you, that even if a person did reveal their heart to you and you feel like you have enough truth to base a judgment on, you are still just a mere human being who has done the very things you are now criticizing. "You, then, who teach others do you not teach yourself? You who preach against stealing, do you steal? You who say that people should not commit adultery, do you commit adultery? You who abhor idols do you rob temples? You who boast in the law, do you dishonor God by breaking the law?" (Romans 2:21-23 NIV). Your judgments on others loses their credibility considering the reality that you too have been a lawbreaker. You're not considered a lawbreaker anymore, but that's only because of the grace of God expressed through Jesus. And lawbreakers who were sentenced to die, but were pardoned, absolved of guilt, and had the written record of wrongs that stood against them cancelled; it would seem that these individuals wouldn't turn around and judge or criticize other people they see breaking the Law in similar fashion. Rather, you'd think these individuals would be the ones who would be broadcasting the Way, the Truth, and the Life, Jesus, because it's only through Him that they have been forgiven!

We've sort of gone off the deep end with this "don't judge me" thing. Instead of it being an admonishment that the Scripture gives to you; we've used it instead to stop anyone from disagreeing with us about anything. Now if anyone doesn't agree with something you do or say, they aren't just in disagreement with you, they are "judging you." But disagreeing is not the same as judging. And disagreeing, even strong disagreement is not the equivalent to persecution. We've lost our heads a little with this. God's Word judges the thoughts and attitude of the heart (Hebrews 4:12). His Word will judge you.

There's a whole book in the Bible called "Judges". Here we see numerous men and one woman, Deborah, who were appointed to lead Israel, to act as a judge in helping to settle disputes and matters between Israelites. Because they were appointed to this office, they had the authority to do this much like judges today that we elect into office have the authority to make judgments and rulings in cases brought to them. Some of these judges in the Bible were good, God-fearing individuals and others were very wicked. Yet it was never God's idea to appoint a king or ruler over Israel (1 Samuel 8). The LORD has and is equipping you to rule and govern, but you are incapable of ruling and governing the Law, of judging the Law, because you aren't the Law's fulfillment, only Jesus is! He is the only One that has the power to save and destroy for all eternity. Help us, LORD, to stop doing what only Jesus is qualified to do!

Father,

> I thank You for Jesus. That He is the Lawgiver and the Judge and that His judgments are based on truth. Would You forgive me for judging others, for condemning others, for

criticizing others when I do those very same things? Help me Holy Spirit not to judge anything before the appointed time, but to trust in Christ for He will reveal what has been hidden in the darkness and He will reveal the motives of the heart. The only heart I need to be concerned about is my own, to make sure my heart is pure, and my hands are clean. Help me, LORD, in Jesus's name, amen.

Day 130: I Am Thirsty!

"...O God, You are my God, I shall seek you earnestly; my soul thirsts for you, my flesh yearns for you, in a dry and weary land where there is no water." Psalm 63:1 NASB

"I am the LORD your God, who brought you up from the land of Egypt; open your mouth wide and I will fill it." Psalm 81:10 NKJV

"The Spirit and the bride say, 'come,' and let the one who hears say, 'come,' and let the one who is thirsty come, let the one who wishes take the water of life without cost." Revelation 22:17 NIV

How thirsty are you for more of the LORD? More of His presence, His Word, His Spirit; a deeper relationship with Him? Do you seek the LORD earnestly? Does your soul thirst for Him, yearn for Him in this dry and weary land where there is no water? Do you crave His presence; do you ache for more of God? Do you want to be with God because, I can assure you, He wants to be with you! When you're physically thirsty depending on how long it's been since you've had water, you can become a little desperate because it's not just about enjoyment anymore, it's about survival. It's like your mind becomes consumed with thoughts of water; how you're going to get to some water; what it will taste and feel like to take a drink and be refreshed. There's an appetite for something and that appetite compels you to find water. It's hard not to enjoy water when you're thirsty! The human body comprised by a significant amount of water (approx. 60% in adults) can only last up to 3 days without water. Whether you like water or not, your body demands and needs water!

The Bible likens the Holy Spirit of the Living God to water! Whether you like it or not, your spirit needs the Holy Spirit of God. In fact, the Bible says that your spirit is dead until you accept Jesus and when you accept Him, your spirit comes alive (Romans 8:10). It's hard not to enjoy the Spirit of God when you are thirsty for it! In John 7, Jesus stood up on the last day of the feast of Tabernacles and says to the crowd, "If anyone is thirsty, let him come to Me and drink. He who believes in Me, as the Scripture said, from his innermost being will flow rivers of living water." (John 7:37 NIV). The feast of Tabernacles was the seventh and last feast that God commanded Israel to observe and it is one of three feasts that the Jews observed each year by going to Jerusalem. The feast lasted eight days beginning and ending with a Sabbath day of rest and worship to the LORD. During these eight days, Israel would dwell in tents or tabernacles as a reminder of God's deliverance from slavery in Egypt and His faithfulness to them throughout the 40 years they dwelt in the wilderness. It was a celebration of the incredible truth that God wants to be with His people. Some great things happened during the feast of Tabernacles in Israel's history. In Nehemiah 8 when Israel returned to rebuild the temple during the feast of Tabernacles, Israel gathered to hear Ezra proclaim the Word of God and revival broke out in the camp as people repented and sought the LORD. Many scholars believe Jesus, the Savior of the world, was born during the feast of Tabernacles, this feast that was largely a celebration of the incredible truth that God wants to be with His people. Here is Jesus, Immanuel, God with us, born during a feast that celebrates this reality. That's hardly a coincidence.

Jesus was born to a Jewish carpenter, so He was present in Jerusalem observing this feast of Tabernacles since all Jewish males were required to observe it each year, but Jesus was also the fulfillment of this feast. John 7 says that Jesus did not go to this feast with His brothers. They went without Him and He went secretly because the Jews sought to kill Him. There were probably thousands of people celebrating this event. There were probably people there just because it was mandated of them, people were there to remember God's faithfulness, and people were there to worship the LORD. But there were also some people there who wanted to be with God in a greater capacity. Jesus stands up amid this crowd on the last day of the feast after everyone had been there all week and says an interesting thing to them. He invites the thirsty to come to Him and drink. Here these people were coming to an annual event that honored God's desire to be with His people and here is Jesus, the very fulfillment of this desire, inviting the people to come and be with Him. Wow! This crowd was doing what they were supposed to do; they were observing the feast, they had stopped their lives and took eight days to dedicate to worshipping the LORD. The crowd had been there all week. It was time to go back to "regular" life, to return to the "real" world so to speak and here is Jesus inviting the thirsty to come to Him. Amid this feast people failed to recognize Jesus, the fulfillment of the feast. Many of them were upset with Jesus; they wanted to seize Him to stop Him from teaching. John 7 makes it clear that when Jesus said this, He was speaking of the Spirit of God whom those who believed in Him were to receive. It was no accident that Jesus spoke of the Spirit during this feast of Tabernacles! God gave you His Spirit, the third Person of the Trinity, equally God to be in you forever. How could you think that God doesn't want to be with you? For God so loved the world that He gave His only begotten Son, Jesus, and He's given you His Spirit! You see, much like society today and even church today, there are people who come to a church service out of duty and obligation, others come because they're upset with Jesus, yet there are some who are there because they are thirsty. They want water. They need water. They want to be with God in a greater way, not just know about Him, but personally know Him. Jesus invited the thirsty to come to Him and drink for He is the Living Water and those who believe in Him, from out of their innermost being will flow rivers of this living water, the Holy Spirit.

Friend, are you thirsty? You have rivers of living water flowing out of you, the Spirit of God. If you have rivers of living water flowing out of you, then you never have to be dry and weary and parched. You never have to go looking for water. You never have to wither or die. You're planted by the stream remember? You have rivers, not a pool or a creek or a pond, but rivers of living water. Pools and ponds tend to stagnate because the waters don't flow, but rivers move, rivers flow, and rivers, every single one of them, lead to a larger body of water, the ocean. And you don't just have a river; Jesus said rivers, plural tense, rivers of living water! Oh friend, there were people in that crowd from John 7 that wanted to kill Jesus, to arrest Jesus, to shut Jesus up. There was a religious spirit present in that crowd that wanted the waters stagnant and calm and predictable and Jesus wasn't just making waves, He was offering people a whole other water source! It's time to let those rivers of living water flow in your life not just for your sake but for the sake of everyone you meet. God wants to be with you. He sent Jesus whose blood brings you near to God and He gave you His Spirit to be in you forever! We live in a dry and weary land. People are thirsty, parched; dying even because they have no water, they can't seem to find any water and the LORD has put rivers of living water in you, the Spirit of the Living God! May they flow to heal, to refresh, to wash, to cleanse, to restore in Jesus's name!

Father,

> I thank You for putting rivers of living water in me. I don't ever have to thirst because I have Your Spirit. Let the rivers flow in my life. I thank You for wanting to be with me. You are so high and holy and awesome, and I am so small in comparison. It humbles me to my core to know that You went to such great lengths just to bring me near to You, to have Your Spirit forever. Your desire to be with me must be incredibly strong for You to clothe Yourself with flesh, endure the cross, despising its shame, for the joy that was set before You. Holy Spirit be like a river in me. I invite you to move, to flow, to lead people to the true source of the living water, Jesus. Let it be in my life in Jesus's name, amen.

Printed in the United States
By Bookmasters